STATE AND SOCIETY IN PAPUA NEW GUINEA

THE FIRST TWENTY-FIVE YEARS

STATE AND SOCIETY IN PAPUA NEW GUINEA
THE FIRST TWENTY-FIVE YEARS

R. J. MAY

E PRESS

Published by ANU E Press
The Australian National University
Canberra ACT 0200, Australia
Email: anuepress@anu.edu.au
Web: http://epress.anu.edu.au
Previously published by Crawford House Publishing Pty Ltd
PO Box 50, Belair, SA 5052

National Library of Australia Cataloguing-in-Publication entry

May, R. J. (Ronald James), 1939- .
State and society in Papua New Guinea: the first twenty-five years.

New ed.
Includes index
ISBN 1 920942 06 8
ISBN 1 9209420 5 X (online document)

1. Papua New Guinea - Politics and government - 1975- .
2. Papua New Guinea - Social conditions. I. Title.

320.993

All electronic versions prepared by UIN, Melbourne
Cover design by Michael Birch with a photo by R. J. May

FOREWORD

Rt Hon Sir Michael Somare, GCMG, CH, MP

A 25th, or silver, anniversary tends to be an occasion for both celebration and reflection. Both activities are apt when, as on the occasion of Papua New Guinea's 25th anniversary of independence, silver itself has contributed significantly both to national revenue, as the third most valuable metal export, and to one of our greatest national tragedies, the violent conflict in Bougainville between 1989 and 1997.

The broad scope of this book on state and society in Papua New Guinea enables the author, Dr R.J. (Ron) May, to draw attention both to some of Papua New Guinea's greatest strengths and achievements and to some of our shortcomings since independence. It also provides an opportunity to explore some of the links between them – a vibrant constitutional democracy and enormous economic potential, especially in agriculture and the resources sector. The accuracy and pertinence of the author's observations are made all the greater because of the way that they draw on his two academic specialties, economics and politics.

In an essay written to explain Papua New Guinea to an Australian audience after 10 years of independence (reprinted here as chapter 2), Ron May writes of 'Port Moresby and the Bush'. In doing so, he refers indirectly to an old Australian dilemma – Sydney, especially (or some other Australian capital city), '*or* the bush'. At the same time, he draws attention to the reality that, for almost all Papua New Guineans, even those who have lived longest in towns, the focus of life is still Port Moresby, Lae, Mount Hagen, Rabaul, Wewak, etcetera '*and* the bush', or home.

In fact, even for the longest-serving Members of Parliament, including myself (I have been elected and re-elected for an unbroken 33 years), national politics and government in Port Moresby are only aspects of political life and public affairs: the clan and village, the local-level government ward where they are located, and (especially since the provincial government reforms) the District, the Province, and sometimes the region are also very important.

The various studies that make up this book recognise the diverse arenas in which Papua New Guineans pursue different interests as well as our national destiny.

In doing so, they draw on the author's detailed research in my home province, East Sepik; his work on the challenges of micro-nationalism; his practical experience in helping to set up two important national institutions, the Bank of Papua New Guinea and the National Research Institute (formerly, the Papua New Guinea Institute of Applied Social and Economic Research); his consultancies to government; as well as his knowledge of other developing countries, especially the Philippines. They also provide a glimpse into his appreciation of the arts in Papua New Guinea, both traditional and modern.

I am, therefore, pleased to introduce this book, which brings together a quarter century of Ron May's scholarly work on Papua New Guinea on the 25th anniversary of independence. Our views have not always coincided, though I appreciate the independence, clarity and knowledge with which the author has expressed his. I continue to value his learning, his contributions to mutual understanding with people in other countries, especially Australia, and his critical analyses of significant events and trends in development.

I commend this book to everyone interested in Papua New Guinea, both for the insights it provides into the first quarter-century of Papua New Guinea's independence and as a valuable stimulus to national self-examination.

Sir Michael Somare, known throughout Papua New Guinea as 'the Chief', was Chief Minister of Papua New Guinea from 1972 to 1975; the first Prime Minister from 1975 to 1977, and Prime Minister from 1977 to 1980 and 1982 to 1985; as well as a senior Minister in subsequent Governments. He was re-elected Prime Minister in 2002.

CONTENTS

PREFACE

In September 2000 Papua New Guinea celebrated 25 years as an independent nation. This collection was put together at the time to mark the occasion, and was originally published by Crawford House Publishing. It comprises papers written over a period of more than 25 years, since I first started working on and in Papua New Guinea. Most of the chapters included here, however, have been written in the past few years and address topics of central political concern: the role of the state, the army, decentralisation, the interaction of traditional and non-traditional authority, and political economy. A few were written more than a decade ago but have been included either because what they have to say is still relevant or because they offer a historical insight into issues of contemporary debate. Since the collection was first published, Papua New Guinea has survived another national election – albeit one marked by increased electoral violence – and Sir Michael Somare has been returned as prime minister. But many of the political and economic problems discussed in this volume remain, and the search for explanations and 'solutions' goes on.

The initial decision to produce *State and Society in Papua New Guinea* was encouraged by my old friend and publisher, Tony Crawford, and was brought to speedy fruition with the expert assistance of Claire Smith, Allison Ley and, especially, Jill Wolf. For preparing the new edition for publication, I am indebted to Richard Thomson, whose editorial and management skills were honed with the *Papua New Guinea Post-Courier*. I would also like to acknowledge the help, stimulation and collegiality I have enjoyed over the years from a number of colleagues in Papua

New Guinea and at The Australian National University, who, like myself, have worked in and on Papua New Guinea for more years than we care to remember, particularly, David Hegarty, Bill Standish, John Ballard, Hank Nelson, Bryant Allen, Anthony Regan and Sinclair Dinnen.

R.J. May
Canberra
March 2004

1

INTRODUCTION: PAPUA NEW GUINEA AT TWENTY-FIVE

On the eve of Papua New Guinea's independence in 1975 there were many – Papua New Guineans, resident expatriates, and overseas observers – who were sceptical about the future of an independent Papua New Guinea. While people in the New Guinea highlands were apprehensive of being dominated by better educated coastal and Island people, and Papuans around the capital, Port Moresby feared being swamped by immigration from the highlands, well informed commentators, looking to the experience of post-colonial states elsewhere, spoke of the likelihood of political anarchy, an army coup or authoritarian single-party dominance, and of economic collapse. Australian journalist Peter Hastings, for example, commented in 1971 on the 'inescapable similarity between Africa and Papua New Guinea', and suggested that after independence 'the Army will inevitably be involved in the political direction of the country' (Hastings 1971:32); the perceptive historian Hank Nelson wrote, around the same time: 'After the formal withdrawal of Australian authority the new government may seem to work well, then, as corruption, inefficiency and secessionist movements become more obvious, the few educated and competent will take over, either dismissing the institutions of government established by Australia or ignoring them', (Nelson 1972:208); and former patrol officer, politician and planter Ian Downs wrote a novel which centred on a Mau Mau style uprising on the eve of independence (see chapter 18 below). Such fears appeared to have been partly justified in 1975 when, prior to independence, both the

North Solomons (Bougainville) and Papua unilaterally declared their independence.

Notwithstanding all this, Papua New Guinea made a smooth transition to independence and in its first decade as an independent state performed well: it introduced several major policy reforms (including the introduction of provincial government and the renegotiation of the Bougainville Copper Agreement); it reelected the Somare government in 1977 and then achieved smooth changes of government in 1980, 1982 and 1985; it enjoyed generally good external relations, including successful intervention by the Papua New Guinea Defence Force (PNGDF) to end a rebellion in newly independent Vanuatu, and it experienced a measure of economic success (the kina actually appreciating against the $A). Papua New Guinea is still one of the few postcolonial states that has maintained an unbroken record of democratic government, avoiding both an army takeover and an authoritarian civilian regime. (An assessment of the first decade of independence is reproduced in chapter 2.)

Nevertheless, from around the mid 1980s several adverse developments became increasingly evident, particularly: a decline in the level of government service delivery (especially in remote areas) contributing, by the late 1990s, to a negative movement in several social indicators; increasing problems of urban and rural lawlessness and the spread of nepotism and corruption; poor economic management, exacerbated by the forced closure of the Bougainville Copper mine and threats to other major resource projects; increasing pressure on land, and environmental degradation associated with mining and logging in some areas, and, of course, the Bougainville conflict itself, which amongst other things brought tensions in Papua New Guinea's relations with its eastern neighbour, Solomon Islands.

The following chapters, written over a period of some 25 years (but mostly over the last decade), look at a number of aspects of Papua New Guinea's political development since independence. Before turning to these, however, the following pages briefly examine some of the key issues facing Papua New Guinea at the beginning of the twenty-first century.

Political institutions

At independence, political parties in Papua New Guinea were embryonic, but though some commentators predicted a transition to a single-party system, most foresaw the natural development of a two-party system. A shift from a preferential voting system to one based on a first-past-the-post poll was implemented partly with a view (informed by political science literature) to encouraging the development of a two-party system. In fact, however, a viable political party system never did develop. Parties, which – apart from pre-independence differences about the speed of the movement to independence – were never sharply differentiated ideologically, remained fluid organisations, lacking a mass base and generally revolving around a small group of prominent politicians. Outside of parliament, they seldom had much presence except at election time. (For a discussion of parties in the first decade of independence see chapter 6.)

Despite predictions to the contrary, over successive elections parties have tended to become less rather than more salient, and as the number of candidates contesting elections has steadily increased, the proportion of independent candidates has also grown; in 1997, 73 per cent of all candidates, and 33 per cent of winning candidates, stood as independents (Electoral commissioner's figures, see Kaiulo 1997:11). Many candidates in fact choose not to align themselves with parties (or at least not to declare alignments) so that, if elected, they are in a better position to negotiate with the political brokers who, in the aftermath of the election, scramble to put together a winning coalition. Every government in Papua New Guinea since the pre-independence election of 1972 has been a coalition government, and because party loyalties are generally weak, and many members can be readily persuaded (by, say, the offer of a ministry in a new government) to change partners, coalitions have shown little stability. Since independence, in every parliament the government has changed mid term. This pattern of parliamentary behaviour has made for a pork-barrelling style of politics which is not conducive to commitment to longer-term national policies. The fact that in every election since 1972 a majority of candidates have lost their seats exacerbates the situation and encourages MPs to use their office to seek immediate gains. Politics, in other words, is widely seen as a form of *bisnis*.

While there is little doubt that most voters expect the candidates for whom they vote to serve *their* interests to the exclusion of others', there has nevertheless been a growing cynicism about the behaviour of politicians, in and out of parliament. By the latter part of the 1990s this was reflected in a growing demand for political reform. Calls for reform focused on two principal features of the political system: the large and growing number of candidates at elections, and the frequency of movement of MPs from one party to another and of parties from one side of the parliament to the other, associated with votes of no confidence against the government in office.

The number of candidates contesting national elections has increased at every election since 1972. In 1977, when the National Parliament first reached its present size of 109 members, there were 879 candidates, an average of just over 8 per electorate; in 1982 the number rose to 1125, in 1987 it was 1513, and in 1992 (notwithstanding a substantial increase in candidates' deposit fees) it had risen to 1655; in 1997 the number of candidates increased again, by over 40 per cent, to 2372. This represented an average of 22 candidates per electorate. In fact, several electorates had more than 40 candidates and one, Northern [Oro] Provincial had 61. This has had two effects. First, with so many candidates, no strong party system, and a first-past-the-post voting system, the winning candidate's percentage of the total votes cast has often been relatively small. In 1997, 16 candidates (14 per cent of all winning candidates) won with less than 10 per cent of the vote; 95 (87 per cent) won with less than 30 per cent of the vote; only four gained an absolute majority (Kaiulo 1997). For some people, at least, this has raised questions about the extent of candidates' mandates: in 1999, under a headline, 'House is full of "rejects"', former prime minister Sir Michael Somare was reported as telling a seminar organised by the Constitutional Development Commission that, with reference to the 1997 elections, 'We were rejected by 80.20 per cent of the population. The national figures do not mandate the current Members of Parliament to make decisions on their behalf' (*Post-Courier* 7 September 1999). Second, with, say, 40 candidates, a candidate can (theoretically) win with just over 2.5 per cent of the vote; in an electorate of (typically) around 30000 voters this translates to around 750 votes. With the possibility that electoral contests might be won with such small numbers, there have been increasing tendencies (especially, it seems, in highlands electorates) for candidates to tie up their 'line' by enforced bloc or clan voting, for supporters of a particular candidate to forcibly prevent rival candidates from entering their area, and for stronger candidates to put up lesser candidates within a rival candidate's home area in an attempt to split a clan or village vote. This sort of behaviour has tended to restrict political campaigning in some parts of the country, and has contributed to increasing electoral violence (see for example the papers by Dinnen and Standish in Saffu 1996). In 1987, with a view to reducing the number of candidates, it was proposed to raise candidates' fees from K100 to K1000 (a figure slightly higher than per capita annual GNP). This was overruled by the judiciary, but before the 1992 elections the legislation was revived, and passed; it did not, however, prevent the steady growth in candidate numbers, which thus remains an issue of concern. In 2000 there was talk of raising the fee to K10000.

The other issue of concern relates to *votes of no confidence*. In 1991, following several votes of no confidence, the constitution was amended to increase, from six months to 18, the grace period within which a government cannot be dismissed through a parliamentary no confidence vote. However, this has had only a marginal impact on parliamentary behaviour: in 1993 Prime Minister Wingti attempted to avoid an impending vote of no confidence by resigning as prime minister and immediately seeking reelection at a parliamentary session at which attendance was dominated by his supporters (this stratagem was subsequently invalidated by the judiciary and Wingti lost office), and in December 1998 Prime Minister Skate adjourned parliament to gain a similar reprieve (but lost office in July 1999). At the time of writing (September 2000) Prime Minister Morauta has announced his government's intention to adjourn parliament for six months beginning December 2000. Ultimately, however, the movement of members across the floor of parliament and the frequency of no confidence votes are a reflection of weak political parties.

Demands for electoral reform were formulated in the 1980s and legislative proposals were put forward, but the proposed reforms did not materialise. Following a change of government in July 1999, the incoming prime minister, Sir Mekere Morauta, declared that a priority of his government was 'to restore integrity to our great institutions of state'. A Constitutional Development Commission was set up to organise public consultation and recommend action. Two principal measures have emerged from this process.

The first is a draft Organic Law on the Integrity of Political Parties and Candidates. In an attempt to strengthen the role of political parties, the legislation provides for: registration of political parties; public funding of registered parties (on the basis of the number of their elected MPs); limitations (albeit generous limitations) on contributions to party funding, from local and foreign sources; financial incentives to encourage parties to nominate women candidates (in 1997 only two women were elected to the 109-seat National Parliament); and restrictions on 'party hopping' and the voting rights of independent MPs. Under the proposed legislation, independents cannot vote on the election of the prime minister (and a candidate elected as an independent may not join a party until after the election of the prime minister), or on amendment to the constitution, or on the budget. Once affiliated with a party, if MPs leave that party their reasons for doing so must be investigated by the Ombudsman Commission, who may refer the matter to the Leadership Tribunal; depending on the outcome of this review, members may lose their seats, or at least be made to refund campaign expenses paid by the party and be barred from holding ministerial or other parliamentary office. Opponents of the proposed measures argue that the public funding of parties will advantage the existing major parties, and that restrictions on the rights of independent MPs and on 'party hopping' are undemocratic; however there appears to be a good deal of support for the legislation, which passed the second reading stage in August 2000.*

The second important measure is a proposal to change the electoral system from first-past-the-post to some form of optional preferential voting (as was introduced at the provincial level in Manus in 1993). This proposal runs counter to the opinion expressed by the Electoral Commissioner, who in his report on the 1997 election said:

> The re-introduction [of optional preferential voting] is premised on the need to reduce the number of candidates to ensure that the MP has a wider basis of support and endorsement, and also to promote collaboration amongst candidates and counter the surge in violence. Whether that system will be able to achieve all these, if it were re-introduced, is a moot point. What is very clear, though, from the point of view of administering the election process, is that it will be more costly, become slower and less tidy. [Kaiulo 1997:13]

It is certainly far from clear that a change in the electoral system, if implemented, will bring about the desired change in elec-

* In November 2000 the government failed to get the bill through the third reading, but the following month it was passed.

toral behaviour, and the arguments against more complex voting procedures are strong. Nevertheless there appears to be widespread support for this measure also, even amongst MPs, on whom it will have an unpredictable impact.

Amongst other measures to restore integrity to the nation's political institutions, the Morauta government has announced its intention to set up a National Anti-Corruption Agency, which will coordinate the activities of several government departments and agencies involved in addressing the problem of growing corruption, and there is support for a separate Independent Commission Against Corruption.

Law, order and state capacity

Questions about politicians' mandates and the susceptibility of governments to votes of no confidence – and thus, ultimately about the legitimacy of the state – have both affected and been affected by what is generally referred to as the 'law and order' situation.

Already in the 1970s Papua New Guinea was experiencing an upsurge of inter-group ('tribal') fighting in the highlands and growing lawlessness associated with 'raskolism' (essentially gang-based petty criminality) in both urban and rural areas. There were even calls for the deployment of the PNGDF in support of police to quell inter-group fighting. Such problems became worse during the 1980s, as inter-group fighting escalated and growing numbers of disaffected young men in both towns and villages joined the *raskol* ranks. In 1984 the PNGDF was first called out during a state of emergency in Port Moresby, and subsequently police and soldiers carried out joint operations during states of emergency in the highlands and other provinces, as well as further operations in the capital. Increasingly frustrated by their inability to counter the rise in criminal activity, police mobile squads resorted to draconian measures, including, on occasion, the burning of houses, killing of pigs, assault of suspects, and even looting and rape. Such actions further alienated citizens from the state, and by the 1990s the state had acquired a sizeable liability for compensation payments to communities, arising from police action.

A number of commentators has suggested that deteriorating discipline within the PNGDF, which became evident both before and after the Bougainville conflict began, was at least in part a consequence of the PNGDF's involvement in internal security operations. Adverse perceptions of the security forces were certainly exacerbated by the politicisation of both police and the PNGDF and by the evidence of declining morale and discipline within both police and the army. On the anniversary of independence, in September 2000, disgruntled soldiers of the PNGDF's Second Battalion in Wewak went on a rampage, burning down the regimental headquarters and officers' mess. A subsequent Ministerial Task Force on Defence headed by Defence Minister Taranupi reported that the basic needs of the PNGDF were not being met, that basic management structures and systems were not appropriate or not working, and that critical issues relating to the mission and purpose, capacity, resourcing and structure of the Force needed to be reviewed. The prime minister overshadowed a 'radical overhaul' of the PNGDF and Defence Department.

By the 1990s private security was one of the fastest growing industries in Papua New Guinea – particularly around urban businesses and big resource projects – and there were suggestions that a Gurkha force be brought in to support police and army in internal security operations. It was a short step from this to the engaging of the 'military consultants' Sandline International in 1997 in an attempt to do what the security forces had proved incapable of doing, namely bringing an end to the Bougainville rebellion. The rejection of Sandline by PNGDF Commander Brigadier General Singirok was popularly acclaimed at the time but set an unfortunate precedent, and in the aftermath of the Sandline affair the PNGDF has been factionalised. These subjects are addressed in chapters 10 and 11.

Within government itself there has been an increasing incidence of nepotism and corruption; in 1996 then governor of the Bank of Papua New Guinea, Mekere Morauta, commented that 'the most corrosive and intractable problem we face now is corruption'. This situation perhaps reached a climax during the government of Bill Skate (1997-1999), despite the widespread demand, during the 1997 elections, for clean government. As noted above, the Morauta government is addressing these issues; it has also handed down guidelines to regulate the controversial Rural Development Funds, which are allocated to each MP for expenditure in his or her electorate. Nevertheless, a number of members of the former Skate government have retained ministerial portfolios in the new government and a culture of exploiting public office for personal gain seems to have become entrenched. This in turn contributes to popular cynicism about politics and politicians, and is frequently cited as a rationalisation for *raskolism* and other criminal activity: if political leaders can steal from the people and get away with it, some argue, *raskolism* is just another form of income distribution.

The same attitudes have contributed to a culture of compensation demands, including rolling demands for compensation for land used for schools, missions, airstrips, roads, and other public infrastructure, which have become a significant source of local tensions and an impediment to development and the provision of government services.

Provincial and local-level government

As described in chapters 7 and 8, in 1976 Papua New Guinea introduced a system of provincial government, in part to counter the separatist threats on Bougainville. Over subsequent years provincial government had a mixed record, working well in some provinces, especially as the capacity of the national government to deliver services deteriorated, but poorly in others.

In 1987 I commented, 'Whatever its shortcomings, provincial government now seems to have become an inescapable part of

Papua New Guinea's political landscape'. By the 1980s, however, many national MPs were beginning to see provincial governments as a threat to their electoral base, and in several instances the suspension of provincial governments seemed to have as much to do with tensions in relations between national and provincial politicians as with poor performance (particularly financial mismanagement) by provincial governments. In 1995 the system of elected provincial governments was replaced, under an Organic Law on Provincial and Local-Level Governments, by a system in which provincial governments were to comprise the national MPs from the province and representatives of local-level governments, up to three 'paramount chiefs or their appointed nominees',[1] a nominated woman representative and up to three other appointed members. A range of functions was decentralised further to local-level governments. At the time, critics of the 'reforms' argued that, in most provinces, local-level governments did not have the capacity to carry out the tasks delegated to them, and that the inevitable effect of the new legislation would be to re-centralise powers under national MPs (see chapter 8). Opposition to the 1995 legislation from within the government resulted in several members being dropped from cabinet, and precipitated a split within the Pangu Pati.

Five years after these reforms were introduced the critiques of the changes seem to have been largely borne out. In May 2000 Prime Minister Morauta observed that the system was not working. The capacity of local-level governments is for the most part weak, and although no comprehensive study has been undertaken to date, in most provinces joint district planning and budget priorities committees appear to have been dominated by national MPs. At a legal seminar held in September 2000 it was claimed that since 1997 all 18 provinces and 284 local-level governments have been operating illegally (reported in *Post-Courier* 11 September 2000). As this volume was going to press, two provincial

[1] The re-discovery of 'chiefs' is discussed in chapter 9.

governments were suspended. A new review of the provincial and local-level government system has been foreshadowed.

Bougainville

Initially, the Sandline affair boosted the peace process on Bougainville. Negotiations between the Papua New Guinea government and the Bougainvilleans were resumed in 1997 and meetings in New Zealand in July and October resulted in the 'Burnham Declaration' and the 'Burnham Truce', which laid the basis for continuing peace talks. A further meeting in Australia produced the 'Cairns Commitment on Implementation of the Neutral Regional Truce Monitoring Group (TMG) for Bougainville'; the TMG, which included unarmed military and civilian personnel from New Zealand, Australia, Fiji and Vanuatu, commenced operations in December 1997. The following month, another meeting in New Zealand culminated in the 'Lincoln Agreement on Peace, Security and Development on Bougainville'; this provided the basis for a ceasefire, which came into effect at the end of April 1998, and paved the way for the Papua New Guinea government's agreement to rescind the call-out of the PNGDF and to establish a demilitarised neutral zone around the minesite town of Arawa. On the Bougainvillean side, it was agreed to establish a Bougainville reconciliation government.

The ceasefire duly came into effect and the TMG was replaced by a Peace Monitoring Group (PMG). The reconciliation government was also established, in the form of a Bougainville People's Congress (BPC), elections for which were held in May 1999. Former premier Joseph Kabui became chairman of the BPC. Peace talks continued throughout 1998 and 1999; at the same time, reconstruction and restoration of services proceeded, and reconciliation processes were undertaken at the local level. The peace process did not go smoothly, however. First, at the end of 1998 the National Parliament rose without passing the necessary legislation to continue to exempt Bougainville from the provincial and local-level government legislation which had been enacted in 1995, thus potentially undermining the situation of the reconciliation government. Second, in 1999 the Bougainville regional member, John Momis (who stood to become provincial governor if Bougainville were to come under the Organic Law on Provincial and Local-Level Governments) challenged the continuing suspension of the provincial government; in November 1999 his appeal was upheld. This could have been a serious threat to the peace process. Once again, however, the various parties were able to come together; the BPC and a Bougainville Interim Provincial Government (BIPG), headed by Momis, have maintained the dialogue with the national government, with the BPC acting as an advisory body to the BIPG.

The main sticking points in the negotiations have been the issues of disarmament and weapons disposal, and the Bougainvillean demand for a referendum, which includes the option of independence. The national government has agreed to grant Bougainville 'a high degree of autonomy' and its chief negotiator, Sir Michael Somare, has ultimately supported the demand for a referendum 'in an effort to avoid a dangerous impasse in the current peace talks'; but the content and timing of the referendum have yet to be agreed upon, and Prime Minister Morauta has maintained the position adopted by his predecessors in rejecting the possibility of independence for Bougainville.

In mid 2000 Bougainville leaders were again expressing frustration at the slow progress of negotiations and apparent lack of commitment on the part of the national government, and former Bougainville Revolutionary Army leaders Sam Kauona and James Tanis were forewarning of a possible resumption of armed conflict if Bougainvillean demands were not met. A substantial agreement was to have been reached by 15 September 2000, the 25th anniversary of independence, but in September the deadline was extended. In short, the peace process has come a substantial way since 1997, but it remains fragile.

External relations

Shortly before gaining independence Papua New Guinea adopted a foreign policy of 'universalism' – 'taking the middle path without veering to either side on questions relating to political ideologies, creeds or governmental systems'. This policy was revised in 1981 to one of 'selective engagement', recognising the significance to Papua New Guinea of its relations to Australia, Indonesia, Solomon Islands, and the country's major economic partners. In the early 1990s Prime Minister Wingti gave the policy a 'Look North' emphasis, acknowledging the economic and potential political importance of relations with Papua New Guinea's Asian neighbours, and implicitly questioning the continuing strength of the 'special relationship' with Australia.

The shift in Australia's development assistance programme, progressively, from one of general budgetary support to one of targetted programme aid has not been well received in Papua New Guinea, and as the Bougainville crisis developed there was a growing sentiment in Papua New Guinea – especially within the PNGDF – that Australian military assistance fell well short of Papua New Guinea's needs. Relations reached something of a low point during the Skate administration, but turned around after the election as prime minister of Sir Mekere Morauta.

Following tensions across the Indonesia-Papua New Guinea border in 1984, Papua New Guinea and Indonesia in 1986 signed a Treaty of Mutual Respect, Friendship and Co-operation (see chapter 14). The same year the Melanesian Spearhead Group was formed between Papua New Guinea, Solomon Islands and Vanuatu. (Fiji, which had experienced its first coup in 1987, was not an initial signatory but the way was left open for Fiji to join.) On Papua New Guinea's initiative, a Joint Declaration of Principles was signed by Australia and Papua New Guinea the following year.

During the Bougainville conflict Solomon Islands became a conduit for escape from Bougainville, and for the supply of weapons, ammunition, medicine and other items to Bougainville.

Consequent heavy-handed actions by the security forces, including raids into Solomon Islands, caused a pronounced deterioration in relations between the two Melanesian neighbours. In 2000, relations had recovered, but the rapid escalation of conflict within Solomon Islands, primarily (but not exclusively) along ethnic lines between people from Guadalcanal and Malaita, has raised possibilities of the Solomons conflict spilling over into Papua New Guinea, particularly if the western Solomons (where there have been longstanding separatist sentiments) gravitate away from the Guadalcanal-Malaita conflict and towards Bougainville.

With the re-emergence of regional conflicts in Indonesia following the fall of Soeharto, and renewed demands for West Papuan independence, there is also increased possibility of new tensions along Papua New Guinea's western border.

The next twenty-five years

Where does that leave Papua New Guinea, 25 years after independence? In chapter 15 I have argued that while the prophecies of doom in 1975 were not borne out in the first decade of independence, developments over the first 25 years have been disappointing. While Papua New Guinea has maintained an unbroken record of democratic government, the promise of the early nationalist leaders has failed to translate into a sense of national identity and purpose: electoral politics remains essentially parochial; national politics has for the most part been dominated by personal politicking for short-term gain; political parties have not developed to play the expected role of selecting candidates, articulating issues and keeping MPs accountable; there has been little development of a civil society, and the quality of governance has been poor. In chapter 15 I have suggested that Peter Ekeh's concept, derived from Nigerian experience, of a primordial culture, was useful in explaining some of the problems confronting Papua New Guinea at the beginning of the twenty-first century; certainly, as is also argued in chapter 16, these problems are not unique to Papua New Guinea.

On the positive side, despite its extreme linguistic fragmentation and potential for conflict along ethnic lines, ethnic tensions have been relatively minor. This is particularly so with respect to language itself: Papua New Guinea does not have an explicit policy on language, with the result that Tokpisin has naturally developed as the dominant *lingua franca,* while English has become the principal language of education, administration and commerce, and the country's 850 or so vernacular languages are being used in early education and adult literacy programs. Another positive element in the situation is that Papua New Guineans themselves are aware of their problems – none more so than Prime Minister Morauta – and are taking steps to address them. What is needed, however, is less institutional reform than a fundamental shift in patterns of political behaviour. If Papua New Guinea can achieve this, it will have done what few other post-colonial states have managed to accomplish.

2

PORT MORESBY AND THE BUSH: PAPUA NEW GUINEA'S FIRST POST-INDEPENDENCE DECADE*

In September 1985 Papua New Guinea celebrated its first decade as an independent nation. The occasion was not without its detractors. Amongst residents in the national capital, Port Moresby, there were complaints that the festivities – stage-managed by a long-serving expatriate – were geared primarily to foreign visitors and neglected ordinary Papua New Guineans. Amongst the foreign visitors some Australian former residents left with a feeling that the place was not what it used to be in their day; they spoke of the scruffiness of Port Moresby, of the high security fences which have gone up around urban residences in recent years, of high prices, and administrative inefficiency. In the country's 19 provinces the celebrations were often very modest and sometimes rather disorganised affairs, partly reflecting a general tightness of budgets and partly because in some provinces the capacity to organise such events is weak. But despite the niggling, Papua New Guineans could point with pride to their country's achievements.

Following Papua New Guinea's third national elections in 1972 Michael Somare became chief minister at the head of a nationalist government. He subsequently led the country to self-government in 1973 and independence in 1975. In a situation which begs comparisons with the Labor government which came into office in Australia in the same year, Somare in 1972 faced a number of

* This paper, which reviews the first decade of Papua New Guinea's independence, was first published in *Current Affairs Bulletin* 63(8), January 1987.

problems. He and his political colleagues were inexperienced in government; they desired a basic social, political and economic transformation of their country in the shortest possible time and they distrusted much of the inherited Australian-dominated bureaucracy. In addition the Somare government seemed to be faced with a serious threat of political fragmentation from a variety of local and regional movements, including a loosely articulated separatist movement on the copper-rich island of Bougainville.

Compared with the Whitlam government, let alone with the experience of other newly independent states in Africa and Asia, Papua New Guinea fared well. Within the framework of a 'home grown' constitution a parliamentary system became firmly established. Somare was returned as prime minister in 1977, as leader of a four-party coalition, and though he lost office through a vote of no confidence in 1980, he was returned after the 1982 elections. He retained office until late 1985 when a split within his Pangu Pati and a further vote of no confidence brought former Deputy Prime Minister Paias Wingti to office. There were, in other words, only three changes of government between 1972 and 1986 and on each occasion the changeover proceeded smoothly along constitutional lines.

Administratively, the public service survived a rapid localisation and some fundamental restructuring, though it remains large and in a number of respects (particularly its ability to deliver services to rural areas) its efficiency has declined. Economically, the government established a viable financial system (at the time of writing, in 1986, the Papua New Guinea kina exchanged at a rate of about K1=$A1.54) and, greatly assisted by Australian budgetary support, successive governments have acted with reasonable fiscal restraint. Although, like many other export-oriented Third World countries, Papua New Guinea's economy has suffered from fluctuating commodity prices and adverse movements in its terms of trade, large-scale mining ventures have provided, and seem likely to provide for some time, boosts to foreign exchange earnings, government revenue and private investment. [Following the outbreak of fighting on Bougainville in 1988, the Panguna gold and copper mine closed in 1990. See chapter 12.] The threat of political fragmentation has subsided, in large part as a result of an ambitious programme of political decentralisation. Despite the problems – and they are not inconsiderable – provincial governments are now well entrenched and are becoming increasingly a source of political and administrative initiative. [A later assessment of the provincial government system is contained in chapter 7.] Externally, apart from recurring flurries along the border with Indonesia, Papua New Guinea has enjoyed cordial relations.

This extremely superficial and generally positive review, however, should not be taken to imply that Papua New Guinea does not have problems. A more balanced assessment of where Papua New Guinea stands after 11 years of independence might be gained by looking in somewhat more detail at developments in five broad areas: party politics; the economy; provincial government; the 'law and order' issue in its broader socio-economic context, and the Papua New Guinea-Indonesia border.

Party politics

In the later years of colonial rule there was a common expectation amongst political commentators that, with the establishment of parliamentary democracy, a stable two-party or three-party system would develop (though some more radical thinkers predicted a democratic one-party state). Indeed, by 1972 there were four political parties with a significant following, as well as a small number of regionally-based popular movements (including the separatist Papua Besena and the Gazelle-based Mataungan Association) which supported candidates in the elections of that year. About a quarter of the candidates who stood in 1972 were endorsed or supported by political parties. Although the highlands-based and generally conservative United Party

(UP) gained the greatest number of successful candidates, the outcome of the 1972 election was a coalition government dominated by the progressive Pangu Pati under the leadership of Somare. The other principal elements of the coalition were the People's Progress Party (PPP) led by Julius Chan, the National Party (NP) led by Thomas Kavali and later by Iambakey Okuk, and the Mataungan Association, whose most prominent spokesman was John Kaputin. Despite some differences, ideological and personal, this coalition survived more or less intact throughout the life of the 1972-77 parliament.

In the country's first post-independence election, in 1977, parties were somewhat more salient but again the outcome of the election was determined by post-election lobbying of successful candidates and the Somare-Chan coalition was returned to power. Okuk, who had been sacked from the Somare ministry and had crossed the floor in 1976, subsequently emerged as leader of the opposition. As the result of a falling out between Somare and Chan, in 1978 the PPP withdrew from the coalition, but a split within the UP brought some of that party's members across the floor and Somare was able to survive three parliamentary votes of no confidence. In early 1980, however, further tension in the coalition led to the withdrawal of prominent islands members Kaputin and Fr John Momis and the creation of a new party, the Melanesian Alliance (MA). Soon after, a successful no confidence motion removed Somare from office and Chan became prime minister at the head of a National Alliance government comprising PPP, NP, MA, Papua Besena and the remnants of UP. This improbable coalition remained in office until 1982, when Papua New Guinea held its second post-independence election.

In 1982 political parties were more visible and more active than in any previous election. Pangu, PPP, UP, NP, MA and the Papua Party (Papua Besena) all fielded candidates, and two new groups – the Papua Action Party and a predominantly Papuan 'Independent Group', headed by former Defence Force commander

Ted Diro – emerged as significant contenders. About 60 per cent of the 1125 candidates were endorsed by one (or more) of these eight parties. In several important respects, however, party structures were tenuous: except perhaps for Pangu, no party had an effective mass organisation and not even Pangu could claim a nationwide organisation; party attachment often meant little more than the use of a label; in a number of cases candidates stood for one party after failing to gain the endorsement of another; some candidates were endorsed by more than one party, and party members frequently stood against endorsed candidates of their own party. Moreover, while party voting was generally agreed to have been significant in 1982, personal, regional and clan loyalties remained critically important for the great majority of voters.

The outcome of the 1982 election was a victory for Pangu and Somare was duly reelected prime minister of a government composing Pangu, the bulk of UP members and some independents. A young highlander, Paias Wingti, became deputy prime minister (his appointment over more senior Pangu members being a recognition of the importance of the highlands vote). Leadership of the opposition passed to Diro, but when in the following year Okuk – who had failed to gain reelection in Simbu in 1982 – was returned in an Eastern Highlands by-election, Diro stepped down in his favour. There are few dull moments in Papua New Guinea politics, however, and early in 1985 simmering dissension within Pangu culminated in a split in the party. Wingti and 15 others crossed the floor, announcing the formation of a new party, the People's Democratic Movement (PDM). Somare subsequently survived a no confidence vote, with support from the NP and, surprisingly, the MA and with the PPP abstaining. MA parliamentary leader Momis replaced Wingti as deputy prime minister.

Meanwhile, the mercurial Okuk, who had lost his new seat in late 1984 following a challenge to his residential qualifications, was voted back again in another by-election in mid 1985 and immediately began pressing for a cabinet post. When Somare ignored these demands Okuk crossed the floor, hoping to take with him the rest of the NP members (two of whom had portfolios in the Somare government). Instead he precipitated a split in the NP.

Somare's victory of March 1985, however, proved to be short-lived. In November there was another vote of no confidence and this time the vote went against Somare. Wingti became prime minister, with Chan as his deputy; Okuk was given the important Primary Industry portfolio.

The new government – a coalition of PDM, PPP, NP, UP and Papua Party – erupted in a series of public confrontations and in 1986 three ministers resigned under pressure, two to face court charges and another following allegations of bribery. Internal friction also continued to plague Pangu. In the early months of 1986 three senior members of Pangu (Tony Siaguru, Barry Holloway and John Nilkare) broke away, forming a group they labelled the Pangu Independent Group (PIG) – and hence the 'three little PIGs'). They were joined by two more disgruntled members and, having been disowned by Pangu, announced the creation of a new party, the League for National Advancement.

Thus, 11 years after independence and 22 years after its first national election Papua New Guinea had a plethora of political parties, and if history is any guide more could be expected to emerge as politicians mobilised for the national election in May-June 1987. Of the eleven groups mentioned in this brief survey, however, only five – Pangu, PPP, NP, UP and the more recent MA – can claim any substantial continuity. Of these, the NP, which began life in 1970 as in effect a highlands-based Pangu equivalent, has had an erratic career whose ups and downs have largely reflected the fortunes of Okuk, and though the UP has survived for almost as long as Pangu, it has lacked cohesion and coherence. All, moreover, are essentially parliamentary parties, coming to life in the electorates only at election time.

While the run-up to the 1987 election may produce a more

effective mass organisation and some geographic broadening of support, at least for the major parties (including the PDM), the fact remains that at present parties tend to be regionalised, not markedly differentiated from one another by ideologies or policies, and to revolve around their parliamentary leadership. It thus seems likely that in 1987, as in previous elections, voting outside the big cities will be determined more by personal, clan and regional loyalties than by party affiliation and that the leadership of the nation will pass to those who are most successful in cobbling together a workable coalition after the votes have been counted. Indeed deals are already being done – Pangu and MA, for example, have agreed not to compete against one another in the East Sepik and North Solomons regional electorates (those now held by Somare and Momis respectively) – and it is a safe bet that over the next few months the activities of politicians both in government and in opposition will be conducted with an eye firmly on the electorate. Some commentators have been critical of this 'fluidity' of the party system, seeing it as a source of 'instability', but it might equally be argued that the absence of sharp ideological or class-type cleavages in the political system has served the young nation well and has contributed to the sustaining of a democratic parliamentary system.

The economy

After something of a boom in the early 1970s, the performance of the Papua New Guinea economy over the decade to the mid 1980s was disappointing in relation both to the earlier period and to the economic performance of other countries in the region. Real GDP has grown at an average annual rate of about 2 per cent, a rate slightly less than the rate of increase in population. On the other hand, estimates of growth in the non-cash economy and various social indicators suggest that the wellbeing of most rural villagers – and that accounts for over 80 per cent of the Papua New Guinea population – has steadily improved: levels of health and nutrition are generally higher; most villagers enjoy better access to services, and participation in the cash economy is greater.

Since coming into production in 1972, the Bougainville copper mine has been a major contributor to Papua New Guinea's development. In the early 1980s exports of gold and copper from Bougainville comprised over 50 per cent of total exports and revenue from the mine provided around 20 per cent of government revenue. A second major gold and copper mine, at Ok Tedi, commenced production in 1984 but the Ok Tedi operations have been plagued by disputes between the operating company and the government over the conditions of the original agreement. Three other major gold prospects, at Porgera, Lihir and Misima, were currently under development in 1986 and there have been promising discoveries of oil in the Southern Highlands.

Tree crops provide the other major source of export earnings, with coffee the most important, followed by oil palm and cocoa. Output and export prices for most of these crops held up fairly well during the early 1980s, though all are subject to sizeable fluctuations in world prices. The discovery of coffee rust in smallholder plantations in the highlands, Madang and the Sepik, however, posed a serious threat to the future of this industry, which in the early 1980s contributed about 14 per cent of total export revenue. Measures to combat the fungus are being taken but climatic conditions and the fact that about three quarters of the output of the industry comes from smallholders, mainly in fairly remote areas, make effective action difficult.

Apart from mining and agriculture, Papua New Guinea's economic prospects do not seem to be particularly promising: fisheries and timber have made significant contributions to export earnings but the development of manufacturing is constrained by lack of skilled manpower and relatively high wage levels.

The government sector plays a major rule in the Papua New Guinea economy – a heritage of the Australian colonial period –

and the high level of government spending has been sustained only by continuing substantial aid from Australia. In the first three years of independence, aid from Australia – mostly in the form of general budgetary assistance – accounted on average for 38 per cent of total budget expenditure. By 1980 the proportion had fallen to 29 per cent, but since then it has remained at about that level. Thus, despite the stated commitment of successive governments and opposition parties to a greater degree of national fiscal self-reliance, Papua New Guinea remained heavily dependent on Australian aid. In July 1985 the two countries negotiated a new five-year agreement to cover the period to 1991. Under this agreement Papua New Guinea was to receive a total of $A1400 million with annual grants declining by 3 per cent per annum and a further 2 per cent per annum being shifted from general budgetary assistance to programme aid. In August 1986, however, in presenting the 1986/87 budget the Australian government announced that aid to Papua New Guinea would be cut by some $A10 million in the current financial year. Less than four weeks later, foreign minister Hayden, while visiting Port Moresby, gave notice that Australian aid to Papua New Guinea may be further cut; a figure of $A45 million per annum was mentioned. The Australian government's decision to renege on its agreement brought a predictable and justifiable sharp reaction from Papua New Guinea's deputy prime minister and finance minister Chan, and from the foreign minister. The impact of further reductions in Australian aid is of particular concern to the Papua New Guinea government in view of warnings from the IMF concerning the growth of the country's external public borrowing.

Papua New Guinea's economic prospects are thus not exactly bleak, but neither do they provide grounds for complacency. The maintenance of sound economic management and fiscal responsibility is thus a prerequisite of the future economic wellbeing of the country, a fact which seems to have been well recognised by the Wingti government.

Provincial government*

The Constitutional Planning Committee (CPC) which drafted Papua New Guinea's constitution in 1974 recommended a 'fully decentralised system of unitary government', partly as a means of maximising popular participation in government and partly to accommodate the demands for regional and local autonomy which had emerged in the years preceding independence. In the event, decentralisation was not written into the constitution but in 1977, under pressure from Bougainvillean politicians who had made a unilateral declaration of independence of the North Solomons, the government passed legislation, in the form of an Organic Law on Provincial Government, which provided the basis for delegation of political and administrative powers to the country's 19 provinces, broadly in accordance with the CPC's recommendations. Interim provincial governments were established in all provinces in 1977 with elections for provincial assemblies to follow as soon as practicable. Selected functions were transferred from the national government during 1977-79 and by mid 1979 four of the 19 provinces had achieved full financial responsibility (i.e. provincial control of all funds available to the province, most of which come in the form of transfers from the national government). It was, however, more than two years before another province attained full financial responsibility and in 1986 fewer than half of the provinces had it. In the meantime two provinces had run into serious financial difficulties as the result of maladministration and had been bailed out by conditional loans from the national government.

The task of establishing viable governments in provinces of widely varying fiscal and administrative capacities, and in an atmosphere of frequently intense local politics, was understandably not easy. It was made more difficult by the resistance which many national government officials offered to decentralisation

---

* For a more recent assessment of provincial government see chapter 7. Also see May and Regan with Ley (1997).

and by frequent opposition from national politicians who saw provincial governments as a challenge to the bases of their electoral support. Critics of provincial government – and there have been many – have described it as wasteful and as failing to achieve the objective of bringing government closer to the people. They have had no difficulty in finding instances to cite of financial excesses and mismanagement, inefficiency, nepotism and corruption. In 1983 the Organic Law on Provincial Government was amended to make it easier for the national government to suspend provincial administrations. Soon after, governments were suspended in four provinces: Enga, Manus and Simbu in 1984 and Western (Fly River) in 1985. (Provincial government was reinstated in Manus 12 months after its suspension, following a new election; Simbu, suspended late in 1984, recommenced operations after the national parliament went into recess without passing the necessary legislation to extend its suspension). Several other provincial governments may consider themselves fortunate not to have been suspended, including Central Province (the province surrounding the national capital, Port Moresby), whose premier is currently facing charges of misusing government funds. In addition, several measures have been taken over recent years which are generally seen as partially reversing the trend of decentralisation, for example the withdrawal of some delegated functions, the allocation of funds to national politicians to spend in their provinces, tighter controls over provincial finances, and a decision to do away with the National Fiscal Commission (which was set up under the Organic Law to mediate on fiscal matters).

In 1984 Somare, whose lack of enthusiasm for provincial government is longstanding, responded to criticisms of decentralisation by proposing a plebiscite to advise on the future of provincial government. This brought a quick reaction from the supporters of decentralisation, however, and in the Islands region the provincial premiers threatened secession if provincial government were abolished. Instead, Somare referred the subject to a select parliamentary committee headed by Siaguru. The parliamentary committee's inquiry was in progress in November 1985 when the change of government occurred and one of the first acts of the Wingti government was to scrap it, ostensibly as an economy measure but also perhaps because the principal movers in the enquiry were his political rivals.

Whatever its shortcomings, provincial government now seems to have become an inescapable part of Papua New Guinea's political landscape. Not only are provincial governments well entrenched politically, they have become, as suggested earlier, important sources of political and administrative initiative in some areas of policy; moreover, as the administrative capacity of the national government comes more closely into question, provincial governments are sometimes seen as having an increasingly important role in the delivery of services to the more remote rural areas.

Apart from the regular intergovernmental contacts provided through the annual Premiers' Council meetings, and informal provincial secretaries and regional premiers' conferences, political linkages have developed between the two levels. Not only does provincial government seem to be emerging as a stepping stone to careers in national politics but a number of politicians who have lost seats in national parliament have re-emerged as influential figures in provincial assemblies. One effect of this (often an offshoot of tensions between national and provincial politicians) has been a 'provincialisation' of national politics. In an extreme case, in Morobe Province, where the outspoken premier Utula Samana seems likely to be a candidate in the 1987 national election, there is talk of a Morobe Independent Group screening the provincial candidates of all major parties in 1987 to ensure their loyalties to the province. On the other hand there also seems to be an emerging tendency to extend (national) party politics into provincial assemblies. Initially, in most provinces there was opposition to political parties, which were seen as potentially disruptive of the small-scale politics of provinces, but in recent years party alignments have become increasingly evident in provincial assemblies.

All this points to a critical need to raise the integrity and efficiency of provincial governments and to provide effective, non-antagonistic lines of communication between the national government and the provinces.

Law and order

In the mid 1980s a good deal of attention was being given – in Papua New Guinea as well as in the Australian media – to the deteriorating 'law and order' situation in Papua New Guinea. In 1981 the government appointed a committee of review on law and order and the following year it initiated a review of the police force. In 1983 another committee was established to review policy and administration on crime, law and order and in the same year a major study of law and order was commenced under the joint direction of the Institute of National Affairs and the Institute of Applied Social and Economic Research; the INA/IASER report became available in 1984. On the basis of these enquiries, in 1984 the government announced a series of measures (the '49 measures') to combat the breakdown of law and order, and appointed a task force to oversee their implementation. Another task force on law and order was created in the following year, which also saw the declaration of a state of emergency in Port Moresby.

There have been three major elements underlying this concern: an increase in tribal fighting, particularly in the highlands provinces; an apparent upsurge in the incidence of urban crime, especially crimes of violence; and the emergence of organised crime networks, particularly what are referred to in Papua New Guinea as *raskol* gangs. Behind all of these developments are some broader questions concerning the changing nature of Papua New Guinea society and the role of the state.

Pre-contact Papua New Guinea society was characterised by

an extraordinarily high degree of social and political fragmentation and by a fairly high degree of violence. During the colonial period much of the energies of the administration were directed at preventing fighting between the numerous small communities and bringing them together within the framework of a modern state. In most coastal areas the period of colonial rule was sufficiently long that the bases of inter-group fighting were resolved or forgotten. However, in the highlands and some other parts of the country, where the period of effective control was historically quite short, as the authoritarianism of colonial rule gave way to the more democratic political processes of the independent state, tribal fighting simply resumed where it had been interrupted. Improvements in transport and communication, the introduction of new political institutions, and the widespread use of alcohol increased the possibilities for tribal fighting and brought some modifications in the way it was conducted.

In the towns, large-scale unemployment, especially amongst young people, a marked imbalance in the ratio of males to females amongst urban migrants, and an increasingly obvious disparity between a relatively affluent urban elite – Papua New Guinean and foreign – and the mass of the urban population all contributed to the apparent upsurge in crime, though it is worth noting that urban crime has affected the poor and the weak in towns at least as much as it has affected the wealthy and the powerful. Not all criminals, moreover, come from the underprivileged. For example, an East European-born resident was charged in 1986 over possession of stolen car parts (he was said to have been the head of an organised car stealing racket). In addition, there has been a disturbing incidence of charges against senior politicians and public servants, ranging from traffic offences and embezzlement to rape.

The other disquieting element of the law and order situation has been the spread of *raskol* gangs. *Raskol*s (the Tokpisin word derived from the English 'rascal', but lacking the jocular overtones of the English word) have been part of the urban and rural scene since at least the early 1970s. Then, it seems, *raskol* gangs mostly comprised unemployed youth from the same village or subdistrict; they were involved both in urban crime, such as theft and rape, and in some forms of rural lawlessness, notably thefts from trucks operating along the highlands highway. Frequently, it was alleged, they stole from the rich (expatriates, truck operators, big store proprietors) and redistributed to the poor, and they were often regarded with a certain degree of indulgence. Nowadays they seem more likely to contain members from different parts of the countryside, they contain older men including some hardened criminals and some educated young men, and there exist extensive and effective networks not only throughout the highlands but across the nation (during the state of emergency in Port Moresby in 1985 it was alleged that *raskol*s in Moresby simply took off to other parts of the country, and following successful police action in which stolen goods were recovered in Moresby in 1986, there were swift retaliatory raids against police in Lae and Mount Hagen). There also appears to have been a rise in the scale of criminal activity: there have been armed holdups of cocoa and coffee buyers, bank robberies, post-election paybacks, a number of pack rapes, and in the Eastern Highlands the small town of Kainantu was virtually held to ransom by *raskol*s. Outbreaks of lawlessness in Port Moresby and the highlands, marking the death of Okuk, took authorities by surprise and underlined the fragility of the law and order situation.

The costs of this breakdown in law and order are considerable. Apart from the immediate damage to person and property, food gardens and cash crops have been destroyed, village enterprises have been forced out of business, schools have been closed down, freedom of movement has been impeded, and it has become almost impossible to persuade public servants to work in some areas; ultimately foreign investment, tourism and overseas recruiting also suffer.

Proposed measures to combat or solve the problem cover a

wide field. They range from the draconian (such as corporal punishment – including the anti-rapists' '*katim bol bilong ol*'; restrictions on the movement of people into towns and repatriation of inter-provincial migrants; tougher police action; use of the military), through the more practical (greater self-regulation through village courts, provincial rehabilitation centres and so on; a larger and better trained police force) to the more ambitious (youth schemes, employment creation, reductions in social inequalities). On one point, however, there is agreement: the law and order problem is complex and not amenable to easy solution. In the highlands provinces several states of emergency have been declared since 1979 and police mobile riot squads, equipped with helicopters and tear gas, have been deployed, without conspicuous success. On the other hand the state of emergency in Port Moresby, which included a curfew and increased police patrolling, brought a dramatic decrease in crime, at least temporarily. And in the Eastern Highlands, low-level liaison with rural communities succeeded in securing the mass surrender of *raskol* gangs who had been terrorising Goroka, Kainantu and travellers on the highlands highway. Whatever action is taken against offenders, however, the problem of lawlessness is unlikely to go away unless something can be done to reverse increasing social inequalities, frustrated expectations, and the breakdown of traditional authority structures.

The border

Located strategically between Southeast Asia and the Pacific, Papua New Guinea is an active member of the South Pacific Forum and has special observer status within ASEAN. The major preoccupation of its external relations, however, has concerned its common border with Indonesia.

In 1969, in an event variously referred to as the 'Act of Free Choice' and the 'Act of No Choice', Irian Jaya, the former Dutch New Guinea, formally became part of the Indonesian Republic.

Incorporation into the Indonesian state was resisted by Melanesian nationalists, who sought a separate state of West Papua; some actively opposed Indonesian rule within Irian Jaya while others 'voted with their feet' by crossing into Papua New Guinea. In the 17 years since 1969 opposition to Indonesian rule, led by the Organisasi Papua Merdeka (OPM – Free Papua Movement), appears to have strengthened rather than diminished and there has been a steady trickle of refugees across the border. In 1984 this trickle became a flood. Indonesian military action against the OPM has also resulted in occasional incursions into Papua New Guinea, where the guerrilla fighters have been known to set up temporary camps.

A basic framework for administrative relations between Indonesia and Papua New Guinea was laid down in a border agreement negotiated on Papua New Guinea's behalf by the colonial government but renegotiated, with some changes, by the independent government of Papua New Guinea in 1979 and 1984. This agreement acknowledges the rights of traditional groups in the border area (including border crossing for traditional and customary purposes – such as hunting, sago gathering, and trade), it contains provisions relating to quarantine, river navigation, development of resources and environmental protection, and it establishes machinery for joint consultation and liaison. Since independence in 1975 successive Papua New Guinea governments have broadly maintained the policies of the former colonial government; Papua New Guinea has accepted unreservedly the sovereignty of Indonesia in Irian Jaya, it has denied the use of Papua New Guinea territory to the OPM, and it has discouraged border crossing while accepting a small number of refugees for resettlement either within Papua New Guinea or, with the assistance of the UN High Commissioner for Refugees, in third countries.

Over the past decade, however, events along the border have created recurring tensions between the two nations and on several occasions relations with Indonesia have loomed large in

Papua New Guinea's domestic politics. There is within Papua New Guinea, even at the highest political levels, a good deal of emotional sympathy with the position of the Melanesians of Irian Jaya, who are seen as having been denied their independence and having fared poorly under a repressive regime. Some educated Papua New Guineans have expressed fears that Indonesia might one day invade Papua New Guinea as it invaded East Timor.

The massive influx of Irianese refugees into Papua New Guinea early in 1984, following an abortive OPM-led uprising and subsequent Indonesian military crackdown, again brought the border into prominence and with subsequent border incursions, and the failure of the formal consultation and liaison arrangements to resolve the problems amicably, Papua New Guinea's foreign minister ultimately felt compelled to raise the issue at the UN General Assembly.

Since then relations between Indonesia and Papua New Guinea have been restored to a degree of cordiality and in October 1986 the two countries signed a Treaty of Mutual Respect, Friendship and Co-operation. [See chapter 13.] There has also been talk of closer military ties between the two countries. There are still, however, some 10000 to 12000 border crossers in refugee camps along the Papua New Guinea side of the border. Although some have been persuaded to return to Irian Jaya, the vast majority have been unwilling to go back. Moreover, in 1986 reports of the arrival of a further 700 border crossers into Papua New Guinea suggests that the problem is a long way from solution. The border thus seems likely to remain a source of occasional irritation and tension in relations between the two countries for some time to come.

The future

The 11 years since independence have thus seen substantial changes in Papua New Guinea's society, economy and politics. Some of these changes have been dictated by external circumstances beyond Papua New Guinea's control; others reflect the passing of the colonial regime and the efforts of the new nation to establish its Melanesian identity. Not all changes have been for the better. Some deterioration in administrative standards, the development of a serious law and order problem, widening disparities between a predominantly urban educated elite and the mass of the population in rural villages or peri-urban squatter settlements, and a degree of economic uncertainty all pose problems for a government pursuing development with equity.

On the other hand, democratic institutions are flourishing, substantial localisation of the workforce has been achieved, the economy appears reasonably sound, and Papua New Guinea has become a significant and independent voice in regional affairs. In the process, there has been a degree of distancing in relations between Papua New Guinea and Australia. This tendency was exacerbated by the Australian government's handling of the aid relationship and by the propensity of some Australian ministers to pontificate on the subjects of Papua New Guinea's economy and regional interests. It may also be accelerated if, as is to be expected, Papua New Guinea's national elections in 1987 produce a new crop of younger politicians who lack the familiar relationship which men such as Somare and Chan have had with Australia. But in any event relations between the two countries are likely to remain close and many Australians will watch with sympathetic interest the unfolding of events in Papua New Guinea's second decade of independence.

3

POLITICAL STYLE IN MODERN MELANESIA*

In recent writing about contemporary politics in Melanesia one frequently comes across the term *style*. The suggestion seems to be that there is, if not a unique, at least a distinctive Melanesian style (or styles) of politics. Hegarty, for example, speaks of an 'essentially accommodative political and governmental style' in Papua New Guinea (1979c:110) and Quiros (1979) speaks similarly of a 'conciliatory style of political leadership' in that country. (Also see Standish 1978:29 and Herlihy 1982:575.) Melanesian political leaders themselves frequently talk about doing things 'in the Melanesian Way' (for example, see Lini 1980).

This paper seeks to identify some of the elements of political style in modern Melanesia and to relate them to broader aspects of the region's political culture.

I begin by accepting that there *is* such a thing as political style; I will not, however, attempt to define the term, except to say that it has something to do with the way in which nations' leaders (and by extension nations themselves) behave within a framework set by formal constitutions and *realpolitik*. The suggestion that one can distinguish a national or regional political style implies the existence of an identifiable *political culture*,[1] though

---

* This paper was presented at a seminar at the ANU in 1980 and published in R.J. May and Hank Nelson (eds), *Melanesia Beyond Diversity* (1982).

[1] On the concept of political culture see Almond and Verba (1963), Pye and Verba (1965), Almond and Powell (1966:chapter 3), Kavanagh (1972). This writing might be compared with the earlier literature on 'national character', of which there is an extensive review in Inkeles and Levinson (1969).

it does not deny the importance of individual personality in political style. By way of crude illustration, from outside Melanesia: I think one might reasonably argue that, say, the Ayatollah Khomeini, Emperor Bokassa, Ferdinand Marcos, and Bob Hawke display a variety of political styles which reflects differences in the respective political cultures from which they have emerged, and which could not be easily transferred from one political culture to another, and that the spectacle of the United States presidential elections reflects a style of politics which varies from that of even such other predominantly Anglo-Saxon Western democracies as the United Kingdom and Australia.

The literature of political science has little to say about political style at an aggregative level, except perhaps in the field of international relations where several authors have referred to national styles as an important factor in determining patterns of international negotiations (for example, see Druckman 1977 and references cited therein; Spanier 1978: chapter 12). There is, on the other hand, a substantial literature on personality and politics (much of it contributed by psychologists), which has a lot to say about individual styles and has occasionally attempted to make the leap from the individual to the group or nation, mostly however in the context of 'developed' societies.[2] The anthropological literature on leadership in Melanesia is also of obvious relevance to the question of style in modern politics, but except for the work of Standish on Simbu politics (especially Standish 1983, 1992) and perhaps that of Finney (1973) on bigmen and *bisnis* – both of which are about Papua New Guinea highlands societies – there appears to have been little interest in the relationship between traditional and modern political styles.

---

[2] The personality-and-politics literature is well reviewed in Greenstein (1969, 1975). There is also an extensive bibliography in Hermann (1977). For specific comments on aggregative analyses of personality and politics see Greenstein (1969:120-140; 1975:60-68). Probably the best known study of personality and politics in 'transitional societies', is that of Pye (1962); there is also some interesting material in Legge (1973).

In approaching the question of political style in modern Melanesia one possible method would be to compile a series of political biographies and attempt to generalise national characteristics from these. Entertaining though such an exercise might be, the prospect of deriving some stylistic equivalent of a 'modal personality' from profiles of political leaders as personally disparate as, say, Walter Lini, Iambakey Okuk, Marten Tabu, John Kasaipwalova, Jimmy Stevens and Ratu Mara seems sufficiently daunting to suggest an alternative approach (a reaction which recent personality-and-politics studies would seem to support).

By way of alternative, it might be argued that if there is a distinctive Melanesian style of politics (or if there are distinctive styles) one might expect to locate its essence in a specifically Melanesian political culture (or cultures). Constraints of time and space prevent me from attempting to draw a comprehensive picture of Melanesian political culture. Instead I will suggest that there is a number of respects in which the culture(s) and the recent political history of Melanesia are, if not unique, at least unusual. Some of these are examined briefly in the following paragraphs.

The scale of politics and the politics of scale

Ward (1982) has touched on the question of the relative smallness and isolation of Melanesian societies and the impact this has had on their politics. This relationship is examined in greater detail in Benedict (1967) and in May and Tupouniua (1980). To quote from the latter:

> The relationships between individuals in a small scale society thus tend to be more intense and social transactions to be dominated by personal relationships reflecting, amongst other things, kinship, village ties and ascriptive status. At the same time, the members of a small scale society tend to be more dependent upon one another's actions than do those of a larger society. Typically, political and economic relations are dominated by series of recipro-

> cal obligations (between equals and between patrons and clients) but it is common, also, for small-scale societies to employ social pressures to ensure individual conformity to the values and objectives of the group. It is often suggested that smallness of scale promotes social cohesion, however there is little evidence for this; indeed as Benedict (1967:49) rightly points out, "intense factionalism" is a common feature of small communities. [May and Tupouniua 1980:423]

Diversity and (a little bit) beyond

Melanesia's diversity is legendary. Linguists have commented on the region's extraordinary linguistic diversity – and have made the interesting suggestion (Laycock 1982:33-38) that this diversity is not a function of isolation but that language has been used deliberately as a means of differentiating one group from another. Prehistorians and anthropologists, while reminding us of the extent of traditional exchange networks, have described a situation in which social units were typically small and in which intergroup relations were limited both in physical range and content.[3] It may be that we are sometimes inclined to overemphasise the extent of isolationism in pre-contact Melanesia; nevertheless the fact remains that even compared with tribal Asia and Africa, pre-contact Melanesia was fragmented to an unusually high degree and that to a substantial extent this fragmentation has survived the colonial period.

Related to this is a provocative suggestion made by Barnes (1962/71:9):

> A characteristic of highland cultures, and perhaps of Melanesia as a whole, is the high value placed on violence . . . . In these circumstances we might expect to find a less developed system of alliances and 'counterveiling' forces, and less developed arrangements for maintaining peace, than we would have in a polity directed to peace and prosperity.

---

[3] See papers in May and Nelson (1982 vol 1).

Bigmen and all that

A substantial body of recent writing on leadership and social stratification in Melanesia seeks to distinguish between a stereotype of the typical Melanesian traditional society as egalitarian and communalistic, with leadership determined by competition between men of influence (what Standish 1978 refers to as the 'Bigman Model'), and the reality of socially hierarchical, status-conscious societies in which heredity frequently played an important part in the selection of leaders. Without wishing to detract from this recent emphasis on social stratification (except occasionally to query the source of the stereotype), I think it is important that we not lose sight of the essential elements of truth in the stereotype: namely, that relative to Polynesia and most parts of Africa (not to mention traditional societies in Europe and Asia) social stratification in Melanesian traditional societies was not particularly formalised and that traditional institutions such as sorcery and warfare, as well as social attitudes to wealth, were frequently used as a means of preventing forceful individuals or groups from rising too far above the common herd (cf. Moulik 1973:123-127).

The exception in this respect, it would seem, is Fiji. There, traditional societies appear to have been more formally stratified and the status ordering, having been consolidated by colonial rule, has so far proved enduring (see Nayacakalou 1975; Nation 1978).

Whatever the situation may have been, there is now a well entrenched (if not universally accepted) belief that egalitarianism and communalism prevailed in pre-contact Melanesia, and that these values are integral to 'the Melanesian Way':

> ... our peoples are communalistic and communalism is the basis for our traditional way of life. Our values therefore must be communalistic. [Gris 1975:137]

The colonial experience

With respect to the impact of colonial rule on Melanesia's political culture, I offer four comments.

The first is the unremarkable observation that the impact of colonialism has itself been diverse. Not only have the colonial *masta* exhibited a variety of political styles reflecting *their* indigenous political cultures (see papers by Nelson, Firth, Hastings, Scarr and Latham in May and Nelson 1982, and Ward and Ballard 1976) but the timing of the colonial impact has been responsible for major differences in the attitudes of colonisers to colonised, and particular circumstances of physical environment and historical events (notably the Second World War) have affected the Melanesian societies in different ways. For example, Australian colonialism in the New Guinea highlands in the 1950s was a very different thing from German colonialism in coastal New Guinea at the end of the nineteenth century, partly because of differences in the political cultures of the two colonisers and partly because of differences in the circumstances of contact, but primarily because prevailing attitudes towards colonialism in the late nineteenth century were rather different from the attitudes prevailing in the mid twentieth century (except, perhaps, amongst French *colons*). Similarly, the impact of the French on New Caledonia might have been very different if that territory had had no nickel.

Second, beyond this diversity colonialism has had a universal impact in breaking down traditional isolationism, facilitating the movement of people, goods and ideas, and fostering a national consciousness within the (largely arbitrary) geographical boundaries of the colonial system. Further, the colonial powers sought to develop this wider consciousness within the framework of institutions and norms imported, for the most part, from outside. (Consider, for example, the comments of Waddell 1973 on the appropriateness of the Westminster model to Papua New Guinea.) At the two extremes of this generalisation: in Fiji the

British administration actively sought to 'preserve' elements of the traditional polity; in Irian Jaya Indonesian policy has been overtly assimilationist and the Melanesian political culture has been suppressed by direct political action and by heavy immigration. As in other parts of the world, however, the attempt to modernise Melanesian societies and to create national polities in the colonialist's image has been only partially successful. For one thing, like colonised people elsewhere, Melanesians have already shown a remarkable capacity for adapting modernity to tradition and tradition to modernity and for maintaining, side by side with occasional overlapping, the forms and institutions of traditional politics with those of the introduced system. For another, in Papua New Guinea, the Solomons and Vanuatu separatist and what elsewhere (May 1975, 1982) I have called 'micronationalist' movements have emerged to contest, actively or passively, the political boundaries of the modern states. [See chapter 3.]

Third, and more controversially, it might be argued that while colonialism is very seldom a pleasant experience for the colonised and although Melanesia suffered its share of forced labour, punitive expeditions and the rest, for most Melanesians the colonial impact, judged against the broad sweep of world history, was relatively benign (Irian Jaya being the notable exception). Without wishing to press the point too far – and recognising that in some respects this is a condemnation of Australian colonial rule: there have been few countries in which, as in Papua New Guinea, the indigenous government, elected on a nationalist platform, has sought to postpone the granting of independence. This observation and the implications of it have been elaborated by the African Mazrui (1970:56).

> Until the recent interest in large scale mining enterprise, Australian indifference denied New Guineans even the advantage of a shared anti-colonial resentment. The British [in Africa], by being exploitative, were also involved in fostering cultural homogenisa-

tion, some economic inter-action, some constructions of institutions for conflict resolution, and above all the beginnings of national consciousness. By the sin of indifference, however, Australia has denied her dependency such an infra-structure for nationhood. And she has denied her own participation in modern imperialism its ultimate legitimation – the legitimation of having laid the foundations of modern statehood.

Finally, in three Melanesian territories a major impact of colonialism (and I include Irian Jaya as a colony) has been the importation of non-Melanesian people. In Fiji and New Caledonia Melanesians are now in a minority of the population; in Irian Jaya non-Melanesians probably account for around 10 per cent of the population *(Pacific Islands Yearbook* 1978:223), but they are concentrated in the administrative and commercial centres and the proportion is probably rising. Obviously this makes for a different style of national politics.

Politics, economics and bisnis

In 1971 R. Kent Wilson wrote:

> When the economic history of Papua New Guinea comes to be written by an indigenous scholar, it is possible that it will be seen in part as the search for a key, a search indulged in by both indigene and expatriate, by both tribes and Administration. Exotic religion, roads, schools, co-operatives, savings societies, information services, business advice and so on, have all been interpreted in some contexts by one or both parties to the dual economy as the key to economic advancement. When frustration or imagination took over, the search was diverted to cargoism, a cult which in broad terms has not been the preserve of the indigene. [Wilson 1971:525]

Nine years later the record of Melanesian business enterprises is little better than it was when Wilson carried out his survey of village industries (Wilson and Garnaut 1968). Equally remarkable is the general failure of the numerous locally-based development movements which emerged in Papua New Guinea in the early 1970s. And although various explanations have been offered (e.g. Nadkarni 1970; Wilson 1971; Andrews 1975; also see Jackman 1977) the questions which plagued business development officers and development bank officials in the 1960s remain largely unanswered. Yet individual and group businesses are still seen – perhaps increasingly – as a road to development and to the acquisition of social and political status, and in Papua New Guinea provincial governments are in the process of setting up business arms, already with some unfortunate results.

Peter Lawrence (1982) has suggested a distinction, in traditional societies, between 'secular or empirical knowledge' and 'sacred or "true" knowledge' and referred to the continued strength – in the face of education and material advancement – of magico-religious thinking as an obstacle to people's understanding of the operation of the modern world. Certainly what Lawrence would refer to as cargoistic thinking, and what might be more generally described as inadequate understanding and unrealistic expectations about business, provides part of an explanation for the failure, in Western terms, of some business ventures; but it is also clear that Melanesians have not always seen the demise of businesses (or, indeed, their *raison d'être*) in the same terms as outsiders (just as Papua New Guinean lawyer, philosopher and consultant to his country's Constitutional Planning Committee, Bernard Narokobi opposed the constitutional provision for an auditor-general on the grounds that such an office was unMelanesian).

The relationship between politics and *bisnis* in modern Melanesia is a complex one, especially as in Papua New Guinea, where a government leadership code seeks to restrict the business activities of national leaders, many of whom argue (with Iambakey Okuk) that the accumulation of wealth is an essential element of political status.

At the national level, also, there is in much of Melanesia an element of unreality in the ideological commitment of self-sufficiency and the fact that Melanesia is, per capita, probably the most heavily aid-assisted region of the world. Commenting on this in 1970 (from the viewpoint of a political party organiser) Michael Somare (1970:490) said: 'our people are so accustomed to getting things for nothing . . . that they do not see why they should organise as political groups to express these demands.'

What sort of a picture does this leave us with and what sort of political style is suggested by these aspects of political culture?

The first generalisation I would offer – which follows on from the comments about scale and about fragmentation – is that politics in modern Melanesia, even at the national level, is essentially personal and group politics. In the absence of basic social divisions cutting across the Melanesian polities (to the obvious frustration of some Marxist analysts) the bases for political support in Melanesia are typically local or personal. With the exception of Fiji, and the qualified exception of New Caledonia (where French colonial attitudes and policies have produced the sort of anti-colonial nationalist solidarity whose absence in Papua New Guinea was noted by Mazrui), the Melanesian political culture has not proved to be a fertile ground for the growth of political parties. Even in Papua New Guinea, where in the early 1970s there appeared to be a well established incipient party system, political parties have not developed as the proponents of the Westminster model assumed they would; indeed in late 1980 the Pangu Pati machinery in both Morobe and East Sepik – probably the strongest examples of political party development in Melanesia outside Fiji – appeared to be in a state of total disarray. In provincial elections in Papua New Guinea during 1979-80 several provinces (including the East Sepik and Western Highlands) decided that they 'would not have' political parties because parties were 'disruptive'. Moreover where incipient party structures have emerged they have tended to display a pronounced regional bias. Even within the West Papuan liberation movement, personal and regional/ethnic divisions have cut across the common cause of Irianese against Indonesian rule.

In the absence of Western-style parties political loyalties have tended to revolve around clan, local or ethnic divisions. This appears to have two major implications. On the one hand it makes for parochial, pork-barrel politics; on the other it ensures the interplay of traditional and modern politics, with the implications this has for the accumulation and distribution of wealth and influence for political purposes, the manipulation of *kastom* to political ends, and occasionally the use of violence (cf. Standish 1983). A corollary of this is the growing incidence of nepotism (in Papua New Guinea, *wantokism;* in Vanuata, 'family government'). As several people (Melanesian and non Melanesian) have argued, there are strengths in a *wantok* system, but when the impact of *wantokism* is to entrench the position of those who for historical or other reasons have gained an initial advantage in the political-administrative system, *wantokism* has a great potential for exacerbating ethnic and regional tensions (cf. McKillop and Standish in May 1982).

A second observation, which derives from the comments about the fragmentation of traditional society, relates again to the importance of regionalism. Apart from the tendency for regionalism to manifest itself as a basis of political organisation within national politics, Melanesian societies have shown a marked propensity towards decentralisation, separatism and micro-nationalist withdrawal. Aside from such separatist tendencies as evidenced by the North Solomons, Papua Besena, Nagriamel and the Western Islands Movement in the Solomons, the formal decentralisation of political power which has taken place in Papua

[4] The closest to a coherent statement of 'the Melanesian Way' which I have been able to locate is a piece by Bernard Narokobi in *Post-Courier* 22 October 1974 but there is constant reference to it in papers in May (1973) and Lawrence (1975) has written about it. A similar philosophy is expounded in *The Pacific Way* (Tupouniua et al. 1975). The Melanesian Way philosophy is, of course, embodied in the Papua New Guinea government's Eight Aims and in the preamble to its constitution. [After this paper was written a volume on the Melanesian Way, by Narokobi, was published by the Institute of Papuan New Guinea Studies, Port Moresby (Narokobi 1980).]

New Guinea and has been mooted in the Solomons is highly unusual in the experience of new states.

A third generalisation concerns the inconsistency between the ideology of 'the Melanesian Way', with its emphasis on equality, communalism, self-sufficiency and consensus, and its respect for tradition,[4] and the reality of political and social change in Melanesia which so often is characterised by social stratification, individualism, dependence and conflict (Standish 1980 uses the term 'jugular politics'), and is so frequently anxious to embrace modern, capitalist development. In part, perhaps, this is evidence of a variety of Melanesian political cultures. In part it is a reflection of the gap between political myth and political reality which exists in all political systems. But it also has something to do with the use of ideologies rooted in a model of harmonious small societies to justify participation in a system imposed during colonial rule. And of course it should be said that 'the Melanesian Way' is not entirely myth. Melanesian politics often does reveal a concern for egalitarianism, a capacity for compromise, and (except perhaps for Fiji) a lack of respect for authority which places it apart from new states in Asia, Africa or America.

In a similar way the emphasis given to *kastom* or *kalsa* in Melanesia is in part evidence of genuine respect for tradition, but it is also a symbol manipulated by politicians (especially young politicians) to legitimate their participation in the modern system and as such, as Tonkinson (1980) has pointed out, can be used both as a force for national unity and a force for ethnic division.

I am aware that this paper does little to capture the spirit of Melanesian political style. And it does nothing to distinguish differential (for example, highlands as opposed to coastal) Melanesian styles. But I hope it does suggest that one might be able to talk about a Melanesian political style, rooted in Melanesian political culture, and that in interpreting contemporary political developments in independent Melanesia non-Melanesian observers should be aware that in part what they are observing is the assertion of that Melanesian style (cf. Quiros 1979 in reviewing Standish 1979).

4

MICRONATIONALISM IN PAPUA NEW GUINEA*

One of the most remarkable aspects of social and political change in Papua New Guinea in the late 1960s and early 1970s was the proliferation of spontaneous local movements, differing in their origins and specific objectives but sharing a broad concern with the achievement of economic, social and political development through communal action. Some of the movements emerged from a background of local cult activity; others were established ostensibly to organise local opposition to particular policies of central government but came to assume wider objectives; still others were specifically motivated by a desire to achieve development through local community action; a few emerged to press for a geographically more broadly based regional autonomy.

In an earlier paper (May 1975) a preliminary attempt was made to provide a brief survey of the more significant of these movements and to place them in some sort of social, cultural and historical perspective. The term 'micronationalism' was introduced in that paper to describe a varied collection of movements which displayed a common tendency, at least at an ideological or psychological level, to disengage from the wider economic and political systems imposed by colonial rule, seeking in a sense a common identity and purpose, and through some combination of traditional and modern values and organisational forms, an acceptable formula for their own development.

---

* This chapter brings together material from the introduction and conclusion to *Micronationalist Movements in Papua New Guinea*, published as Political and Social Change Monograph 1 in 1982.

In employing this term to describe so disparate a group of movements it was our principal intention to draw attention to the convergence in objectives and organisational style of movements with often widely divergent origins and in particular to emphasise their common tendency towards disengagement or withdrawal (but not, as a rule, formal secession) from the larger, national community. Although most of the movements described possessed a loosely defined ethnic base, many of them cut across linguistic and tribal boundaries and few placed much emphasis on ethnicity, some even specifically seeking a multiracial membership; for these reasons (and also because 'ethnicity' is at best a slippery concept,[1] especially in the culturally complex situation of Melanesia) we avoided the term 'ethnonationalism', which has been employed by some authors to describe somewhat similar movements in other countries.[2] We also rejected the term 'primordial' (Shils 1957), which has been attached to comparable movements in other new states but generally seems to imply greater internal coherence and intensity than most Papua New Guinea movements have possessed; similarly, terms such as 'communal association' and 'voluntary association', used to describe groups in Asia, Africa and Latin America, seemed to suggest more clearly defined membership and organisational structures than was the case with movements we described for Papua New Guinea in 1975.

An anatomy of micronationalism is attempted below; for the present, the essential characteristics of the movements we have described as micronationalist might be summarised: (1) membership is based on community or region and is typically fairly loosely defined; (2) objectives are universalistic but place major importance on broadly based and generally egali-

---

[1] For some cautionary comments on the use of this term see various papers in van den Berghe (1965), especially that by Mercier; Connor (1973); Cohen (1978). Also see Heeger (1974:88-94).

[2] And by at least two authors (Premdas 1977 and Griffin 1975) in reference to movements described in May (1982).

tarian 'development'; (3) ideologically (if not always in practice) emphasis is on achieving objectives through communal self-help, rather than through dependence on that colonial creation, 'the state'. It is in this last sense that we speak of 'disengagement' and 'withdrawal' (and by implication distinguish micro-nationalist movements from pressure groups and political parties[3]). At the same time, although we have included in the category 'micronationalist' some movements which might be described as 'separatist' (see below), micronationalism does not imply political separatism in the usual sense of that term (cf. Griffin 1973, 1976; Premdas 1977; Woolford 1976:chapter 11); nor does political separatism necessarily imply micronationalism.

By way of further clarification it might be useful to say what we have not included within the ambit of micronationalism. We have not included relatively narrowly-focussed interest groups (such as farmers' clubs and cattlemen's associations), whose membership tends to be restrictive, whose objectives tend to be specific, functional and individualistic, and whose activities are primarily concerned with access to government services. We are not concerned with political parties[4] (though the fact that some micronationalist movements have sponsored electoral candidates does not disqualify them from our definition). Nor are we looking at 'cargo cults'.[5] More tentatively, we have sought to con-

---

[3] Cf. Wolfers (1970) and Stephen (1972) both of whom included the *Mataungan Association* and Napidakoe Navitu in their surveys of political parties.

[4] For a comment on the definition of political parties, with reference to Papua New Guinea, see Wolfers (1970).

[5] 'Cargo cults' might be broadly described as movements which seek to achieve a substantial increase in material welfare ('cargo') through mystical or quasi-mystical means (cf. Jarvie [1963:1]:'Cargo cults are apocalyptic millenarian movements, primarily of Melanesia, which promise a millenium in the form of material and spiritual cargo'). Outside the more precise anthropological literature, however, the term has been attached loosely, and often pejoratively, to a variety of spontaneous local movements, many of which have had little to do with cargo expectations narrowly defined (cf. Walter 1981). The extent of a link between cargo cult

fine the term to movements which extend beyond the level of a single village or clan, thus excluding the numerous small 'village development associations' which have sprung up (partly in response to government stimulus) since around the mid 1970s. (Information on grants approved by the Office of Village Development up to 1978 suggests that there were probably well over a hundred such organisations scattered throughout the country towards the end of the 1970s.) Finally, though they are closely related to the micronationalist phenomenon, we have excluded from our definition ethnic and regional associations formed amongst urban migrants.

In retrospect, 'micronationalism' may seem an overly dramatic term to use in the description of the local movements we have identified, especially in a country which has displayed the high degree of political stability which independent Papua New Guinea has; nevertheless the term has gained some currency and we will continue to use it in this volume as a convenient umbrella, albeit one which casts a wide and perhaps poorly defined shadow.[6]

The emergence of micronationalism

Before European contact Papua New Guinea's population consisted almost entirely of small, largely independent communities of subsistence cultivators. Within these communities social, political and economic relationships were generally close and fairly well defined. Between them, notwithstanding some extensive trading networks and enduring political alliances, relations tended to be limited.

---

and micronationalist movement is a subject to which we will return.

[6] Gerritsen, also writing in 1975, used the term 'dynamic communal association' in reference to at least some of the movements included in our 1975 survey (contrasting such community based organisations with '"class" based' interest associations) (Gerritsen 1975:14). More recently, Walter (1981) has used the term 'community development association' in a similar context.

Under the impact of missions, traders and colonial administrators the situation gradually changed. As tribal fighting diminished and as plantations and commercial and administrative centres were established people began to move outside traditional tribal boundaries and to take up wage employment in the colonial economy. Later, encouraged by the colonial administration, rural villagers turned increasingly to cash cropping, producing mostly export crops whose income provided the means with which to acquire the goods and services of the modern sector and sometimes also to buy into traditional systems of status attainment. In time cooperatives were introduced as a method of promoting collective local enterprise and steps were taken to foster individual and group enterprises in secondary and tertiary as well as primary production. As in other parts of the developing world, a growing proportion of the population shifted at least temporarily to towns where they became wage earners or used established networks of kinsfolk to stay on as *pasindia*.[7]

Politically, the colonial administration sought to foster participation in the imposed system through local government councils at the local level and through a systematic programme of political education to reinforce the introduction of Westminster style political institutions at the national level.

The early relationship between the colonial regime and its subjects was, however, essentially exploitative. Traditional villagers and those on the periphery of the colonial society sensed an inability to bridge the gap between their own situation and that enjoyed by their colonial masters; this in turn generated a sense of deprivation and frustration which manifested itself from time to time in spontaneous local movements which sought, through a variety of means, to remove the blockages to the people's enjoyment of material wealth and power. Usually such movements were mystical and millenarian in nature but sometimes too they expressed themselves through acts of defiance

[7] From the English, passenger; hence one who is 'carried', dependent.

against government and mission. With rare exception the colonial regime regarded such movements, loosely lumped together under the term 'cargo cults', with suspicion and hostility and frequently they were repressed under the various regulations which prescribed against illegal cults, illegal *singsing* and spreading false reports.

As in other parts of the Pacific, the experience of the Second World War stimulated the growth of spontaneous local movements seeking change: it demonstrated the vulnerability of the colonial regime, it diminished at least temporarily the status inequalities between colonisers and colonised, and for many Papua New Guineans who came into contact with large numbers of people from other parts of the two territories for the first time it brought a vague sense of national identity. It also helped to produce a number of men with a broader world view and better understanding of the process of modernisation than their elders, some of whom returned to their villages after the war with ambitious plans for social, economic and political reorganisation and improvement for their people through communal effort.

Despite the fact that many of these movements displayed a fairly high degree of economic pragmatism and political moderation (even though a large number expressed opposition to incorporation in local government councils), official attitudes towards them remained, at best, guarded. Other observers, however, recognised in their objectives and organisation a change from cargo cult to political movement, a shift 'from religion to pragmatism, from myth to self-help'.[8]

The record of these early postwar movements was generally disappointing. Some degenerated into a pattern of behaviour reminiscent of prewar cults; others simply fizzled out as expectations failed to materialise and popular support gradually dissipated. The histories of the two best documented movements,

[8] See, for example, Belshaw (1950), Bodrogi (1951), Guiart (1951b), Lawrence (1955, 1964), Worsely (1957), Mead (1964) and Cochrane (1970). The quotation is from Cochrane (1970:157).

that founded in Manus by Paliau Maloat (Schwartz 1962; Mead 1956, 1964) and that formed in the Papuan Gulf by Tommy Kabu (Maher 1958, 1961; Oram 1967), are illustrative of a general pattern.[9]

Paliau, a former policeman, came back to Manus at the end of the war with plans for a comprehensive social, economic, political, religious and cultural transformation. His 'New Way' *(Niupela Pasin)* envisaged a break with traditional social organisation and religion, the construction of new villages, a programme of organised communal work and saving, and the establishment of schools, councils and village courts. The movement also sought to bring together traditionally conflicting tribal groups within the Manus Province. It sought cooperation with government but was antipathetic to the missions. In 1947 and again in 1952 supporters of Paliau were caught up in cargo cults which emerged in the area in competition with the Paliau movement. These cults involved expectations of a 'Second Coming' of Christ, destruction of property, and cemetery rituals; cultists had visions and experienced 'shaking'. Paliau resisted these manifestations of cargo cult but as prophecies went unfulfilled he was able to capture most of the large membership they mobilised. At its peak the Paliau movement had about five thousand supporters (around a third of the total population of Manus) and included several of the province's 25 language groups. However, with the establishment in 1950 of the Baluan Local Government Council (of which Paliau became president) and with the general failure of the Paliau movement to fulfil its economic objectives, the movement began to decline from around the mid 1950s, though Paliau went on to become a member of the House of Assembly and gain the respect of the colonial administration.

[9] For accounts of similar movements in other parts of Melanesia in this period see Guiart (1951a) on the Malekula Native Company (Vanuatu) and Cochrane(1970) and Keesing (1978) on the Marching Rule (Solomon Islands).

Tommy Kabu was another whose wartime experiences inspired him to reorganise his people to improve their welfare and status. Like Paliau, Kabu was a former policemen. On his return to the Purari delta after the war Kabu set up a movement, known as 'the New Men', whose principal objective was to further the economic development of the area on an autonomous, cooperative basis. Traditional customs were rejected; new, decentralised, villages were built; produce associations were established with a view to marketing sago and copra in Port Moresby, and a *kompani* was formed and some shares issued. Income from produce sales was to be divided between returns to producers on a cooperative basis and investment in new undertakings. The movement brought together villages from several language groups and Hiri Motu, the *lingua franca* of Papua, was adopted as a common language. For a while the movement 'suspended' Australian administration in the area, establishing its own police force and village courts and organising military style ceremonies, but this was quickly and peacefully stopped by the government. Within a few years, however, it was clear that the economic programme was a failure; the intertribal *kompani* collapsed, though several supporters of the movement went into individual business ventures; and around the mid 1950s the movement seems to have faded out.

Another well documented movement, which emerged a few years later provides something of a link between the early postwar movements and those which sprang up in the late 1960s and early 1970s. The Hahalis Welfare Society was created in 1960 as a breakaway from the East Coast Buka Society established a few years earlier. The East Coast Buka Society was formed by traditional leaders in opposition to the introduction of local government councils and cooperatives; when the majority of its members was persuaded by the government to support the council, the Welfare was set up on the initiative of some younger villagers to continue the resistance and pursue development instead through local communal action. Its broader aims have been described as being to integrate the whole community as a productive unit; to invest the group's income in an enterprise in which all would share equally; and to establish a relation of mutual respect and assistance between traditional leaders, the younger men and women with education, and government-appointed officials (Rimoldi 1976:2). Although there seems to have been a millenarian streak in the movement's activities during the early 1960s, the Welfare had a firm business orientation, being involved in copra and cocoa production and marketing, trade stores, trucks, road building and a credit union. Its leaders expounded a communalistic social philosophy – the most publicised aspect of which was the Hahalis matrimonial clubs, or 'baby gardens' – which incorporated both traditional and Western elements. In 1962, following a decision not to pay annual head tax, there was a violent confrontation between the government and the Welfare, which resulted in the arrest of the movement's leaders, John Teosin and Francis Bagai, and almost 600 supporters, most of whom were released after a court appeal. Subsequently Hahalis supporters resumed the payment of taxation and the government left the movement pretty much to itself. With the construction of a road across the island in the early 1960s, the provision of a high school, and improvements in government services, some rapprochement was achieved. In 1966 the Hahalis Welfare Society was registered as a private company. While shareholders provided a membership core, its adherents were said to comprise half the population of Buka in 1973 (that is, half of about 25 000) (Oliver 1973:153) and some villagers on northern Bougainville. Since then, and especially since the death of Hagai in 1976, the Welfare seems to have gone into decline, though it supported Bougainville separatism in 1975 and cooperated with the provincial government in the latter part of the 1970s and early 1980s.[10]

[10] For a more detailed account of the Hahalis Welfare Society see Rimoldi (1971, 1976), Hagai (1966), Kiki (1968:chapter 7) and Oliver(1973). [A more recent publication is Rimoldi and Rimoldi (1992).]

During the 1960s and early 1970s there was a pronounced acceleration in the pace of social, economic and political change in Papua New Guinea. Amongst the important elements of this were a marked increase in the absolute level of Papua New Guinean participation in the cash economy, a belated – and correspondingly rapid – localisation of the bureaucracy, and a conscious effort on the part of the colonial administration to promote a sense of national unity. Inevitably, the structural adjustments which accompanied these developments created tensions in the society and the rapid movement to self-government and independence in the 1970s served to focus these tensions, much as Geertz had described in his much quoted study of primordial tendencies in new states (Geertz 1963; also see Ake 1967).

This reaction took different forms. Some groups, displaying a higher degree of continuity with historical antecedents, turned to a mixture of mysticism and modern business aspirations, with varying degrees of antipathy towards government; these groups might be loosely described as marginal cargo cults.[11] Others emerged as organised opposition to existing or proposed local government councils or to large scale development projects in the area, but came to assume wider objectives. A third type of response, probably the most common, was the formation of what might be termed self-help development movements. These typically drew their membership from a small number of clans or villages and their broad and often vaguely expressed objectives were to achieve social and economic improvement through communal effort. A few groups, for whom questions of political status seem to have been particularly important, sought to mobilise a broad regional consciousness as a basis for demands for greater autonomy. The following paragraphs briefly describe some of the movements which were active during the 1970s, using the categories suggested above. But as we have argued earlier, these categories are fluid; indeed what is interesting about

[11] Cf. Guiart's description of the Malekula Native Company (Vanuatu) as being '*en marge du* "Cargo Cult"' (Guiart 1951a).

the movements which proliferated in the late 1960s and early 1970s is not so much their differences as their convergence, over time, on similar objectives and behaviour.

Marginal cargo cults

Amongst the movements which came into being in the early 1970s two attracted particular popular attention because of their large scale, broadly-based membership, and their association with movements in which mystical practices designed to increase money or improve material conditions played an important part. These were the Peli Association and the Pitenamu Society.[12]

The Peli Association was established in 1971 in the aftermath of what was described at the time as one of the biggest and most explosive cults in the country's history. It quickly gained massive support throughout the Sepik provinces but following a split in the leadership and growing disillusionment amongst its members, it declined. Before its decline the Peli Association had successfully contested a national election and by-election and had taken faltering steps towards the establishment of orthodox business enterprises.

Pitenamu first came to public notice in the same year. Having its origins in the Morobe highlands and, like Peli, strong links with earlier cargo cults in the area, the movement soon won widespread support throughout the province. Although it is sometimes difficult to disentangle Pitenamu's more 'secular' from its more 'cargoistic' elements, like other micronationalist movements it expressed a clear demand for greater political autonomy – reflected in antipathy to local government and in its early self-identification with the Pangu Pati – and for economic development, to be achieved through communally supported

[12] Detailed studies of the Peli Association and the Pitenamu Society are included in May (1982). [On the Peli Association, also see Gesch 1985.]

modern business enterprise. By 1976, however, the movement was in a state of decline with little to show in material terms other than a small shareholding in a foreign-owned company.

Another movement with strong linkages to an earlier cargo cult is the Tutukuvul Isukal Association (TIA) of New Ireland (though TIA in its present form might more properly be regarded as a self-help development movement). In the early 1960s there was unrest in the Lavongai Council area on New Hanover and extensive government action was taken against tax defaulters. Then in the 1964 national elections people in the area insisted on voting for 'Johnson of America' and after the election about K1000 was collected to pay for the United States' president's fares to New Hanover, where it was hoped he would set up a new administration. The Johnson Cult, as it became known, was led by young but uneducated villagers. It had no specifically cargo philosophy and emphasised work rather than ritual; between 1965 and 1967 there was some organised communal planting of coconuts as a cash crop. However, its main objective was to get rid of the Australian administration and to bring in the Americans as a means of improving the welfare and status of the people. The movement quickly attracted several thousand supporters in southern New Hanover and on the mainland of New Ireland. Its members refused to pay council taxes and boycotted government cooperatives, and there were violent confrontations with government field officers (Billings 1969). In an attempt to divert the people's energies along more profitable lines, in 1966 TIA was formed as an 'investment society' by an expatriate catholic priest at Lavongai. The Association received strong support from the cultists, as well as from opponents of the cult, and by 1967 had collected K12000. Initially it sought development through communal copra production and development of unused land (*tutukuvul i sukal* may be translated as 'stand together and plant'); subsequently it acquired a freezer, a small sawmill, workboats, and in 1977 three plantations. In 1968 a TIA candidate easily won the national election in the

Kavieng Open electorate. Payment of local government council taxes was a condition of membership of TIA; however, many members were antipathetic to the council and this antipathy seems to have increased after 1975 when university students from New Ireland worked with the movement during a university vacation.

Local protest movements

Several of the more prominent micronationalist movements of the 1970s had their origins in organised local opposition to government policies. Amongst these may be listed the Napidakoe Navitu of the North Solomons (Bougainville) Province, the Mataungan Association of East New Britain, the Nemea Landowners' Association of the Central Province, the Koiari Association of the Central Province, the Ahi Association of villages near Lae, and the Musa Association of the Northern (Oro) Province.[13]

The establishment of Napidakoe Navitu was the outcome of a series of public meetings held at Kieta in 1969 to protest the government's proposed resumption of Arawa plantation and press for a conference on other land problems associated with the Bougainville copper mine. Subsequently it represented the people of Rorovana and Arawa villages in an unsuccessful legal action against the government's resumption of land and in the successful negotiation of compensation. Navitu, however, assumed objectives beyond the immediate issue of land. Its main aims were said to be the economic, social and political development of Bougainville, political autonomy, and better education; a supplementary list of objectives included the unity of all racial groups and political and religious bodies on Bougainville, promotion of traditional culture, maintenance of respect for marriage and the stability of the family, early self-government, and

[13] Detailed studies of Napidakoe Navitu, the Mataungan Association, the Nemea Landowners' Association and the Ahi Association are included in May (1982).

the nomination of candidates for election to the House of Assembly. The Navitu also became involved in business enterprises, though these did not prove to be particularly successful. Support for the movement, which initially came almost entirely from the Nasioi people, grew rapidly; within 12 months it claimed 6000 members from 116 villages in the Kieta District (Middlemiss 1970:101) and support cut across linguistic and religious divisions.

Napidakoe Navitu was generally hostile to the government and it saw the Kieta Local Government Council as 'dominated by *kiaps* [government field officers]' (Middlemiss 1970:101). Expatriate domination of local business enterprises also came under fire. The movement was critical of many aspects of the mining project on Bougainville, especially the share of profits retained locally, but did not oppose the mine or the operating company. Increasingly the Navitu became an advocate of Bougainville secession and a supporter of a referendum on the issue of separatism. By the early 1970s, however, other developments in Bougainville – particularly the emergence of a more broadly-based Bougainville nationalism – and internal dissention began to undermine the political significance of Navitu; it also suffered an economic decline.

The Mataungan Association was founded in the same year as Napidakoe Navitu. Its formation came after a series of public meetings organised to protest the government's decision to form a multiracial local government council on the Gazelle Peninsula. The Association's interests, however, soon spread to a range of other issues, including land matters, economic enterprises, education, and the preservation of certain aspects of traditional Tolai culture. Opposition to the proposed multiracial council was expressed through mass meetings and marches and a partially successful attempt to have the council elections boycotted; subsequently Mataungan officials seized the keys to the council building and there were physical attacks on a number of Tolai leaders who supported the multiracial council, resulting in the arrest of several Mataungan Association executives. After the council was elected, Mataungan supporters refused to acknowledge it and instead of paying council taxes paid equivalent amounts to the Association, which in due course set up its own 'council', the Warkurai Nigunan. They also boycotted the council-run Tolai Cocoa Project. In 1970 the Association's patron, Oscar Tammur, presented a submission to the Select Committee on Constitutional Development calling for an independent government for the Gazelle Peninsula and threatening that 'the Association and its followers would break away from the Territory of Papua and New Guinea if its wishes were not satisfied' (Select Committee on Constitutional Development 1971:3).

The government's initial reaction to the Mataungan Association was a show of force. Large numbers of police were flown in and some villages known to be sympathetic to the Association were raided. A Commission of Inquiry into local government and other matters in the Gazelle Peninsula was set up in 1969, but its report did nothing to ease the situation. Eventually the government acceded to demands for a referendum on the council issue but the Association refused to accept the government's condition of a secret ballot. A further attempt to settle the issue by negotiation between the Association and several prominent Tolais (the Warmaram group) also failed. The Gazelle Local Government Council was suspended in June 1972. Three months later, in what was generally regarded as a victory for the Mataungan Association, the government introduced legislation designed to create 'a new type of local self-government for the Gazelle'.[14] The legislation provided for a trust to manage the property of the council and for the recognition of three groups: the Warkurai Nigunan, the Warbete Kivung (a group of Tolai who have refused to participate in local government since its inception) and the Greater Toma Council (comprising groups loyal to the Gazelle Council, who had held informal elections towards the end of 1972). These groups,

[14] *House of Assembly Debates* (HAD) III (8):1011, 29 September 1972.

to be represented on the executive of the trust, were given power to tax registered members and the executive of the trust was given responsibility for deciding on economic and community projects.

Mataungan Association candidates successfully contested the 1972 and 1977 national elections and held senior portfolios in both the coalition governments of Michael Somare and of Julius Chan. From an early stage, too, the Mataungan Association was involved in economic enterprise, establishing a market (in competition with the Rabaul Council's market), and acquiring interests in plantations, cocoa and copra marketing, trade stores and a tavern. In 1972 a New Guinea Development Corporation was registered, with authorised share capital of K250 000, to carry on the Association's business activities.

Mataungan Association leadership came mostly from young educated Tolai and support for it cut across traditional intertribal enmities. In late 1973 an official estimate of Mataungan Association supporters on the Gazelle Peninsula was 15 000; the Mataungan Association became a movement of substantial political importance locally and the Development Corporation, for a while, a successful model of local capitalist enterprise.

The Mataungan Association was a source of inspiration to a number of individuals and groups with feelings of grievance against the government and a desire to see economic, social and political development take place through local community action. Amongst movements which acknowledged the influence of the Mataungan model were the Kabisawali Association, the Boera and Hiri Associations and Komge Oro (see below).

The Nemea Landowners' Association emerged in 1970 near Abau in the Central Province to express dissatisfaction both over land alienation in the area and with the government's closure of the Cloudy Bay Local Government Council. Its members sought to form their own 'government' and to achieve economic and social development in the area, with financial assistance from the central government. Two smaller movements appeared in the same district at about the same time. The Wake Association was formed ostensibly, like Nemea, to secure registration of tenure over tribal land, though clearly it was strongly motivated by a desire to counter Nemea influence in the area. The Ganai Association, whose establishment probably also owed something to Nemea activities, was set up to oppose prospecting and timber exploitation in the area.

Demands for a separate local government council and for compensation for tribal land taken over by the Papua New Guinea Electricity Commission appear to have motivated the formation in 1973 of the ethnically-based Koiari Association. The Koiari, who occupy the foothills of the Owen Stanley Range behind Port Moresby, also voiced general aspirations for local social and economic development. In 1973 a deputation from the Association, accompanied by the regional MA, Josephine Abaijah, presented a schedule of demands to the Electricity Commission; the Association secured the promise of a road link to Koiari villages and in 1976 the Koiari were given their own council. Subsequently they received a substantial cash compensation.

The Ahi Association was established in 1971 following release by the government of an urban development plan for Lae. The Association, which represented five peri-urban villages, was created in the first instance to prevent the imposition of town plan proposals which were considered contrary to the interests of the villages and to take up claims against the government for compensation in respect of alienated land. A compensation settlement was negotiated in 1974 and funds received were subsequently invested in the purchase of a large commercial building complex in Lae. Other social and economic ventures included the construction of a market and the establishment of a provincial cultural centre. The Ahi Association also provided a means of political expression for these peri-urban villages.

The Musa Association comprised people of several tribes in the upper and middle Musa River area of the Northern (Oro) Province. Its formation in 1975 appears to have been prompted by local opposition to a government decision to dam the Musa River and relocate the affected villages. However, the movement declared its main objective to be communal economic development. To this end it collected subscriptions which were used to finance the establishment of a wholesale store and to start cattle projects in the area. Leadership of the movement came primarily from older villagers, though the Association was assisted by a young educated 'adviser'.

Two other local protest movements merit brief mention. The Purari Action Group was established in 1974 by a group of young educated Gulf Province people in Port Moresby to organise opposition to a large-scale hydro electric project in their province.[15] In opposing the scheme the Group called for 'alternative development on a more realistic scale, based on agriculture and farming' (Pardy et al 1978:216). The West New Britain Action Group emerged about the same time to protest against development projects in that province based on resettlement of migrants from other provinces. Unlike the local protest movements already mentioned, however, neither the Purari Action Group nor the West New Britain Action Group appears to have extended its activities beyond the immediate objective of protest.

Self-help development movements

While a number of the movements which began ostensibly as movements of local protest subsequently adopted broader objectives of autonomous local development, many of the movements which emerged in the late 1960s and early 1970s were established specifically to pursue development through communal action (though, to complete the circle, some later acted as local protest groups).

One of the most prominent of these was the Kabisawali As-

[15] For a more detailed discussion of the Purari issue see Pardy et al. (1978) and Kairi (1977).

sociation. The aims of the Kabisawali movement, as stated by a supporter (Mwayubu 1973), embraced political, economic and social aspirations:

> First it's a move to tell the government and the leaders we do exist as it seems we have been overlooked for any development. Secondly to fulfill the meaning of the Association broadly speaking, wants to run its own affairs like running the Tourist Industry with hotels and tourist amenities. It wants to revive the islands happy life with festivals and traditions without too much of a loss to the western world.

In 1972 supporters of the Association established a Kabisawali People's Government. The following year Kabisawali candidates contested the Kiriwina Local Government Council elections and having won a majority proceeded to dissolve the council, a move which was tacitly accepted by the central government. The movement's business activities have included involvement in trade stores, trucks, road building, tourism, artefacts trading, and a variety of more ambitious projects. Following the Mataungan model, a Kabisawali Village Development Corporation was established in 1974 to undertake business and other activities, including traditional *kula* exchanges, artistic and cultural activities, and promotion of youth and adult education. Compared with other self-help development movements, relatively little emphasis was placed on subsistence agriculture. From about 1975, and especially following the imprisonment of the movement's effective leader, John Kasaipwalova, in 1977 on a charge of stealing funds allocated by the National Cultural Council, Kabisawali declined as a popular local movement and its organisational centre of gravity shifted, for a while, to Port Moresby and Lae. In 1973 Kabisawali's successes prompted the movement's opponents in the Trobriand Islands to form a rival organisation, Tonenei Kamokwita (TK), with similar social and economic aims but without Kabisawali's hostility towards the central government.

The other conspicuous followers of the Mataungan-Kabisawali model were the Boera and Hiri Associations, and Komge Oro. The Boera Association was established in 1972 at Boera village near Port Moresby to promote village development on a self-help basis.[16] The main initiative for its formation seems to have come from young university graduate, former public servant and Pangu Pati chairman, Moi Avei. The Boera Association subsequently extended its activities to other nearby Motu villages and a larger, ethnically based, movement, the Hiri Association, was formed. Later a Hiri Village Development Corporation was set up to manage the organisation's economic interests, which included passenger motor vehicles, trade stores and an artefact and local fabric fashion shop in Port Moresby. The Hiri Association had little success with its business activities and from about 1976 support for the movement gradually fell away.

Komge Oro claims to have been formed in 1969, consisting mainly of people of the Binandere, Aega, Chiriwa and Biage groups in the Northern (Oro) Province. (Komge is an acronym from the five rivers in the region and *oro* is the Binandere word for the traditional men's house). However the movement did not attract public attention until 1974 when it successfully organised local opposition to a proposal to establish a large timber processing plant in the area.[17] As stated by its principal spokesman, John Waiko:

> . . . *Komge Oro* and its members are committed to pursuing cultural, social and economic activities based on village community initiative, and to developing resources with village leadership . . . The emphasis is placed upon subsistence living as a basis for self-reliance, and the acceptance of cultural activities that are bound up with that way of life. Any other innovation, be it in the form of technology, crops or techniques, must be geared towards supporting and improving the subsistence basis rather than distort-

---

[16] For an analysis of the impact of the Boera Association on the village people see Moi (1979).

[17] See Waiko (1977).

ing or replacing it with a cash economy. [Waiko 1976:17-18]

Under the guidance of two vocational school graduates, village pig and poultry breeding centres were established and village youth clubs were organised to help clear and plant gardens large enough 'to hold ceremonies not only within a village or a clan but beyond the tribal and indeed the regional level'; appropriate technology was to be promoted, small village industries established, and a village barter system encouraged (Waiko 1976). Waiko was also reported as saying that members hoped that Komge Oro would be a springboard for the mobilisation of the whole Northern Province, 'leading the people towards true self-reliance and control over their own destiny' and called on the Province's trained leaders throughout the country to 'come home'.[18]

One of the Northern Province's trained leaders, senior civil servant Simon Kaumi, did return home in 1974 after being suspended for making public attacks on the government. Kaumi became patron of another local self-help development movement, the Eriwo Development Association. The Association, formed in 1974, expressed antipathy towards the central government (Kaumi was reported[19] as saying in 1975 that if Papuan separatism failed his people would try to set up a 'Northern Province Republic') and to local government councils (the Eriwo established their own 'council', named Bubesa). Soon after the formation of the Association, a wing of it, adopting the bold title of 'Papuan Republic Fighters' Army' and led by Kaumi, seized an expatriate-owned plantation and occupied it in the name of the Association. Plans were subsequently announced for village redevelopment, cattle projects, supermarkets, and tourism development on the seized plantation. The central government responded by negotiating the purchase of the plantation for the

[18] *Post-Courier* 12 August 1974. For some critical assessments of the Movement see Yaman (1975).

[19] *Post-Courier* 16 January 1975.

Eriwo people, but the development plans were never fulfilled and popular local support for the movement dissipated.

Another self-help development movement which achieved some prominence in the early 1970s is the Damuni Association of the Milne Bay Province. [The Association is described in detail in May (1982).] The Association was created by prominent councillors in the province in the late 1960s following rejection by the commissioner for local government of proposals for council involvement in certain business interests. Through an associated company, Damuni Economic Corporation Limited, the Association acquired plantation interests in copra and cattle, and a freezer. In 1975 the movement's leader was elected to the National Parliament. Since about 1976, however, this movement, too, seems to have been in a state of decline.

On Goodenough Island in the Milne Bay Province three communally-based self-help movements appeared at about the same time. The Kobe Association, formed around 1970 on the initiative of an expatriate schoolteacher, sought to promote self-reliant development but was also an outspoken critic of government policy generally and local government council activity specifically. The Island Development Association, set up in 1971 by Goodenough Islanders working in Port Moresby, had similar aims but was stronger in its criticisms of central government, local government and expatriate business, its president at one stage threatening to chase government personnel and expatriate businessmen from the island (Kaidadaya 1974). In 1974 a third organisation, the Aioma Association, was established along similar lines. None of the Goodenough movements, however, appears to have been very active.

Amongst a number of smaller self-help movements which sprang up in the Central and Milne Bay provinces the Hood Lagoon Development Association is notable primarily because it was the subject of a pamphlet circulated by the government in 1976 as part of its Government Lliaison (political education) Programme (Office of Information 1976). The Association, established in 1974, mobilised communal labour and capital for a self-help development effort which included road construction and the purchase of a truck and freezers to facilitate the marketing of fish in Port Moresby.

Self-help development movements were slow to emerge in the highlands but by the mid 1970s there were several, mostly small, local movements. One of the larger and more successful of these was the Piblika (or Pipilka) Association. The Piblika are an ethnic group, comprising a number of clans which claim common ancestry, in the vicinity of Mount Hagen in the Western Highlands Province; they number about 6000. Formation of the Association followed a meeting in 1974 organised by a local bigman in an attempt to bring an end to a long period of tribal fighting in the area (Timbi n.d.; also see Mark 1975). Having succeeded in engendering a sense of Piblika solidarity, the bigman went on to suggest that the Piblika combine in a joint business venture. Initially trade stores and a petrol station were mentioned, but following advice from two young educated Piblika men then in Port Moresby more ambitious plans were formulated. In 1975, having raised K11 000 from members and with a government loan of K212 000 the Piblika Development Corporation acquired a local plantation which the government had purchased from its expatriate owners. Aided by unusually high coffee prices in 1976-77, the group repaid its loan within a year, declared a 100 per cent dividend to its shareholder members, and proceeded to purchase another, smaller plantation, make a substantial downpayment on a large motel in Mount Hagen, and purchase several trucks to be used mostly for coffee buying. There was also talk of establishing a special fund to provide loans to member clans for village development. Until 1977 the enterprises were run as before by European managers with plantation labour mostly from outside the province. In that year, however, inter-clan disputes led to the subdivision of the large plantation and its partial reorganisation on a smallholder basis.

Regional separatist movements

Opposition to existing local government councils and general antipathy to central government characterised many of the movements which have been described in the foregoing paragraphs. In a few instances such autonomist sentiments expressed themselves through the creation of what might be termed regionally-based separatist movements. In describing these movements as 'separatist', however, it should be said that, with the possible exception of the North Solomons, what the movements seem to have been after was not secession (which except for the North Solomons was not a practical option) but recognition by the national government of specific regional interests. The threat of separatism, in other words, was probably more strategic than real – even though not all the supporters of 'separatist' movements appreciated such a distinction. The two most commonly cited examples of separatist movement are the North Solomons (Bougainville) and Papua Besena.

The existence of a strong separatist sentiment in Bougainville was evidenced at least as early as 1968 when a group of Bougainvillean leaders and students, meeting in Port Moresby, called on the government to hold a referendum to determine Bougainvillean feeling towards separation. This request was not granted but the issue remained a lively one and in 1973 a Bougainville Special Political Committee was established, under the chairmanship of university graduate Leo Hannett, to help define Bougainville's political aspirations and act as a pressure group for political change (Mamak and Bedford 1974:22). The committee brought together traditional leaders and young educated Bougainvilleans, including MHAs, presidents of local government councils, representatives of non-council areas and outlying islands, and representatives of the Hahalis Welfare Society, Napidakoe Navitu and the Mungkas Association (an urban-based association founded by Bougainvillean students in other provinces). After protracted, and often acrimonious, negotiations with the central government, an interim district government was established in 1973 and a provincial government (the first under the new constitution) in 1976, the latter, however, not before frustrated Bougainvilleans had made a symbolic unilateral declaration of independence for the 'North Solomons Republic'.[20] Although North Solomons nationalism in the 1970s had much in common with the micronationalist phenomenon described in this paper, it was much more a coalition of political forces at a point of time than a coherent single movement. Moreover, while the movements described as micronationalist were characterised by a package of broad social, economic and political objectives, North Solomon's nationalism appears to have had the specific objective of political separatism, and with the granting of provincial autonomy the 'movement' lost its coherence.

Papua Besena emerged in 1973 under the leadership of Josephine Abaijah MRA, in opposition to the Australian government's commitment to granting independence to a unified Papua New Guinea, and with the stated aim of liberating Papua not only from Australian colonial rule but also from domination by New Guineans.[21] But apart from the broad objective of 'liberating the minds of the Papuan people', the aims of Papua Besena were vague and sometimes apparently inconsistent. Papua Besena claimed to be a Papua-wide movement with supporters in all the Papuan provinces. Lacking a coherent organisational structure, it chose to work with and through a number of Papuan organisations with similar objectives. (These included the Social Workers' Party of Papua New Guinea, the Papuan Black Power Liberation Movement, the Papua Group, Simon Kaumi's Papuan Republic Fighters' Army, and the Koiari Association.) But in fact the movement drew most of its support

---

[20] The most comprehensive account of the North Solomons nationalism in the period to 1974 is that of Mamak and Bedford (1974). Also see Griffin (1973, 1974, 1976), Hannett(1975) and Conyers (1976).

[21] The Papua Besena movement is examined by McKillop in May (1982), and also in Daro (1976).

from villages in the National Capital District and Central Province and served, primarily, the interests of an educated elite. In March 1975, six months before Papua New Guinea's independence, Papua Besena staged a unilateral declaration of independence, but no attempt was made to take this declaration beyond the symbolic act and in 1977 Besena candidates successfully contested the national elections. The movement's 'parliamentary wing' subsequently became part of a highlands-dominated coalition which, following a vote of no confidence against prime minister Somare in 1980, formed the new government.

A rather different sort of separatist movement was the Highlands Liberation Front (HLF).[22] It was set up towards the end of 1972 amongst students from the (then) four highlands provinces at the University of Papua New Guinea with the principal aim of liberating 'all highlands people from white and coastal domination in the public service, private enterprise and the armed forces'.[23] As well as demanding the appointment of highlanders to senior administrative positions in the central government, it advocated a high degree of political decentralisation and a majority local equity in all business enterprises in the highlands; there was talk of establishing a highlands development corporation to control tourism and to establish small businesses. Acknowledging inspiration from the Mataungan Association and Napidakoe Navitu, the HLF supported economic development through local community efforts and economic self-sufficiency, was concerned with adult education, and identified with traditional social forms. In 1972 a model village project, initially designated 'HLF Demonstration Village No. 1', was established at Olu Bus in the Western Highlands Province to give practical expression to the self-help philosophy of development (see Kaman 1975; Reay 1979). The HLF claimed to have the support of about one thousand highlanders in the public service and tertiary institutions and from several highlands members of par-

[22] The HLF is described in detail, by Standish and Mel in May (1982).

[23] *Post-Courier* 28 November 1972.

liament but it failed to attract a significant following in the rural villages, remaining essentially a movement of the educated elite, and by 1976 was moribund.

On a smaller scale, the Wahgi Tuale was created in the Western Highlands in the early 1970s to press for a separate province in the Wahgi-jimi area. The Tuale appears to have been a loosely structured organisation with both local bigmen and university students occasionally acting as spokesmen. At least some of the latter, including Philip Kaman, the founder of Olu Bus, seem to have seen the Tuale as a potential self-help movement with broad social and economic goals. Other, less articulated, movements emerged at about the same time to press for separate provinces within the existing West Sepik (Sandaun), Eastern Highlands and Morobe Provinces (May 1975:40).

Two associated developments of the late 1960s-1970s which were clearly related to the micronationalist phenomenon merit a brief note. One was the emergence of ethnic associations amongst urban migrant groups (see Skeldon 1977). This did not occur in Papua New Guinea on the scale it did in parts of post-independence Africa and Latin America, and the objectives of such associations were generally confined to a limited range of welfare and sporting activities. The other concerns the establishment of at least one regionally-based women's movement. The movement, best known by the titles Wok Meri or Kafaina had branches throughout the Chimbu Province and in the Eastern Highlands. It had much in common, ideologically and organisationally, with the micronationalist movements described here (see Munster 1975; Anggo 1975; Sexton 1980; Warry 1987).

Micronationalism and government policy

It has already been observed that the historical attitude of colonial governments towards spontaneous local movements was one of suspicion and hostility. Apart from the facts that they frequently followed practices unacceptable to officialdom and that their leaders were often suspected (sometimes with good reason) of exploiting their followers, such movements were commonly regarded as a threat to the authority of government and church. Official policy towards them was at best neutral and more often actively repressive.

By the 1960s government policy had become rather more tolerant but movements were still seen primarily as a source of local disturbance and a potential threat to the orderly progression to self-government and independence as a united country (cf. Rowley 1969). As late as 1971 an official review of the political education programme in Papua New Guinea recommended that the recent development of micronationalist movements such as Napidakoe Navitu, the Mataungan Association, and the Papuan Front organisation must be resisted and countered, and the same year Papua New Guinea's deputy administrator told the House of Assembly that separatist movements would be discouraged no matter who started them.[24] A particular source of concern was the frequent opposition of micronationalist movements to local government councils and refusal by their members to pay council taxes. It was this more than anything else which prevented the Australian administration from taking a more sympathetic attitude to the movements and it was this which led to the early violent confrontation with Hahalis and the Mataungans.

The accession to power of a national government, following the country's third general elections in 1972, produced a more substantive shift in attitudes and policies. In 1975 prime minister Somare wrote in his autobiography,

> During recent years one of the most important developments in Papua New Guinea has been the emergence of spontaneous efforts by village and ethnic based organisations encouraging self-

[24] *House of Assembly Debates* 11(17):123, 20-24 September 1971.

> reliance. The government recognises the importance of [such] groups. [Somare 1975:139]

In relation to individual movements, the new government displayed a willingness to negotiate at ministerial level and to make settlements (as it did with the Mataungans, Kabisawali, Ahi, the Nemea Association, the Koiari Association and, eventually, the North Solomons) to meet the circumstances of particular situations. It also provided a good deal of financial and technical assistance to particular movements.

In the area of national policy making, a specific commitment to decentralisation and self-reliance was embodied in the Eight Point Plan announced by the government in 1972, and the potential importance of local movements as a means of implementing the Eight Aims was recognised in a number of policy decisions which gave positive encouragement to local groups. The most important measures in this context were the creation in 1974 of a Task Force on Village Development (initially headed by Moi Avei, the organisational force behind the Boera Association), whose purpose was to assist village groups, and the establishment of a Village Economic Development Fund to provide grants for village group (but not individual) projects. Village groups also received assistance through favoured access to the Rural Improvement Programme,[25] through the establishment of a Plantation Redistribution Scheme, the administration of which favoured village groups, and through grants from the National Cultural Council to support local cultural projects. Development Bank lending policy was also revised to favour village self-help movements and requests from them for technical assistance were received sympathetically. Other relevant measures included the introduction of village courts and the establishment of experimental *Komuniti Kaunsil*

---

[25] Note, however, the comment of Colebatch (1979:120), that 'few of the local development associations appeared as [RIP] project sponsors'.

in Kainantu (Uyassi 1975; Mogu and Bwaleto 1978; Warren 1976) and, under the North Solomons provincial government, of village government (Anis 1976; Connell 1977) as alternatives to local government councils.

In 1974 Papua New Guinea's Constitutional Planning Committee gave consideration to the possibility of making special provision for local movements within the constitution. But while welcoming the growth of associations spontaneously formed by the people outside the framework of local government it was 'unable to foresee a situation in which these bodies might act as the main link between the national government and village people'; the Committee, however, expressed the belief that 'such bodies should seek representations on district-level [i.e. provincial] assemblies' (Constitutional Planning Committee 1974:10/3).

There is little doubt that the Somare government's more sympathetic attitude to local movements encouraged their proliferation. At the same time, it seems likely that the shift in government attitudes and policies to local movements did something to modify the micronationalist response. It is arguable that the government's apparent sympathy towards micronationalist movements enabled it to divert the energies of at least some potentially troublesome movements into social, economic and even political activities which accorded with the changing priorities of the government and so incorporated them into the system. In this way, paradoxically, the government may have contributed to a decline in micronationalism.

An anatomy of micronationalism[26]

Objectives

The objectives of micronationalist movements reflect the circum-

[26] This section draws on material presented in a preliminary form in May (1975, 1979).

stances of their origins. For the most part they were broad, ambitious and ill-defined. This is only slightly less true of the comparatively sophisticated movements whose objectives were spelt out in corporate charters than it is of the marginal cargo cults, and it is a generalisation which applies both to village level organisations and to regional movements like the HLF and Papua Besena. Nearly all the movements were 'universalistic', embracing a package of political, economic, social and cultural objectives. Even those such as the Mataungan Association, Napidakoe Navitu, and Wahgi Tuale, which began with fairly narrowly political aims, soon acquired economic and cultural objectives; and the majority of those, like Damuni and Piblika, which saw themselves in narrow economic terms had a clear political aspect.[27]

If one can distinguish a common primary objective it is that of material improvement through the mobilisation of local resources. In those movements with a more coherent ideology (principally those with young educated leadership) there was a general emphasis on improving subsistence living, but most movements aspired to take over expatriate plantations and businesses and most were quick to take advantage of government assistance through financial and technical support; indeed probably the most successful of the movements were those, like the Mataungans, Ahi, and perhaps Damuni, which managed to invest in fairly large-scale capitalist enterprises.

The demand for material returns, however, cannot be interpreted in simple economic terms. The desire for improvements in subsistence living and for success in modern business was motivated also by considerations of status: micronationalist groups were anxious to demonstrate that they could achieve for

[27] McSwain (1977:183) makes the general comment on the people of Karkar: 'One of the important differences [between the Karkar and Europeans] was the Karkar merging of economic, political and educational institutions into one generalised social system oriented towards the traditional value of local communalism as against European specialisation and compartmentalism'.

themselves what government had failed to provide for them, and the takeover of foreign-owned plantations and businesses was probably as much a symbolic assertion of independence as an attempt to secure monetary returns.[28] Indeed it is perhaps only in these terms that one can account for the continued existence (for a time, at least) of movements whose performance, in material terms, was so poor.

Amongst social objectives, special importance has frequently been attached to education, including adult education, and to providing useful occupations for the already large and potentially politically significant group of school leavers, though few seem to have achieved much in this regard.

Although the movements were essentially modernising in their outlook, most also emphasised traditional values and some, such as Kabisawali and Komge Oro, actively sought to maintain traditional social and cultural forms.[29] In this they differ fairly sharply from most of the earlier postwar movements. In part the emphasis on traditional values and forms is a symptom of withdrawal[30] and in part it reflects a genuine desire to cull the best from both traditional and Western cultures; but also it represents a manipulation, conscious or unconscious, of traditional cultural symbols to legitimise the activities of movements whose main objectives and organisation were foreign to the traditional culture and whose leaders frequently lacked status within the traditional social framework.[31]

---

[28] For an interesting critique of the materialist interpretation, from the viewpoint of a missionary discussing cargo cults, see Heuter (1974).

[29] Adas, in his study of 'millenarian protest movements', observes similarly that 'prophetic ideologies are normally eclectic both temporally and culturally' (1979:114).

[30] Compare Jarvie's comment, in relation to the revival of old customs by cargo cults:' . . . the revived culture is a symbol reminding people of a time of freedom or happiness when there were no frustrations' (Jarvie 1963:12). Similarly Smith (1979:176-179) sees 'ethnic nationalism' as a romantic reaction to the centralised, modernising state.

[31] In his analysis of the leadership of millenarian protest movements

In this context, it should be observed that the various participants in a movement may interpret the objectives of the movement quite differently. Studies of Peli and Pitenamu (in May 1982) illustrate how spokesmen for movements can exploit ambiguity in their pronouncements, presenting the movements for the most part in modern, secular terms but at the same time tapping the rich vein of magico-religious explanation which moves many of their followers. Griffin (in May 1982:135) suggests that Lapun may have acted similarly. Leach (in ibid.:284-285) similarly comments on the differences between Kasaipwalova, and other Kabisawali leaders and followers in the interpretation of that movement's broad aims.[32]

Leadership and organisation

In the majority of the movements described here (and in May 1982), initiative and leadership came mostly from the younger, better educated and more sophisticated members of the community, though in several cases their main function was to help articulate demands already expressed by village leaders and to provide the organisational impetus of the movement. Just as in the immediate postwar period new movements were frequently initiated by men whose outlooks had been widened by their wartime experiences, so in the late 1960s and 1970s several micronationalist movements were launched by university students or recent graduates who returned to their village or dis-

---

Adas (1979:112-119) distinguishes between, at one pole of a continuum, 'displaced indigenous leaders', who 'emerge as defenders of the customary, precontact cultural order' and respond to well-established models of behaviour, and at the other, 'men of low birth' who have no established place in either the precolonial or the colonial order but whose exposure to both allows them to act as 'cultural brokers' and who draw on both for their ideologies, leadership styles, and modes of organisation.

[32] Lawrence comments similarly on the Yali movement (1964:255):'... in 1945, when Yali tried to introduce a programme that did not include ritual activity ... the people distorted his propaganda ... it had to be made consistent not only with their economic and sociopolitical aspirations but also with their intellectual assumptions'.

trict to work with their people. This educated group brought with them a mild radicalism and an ideology which placed emphasis on self-help and political decentralisation. Frequently, too, (self-help notwithstanding) they brought a greater awareness of the possibilities of government assistance and a knowledge of the means by which access is gained to it. Young men like Kasaipwalova, Kaman, Mel, Avei, and Waiko owed their leadership largely to their effectiveness as brokers between village people and a central government anxious to encourage local development initiative. (Compare Enloe 1973:162.)

There may also be something of relevance to Papua New Guinea in the observation of Ake (1967:97) that in the social transformation brought about by modernisation, 'Those obliged to leave their folk culture may become lonely and insecure and inclined to doubt the meaning of their new life', and that such loneliness and insecurity 'tend to breed alienation and extremist political movements'. Though micronationalism in Melanesia has seldom taken the form of 'extremist political movements', for the educated elite, participation in micronationalist movements has probably been motivated often by a felt need to justify themselves to themselves and to their village peers.

The outstanding exceptions to the generalisation of youthful, educated or sophisticated leadership are those movements like Peli and Pitenamu, which we have categorised as marginal cargo cults. In these, as in earlier cult movements, leadership has usually been vested in personal charisma or believed 'special powers' rather than in educational qualifications, experience of introduced institutions, or leadership within a traditional social context, which have generally been slight. And in the Peli case, at least, there is an illustration of the division, observed by several students of cargo cults (for example Thrupp 1962, Talmon 1966), between a prophet-leader (Yaliwan) and an organiser-lieutenant (Hawina).

Sometimes, as in the case of the Mataungan Association, Kabisawali, Komge Oro and Wahgi Tuale, the initiative of young people resulted in clashes between the younger activists and traditional leaders. In no case, however, can a movement be explained simply in terms of a conflict between young radicals and old conservatives;[33] while the Mataungan case study provides perhaps the best illustration of the general complexity, all movements have found some support amongst the older people (frequently deliberate efforts have been made to involve traditional leaders in the movements' activities) and many have found opponents amongst the young.

With regard to the general membership, a common characteristic of the movements is the looseness of their organisational structure. Most had some sort of executive, though the members of this seem more often to have 'emerged' or to have been self-appointed or chosen by the leader or patron of the movement than to have been the product of a formal election. Commonly these executives were dominated by one or two individuals who acted as spokesmen for the movement. The majority of movements had a formal membership core defined by fee paying or shareholding, but records were not always rigorously maintained and non-contributors were not necessarily excluded from the movement's general activities. Papua Besena, in fact, specifically rejected any idea of formal membership or organisational structure and deliberately kept no records. In some instances a broader membership was defined by ethnic or regional boundaries: in a loose sense all Piblika people were regarded (or at least, at the outset were regarded) as 'members' of the Piblika Association, all Koiari were regarded as 'members' of the Koiari Association and all Papuans as 'members' of Papua Besena. But movements were seldom overtly exclusive and even those which appear to have had a distinct ethnic basis might admit

---

[33] Pye (1962:22) argues that 'sharp differences in the political orientation of the generations' are typical of 'transitional politics'. In the Papua New Guinea context, Townsend (1980) posits 'difference in the attitudes of the generations' as explanation for the contrasting post-colonial reactions of 'disengagement' and 'incorporation'.

outsiders even occasionally, Europeans.

In most cases the movements drew most of their energy from a small number of activists, usually recruited by the founder and sometimes, as in the Pitenamu case, held together by preexisting interpersonal ties. Next to these was a larger group of members with a fairly strong psychological and sometimes financial commitment to the movement. In most movements, and especially in the marginal cargo cults, there was then a still larger group of 'supporters', who may or may not have been fee-paying members, whose attachment to the movement was tenuous; they were there either through communal pressures to conform or because, while not really expecting much of the movement, they did not want to miss out if it did somehow succeed – as many Peli supporters expressed it, '*mipela traim tasol*' ('we are just giving it a go').[34] These floating supporters accounted for a large part of the membership claimed by movements at their peak (and in the cases of Peli and Pitenamu the numbers were considerable) but they were quick to let their membership lapse when it appeared that the material returns were not quickly forthcoming, and this largely accounts for the apparent instability of so many of the movements.

What does not emerge from the case studies is a clear picture of who joined and who did not join micronationalist movements. Worsley (1957) and others have commented on the strong integrative aspect of popular mass movements in Melanesia. Morauta (1974) on the other hand argues that such movements may link people across villages but divide them within villages. Walter (1981) takes this latter view further, seeing cult movements, and by extension 'community development associations' (roughly equivalent to our micronationalist movements) as movements of small men against traditional leaders. The data provided by the studies in May (1982) suggest that both

[34] Compare Bailey's (1969:chapter 3) distinction between 'core', bound to a leader through multiplex ('moral') relationships, and 'following' whose attachment is transactional.

Worsley's and Walter's interpretations oversimplify. Micronationalist movements – even those with a specifically ethnic base – seldom if ever united all of the people within the group, and many, like the Mataungan Association, Kabisawali and Nemea, were highly divisive. Nor is there conclusive evidence for the view that micronationalist movements were revolutionary within their own smaller societies: not only did many micronationalist movements make deliberate efforts to involve traditional leaders (Kabisawali and TK actually coming together in their support for establishing a council of chiefs), frequently leadership came from people who either possessed status in traditional terms by virtue of 'special knowledge' or 'powers', or (like educated elites) had other avenues to status achievement.

Finally with respect to organisation, micronationalism in Papua New Guinea was overwhelmingly a non-urban phenomenon. The urban ethnic associations which have been so prominent in Africa, Asia and Latin America, had some counterpart in Papua New Guinea (Skeldon 1977); but, with the possible exception of the Mungkas Association (an organisation created by young North Solomons people living outside their province), their social and political significance was slight. Apart from these, nearly all the movements were rurally based. The obvious exception is the Ahi Association, which however represented the interests of peri-urban villages against urban intrusion. Possible exceptions, also, were the two regional separatist movements. Papua Besena, while seeking a rural base, drew much of its support from an urban elite and from villages close to Port Moresby; similarly, although the HLF earnestly sought a rural base, it remained, by Standish's account, a movement of the urban-based elite (see Standish in May 1982).

Strategies and achievements

It is more difficult to generalise about the strategies by which

[35] Compare Pye's comment (1962:24), that the 'functionally diffuse character' of groupings in the transitional political process 'tends to force each

micronationalist movements pursued their broad objectives,[35] and about their achievements, than it is to generalise about other characteristics. In part this reflects a fundamental contradiction inherent in the concept of withdrawal from the political system: the more positively movements 'withdraw' from the larger system the more inevitable it becomes that they will attract the attention of government. Sometimes this led to confrontation, but more often it attracted the sympathetic concern of the central government, a concern which few micronationalist leaders seemed willing to reject. Thus, paradoxically, the ultimate effect of withdrawal was often to foster accommodation between the movement and the state and eventually to bring about a degree of incorporation. With these qualifications in mind, some common patterns may be discerned.

As we have argued above, the philosophy of micronationalism, while fundamentally a revolutionary philosophy, is one of withdrawal or disengagement rather than of active confrontation. Consequently, the movements discussed here typically tended to reject the institutions of the imposed system – government, mission and, to a lesser extent, private business – rather than seek to capture them (possible exceptions are, again, the HLF and Papua Besena) or deliberately enter into conflict with them. Some confrontation, however, was inevitable, especially in the early years of the period when the colonial government often regarded such deviant behaviour, particularly refusal to pay local government council taxes, as a threat to its authority and responded repressively. The histories of Hahalis, the Mataungan Association and Kabisawali all contain instances of violent clashes with central government, and in the mid 1970s clashes with Papua Besena and the Eriwo Association were avoided only by considerable tolerance on the part

---

group to develop its own ends and means of political action, and the relationship of means to ends tends to be more organic than rational or functional'.

of the central government.

A particular aspect of the micronationalist withdrawal was the general antipathy, and occasional open hostility, which movements showed towards local government councils. In a few instances such antipathy was bound up with, or became bound up with, local political differences; Kabisawali provides the most obvious example. More often it was a fundamental aspect of the micronationalist outlook. Local government councils were commonly seen more as survivals of colonial administration and agents of a distant and impersonal central government than as custodians of village interests. To many village people they were the most tangible element of an imposed system which had undermined traditional social and political structures and, having imposed taxes, failed to deliver the hoped-for material benefits of development.

In several instances micronationalist leaders sought to use their local support base to gain election to the national parliament – though, as the Peli case illustrates, without necessarily accepting the rules of the parliamentary game. Mataungan Association leaders stood successfully as Mataungan candidates in the national elections of 1972 and 1977 and in the East New Britain provincial elections of 1977, and unsuccessfully in the 1981 provincial elections. Papua Besena leader Abaijah became a member of the House of Assembly in 1972 and the movement subsequently mobilised support in Central Province provincial elections and scored a notable success in the 1977 national elections, which however it exploited in an unlikely coalition with highlands-dominated parties. Prominent members of Napidakoe Navitu, Peli and Damuni also contested elections successfully, and some others, notably Stephen Ahi and some of the 'young radicals' of the early 1970s, did so unsuccessfully. Apart from these, the HLF claimed support from the United Party and the National Party; the Nemea Association and Pitenamu both identified themselves with the Pangu Pati, and in 1973 the short-lived Social Workers Party listed amongst its objectives 'support for the Free Papua Movement and for the liberation struggles of the Mataungan Association and Kabisawali People's Government'. There was even an idea, which seems to have had some currency amongst educated spokesmen for movements in the early 1970s, that micro-nationalism might be used as a basis for political action at the national level (in 1977 John Kaputin was quoted as saying that, 'Development groups and not political parties should organise Papua New Guinea's Government'[36]). For the most part, however, micronationalist movements chose to operate outside existing formal political institutions and independently of political parties, and where micronationalist spokesmen were elected to parliament, the tendency (with Peli the notable exception) was for them to become incorporated into the larger system and to act largely independently of their micronationalist origins.

On the economic front, most movements were ambivalent. Despite the common ideological emphasis on self-sufficiency and subsistence, movements were active seekers of financial and other assistance from government and many of them took over expatriate plantations and businesses; on the other hand the frequent commercial failure of trade stores, trucks and other businesses can be largely attributed to a lack of commitment to orthodox business methods.

Conceptual problems aside, measurement of the achievements of micronationalist movements is made difficult both by lack of information and by the fact that the generality in which most movements described their aims makes it difficult to evaluate the extent of their successes even in terms of their own stated objectives (and this itself is a dubious criterion). Nevertheless a few generalisations can be offered.

The first is that micronationalist movements were remarkably successful in quickly bringing together groups of people as

---

[36] *Post-Courier* 16 March 1977. A similar view was expressed to me by John Kasaipwalova in 1975. Also see the comment by Nemea leaders in 1974 (quoted in May 1982:183).

members and supporters, groups which in many instances extended across tribal and linguistic divisions and prevailed over traditional enmities. They were also notably successful in raising funds from supporters and in many cases pursued successful applications for financial (and in a few instances technical) assistance from the Development Bank, VEDF, Plantation Redistribution Scheme, and other sources. As against these achievements, in the majority of cases the initial enthusiasm was shortlived; few self-help movements were able to sustain the active interest of members for more than three or four years.[37]

The apparent falling away of support for the movements might be explained by several factors. In most cases, it would seem, support declined because the movements failed to fulfil the expectations which they generated; this will be discussed further below. A more fundamental failure is suggested by Gerritsen's comment (1982:326), made in relation to Damuni but applicable, eventually, to several movements: 'there was no real mobilisation of people in any activity (other than joining) and thus no broadly-based developmental endeavour'. Paradoxically, another major reason for decline in support was the early success of some movements in achieving limited objectives. This applies particularly to the smaller self-help groups whose immediate objectives centred on, for example, buying a truck or boat or freezer, or taking over a local plantation: once the immediate objective of the group was achieved, enthusiasm waned and the commitment necessary to keep the project going proved difficult to sustain. Other reasons for decline (which relate to the common importance of individual leadership) have been departure of the initiators of the movement and loss of momentum through internal dissention. Interestingly, considering the history of cooperatives (Singh 1974), misuse of funds by movement leaders does not seem to have affected movements on a large scale.

[37] Compare this observation with the comments of Wilson (1972) on the performance of village industries.

The achievement of micronationalist movements in relation to broad social and cultural objectives appears to have been modest. A few initiated adult education programmes. Some may have encouraged an interest in their traditional cultures but of three proposed cultural centres for which government funds were allocated to self-help movements (Kabisawali, TK and Ahi) none materialised.[38]

Few of the movements admitted political objectives. Of those which did, Kabisawali and the Nemea Landowners' Association both proposed to establish their own autonomous 'governments' and both did (after a fashion), though neither seems to have been very effective. Several, like the Mataungan Association, Napidakoe Navitu, the Ahi Association and Komge Oro, were concerned to protest particular local issues, and seem to have been fairly successful in persuading the first Somare government to accommodate their demands. Where micronationalist leaders attempted to use the movement as a support base in seeking election to the national parliament the results were mixed (see below); whether, as the Constitutional Planning Committee (1974:10/3) suggested, provincial government provides a more effective stage for micronationalist politics remains to be seen.

We have suggested above that a major reason for decline in micronationalist movements was their failure to fulfil the expectations which they generated. Often the expectations of supporters were unrealistic; they expected radical transformations in village economy and society when, by their nature, the most that the movements could offer was a modest improvement in village conditions. But equally, few movements returned to their supporters, in terms of continuing material benefits, as much as their supporters had been encouraged to expect.

Concern for improving subsistence living (including the introduction of appropriate technologies) generally produced more

[38] This is perhaps not quite fair in the case of Ahi. A Morobe Cultural Centre was established in Lae – but only with substantial initiative from sources outside the Ahi Association.

rhetoric than action. Komge Oro, which placed particular emphasis on this aspect, planned village pig and poultry breeding centres and sought to organise village youth clubs to clear and plant communal gardens, but these projects do not seem to have made much progress. Olu Bus established a pig-breeding waste-digester project but the project was heavily dependent on the encouragement of a Canadian volunteer and when he left the project ran down.

Business ventures, especially takeovers of expatriate enterprises, were probably more successful; however most seem to have suffered from deficiencies in managerial competence, due in part to the inexperience of local managers and in part, as we have already suggested, to ambivalence about pursuing development through orthodox Western methods (Kabisawali providing an instructive case study). Where existing outside management was retained (as, for example, in the case of TK and Piblika) the record seems to have been better, but even then performance was often disrupted by conflicts over the direction of control. In the specific instance of plantation takeovers, poor performance by local groups threatened the viability of the government's Plantation Redistribution Scheme, which was suspended in 1980.

An alternative 'development' strategy was investment outside the group (for example in real estate or company shares). In general this yielded steady but unspectactular returns; but while it proved a useful way of generating income, especially for groups (like Napidakoe Navitu, the Mataungans and Ahi) close to urban centres, it was a dubious form of self-help.

It might be argued that outside observers are prone to overestimate the importance of material returns, that for most village people what was important was the demonstration of their ability to organise a coherent movement, and that the take-over of foreign-owned plantations and businesses was, as we have suggested above, as much a symbolic assertion of independence as an attempt to secure monetary returns. But this provides little consolation either for those responsible for distributing government resources to micronationalist movements or for a number of sympathetic observers who regarded such movements as potential vehicles for social change in accord with the government's eight aims and five national goals and directive principles.

At a more abstract level (not reflected in movements' own definitions of their objectives) it might be argued that substantial positive achievements of micronationalist movements lay in their contribution to a shift in development initiative from the centre to the village, their influence in the move towards political decentralisation (see, for example, Constitutional Planning Committee 1973a:A/4) and in helping to bridge the growing gap between a largely urban-based elite and the predominantly rural masses.[39]

Explaining the micronationalist phenomenon

Granted both the similarities and the differences which are discernible in the movements which proliferated in the 1960s and 1970s, two important questions are posed: (1) Why did the movements emerge on this scale when they did? (2) How are they to be placed in the broad process of political and social change in Papua New Guinea?

(1) The question of timing

We have already suggested that the movements which sprang up in the late 1960s and early 1970s had precursors amongst the spontaneous local movements which appeared from time to time throughout Melanesia since European colonisation (and perhaps before), but that the increase in what we have termed 'micronationalist' activity coincided with a marked increase in the pace of modernisation and of political development directed towards

[39] On the last point compare Wallerstein (1960) and Ake (1967).

the establishment of a unified, and unitary, independent state.

It was inevitable that modernisation, and especially the indigenisation of the political and (to a lesser extent) the economic system, should stimulate the growth of political, social and economic organisations.[40] And the great diversity of traditional cultures and the lack of obvious major social or economic divisions at the national level provide strong reasons why such mobilisation should have taken place predominantly at the local level. Further, the fact that Papua New Guinea achieved independence without significant resistance from the colonial power probably acted against the growth of strong nationalist movements,[41] and tended to direct energies towards more parochial concerns. Even at the height of nationalist feeling at the University of Papua New Guinea (UPNG), for example, it was reported (Morgan, quoted in Davis 1970:291) that

> . . . integration has been surprisingly poor. No genuine attempt has been shown in learning about and understanding a person from another area . . . Tribal bias and snobbishness is prevalent.[42]

It was equally inevitable that the increased pace of development would leave some groups feeling relatively disadvantaged, frustrated or threatened; for these groups the formation of movements with ethnic or regional boundaries and emphasising group identity and self-determination was a natural, and a historical, reaction.

---

[40] For an interesting discussion of the effects of 'size' on political activity, see Dahl and Tufte (1974, especially chapter 3).

[41] Cf. Mazrui (1970:56):'Until the recent interest in large scale mining enterprise, Australian indifference denied New Guineans even the advantage of a shared anti-colonial resentment'.

[42] Six years after Davis wrote, of thirty-one student groups affiliated with the University's Student Representative Council eleven were university-wide sporting clubs, fourteen were provincial associations (Central Province Students Association, East Sepik Students Society, etc.) and five represented sub-provincial regional groups; the remaining group was an association of (non Papua New Guinea) Pacific Islands students. Ballard (1976) has also commented on student parochialism at UPNG.

The variety of responses in the 1970s compared with earlier periods can probably be explained in terms of greater complexity of the society in the 1960s and 1970s, increased involvement of Papua New Guineans in government and the cash economy, and growing sophistication amongst both rural villagers and an educated elite which was able to act as broker between the village and the centre.

Hegarty (1973:440), following Geertz (1963:120), has suggested a more specific explanation of the surge of micronationalism in the early 1970s:

> One of the characteristics of the period of transition to independence is the rapid formation of political groups and movements. An awareness of the imminent withdrawal of the colonial power develops, movements – some with formal organisation, some without – begin to make demands of government on a wide range of issues. Communal groups with only vague and unspecified economic objectives tend to proliferate. Minorities fearful of their vulnerability at independence seek constitution or political safeguards . . .

Certainly the well publicised approach of self-government and independence must have sharpened the sensitivities of groups which felt disadvantaged, frustrated or threatened. The Nemea Association, and on a rather larger scale Papua Besena and the HLF, were specifically concerned to define their rights and secure their positions before the departure of the colonial government; in several instances (including Napidakoe Navitu, the Ahi Association, MODIPE, Papua Besena, the Nemea Association, the Purari Action Group and the West New Britain Action Group) fears of large scale inmigration were a particular source of insecurity and a stimulus to ethnic or regional solidarity.

In looking for more particular reasons for the growth of these movements, another factor of obvious importance is the intellectual climate of the period. Already in the latter part of the 1960s there was some questioning in Papua New Guinea of the dominant development strategy, endorsed in 1964 by a visiting World Bank team, of concentrating resources in areas of expected greatest short-term productivity, and at the University of Papua New Guinea (created in 1966) students were being introduced to critiques of capitalist, urban-oriented development and to theories of small-scale socialist development with Tanzania and China as models. There is some evidence of a growing concern with self-reliance and decentralisation in papers presented to the fifth Waigani Seminar, on rural development, in Port Moresby in 1971 (Ward 1972) but at the following year's seminar, which was dominated by the presence of Lloyd Best, Rene Dumont and Ivan Illich, these principles were swept forward on a wave of popular enthusiasm. (See May 1973.) After the seminar the Students' Representative Council endorsed a proposal by its president, John Kasaipwalova, to set up a student vegetable garden and pig farm beside the campus (a garden project was commenced but it was shortlived) and in 1972 and later years, encouraged by their university supervisors (who gave course credits for 'action research' in rural areas during vacations), a number of students returned to their villages to initiate or assist local development projects. In 1973, as an outcome of a workshop of students, staff and recent graduates of UPNG, the Melanesian Action Front was established, with a manifesto which emphasised equality, self-reliance and village development. The following year a joint staff- student Development Investigatory Group was established at UPNG with a view to supporting student involvement in village development projects. Many of these efforts produced more enthusiasm than action but they exercised a lasting general influence over village development in a number of areas.[43] Somewhat ironically these 'radical' influences were complemented by the propaganda of the retiring colonial administration, which emphasised the importance of self-reliance as a precondition of effective political independence (Parker 1971).

[43] For a more detailed description of the mood of this period, see Ballard (1976) and Standish (1982).

The principles of small-scale development and self-reliance were further endorsed in 1972 by a visiting United National Development Programme-sponsored team which reported on development strategies for Papua New Guinea (Overseas Development Group 1973). Following this, in December 1972 chief minister Somare announced his government's 'Eight Aims for Improvement', which included decentralisation of economic activity and (national) self-reliance.

It may be argued that the announcement of the Eight Aims, and subsequently the embodiment in the Constitution of a sympathetic 'Five National Goals and Directive Principles', merely gave official recognition to already prevalent sentiments and provided no clear basis for action. However Somare recognised the potential importance of local self-help movements as a means of implementing the Eight Aims and in a number of policy decisions his government gave positive encouragement to them (see above).

Finally, the apparent success of some of the early movements encouraged the growth of others. This happened in two ways. On the one hand, groups in one part of the country emulated movements which appeared to have succeeded elsewhere. Thus, for example, in the early 1970s a number of the young radicals were strongly influenced by the example of the Mataungan Association: Kasaipwalova's Kabisawali Village Development Corporation was closely modelled on Kaputin's New Guinea Development Corporation, as was Avei's Hiri Village Development Corporation, Waiko's Komge Oro, the (Goodenough) Island Development Corporation, and a number of other village self-help charters. In a more general way, the Mataungan example also influenced the leaders of both the Nemea Association and the HLF (and possibly others) and there were various supportive contacts between all these movements, and between Papua Besena and the Koiari, Eriwo and Nemea Associations. On the other hand, the success of one group – especially in gaining access to government assistance – sometimes prompted a competitive (one might even say defensive) reaction from other groups in the area. The outstanding instance of this is the TK reaction to Kabisawali; the establishment of the Wake and Ganai Associations in the Abau area and the proliferation of local ethnically-based movements in Manus (Pokawin 1976) provide others.

(2) Rot bilong development

We have already observed that several commentators saw in the movements which emerged in the early postwar years a shift from cargo cult to secular development movement. This view received 'official' endorsement when in 1972 the administrator of Papua New Guinea, Mr L.W. Johnson, went so far as to suggest that cargo cults might be dying out and being replaced by economic development associations.[44] Some, more specific, saw the postwar movements in political terms as evidence of an emerging anti-colonial nationalism.

Such comments suggest two, related, questions. First, what sort of a link is there between micronationalist movements and cargo cults? Second, does micronationalism represent a passing historical phase, an element perhaps of transition from colonial to new-state politics, or is it a reflection of more fundamental aspects of Papua New Guinea's changing society?

(i) The cargo cult connection

The data presented in May (1982) leaves little doubt that there is some continuity between the movements we have described as micronationalist and those earlier movements (and some

[44] *Post-Courier* 14 January 1972.

[45] A definition of 'cargo cults', and a comment on the usage of the term, is offered in note 5 above. Also noted is Walter's (1981) objection to the term. It is not our intention here to debate the semantics of the cargo cult literature; however, as Strelan (1977:11) argues, cargo is an inadequate translation of the Pidgin term *kago,* and in the following discussion we will use the term in the broad sense elaborated by Strelan (ibid.):'Cargo cults have to do with Melanesian concepts of power, status, wealth, and the good life'.

contemporary movements) loosely referred to as cargo cults.[45] The link is most obvious in cases like Peli, Pitenamu and TIA where there is a direct historical connection between prophet-led millenarian movements promising some form of *kago* and more recent secular movements pursuing 'development' through more or less conventional means. But even in the more obviously 'modern' movements, with educated leadership and impressive corporate charters, there are clear similarities of objective, organisation and strategy with the more 'primitive' cult movements.[46]

These similarities of form reflect fundamental similarities in the nature of the movements. In a review of the literature on cult movements, for example, Lanternari distinguishes four aspects of 'nativistic and socio-religious movements': religion; search for cultural self-identity; acculturation, and the psychological aspect (the last being expressed in such terms as 'deprivation' and 'crisis') (Lanternari 1974:487).[47] All but the first of these is equally pertinent to micronationalism, and in the more recent movements 'development', or more narrowly *bisnis*, has in effect become a substitute for religion. The basis of this coincidence has been suggested by several writers who have seen cargo cults, rightly, as a particular form of a more general class of revolutionary social movement. Hobsbawm (1959), for example, places 'millenarian movements' in the middle of a hierarchy of social movements ranked 'in order of increasing ambition', but observes:

> The essence of millenarianism, the hope of a complete and radical change, in the world . . . is not confined to primitivism. It is

[46] Gerritsen similarly sees his 'dynamic communal associations', as 'the spiritual if not the lineal descendants of the cargo cults', even to the point of describing the Mataungan Association as 'the heir to earlier cargo cults' (1975:8-9, 14, 18).

[47] Comparable lists of the 'characteristics' of cargo cults are presented and discussed in Stanner (1953), Hogbin (1958), Hobsbawm (1959), Mead (1964), Jarvie (1964), Brown (1966), Talmon (1966), and elsewhere.

present almost by definition, in all revolutionary movements of whatever kind . . .[48] [ibid.:57]

In an otherwise not particularly illuminating paper on the explanation of cargo cults, Inglis (1957) also hints at the continuity between cults and modern development movements when she suggests that cults might be arranged on a scale according to degree of sophistication, 'And by sophistication, in this context, I mean the capacity of the natives to understand what kind of effort will enable them to gain their ends' (ibid.:249-250). Similarly Brown (1966) distinguishes between cults and secular movements but observes that cults may alternate with secular movements and that 'Movements which are practical both in their ends and in their means may incorporate the sort of false beliefs which are common in cults' (ibid.:161). (See also Wallace 1956; Brookfield 1972; Stephen 1977; Adas 1979.)

At the risk of oversimplifying an extensive and often subtle body of scholarly writing, one might summarise the relationship: both cargo cults and micronationalist movements have their ori-

---

[48] Hobsbawm suggests three main characteristics of the 'typical old fashioned millenarian movement in Europe': 'First, a profound and total rejection of the present, evil world . . . Second, a fairly standardised "ideology" of the chiliastic type . . . Third . . . a fundamental vagueness about the actual way in which the new society will be brought about' (1959:57-58). Being essentially revolutionary, however, millenarian movements are easily modernised or absorbed into modern social movements. Once so transformed or absorbed, Hobsbawm argues, they normally retain the first of these characteristics (rejection of the present order); abandon the second at least to some extent, substituting a modern, generally secular, ideology; and add a superstructure of modern revolutionary politics (ibid.:59). In the Papua New Guinea case, it might be argued that in the 1970s political responsibility was already being transferred from the colonial government to 'the people' – but without a corresponding transfer of economic power, and that in consequence what was added to the armoury of local mass movements was not a superstructure of revolutionary politics but one oriented to 'development' through a combination of modern *bisnis* and a somewhat romanticised ideology of communal self-help.

gins, at least in part, in a sense of relative deprivation, whether in terms of material goods, status, or political power;[49] both seem to occur with greatest frequency in periods of rapid change; and both, in seeking ultimately to remove the blockages which prevent their supporters from enjoying those things of which they believe themselves to be deprived, do so, in varying forms and to differing degrees, through 'withdrawal' or 'disengagement', redrawing the world, as it were, within their own perspective and on their own scale.[50] With regard to modern movements, it is this tendency to withdrawal which principally distinguishes micronationalist movements from, for example, pressure groups or political parties.

Within this framework, what differentiates micronationalist movements from cargo cults is essentially their reliance on a secular rather than a magico-religious world view and their use of 'modern' means over ritual. This is not, however, to draw too sharp a distinction. As we have already implied by the use of the term 'marginal cargo cult', the dividing line is not always precise.[51] Moreover, it requires a certain amount of ethnocentricity to believe that because the behaviour of recent movements corresponds more closely than that of cults to economic and political norms familiar to Western trained observers, there is necessarily a greater 'rationality' on the part of the mass of support-

[49] The concept of relative deprivation is explored in Aberle (1962). Note, however, Aberle's warning that analysis in terms of deprivation does have 'a certain excessive flexibility. It is always possible after the fact to find deprivations' (1962:213).

[50] Compare Aberle (1962:214): '. . . the deprivations which form the background for the [millenarian movement not only involve the sense of blockage . . . but also the sense of a social order which cannot be reconstituted to yield the satisfactions desired. The millenarian ideology justifies the removal of the participants from that social order . . . [It] justifies withdrawal, and that is its functional significance'.

[51] Stent (1973:2), in proposing a definition of cargo cults, has some interesting comments on what, in the Papua New Guinea context, is and what is not a cargo cult.

ers, to whom the rituals of business organisation and parliamentary politics may be no less exotic than those of 'money houses' and 'memorial gardens', and for whom expectations about material returns may be no less unrealistic.[52]

Nor do we support the view that cargo cults are on the verge of extinction. With increasing sophistication amongst village people it is to be expected that economic development associations, self-help movements, and suchlike 'modern' organisations will be seen as more potent, more officially acceptable and more fashionable than movements which begin from a magico-religious world view (even the leaders of Peli and Pitenamu vigorously denied charges of cargo cultism). But the magico-religious world view is a persistent one. Lawrence wrote in 1964 that 'many natives in the southern Madang District seem to have accepted development as a potentially satisfactory alternative to cargo cult' (1964:274); in a preface to McSwain (1977), however, he acknowledged that cargo belief had not disappeared with economic and sociopolitical development, adding that 'cults as such are relatively unimportant. What is important is the general condition of cargoism, which is interwoven with everyday events . . . the distinction between religious and secular may have little meaning for [Papua New Guineans]' (McSwain 1977:xii-xiii).[53] Moreover, whether or not we can expect some decline in magico-religious thinking, both cargo cults and micronationalism derive from similar feelings of deprivation, frustration and insecurity, and so long as the underlying social and economic forces which

[52] On the subject of 'rationality' in relation to cult behaviour see Jarvie (1964:chapter 5), Jarvie and Agassi in Wilson (1970), Brookfield (1972:chapter 13), and especially Adas (1979:160-164).

[53] Lawrence has further elaborated his 1977 comments in Lawrence (1982). Similarly see Strelan (1977:10): 'Cargoism in Melanesia is endemic; it exists even when and where there is no overt cargo movement or cargo activity'. McSwain (1977) and Stephen (1977) are amongst others who have recently documented the coexistence of cultic and secular beliefs and social action.

[54] Similarly, see Gerritsen (1975:8-9).

generate these feelings continue to operate, such movements will continue to appear.[54]

(ii) Nationalism and micronationalism

This brings us to the second of the two questions posed above, namely that concerning the relationship between the movements which proliferated in the 1960s and 1970s and the emergence of a broadly based nationalism.

Amongst those who saw a transformation in cargo cultism in the early postwar years, many interpreted the change in terms of a shift from cult to political movement. Worsley, for example, wrote:

> . . . we have seen a general trend in the development of the cults away from apocalyptic mysticism towards secular political organisation, a trend from religious cult to political party and cooperative . . . We are, in fact, witnessing the early stages of formation of national groupings in Melanesia. [Worsley 1957:231, 254]

Worsley referred to such groupings as '"proto-nationalist" formations of a transitional kind', endorsing Guiart's earlier description of movements as 'forerunners of Melanesian nationalism' (Guiart 1951b; Worsley 1957:255). Similarly, Lawrence (1955:20; 1964) referred to cargo cult as 'an embryonic nationalist movement', and Mead (1964:197) commented that 'Whereas cargo cults had become endemic in the New Guinea area, political movements were epidemic in the immediate postwar atmosphere'. This interpretation of events was shared by such other prominent and enlightened observers of the Papua New Guinea scene as Belshaw (1950), Bodrogi (1951), Hogbin (1958), Rowley (1965), and Brown (1966).[55] Indeed Hogbin (1958:232) warned that 'The governments of Melanesia may in the future

[55] It was not, however, universally accepted; see, for example, Stanner (1958) and Jarvie (1964:61). A more recent critic of the hypothesis is Smith (1979:chapter 2).

find themselves confronted with a Mau-Mau cult or . . . with a serious attempt to obtain political independence', while Rowley optimistically saw 'The solution . . . being worked out largely through the extension of the Local Government Councils' (1965:186).

Developments in Papua New Guinea in the 1970s could have been interpreted as supporting such a viewpoint: at a superficial level, micronationalist movements proliferated in the period leading up to independence, and in at least some respects (the emphasis on communal self-help, local political autonomy, and traditional values, for example) most did express an emerging Melanesian nationalism. More specifically, in several instances movements confronted the colonial government or had prominent members contest elections. There was even the suggestion that micronationalist movements might provide a basis for political action at the national level, which suggests that some people within micronationalist politics saw the movements in proto-nationalist terms, and in 1973 the Pangu Pati, the leading nationalist political movement in the country, invited representatives of movements to the Pangu Pati Congress.[56] Thus, Grosart argues (1982:174,149) that Mataunganism was both a nationalist and a micronationalist movement, Adams (1982:240) attributes to the Ahi Association 'strong nationalist sentiments' and Gerritsen describes the ideology of Damuni as '"early independence" nationalism' (1982:311).

As against this, however: first, the spread of micronationalist movements, and the form they took, can be explained (as we have attempted above) in other terms, relating more to 'primordial' differentiation in the period leading up to, *and in the period following*, independence than to an emerging pre-independence nationalism; second, rather than metamorphose into segments of a fully-fledged nationalist movement, the tendency was for micronationalist movements simply to lose

[56] David Hegarty, personal communication, 1976.

their initial impetus and dissipate their support. The possible exceptions to this latter generalisation were the Mataungan Association and Papua Besena, both of which participated successfully in national politics; but even these two movements remained essentially local or regional in their orientation. And the idea of a pan-micronationalist group in national politics was never made operational, and was effectively rejected in 1974 by the Constitutional Planning Committee, of which the North Solomons' John Momis and the Mataungan Association's John Kaputin were prominent members. Thus, without denying that an emerging broader Melanesian nationalism may have been one element of the micronationalist phenomenon in the 1970s, and bearing in mind also that a period of colonial struggle might have brought micronationalist movements together in a more concrete way than in fact occurred, the general conclusion must be that micronationalism in Papua New Guinea cannot be seen simply as a transitional phase of 'nation-building', but rather reflects the continuing strength of localism, regionalism, and ethnicity in Papua New Guinean society. To the extent that micronationalism in Papua New Guinea was a revolutionary force, in other words, the micronationalists sought their new order not so much in the overthrow or capture of the colonial regime, as Worsley and others seem to have anticipated, as in withdrawal from it.

Going from the particular to the general, in retrospect the view expressed by Worsley and others might be seen as belonging to a more general school of thought, dominant in much of the 'development' literature of the 1950s and 1960s, which saw political and social change as an *evolutionary* process in which particuliarisms like micronationalism and ethnicity inevitably gave way in the face of emerging nationalism, and in which (in some formulations) social class superseded ethnic and local divisions as a fundamental basis for political organisation.[57] But

[57] For a recent formulation of such an 'evolutionary' viewpoint, with

the tendency to regard micronationalist and similar movements as a feature of transition, by aggregation, from tribal societies to an integrated nation-state underrated the persistence of ethnic and regional divisions, not only in the new states but in the longer established states of Europe and North America as well. In Africa, Asia and Latin America micronationalist-type movements have not disappeared, despite the frequent efforts of independent governments to eliminate them, and in Europe and North America there has been a resurgence of what Birch (1978:331-332) refers to as 'minority nationalist movements'.[58]

Reflecting the historical facts, from the 1960s a number of scholars rejected the evolutionist idea of 'nation-building',[59] arguing not only that (in the words of Melson and Wolpe 1970:112) 'communalism may . . . be a persistent feature of social change', but that

> To ask whether new national identities will replace or be built upon existing 'primordial' identities is to miss the point that these 'primordial' identities are themselves in the process of being created. For many of the same factors generating national identities . . . are generating sub-national identities as well. [Weiner 1973:253]

This view was well elaborated by Heeger (1974). In non-Western societies, Heeger argued (ibid.:5), 'Social change, far from being inevitable and ultimately modernising, is sporadic, erratic and unpredictable in its consequences'. In much the same terms as Shils (1963) had employed a decade earlier, Heeger characterised 'underdeveloped societies' as highly segmentary ('segmented by region, community, kinship and the pace of social change', ibid.:23) and their politics as amorphous and inherently

specific reference to Papua New Guinea, see Townsend (1980). Townsend sees 'the present disengagement in some rural areas' as 'a transitory phase' (ibid.:16), preceding eventual incorporation into the world system.

58 Also see Smith (1979) and Gourevitch (1979).

59 See, for example, Wallerstein (1960), Geertz (1963), Connor (1967-68,

unstable, being held together at the centre by a tenuous cohesion of political elites.

Much of the 'post evolutionist' writing on political and social change in new states has drawn on experiences in Asia and Africa, and this has influenced the respective emphases which different authors place on such questions as ethnicity, stability and the role of elites. But the general emphasis on the persistence of segmentary elements in the political process, and on the importance of understanding these elements if one is to comprehend the nature of political and social change, has an obvious relevance for Papua New Guinea (and one which Papua New Guineans have not been slow to realise).[60]

Conclusion

What, then, is the likely future of micronationalism? If the analysis of Heeger and others is broadly correct – and I believe it is[61] – then we may expect to see movements of this type playing a continuing role in the expression of regional, communal and ethnic elements in Papua New Guinean society. Obviously their future form and activities will depend largely on the way in which the country's political and social institutions develop. Of particular importance will be the institution of provincial government: in part at least, the introduction of provincial government was seen by its proponents as a means of containing the centrifugal tendencies which micronationalism seemed to present; in fact, however, provincial government may provide a favourable environment for micronationalist movements – especially in view of the decision in several provinces 'not to have' political parties in provincial elections.

1971-72), Roth (1968), Melson and Wolpe (1970), Enloe (1973), Heeger (1974), Birch (1978), Smith (1979).

[60] See, for example, Somare (1970).

[61] For one thing, it helps explain the non-development of a coherent national political party system.

It must remain a strong possibility that micronationalist movements will turn increasingly to more conventional methods of political and economic activity and thus be gradually incorporated within the system, at the provincial if not at the national level. Equally plausible, however, is that micronationalist movements (and also perhaps cultic movements) will continue to emerge, sporadically, as a form of protest amongst groups who consider themselves relatively deprived, slighted or threatened.

For the country's political leaders the central problem will continue to be much as it has been over the past decade or so, namely one of minimising the unproductively disruptive effects of movements locally while maximising their undoubted potential as innovative indigenous responses to political and social change.

5

THE POLITICAL EDUCATION PROGRAMME*

Before both the 1964 and 1968 general elections in Papua New Guinea, the Australian colonial administration embarked on a programme of political education intended to acquaint voters with some of the broader aspects of the political system it was introducing and thus to increase their appreciation of what the election was all about (Bettison 1965:53-69, Parker and Wolfers 1971:41-45). There was widespread criticism of both programmes, both for what they sought to do and for what they failed to achieve. Reviewing the achievements of the education programme which preceded the 1968 election, in mid-1968 an inter-departmental committee recorded a general feeling that while it could not be said that the programme had failed, its impact had perhaps been slight; this was attributed to a lack of funds and resources to enable a more ambitious programme to be carried out. Subsequently, the report of the United Nations mission which had visited Papua New Guinea in 1968 recommended 'that there should be a more vigorous programme of political education through all available publicity media' (United Nations 1968:113). Even while the 1968 election was in progress there were proposals to set up a continuing programme of political education. These were generally accepted and in July a reconstituted interdepartmental

* This study was undertaken in 1972, as part of a broader study of the last pre-independence national election, and was published in D. Stone (ed.), *Prelude to Self-Government: Electoral Politics in Papua New Guinea 1972* (1976).

Political Education Committee (hereafter PEC) held its first meeting. The Committee was instructed to plan and recommend to the administrator a long-term programme of political education and to implement an approved programme.[1] It was to liaise with the administrator's Public Relations Advisory Committee (PRAC), through whom its report was eventually to be submitted. Subsequently, the Australian Minister for External Territories approved the re-establishment of the inter-departmental committee, but noted that it should not make statements concerning the meaning and implications of self-determination or about future financial and technical assistance from Australia.

A report from the PEC was passed on to the administrator, with comments by the PRAC, in October 1968; about two months later a statement was approved by the Administrator's Executive Council (AEC) and tabled in the House of Assembly (HAD, II (3):808-9). The statement outlined a programme designed

> to cover the whole spectrum of political education from involvement in current events and the practical use of political institutions to the improvement and understanding of the principles of democracy.

The administration, it said, aimed to bring the programme to the people in the rural villages; to do this use would be made of radio, publications, films and the talks of administration officers and others who regularly visited the rural areas. This provided a broad framework for the administration's political education efforts during the next three years; within this framework, however, there were notable shifts in both the content and direction of political education. Formal political education ceased with the issue, in November 1971, of writs for the election, but

[1] The following account draws on the records of the PEC, kindly made available by the Government Liaison Branch of the Department of the Chief Minister and Development administration.

field officers were told that they could answer questions on politics and electoral matters.

Objectives of the programme

The objectives of the political education programme as set out in the November 1968 statement were somewhat vague. In introducing the statement the director of district administration said that the purpose of the programme was to help people understand the principles of democratic government and to know their rights and duties as individual citizens. There were two elements to the proposed programme: one, aimed at increasing the general level of political awareness, the other, 'a formal educational programme dealing more directly with the principles and structures of democratic government' designed both to increase people's understanding of concepts and to improve their ability to work the system.

With respect to the formal part of the programme, the director listed as topics to be included: 'Majority Rule; Local Government – how it works and how it is paid for; Central Government – how it works and how it is paid for; the Legislature – the responsibility of Members of the House and political parties and so on; the Executive; Ministerial Members; the Public Service; and the Judiciary'. To this extent, the programme outlined in 1968 was a continuation of that which preceded it, whose content was broadly indicated by publications prepared during 1966-68 (Parker and Wolfers 1971:43-44). Its essential aim was to instruct people in the theory of Westminster government and its practice as applied in Papua New Guinea. (It was a specific recommendation of the PRAC in 1968 that the political education programme should not 'at the present stage' embrace any political systems other than the Westminster system). Towards the end of 1969, however, with the House of Assembly's Select Committee on Constitutional Development planning to tour the country seeking popular views on that subject, the administrator suggested that the time was now appropriate for a booklet to be written on other systems of government and asked the assistance of the Department of External Territories in preparing such a booklet; but nothing appears to have come of this. An effort was made also to extend the political education campaign in districts to provide some basis for discussion of issues to be raised by the Select Committee. In early 1970 administration field officers could occasionally be found conducting discussion groups in villages on such topics as the advantages and disadvantages of unitary and federal systems and of unicameral and bicameral parliaments.

Instruction in political matters was to be objective; at its first meeting the PEC agreed that political education should not become government propaganda and in a circular to district commissioners in March 1970 the head of the Division of District Administration said:

> Our task is to give the facts and remain neutral. Questions of the merits or otherwise of political matters should be avoided and officers should advise the people to make their own minds up after due consideration of the facts.

Around the beginning of 1971 there was a shift in emphasis in the political education programme.

Tours of the country in 1970 and early 1971 by both the Select Committee on Constitutional Development and a United Nations visiting mission, as well as visits from the then leader of the Australian parliamentary opposition, Gough Whitlam, had stimulated political consciousness in the rural areas and both the Select Committee and the UN mission noted that there was some apprehension and confusion, especially in the highlands, about self-government and independence. An earlier UN mission had already called for greater effort to explain what was meant by the terms 'self-government' and 'independence' (UN 1968:113); though the 1971 mission did not repeat this specific demand, it did call for more intensive political education and said that it would be important to ensure that self-government, as it approached, was fully understood and accepted as a step in a steady process of political evolution (UN 1971:108). The Select Committee on Constitutional Development, for its part, in a report tabled in the House of Assembly in March 1971, recommended (p.2), 'that the development of the Territory be geared to preparing the country for internal self-government during the life of the next House of Assembly'. This was endorsed by the House of Assembly and accepted by the Australian government.

Also, early in 1971 the administration officer who had accompanied the UN mission (and who had been the first executive member of the PEC) recommended a change in content in the political education programme to take account of the apparent uncertainty in the minds of the people regarding self-government. His recommendation was accepted. In a circular dated March 1971 the secretary of the Department of the Administrator told district commissioners that steps must now be taken to prepare the people for self-government and, more particularly, to allay the fears and misconceptions which had arisen. District commissioners were asked to compile a list of fears and misconceptions as they affected each district, to plan a programme aimed at clarifying the issues involved, and to organise seminars aimed at 'thought and opinion leaders' and designed to '(a) Explain the concept of self-government and independence; (b) Assuage the fears and anxieties [termination of Australian aid and assistance and breakdown of law and order were quoted as examples]; (c) Counter rising and dangerous expectations that self-government or independence will result in a wholesale takeover of expatriate assets, and that impossibly high salaries and unrealistic living conditions will automatically be achieved ... (d) If possible, point to the inevitability of self-government and of independence, and the implications thereof'. The following month a survey of the political education programme noted that the whole tenor of the programme was based on the resolution of the Select Committee to prepare the country for self-government.

At about the same time, the promotion of national unity seems to have been given greater importance as an objective of the political education programme. The PEC had been given such a mandate in 1968 when the House of Assembly declared that national unity was essential to the progress of the country and called on the administration 'through the use of field staff, administration radio, and lessons in schools to tell the people what they will gain by keeping together as a single country' (HAD, II (3):616, 654); and such a charge was laid upon the administration by the United Nations. But although it was claimed in 1970 to be first amongst the aims of the political education programme (Baker 1970:38), and was indeed emphasised during the first training course for political education officers in April 1970, the promotion of national unity does not appear to have been a major concern in district programmes at that time. The increased attention given to this objective from early 1971 seems to have been prompted in part by the House of Assembly's endorsement of a recommendation on national unity by the Select Committee on Constitutional Development (1971:7), in part by a further resolution on this subject by a UN visiting mission (UN 1971:109) and especially by a press statement by the administrator in May (*Post-Courier* 21 May 1971) which, following demands for Papuan separatism, reaffirmed the Australian government's commitment to the unity of Papua and New Guinea. There were suggestions, too, that the programme should now be placed on a national basis (see below) and in July 1971 a draft programme for a national political education campaign was drawn up which called for emphasis on (i) self-government and (ii) national unity, adding that 'The development of a positive nationalism, in contrast to oppositionalist or obstructionist nationalism, is aimed for'.

Along with the shift in emphasis in the content of the political education programme came some shift in direction. In introducing the statement by the PEC in November 1968, the director of the Department of District Administration had expressed the aim of bringing the programme to the people in the rural villages and of concentrating particularly on local government councils, women's clubs and similar groups, and school students. Early memoranda to field officers stressed the importance of face-to-face contact at the village level; in one memorandum they were advised that 'the method to be adopted is that of listener, engaging in discussion with village people at their leisure and attempting to bring home points indirectly'. But with the months going by and the difficulty of reaching large numbers of people becoming more apparent, in late 1969 it was recommended that increasing attention be focused on 'thought and opinion leaders' who would be depended upon to spread the message amongst villagers. This was described as a policy of 'educating the educators'. In the latter part of the period much of the political education effort was devoted to seminars for thought and opinion leaders, amongst whom were listed local government councillors, local public servants, school students, local entrepreneurs, local catechists and village leaders.

Organisation and implementation

Initially the Political Education Committee consisted of five people: two representatives (including the chairman) from the Department of District Administration[2] (DDA) and one each from the departments of Education, Information and Extension Services (DIES) and the Department of the Administrator; the Administrator's Department representative was to carry out executive duties for the committee (the initial appointee was also executive member of the PRAC). With the transfer of one of the DDA representatives to the Department of Social Development and Home Affairs, the Committee was widened to retain his membership. All the original members of the committee were

[2] In 1969 district administration ceased to be a separate department and became a Division within the Department of the Administrator. (The abbreviation DDA is used here for both.)

expatriate; in mid-1971 it was suggested that there should be a local member and in September that year a local officer, the then deputy chief electoral officer, was appointed. The chief electoral officer, however, objected to this appointment on the grounds that electoral education should be the only educational function of that office, and the appointment was withdrawn. Another local officer, from the Department of Labour, was appointed instead, but after attending few meetings, in July 1971 he resigned. Subsequently he was replaced by two Papua New Guinean officers, one a woman.

The PEC's role was largely one of coordinating and directing the efforts of the departments involved. As was made clear in a note by the administrator dated December 1970, it was a purely advisory body, advising the administrator on a subject the functional responsibility for which rested (after District Administration was transferred to the Department of the Administration) with the head of the Department of the Administrator.[3]

The Department of Education did not play a major role in the PEC. It ensured that the objectives of the political education programme were taken into account in a revised school social science syllabus, increased the political education content of school magazines and broadcasts, introduced practical exercises in politics in schools (democratic elections, debates on current issues, etc) and, at the instigation of the PEC, in 1969 carried out a survey designed to test the political knowledge and awareness of pupils in four high schools; but apart from this it seems to have contributed little to the programme. A proposal to have teachers organise discussion groups for villagers does not seem to have come to anything. DIES was largely responsible for the preparation of political education materials (see below) and for the dissemination of information through administration radio

[3] Before district administration became a division with the Administrator's Department there appears to have been occasional tension between the department (and the PEC) and DDA. During the 1966-1968 campaign DDA provided both the chairman and the executive member of the PEC.

stations in the districts. Appointment of an officer from the Department of the Administrator as executive member reflected the fact that the Committee's function was to advise the administrator; the first executive member was an important source of initiative in the political education programme, both in that position and subsequently as senior liaison officer in the same department. The bulk of the responsibility for carrying out the programme, however, rested with DDA.

As the director of DDA (and subsequently secretary of the Department of the Administrator) frequently pointed out, political education had been a longstanding function of DDA field staff and DDA field staff continued to be the main agents of the political education programme. At an early meeting of the PEC it was agreed that district commissioners should be the focal point in districts and that the PEC should work through them. Each district commissioner was to be responsible for organising the political education programme in his district and for coordinating the activities of administration officers and others in the field.

In a circular from the director of DDA, dated January 1969, district commissioners were reminded that political education was a prescribed function of the department, and a particularly important one, and officers in the field were asked to keep in mind that it was vital to spread a knowledge and understanding of the nature of government, how it works and its importance in the daily lives of the people. 'The material distributed before the last House of Assembly elections', they were told, 'contains all the information necessary to enable action to continue'. It was not for another nine months, however, that anything was done to appoint officers with a more or less fulltime responsibility for political education. In September 1969 there was still little evidence of political education activity in the field and the administrator called on the PEC to step up the programme without delay. The following month each district commissioner was requested to nominate two experienced officers to be specially briefed about the political education programme and afterwards to spearhead activity in the district. Later that year, after attending two-day briefing sessions, a number of DDA officers appear to have taken up duty as political education officers, 'educating the educators', conducting special political education patrols, and arranging seminars for selected groups. But it was not until April 1970 that the first training course for political education officers was held and though a total of 33 officers attended this and a second four-week course in July, by August 1970 there were only 16 full-time political education officers in the field and three districts were without political education officers. Commenting on the situation at the end of the year a memorandum noted that

> . . . wastage amongst political education officers had been considerable but not surprising considering that all had been appointed by their district commissioner with many having little real interest in political education and even less aptitude for this work.[4]

Political education officers were responsible to their district commissioners, whose task it was to direct the programme within the district and who in turn were responsible to the head of district administration, who provided a link with the PEC. After the two training courses in 1970 a newsletter was distributed amongst political education officers to provide a more direct means of communication amongst them and between them and headquarters staff.

At about the same tune as it was decided to appoint full-time political education officers, the PEC also recommended the appointment of a fulltime officer to coordinate and expedite the overall programme. (Shortly before this, it seems, the executive member was employed full-time in this role.) A joint report on the political education programme in mid-1971 by the executive member and an overseas public relations and communications consultant also suggested that political education officers had been left too much to their own devices and recommended that

[4] The 20 officers attending the April 1970 course were given gradings: three-quarters were rated competent for the task.

'emphasis should now be on a national approach and that organisation and capacity at headquarters level be enlarged and strengthened. Subsequently, a formal submission was made to the Public Service Board to establish, as a matter of priority, a Political Education Section within DDA, with an assistant secretary, six headquarters staff and 18 political education officers in the field. The move for such a headquarters section was motivated in part by belief in the need for a more effective coordination of the enlarged programme, but it also reflected a growing feeling that something as important as political education should not be left to the initiative of 18 district commissioners, whose commitments to political education varied. However, when the 1972 elections began, this submission was still with the Board.

After 1969 district commissioners were required to report regularly on the political education programmes in their districts. Reports summarised political education activities within the district (seminars, political education patrols, radio programmes, visits to schools, essay competitions, quizzes, film showings, etc.), commented on publications, gave an account of cooperation with other administration departments and involvement of missions, private enterprise and others in the programme, and sometimes attempted to review attitudes and opinions within the district. Judging from reviews based on these reports in 1970 and 1971, the programme placed heavy reliance on the use of two-to five-day seminars for thought and opinion leaders (in the three months to February 1971, 200 courses for thought and opinion leaders were held at sub-district and patrol post level). Little recourse was had to special political education patrols and there was little training of DDA staff, and radio was used fairly extensively in most districts for talks by district commissioners and political education officers and for quiz programmes, but with varying assessments of its worth. Similarly, large numbers of publications were distributed though many doubted their effectiveness. These reports also gave an indication of the disparities in effort between districts (see below).

Involvement of people at the district level was an important element in the political education programme. The PEC was empowered in 1968 to seek comment, advice and assistance from outside the administration and to co-opt the assistance of specialist administration officers as the need arose. From the outset the Committee made it clear that it intended to do this and listed as possible participants in the programme patrol officers, agricultural extension officers, aid post orderlies, council advisers and councillors, welfare officers and women's clubs, officers running community education courses and officers in contact with urban associations of all kinds, teachers, missionaries, and senior school students and their parents. The lack, for some time, of full-time political education officers and the delay in producing a field manual limited the effectiveness of this strategy, but by about mid-1970 most district administrations had secured some local involvement in the programme. One district commissioner, reporting in 1971, said practically everybody who is physically capable of moving about amongst the public is invited to participate. Late in 1970 arrangements were made to employ 24 first and second year students from the University of Papua and New Guinea as political education assistants during the long vacation. They were given a training course on political education and communication techniques and were directed to keep diaries in which they were to record people's attitudes, fears and misconceptions and their own comments on, and criticisms of, the programme. District commissioners were asked to ensure that the students were given interesting and creative work. Reviewing the scheme in August 1971 the PEC agreed that it had been an overall success and would probably be repeated in future years.

Materials

One of the prime concerns of the Political Education Committee was the planning and organising of production of political education materials. This included material for radio, films and film strips, and printed publications.

The content of radio programmes was left largely to the administration radio stations in each district. For the most part the political education effort consisted of increases in the number of news items dealing with the activities of the House of Assembly and its members but some stations broadcast political education talks by DDA officers and ran question and answer or quiz programmes.

A film of the 1964 elections, which had become available in 1967, was shown during the campaign and in late 1969 this was supplemented by a film dealing with local government *A Community Develops* with soundtracks in English, Tokpisin and Motu. However, a film on the House of Assembly, planned in 1968, was not distributed until late 1971 and probably was seen by very few voters in the 1972 election. Two strip films appear to have been produced, one dealing with council taxes and one entitled *Pesman bilong Yumi* ('Our Representative') but a projected series on the people of the 18 districts, with a national unity theme, had not been completed when the campaign closed.

In the period before the 1968 elections eight booklets (including a series of six school-level booklets) and 20 one-page leaflets had been produced for political education purposes (Parker and Wolfers 1971:43-44). In the early months of the new campaign additional copies of these were distributed, but in due course they were replaced or supplemented by six publications: *Towards a United Country* (a 106-page basic text in English, which explained how government worked in Papua New Guinea and was intended to serve as a field handbook), and five narrative style booklets with political themes *(Matthias Talks About Government, Minga and Magete Start a New Life* – a story about highlanders who became oil palm scheme settlers in West New Britain, *A Mountain Villager Grows Pyrethrum, A Highlander Grows Tea,* and *Loa Becomes a Teacher).* A booklet setting out political party platforms (projected as early as May 1971 as a pamphlet explaining political parties) was produced early in 1972, too late for adequate distribution before the election. From February 1969 *Our News*, a fortnightly newspaper produced by the administration, in English and Tokpisin, carried stories, news items and quizzes geared to the political education programme. (A DIES survey of *Our News* readers in September 1969 showed that 55 per cent had read the serialised narrative (Matthias) stories, while 72 per cent had read straight articles on government and the House of Assembly.) In addition the PEC obtained some copies of a pamphlet explaining the Administrator's Executive Council, which was produced for the Select Committee on Constitutional Development. It also bought a large number of copies of Brian Jinks' *New Guinea Government: An Introduction*[5] for distribution amongst field officers and made use of several booklets published by the Reserve Bank as part of its financial education programme for Papua New Guinea. Political education officers were also supplied with a collection of papers on 'recent constitutional development', a 'National Unity' wall-chart, and with occasional press statements and journal articles.

Highest priority in the PEC's publication programme was given to *Towards a United Country*. Notwithstanding this, although the publication was commissioned from DIES at one of the first meetings of the PEC it was not distributed until May 1970 (when 10 000 copies became available). Since *Towards a United Country* was intended as a basic text and handbook for patrol officers and others spreading the word in the field, the delay in producing it was a significant set-back for the programme. (The circular to district commissioners in October 1968 which called for greater effort in the field noted, 'This has not hitherto been pressed, as some written guide to field staff officers was considered an essential pre-requisite'; and the first training course for political education officers seems to have been delayed pending publication of the booklet.) Moreover when it did appear, despite the

---

[5] Angus and Robertson, Sydney 1971. This book, written by a former DDA officer, was intended as a text for junior secondary school students in Papua New Guinea.

fact that the draft manuscript had been examined by district commissioners, several administration departments, the Department of External Territories, and academics in Papua New Guinea, *Towards a United Country* was widely criticised by both field officers and outside critics of the political education programme, as being poorly organised, containing errors of fact, and being generally unsuitable for use in the field; after it had been only a couple of months in circulation political education officers generally ceased using it.

Assessment

In the absence of fairly precise data about the state of political awareness before and after the 1968-71 political education programme, it is impossible to measure the impact of the programme in anything but the most impressionistic terms. And such an assessment is further made difficult by the apparent shift in objectives during the life of the programme – indeed the fact that there were perceived fears and misconceptions which needed remedying is perhaps a measure of the effectiveness of the early political education effort in creating an awareness that political change was under way and fostering discussion of it. The PEC itself claimed as a measure of its success the observation of the Select Committee on Constitutional Development, that during its second tour of the country in January-February 1971 it had encountered a greater degree of political awareness and willingness to discuss self-government than had been the case during its first tour in April-May 1970. On the other hand, several attempts at measuring the political knowledge and attitudes of select (elite) groups purported to see, in the dismal results obtained, the failure of political education, and there was no shortage of general critics of the campaign.

But while it is difficult to comment on the overall impact of the programme, there are some obvious comments to be made about aspects of it.

In the first place there was a good deal of criticism of the general concept of 'political education' and objection that a political education programme – especially one in the hands of *kiap* – amounted to administration brainwashing of the people. The administration was not insensitive to these criticisms. In a paper presented to the annual Waigani Seminar in Port Moresby in May 1970 the principal training officer of DDA made the following statements:

> . . . I should clear up any misconception that the administration is or regards itself as the sole or even the major vehicle for political education.
>
> . . . the role is that of political education not, and I repeat NOT, political indoctrination. There is no intention in this programme to push any one structure or form of government.
>
> The possible role conflict inherent in the DDA field officer-political educator role was recognised and an attempt was made to obviate this by ensuring that, short of major emergency, officers engaged full time in political education would not exercise their police and magisterial functions. [Baker 1970:37, 39, 42]

In March 1970 the title of the programme was changed to 'community education', in the hope of diverting critics, but following representations from political/community education officers attending the first training course, the title was changed back to its original form two months later. (Soon after the election in 1972 of the Somare government the title was changed to 'government liaison'.) There was also a suggestion, which was supported by the speaker of the House, that the political education function should be shifted from the administration to the House of Assembly, but apart from notice of a motion which was subsequently withdrawn before debate, nothing came of this. For the most part, however, criticism on these grounds was simplistic. Even the firmer critics of political education seem to have been prepared to admit that given a choice between introducing new, more broadly-based political institutions with or without an attempt at explanation of their operation and the principles behind them some educative effort is preferable to none. In such a situation, 'education' inevitably becomes supportive of the system being introduced. Despite his disclaimers, speaking of the use of films Baker said (1970:41), 'The aim, of course, as with so much of political education is towards increasing the commitment of people to the institutions of government'. The argument then becomes whether the administration should have fostered more discussion of alternative systems rather than concentrating on the explanation of a particular system – and this then becomes largely a question about the effectiveness of the work of the Select Committee on Constitutional Development – and whether the content of the political education programme was appropriate (which is discussed below). In any case, political education was urged by the United Nations Trusteeship Council and seems to have been given a clear mandate by the Select Committee on Constitutional Development, as well as being requested by several local government councils and some politicians.

The argument against 'political education' is much stronger, however, when applied to the objectives emphasised later in the programme: assuaging fears and anxieties about self-government and independence and promoting national unity. On the first of these, the district commissioner of one of the poorer districts pointed to one of the difficulties which could arise, when, commenting on the new emphasis in the programme, he said:

> This fear (of self-government and independence), centred on the lack of economic development, is real to the people (of his district) . . . there is a danger in attempting to nullify this particular fear insofar as such an attempt could be interpreted as an attempt to deceive the people.

With regard to the other, the promotion of national unity posed some obvious difficulties for those involved in political education in areas (such as Bougainville, the Gazelle Peninsula and parts of Papua) where separatist or 'micronationalist' movements were seen to be incompatible with Papua New Guinea nationalism.

But even if the general principle of political education is accepted, the content of the programme can be questioned. Three aspects of it were notable. First, the initial efforts to be factual and objective seem to have resulted in an excessive emphasis on instruction in the formal elements of the Westminster system rather than on demonstrating the universality of political activity and fostering a sense of participation in the new institutions. (An extreme example of this was the early neglect of the subject of political parties.) Second, the training courses which were arranged for political education officers dealt more with techniques of communication than with the substance of the message. Third, most of the political education material approved by the PEC was poor both as political science and as teaching aids; *Towards a United Country* was only the most obvious example of this. In some cases field officers realised this and prepared their own material, but with commitment to a policy of widespread involvement in the programme and with largely untrained political education officers, the inadequacy of the material imposed a serious limitation on the effectiveness of the programme.

This raises another aspect of the programme. The fact that so much responsibility for the organisation of political education, initially at least, rested with the district officers resulted in unevenness in the political education effort from district to district. In some districts the political education programme was carefully planned and conscientiously and intelligently executed; in others it appears not to have been taken very seriously – indeed in their joint report in mid-1971 the executive member and overseas consultant told the PEC that in discussion with one district commissioner, they were 'made aware from the start that political education was something of a joke'. On the basis of the reports submitted by district commissioners in 1970 and 1971 it seems that political education activity was consistently at a fairly satisfactory level in six districts (Bougainville, Central, East Sepik, Eastern Highlands, Southern Highlands, Western Highlands); practically non-existent in four districts (East New Britain, Gulf, Manus, West New Britain) and at an intermediate – and probably variable – level in the other eight (Chimbu, Madang, Milne Bay, Morobe, New Ireland, Northern, West Sepik and Western).

Differences in performance may have been due to a number of factors, but this breakdown suggests that population density, terrain, language, and differential levels of development were not major determinants; differences of attitudes between district commissioners undoubtedly provide a large part of an explanation and differential abilities and enthusiasm on the part of patrol officers and local radio stations probably account for another significant part. And, of course, the paucity of well-designed political education material and, at least until the last months of the period, the lack of systematic coordination at the national level exacerbated the situation. Given all this, it is difficult from what little data is available to discern what effects the unevenness in the district political education programmes had on the level and nature of political activity in the districts. There is some correlation between the extent of political education activity (as classified above) and the number of candidates nominated per seat but it is doubtful whether the two were causally related.

As in 1968, it seems that what worthwhile political education efforts were made came only shortly before the elections themselves. Although the programme got off to an early start, it was slow to get moving: it was over a year before the first new publications appeared, and the text, intended to be a basic element of the programme, was not distributed until mid-1970. The record with regard to radio and films was not much better. In the field, little was achieved until after the appointment of political education officers in late 1969, and training courses for them were not arranged until some months later. In March 1970 it was reported that efforts were generally under way but in

December that year a DDA circular was issued with the aim of revitalising district programmes and reemphasising the priority to be given to political education. One factor relevant to this delay was the early lack of a clear statement by the Australian government of its policy towards self-government and independence (this came after the report of the Select Committee on Constitutional Development). Other important factors were a shortage of DIES personnel, despite application in 1968 for an additional staff establishment for political education work, and the failure, despite repeated recommendations, to establish an adequate headquarters political education section within the Department of the Administrator. Finally, it is clear that in a number of districts district commissioners felt no real commitment towards political education and, in the absence of firm direction at the national level, did little to promote it.

On the positive side, there can be little doubt that the political education programme contributed to a significant increase in the level of political awareness, especially amongst so-called thought and opinion leaders, sharpened interest in political issues, and provided a useful demonstration of the possibilities of cooperation between departments and others at the district and sub-district levels.

6

CLASS, ETHNICITY, REGIONALISM AND POLITICAL PARTIES*

Political parties were slow to emerge in Papua New Guinea and in 1984 – 20 years after the first general elections – it still requires some stretch of the imagination to speak of a party system in Papua New Guinea. This paper seeks to answer the questions: why has a party system been slow to develop? Is the (further) development of a party system inevitable? And, if so, what are the likely bases (Class? Ethnicity? Regionalism?) for the articulation of party interests? Behind these three fairly specific queries lies a larger question. In both the more 'orthodox' liberal approaches to political analysis and in Marxist accounts of Western-style political systems, political parties are generally assumed broadly to reflect and to represent fundamental socio-economic or class divisions within the society. Is this an appropriate assumption for Papua New Guinea? And if so, what is the relationship between the state of political party development and existing or emerging lines of social stratification?

The development of parties[1]

The first of these questions has been substantially answered by Hegarty (1979a): Papua New Guinea's political independence was not the product of struggle, and in the absence of a struggle the sort of nationalist movements which emerged in other new

---

* This paper was first published in R.J. May (ed.), *Social Stratification in Papua New Guinea* (1984).

[1] For a history of political parties in Papua New Guinea see Parker (1967a) Wolfers (1970), Stephen (1972), Stone (1976) and Hegarty (1979b).

states, and which provided the milieu in which party systems developed, were simply not evident in Papua New Guinea. 'The development of nationalism', Hegarty argues (1979a:188-190), was 'inhibited by a number of factors':

> Firstly, the country has no common history of statehood; its people are fragmented into hundreds of often mutually antipathetic ethnic groupings, there is no single common language and the various regions have experienced different colonial rulers . . . Secondly, the nature of Australian colonial rule has militated against the appearance of a nationalist movement: in style heavily authoritarian and thoroughly paternalistic; in substance highly restrictive of autonomous political activity, and non-participatory . . . [Thirdly] . . . was the absence of a sufficiently large and independent class or group to sustain [a nationalist movement].

More specifically,

> . . . with the transfer of power coming so soon after parties had developed, the incentive to mobilise disappeared. As the new political elite acquired a material interest in the continuation of the colonial institutions and economy, mobilisation became, in its eyes, unnecessary.

In a paper written in 1970, a frustrated political organiser, Michael Somare, presented a similar list of problems of political organisation. 'The administration', Somare said, 'is the giver of all things and people do not care so long as they are at the receiving end. Our people are so accustomed to getting things for nothing that . . . they do not see why they should organise as political groups' (Somare 1970:490).

We will return to the question of class and elites below. Meanwhile, the attitude of the Australian administration to political parties deserves some elaboration. There is no doubt that until quite late in the colonial period the administration was antipathetic to any mass movement of a 'political' nature – and that could include anything from a 'cargo cult' to a local government council breakaway group. In part this was a defensive response to forces which were seen as potentially disruptive of the colonial order. In later years it was increasingly a reflection of anxiety over possible threats to an orderly progression towards national unity and a stable, independent state. Wolfers records that Special Branch police 'were regularly to be observed taking notes' at meetings of political parties in the 1960s (Epstein, Parker and Reay 1971:30; see also Wolfers 1970:445) and as late as 1967 (as steps were being taken to establish indigenous political parties) the then minister for Territories, Charles Barnes, was reported as saying, 'At this stage of its development the Territory would be better off without parties' (*Canberra Times* 23 June 1967). During the 1968 elections the derogatory statements of the minister and of some administration officers gave strength to the suspicion and hostility with which political parties were generally regarded (Epstein, Parker and Reay 1971:337) and even in the months prior to the 1972 elections, according to Stone (1976:51), 'Administration officers outside the House continued to foster the attitude that parties were detrimental to the country'. (See also Somare 1970, 1977.) Nevertheless, in a political education programme mounted before the 1968 election, and continued after it, the administration commended political parties (specifically commending two or three parties over many or one) (see Epstein, Parker and Reay 1971:373-375; May 1976 [chapter 5 above]) and in 1972, after a visiting UN mission had recommended that parties be promoted on a nationwide basis (it expressed fears that differences between the existing parties might solidify on a purely regional [coastal/highlands] division, UN 1971:66), the administration distributed, as part of its political education programme, a booklet on political parties which contained the platforms of the three major parties. Indeed, by the early 1970s it might be said that the administration was propagandising for the institution of political parties at a time when some well informed Papua New Guineans were arguing against parties as being potentially disruptive. Ironically, those who in the late 1960s and early 1970s might have appeared progressive in their support of political parties are now liable to find themselves condemned as having been the apologists for a conservative and essentially ethnocentric doctrine of political 'modernisation'.

Inhibiting factors aside, however, mass-based political movements did emerge in the pre-independence period. Amongst the various political organisations to appear on the scene prior to the elections for the second House of Assembly in 1968, two – the United Christian Democratic Party (later United Democratic Party – UDP) and the Pangu Pati – might be described as the first indigenous, mass-based parties. The UDP, however, proved to be shortlived. Formed in the East Sepik, where it was identified with the Catholic mission, and ideologically conservative and parochial, it was unable to attract significant support outside the province and faded away after a disappointing showing in 1968. Pangu, of course, was, and has remained, more successful. But it is perhaps worth noting that although the founders of Pangu (themselves an educated bureaucratic elite) represented a broad geographic cross-section of the population, the mass base of the party was (and has remained) geographically concentrated – in the East Sepik and Morobe provinces, Port Moresby and, at least in the early years, North Solomons. Moreover, the most effective organisational network which the party has had – the branch system in Morobe which Toni Voutas developed in 1966 – was based on individual village organisations with little or no coordination below the provincial level (Voutas 1970).

In 1968 parties were evident, but their influence on the election was minimal:

> Outside a handful of towns, there was little sign of the "political parties" so hastily inaugurated during 1967 . . . At worst . . . it was an electoral liability for a candidate to be publicly associated with them, and candidates . . . avoided or even denied such association. [Epstein, Parker and Reay 1971:326]

Nevertheless when the second House of Assembly sat in 1968,

10 of its 84 members were supporters of the Pangu Pati, which duly declared itself to be the 'loyal opposition'.

During the course of the second House two other mass-based movements appeared which subsequently contested elections and have been described by both Wolfers (1970) and Stephen (1972) as political parties. These were the Mataungan Association of East New Britain and Napidakoe Navitu of the North Solomons. But though both movements fielded candidates in 1972 (and the Mataungans again in 1977), these movements were not political parties in the usual sense of that term, in that they were not formed to contest elections. Nor were several other, 'micronationalist' movements which appeared about this time, even though some of their leaders did contest elections (see May 1982:429-30).

Before the end of the 1968-72 House of Assembly, however, three organisations emerged which clearly were political parties. The first of these, the United Party had its origins in an Independent Members' Group (IMG) established in the House in 1968 amongst a group of members brought together essentially by their opposition to Pangu's demand for early independence. The group consisted largely of highlands members together with some of the more conservative expatriate members. During 1968-69 some attempts were made by members of the IMG to create local groups to support a political party centred on the IMG and in early 1970 the formation of a coordinating body, Combined Political Associations (Compass) was announced. Later that year, at a meeting in Minj attended by some members of the IMG and by local government council leaders and representatives of other highlands groups, a Compass organisation was established and a chairman and secretary appointed (both were highlanders); in early 1971 Compass changed its name to United Party (UP). The circumstances under which Compass was established, however, and specifically its dominance by highlanders resulted in the emergence of a second party from within the IMG. In mid 1970 a Business Services Group, under the leadership of

Julius Chan and comprising mostly members from the New Guinea Islands, was formed within the IMG. Following the Minj meeting this group founded the People's Progress Party (PPP), a move which, in the words of Loveday and Wolfers (1976:21), 'seemed to represent a regional distrust of the highlands leadership implicit in Compass'. The association of highlanders with a 'go-slow' attitude to independence, which Compass represented, also prompted the formation of the New Guinea National Party (NP) amongst a group of generally younger and more progressive highlanders. To quote Loveday and Wolfers again, the NP 'was soon regarded as the highlands equivalent of Pangu' (ibid.).

The 1972 election was thus, for the first time, contested by parties. About 150 of the 611 candidates who nominated were endorsed or selected and helped by parties (Loveday and Wolfers 1976:74), though some candidates were still hesitant about publicly admitting party membership. Some electorates fielded more than one 'endorsed' member from the same party, and no party had a nationwide organisation.

In the event no party emerged from the 1972 elections with a clear majority and, notwithstanding the expectations of the UP (as the largest group in the 1968-72 House), Pangu leader Somare was able to cobble together a coalition government which embraced Pangu, NP, PPP and the Mataungan Association. The UP accepted the role of opposition (though in 1975 some UP members supported the government on critical divisions).

This party alignment was broadly maintained during the life of the 1972-77 House. There were, however, at least four developments of some significance with respect to political parties. One was the formation in 1974 of a Country Party, whose supporters were recruited primarily from amongst UP, highlands members. The Country Party, however, had little effect on members' voting patterns (Loveday and Wolfers 1976:91) and appears to have faded away by the time of the 1977 elections. A second development was the emergence of the Nationalist Pressure Group (NPG) in 1974. The NPG represented a coalescence of members who supported the proposals of the Constitutional Planning Committee against the modifications put forward by the government (see Hegarty 1975). But although it voted as a cohesive group on 'national' issues in 1974-75, the NPG specifically avoided the label 'party' and its 18 core members – drawn from the four major parties plus the Mataungan Association and the newly-formed Country Party – retained their party affiliations. A third development was the split and virtual collapse of the NP in 1976, after Somare had dismissed from cabinet its leader and deputy leader, and a move by them to withdraw all NP members from the coalition had failed. The fourth, which foreshadowed the emergence of Papua Besena as an electoral force in 1977, was the election in a by-election of 1976 of a second Papua Besena member and the subsequent announcement of a Papua Party (McKillop 1982).

In 1977 the party mass organisations, which had generally atrophied since 1972, were revived for the country's fourth, and first post-independence, election. This time, of the 879 candidates who contested the 109 seats, 295 (30 per cent) were endorsed by one, or more, of the three major parties (Hegarty 1977:457). In addition, a number of Papuan candidates stood for Papua Besena, which in 1977 appeared to have evolved from an ill-defined separatist movement to a fully-fledged political party. Observers of the 1977 poll seem to have been generally agreed that political parties had a substantial impact on the election (Hegarty 1977, 1983), though in an interim report on the election Standish (1977:4) concluded that while in the towns competition 'was more in terms of modern associations', in rural areas 'clan voting prevailed'. Nevertheless, in 1977 as in 1972 uncertainties about the political allegiances of some candidates resulted in intense post-election lobbying amongst those who hoped to be able to put together a government. One proposal was for a 'National Alliance' comprising former governor general Sir John

Guise and members of UP, Papua Besena, Country Party and NP. Another was for an Islands-based Alliance for Progress and Regional Development, led by the two former NPG spokesmen, Momis and Kaputin.

In the event, the successful combination was a coalition of the enlarged Pangu and PPP membership with most of the Mataungan and North Solomons members. After several months of dispute within the opposition over the leadership performance of the UP's Sir Tei Abal, in 1978 former NP minister Iambakey Okuk (who had been reelected in Simbu with UP support) emerged as opposition leader. After attempting unsuccessfully to bring together his highlands supporters, Papua Besena members and some others in a People's United Front, Okuk revived the NP and as its leader waged an aggressive campaign against the coalition.

In November 1978, following a growing unease in the relationship between PPP and Pangu (which had probably more to do with personalities and leadership styles than with policies) PPP withdrew from the coalition. Pangu was maintained in office, however, by a split within the UP which brought about half of that party's members across the floor to the government. In 1978-79 the Somare government survived three no-confidence motions initiated by Okuk, but in January 1980 both Momis and Kaputin withdrew from the coalition, forming a new party, the Melanesian Alliance (MA), and two months later, with their support, a no-confidence vote against the Somare government succeeded. Chan became prime minister as the head of a National Alliance government comprising PPP, NP, MA, Papua Besena, and part of UP. The Alliance was able to hold on to office until the scheduled elections of 1982, but it was, to say the least, an improbable coalition. PPP and NP, broadly aligned in support of capitalist development and foreign investment (though with little personal empathy between Chan and Okuk – see, for example, *Post-Courier* 21 June 1983), were at one end of a political spectrum from the MA, which regarded itself as being to the left of Pangu and whose leaders were strongly identified with economic nationalism and the aim of self-sufficiency; and Papua Besena, which owed its origins in large part to fear and distrust of highlanders (Daro 1976; McKillop 1982), was a strange bedfellow for a coalition in which highlands members were a large component and whose deputy leader (Okuk) was a staunch highlands nationalist.

When in 1981 I visited East Sepik and Morobe provinces even Pangu party organisation appeared to be in a shambles. Nevertheless, as in previous elections, party organisations were resuscitated in late 1981-early 1982 and several new groupings appeared on the scene; indeed in the 1982 elections parties seemed to be more salient than ever. Pangu, PPP, UP, NP, MA and Papua Besena/Papua Party all fielded candidates, while two new groups – a Papua Action Party (which had links with the NP), and a predominantly-Papuan 'Independent Group' headed by former Defence Force commander, Ted Diro – emerged as significant contenders. About 60 per cent of the 1125 candidates who stood in 1982 were endorsed by one or more of these eight parties (Hegarty 1982). My own observation of the 1982 campaign in the East Sepik suggested not only that nearly all candidates sought a party label (some, indeed, more than one) but that a high proportion of voters could accurately attach party labels to most candidates. As against this apparent evidence of the arrival of parties as an important political force, however, there remained some indications that perhaps things had not changed as much as might seem. For one, party attachment for most candidates seemed still to be loose and it was not rare for a candidate who failed to get endorsement or assistance from one party to turn to another. Second, for some parties and in some electorates party attachment meant little more than the use of a label. Third, in a number of instances party members stood against endorsed candidates of their own party against their party's interests (though in some cases parties – especially Pangu – supported more than one candidate in order to split the local vote of opponents of their endorsed candidate). Finally, although the available evidence does not permit a strong conclusion, it would appear that while there was in 1982 some increase in party voting, personal and local loyalties were still considerably more important for the great majority of voters (Hegarty and King 1982).

The outcome of the 1982 election was a victory for Pangu, which – apart from the recently established MA – was the only party to increase its representation in the parliament. In August 1982 Somare was duly reelected to the prime ministership, heading a government comprising successful Pangu candidates, UP members and a number of members who were either elected as independents or switched from other parties after the election. Although Momis was the opposition's nomination to stand against Somare in the initial vote, he was subsequently passed over as opposition leader; this position was given to Diro whose group had thrown its weight in with the NP. But when in 1983 Okuk – who had lost in Simbu in 1982 – was returned in a by-election, Diro stepped down in his favour.

From even so brief an account as this, four characteristics of political party development in Papua New Guinea are apparent.

First is the fluidity of party alignments. Amongst the major parties which have contested elections since 1968 (that is, leaving aside a number of small parties not mentioned here which have flashed briefly across the political scene) only Pangu, and PPP have had a continuous, cohesive existence lasting over several years. The UDP disappeared, within about two years, soon after its failure in the 1968 elections; the UP, the largest group in the 1968-72 parliament, split in 1978 and appears to be on the wane; the NP has come and gone and come again, its future probably closely tied up with the political fortunes of Okuk; the Country Party proved to be short-lived; Papua Besena/Papua Party enjoyed at least one reincarnation but has been faction-ridden for most of its existence as a party, with its founder, Josephine Abaijah, denying that Papua Besena is a party; the Papua Action Party appears to have dissolved after its failure at the polls in 1982; and the Melanesian Alliance has yet to prove its capacity for survival, though in 1984 it seems likely to remain a substantial political force. Moreover, apart from the question of candidates holding multiple party endorsements, in 1982, as in 1972 and 1977, the real test of party loyalty came after the elections in the politicking to get the numbers to form a government. Thus in 1982 the MA lost two members to Pangu after the elections, UP lost 3, and in the vote for the prime ministership only four out of seven of Diro's Independent Group voted with him.

A second notable feature of parties has been their general lack of effective mass organisations. Although most of the larger parties have, on paper, organisational structures based on party branches, in fact the majority have their origins in parliamentary alliances and remain dominated by parliamentary members, and between elections party organisations in the electorates tend to atrophy. The main exception to this – apart from the Mataungan Association and Papua Besena, which began as popular movements without the specific objective of contesting elections – is probably Pangu, but even it is essentially a parliamentary party except when elections are approaching.

Third, as various commentators have observed, parties in Papua New Guinea have not been particularly concerned with ideology. In the period before independence, Pangu (together perhaps with the NP) was differentiated from the other parties primarily by its critical attitude to the Australian administration and its demand for early independence. By 1974-75, however, in the interests of political stability Pangu was in the position of pressing the Australian government to delay the granting of independence, and with the achievement of independence in 1975 this ceased to be an issue. The UP and PPP, on the other hand, were generally regarded as more 'business' oriented and more favourably disposed towards foreign participation in the economy, though in practice the differences appeared not substantial, as the record of the 1972-1978 coalition government indicates. (Hegarty, in fact, speaks of a general 'pro-capitalist convergence' (1979a:199-201).) On the one occasion that substantial differences on important policy issues did arise – namely during the constitutional debates of 1974-75 – alignments cut across party lines. The split which occurred within the coalition in 1978, on the other hand, seems to have had more to do with personal relationships and political styles than with any ideological differences. And the nature of the coalition which replaced Somare in 1979 – accommodating as it did such widely different viewpoints as the 'open economy capitalism' of Chan and Okuk and the economic nationalism of Kaputin; the highlands nationalism of Okuk and others and the (anti-highlander) Papuan nationalism of Papua Besena – suggested further that questions of ideology were secondary to considerations of parliamentary office, a suggestion reinforced in 1978 by the split of the UP, and in 1977 and 1982 by the lobbying which followed the polls.

Fourth, even leaving aside those movements and parties (such as the Mataungan Association, Papua Besena, the Papua Action Party) which were specifically locally or regionally focused, and a number of small parties in the late 1960s and early 1970s which never grew beyond their local origins, there has been from the inception of parties a clear regional orientation in political party organisation. As has been noted, the UDP never managed to establish itself beyond the Sepik; the UP, NP and Country Party have drawn their support predominantly from the highlands; PPP and MA have been largely Islands based; even Pangu has little party organisation outside of East Sepik, Morobe and Port Moresby (though the support it received in the highlands in 1982, and its association with the UP, may change this). Mention might also be made in this context of the Morobe District People's Association (MODIPE), a provincial organisation which was established in 1973 with the specific objective of preventing people from outside the province becoming parliamentary members for Morobe electorates (at this time the Pangu member for Lae was a Papuan). The visiting UN mission of 1971 expressed concern at the regionalist tendencies in political party development (UN

1971:176). Stephen (1972:175) also observed, 'Pangu and the United Party are regionalistic . . . The smaller parties are regional too'. Writing in 1972 Waddell (1973a:96) forecast that 'it will not be ideology or class interests which separate the parties – if there are more than one . . . regional interests are the most likely source from which political parties will derive their mass base'. Commentaries on the 1977 election tended to support this judgement. Hegarty (1977:454, 461) observed that in the pre-election period 'considerable social differentiation had become apparent', but went on to conclude, 'The basic cleavages in PNG politics are not ideological or class based but regional'. And Premdas and Steeves (n.d.:35) ventured the opinion, 'It would be difficult for anything but an ethnically-based party system to emerge', and figures of candidates by party and region provided some basis for such a view. By the time of the 1982 elections the regional concentration of party support appeared to have been diluted somewhat. Jackson and Hegarty (1983), in fact, entitled a paper on the 1982 elections, 'From geography to ideology?' Nevertheless there was still evidence of a regional element in party support, as shown in the following table.

Party Voting, by region, 1982

	North Coast	South Coast	Highlands	Islands
Pangu	54.7	22.0	30.0	24.5
PPP	6.3	8.4	11.5	14.9
NP	10.1	3.2	13.3	7.6
Diro Independent Group	-	18.3	6.7	5.2
Papua Action Party	-	4.7	-	-
MA	11.5	7.1	2.2	28.1
UP	5.1	6.8	9.3	4.5
Papua Besena/Papua Party	-	9.0	-	-
Independent	12.3	20.5	27.0	15.2
	100.0	100.0	100.0	100.0

Source: David Hegarty, personal communication 1982

Moreover, while the PAP and Papua Party campaigned for Papuan solidarity and a Papuan prime minister, in the highlands the NP complained that the government had been dominated by coastals, and called on voters to help elect a highlander prime minister.

The introduction of provincial government, commencing in 1976, created another level of political institutions and raised the possibility that provincial elections might stimulate the development of existing party organisations at provincial level.

In fact, and although stories vary from province to province (and to date there has been little documentation of provincial politics[2]), two patterns seem to be common. One is a tendency to reject parties at the provincial level: within several provinces (amongst them Eastern Highlands, Western Highlands, East Sepik) the view has been expressed that parties are 'disruptive', are 'not appropriate' for provincial assemblies and provincial elections (see, for example, the statement by the East Sepik Provincial Minister for Commerce, reported in the provincial government's *Wama Nius* 5(4), April 1983). The other has been the discouragement of the projection of 'national' parties into provincial politics has been a frequent antipathy between national politicians and provincial politicians (even those identified with the same party). This antipathy is rooted in uncertainties about the respective roles of national and provincial assemblies, and in a common fear on the part of national politicians that provincial members (seen by at least one highlands politician as failed national political aspirants) undermine their power bases in the province. That is not to say that factions have not emerged in provincial assemblies, nor even to deny that such factions are sometimes identified with parties (for example, Pangu, and non-Pangu factions in East Sepik Province). But I would suggest that where systematic divisions, other than limited personal followings, have emerged in provincial assemblies, the basis for

---

2 [However, see May and Regan, with Ley (1997).]

such divisions has more commonly been regional. Thus, for example: Standish (1984) has described the 1980 provincial and 1982 national elections in Simbu in terms primarily of a conflict between Bomai (southern) and northern regional blocs in the province; in the East Sepik an emerging division between the people of the river, the people of the coast and islands, and those of the hinterland has, to a degree, been formally accommodated by writing into the constitution specific provision for area ministers (representing Ambunti and Angoram, Wewak, and Maprik); in the Southern Highlands Ballard (personal communication 1982) has described provincial politics in terms of differences between three main regional blocs – Mendi, Ialibu and Tari. And it seems that similar patterns are discernible elsewhere (Central Province? Morobe? Eastern Highlands? New Ireland?).

Moreover, I believe that the creation of provincial governments, and more recently the emergence of regional provincial political organisations, have tended increasingly to 'provincialise', or at least to 'regionalise', national politics, a factor which is reflected, for example, in the allocation of cabinet portfolios and of senior public service positions.

Is the development of a party system inevitable?

If the foregoing has established that Papua New Guinea does not have a 'developed' party system, based on fundamental social cleavages, the big question remains: is this situation likely to endure or is it simply a reflection of Papua New Guinea's present, transitional, 'stage of political development'?

Several commentators have suggested the latter, generally implying that a two- or three-party system will develop as social classes emerge (see, for example, Jackson and Hegarty 1983). Such a view is in accord with the general thrust of the political development/'modernisation' literature of the 1960s and early 1970s. It is also consistent with the mathematics of competitive representative government (for example, see Riker 1962;

Groennings, Kelley and Leiserson 1970), which suggests the formation of coalitions to aggregate the preferences of like-minded people.

As against this, the view of political development as an inevitable, evolutionary, process, in which competing political parties play an essential role in organising mass participation in the processes of social choice – and more particularly the suggestion that there is a 'natural movement of societies . . . towards the two-party system' (Duverger 1954:21); see also Huntington 1968:423-433) – has not been borne out by the historical experience of the 'new states', nor even perhaps of developed states in which social stratification is clearly articulated. Over the past two decades there has been a pronounced tendency towards authoritarian regimes, in which the functions of interest articulation, interest aggregation, recruitment of a political elite, political socialisation, and so on have been performed by one-party or dominant-party structures, by the military, or by the bureaucracy. There has also been a growing recognition that, where they do exist, political parties in developing states are often, to quote one commentator, 'little more than coalitions of elites and, at their outer reaches, complex sets of highly personal face-to-face relationships, all momentarily integrated by access to government and its patronage' (Heeger 1974:70). This pattern – the predominance of personal and factional (kin, ethnic or regional group) politics – may be particularly appropriate to the politics of small-scale, as well as poorly integrated, societies (cf. May 1982; May and Tupouniua 1980).

Addressing the question, 'what sort of a party "system" could emerge' in Papua New Guinea, as early as 1966-67 Robert Parker warned that the constitutional, democratic party system, represented by Australia, was rare, and that there was no basis for expecting such a system to develop in Papua New Guinea. Recognising the general tendency to one-party states elsewhere, and in the light of his analysis of interest groups, issues, communications and potential leadership in Papua New Guinea,

Parker went on to suggest that there appeared to be 'powerful considerations favouring the emergence of [a "democratic one-party" system] after independence' (1967b:15; see also 1966-67, 1967a). In a later paper, Waddell (1973a) also appears to have seen a one-party regime as a likely development, though he himself advocated 'a co-operative government in which all major, and perhaps even minor, parties are automatically involved' (1973b:30). Premdas, on the other hand, arguing against a 'no-party state', believed that 'a wide range of party systems is available from which a choice can be made' (1974:130; see also 1975).

In 1984 it would appear that a one-party, or no-party, regime is unlikely. Although the 'party system' has not been particularly stable, parties have been in evidence now for some time and a small number has survived for over a decade. The answer to the question posed in this section would therefore seem to be that, while mass-based, issue-related political parties are not logically essential to the working of a parliamentary system like Papua New Guinea's, some sort of political coalescing probably is inevitable and in Papua New Guinea parties of one form or another now seem to be a well established feature of the political landscape. Such an answer, however, still leaves us with the other big question, namely what are the likely bases for the articulation of party interests?

Bases for a party System

Amongst those who in the 1960s and early 1970s anticipated the development of political parties, both in new states generally and in Papua New Guinea, there seems to have been a presumption that, as in Europe (and Australia), the development of parties would be associated with the articulation of social classes and the emergence of a nationwide socio-economic stratification which would supersede politically other divisions of society such as region or ethnicity. Indeed political parties were often seen as agents of integration and national unity. (In the Papua New Guinea context, for example, Premdas (1974), in arguing for political parties, listed integration and unity as one of four 'critical areas' in which parties had a role to play.)

Three assumptions seem to be implicit in this view: (i) that the emergence of social classes is inevitable; (ii) that class divisions are generally a more likely basis for political parties than other divisions in society, such as ethnicity or region; (iii) that political parties must relate to certain fundamental divisions of society and be differentiated from one another on the basis of such divisions.

The first of these assumptions is discussed elsewhere (see May 1984); I will not buy into the debate here except to offer the opinion that even though there is evidence of emerging social classes in the rise of 'big peasants', the growth of a largely-urban 'salariate' or 'bureaucratic bourgeoisie', and perhaps the emergence of a rural and an urban proletariat, the prospective picture of social class in a predominantly rural, fragmented society like Papua New Guinea's, in which traditional elements of social structure are still important, is more complex than that which is offered by a simple Marxist model (cf. Hyden 1980).

Second, on the evidence to date from Papua New Guinea, and having regard to experiences elsewhere (in Europe and North America as well as in the 'new states'), I am far from convinced that class divisions, even where they are clearly articulated, must necessarily outweigh ethnic or regional differences as a basis for political organisation.

Third, to the extent that Papua New Guinea's political parties conform to what Heeger sees as often little more than coalitions of elites – and on the basis of the description presented earlier in this paper I think they do – the question of a mass base becomes relatively unimportant; it might then be argued that regionally-focused patronage systems are a more effective way of gaining electoral support.

Finally, to have a small bet each way, it might be pointed out that in Papua New Guinea socio-economic status and region are not entirely without correlation: capitalist penetration has probably been most extensive in the Islands and the Highlands regions, which have also been the primary areas of support for the generally pro-capitalist UP, CP, reorganised NP, and PPP, though the more recently contacted – and thus in some respects 'less developed' – highlands provinces are historically most closely associated with the relatively conservative (initially pro-administration) UP and CP; the less advantaged Mamose (North Coast) region has predominantly supported Pangu, while Papua Besena/Papua Party and PAP have in part sought to protect the interests of a largely Papuan urban salariate. Moreover one can think of tendencies which could strengthen such a correlation: for example, growing regional disparities in levels of economic development (cf. Berry and Jackson 1981), competition over central government funding of provincial governments (cf. May 1981), administrative breakdown at the centre, increasing *wantokism* within the bureaucracy.

Conclusion

For some time commentators on Papua New Guinea have spoken of the imminent emergence of a social class system and have frequently suggested that as social classes finally emerge the country's currently fluid party 'system' will solidify along class lines.

In this paper I have attempted to suggest that there are no good grounds for regarding Papua New Guinea's present party system as 'transitional' between an 'undeveloped' and a 'developed' system, and that even if there is an articulation of social classes which cut across regional divisions there is no necessary reason to suppose that parties will follow the class divisions. Ethnicity and regionalism are significant and convenient bases for political organisation in Papua New Guinea and are likely to remain so. To the extent that political parties remain essentially parliamentary organisations, coalitions of political elites, the more successful undoubtedly will widen the geographic base of the coalition but I believe this is more likely to be reflected in the linkage of personal and regional followings than in appeals to what some observers see as emerging social classes.

7

DECENTRALISATION: CONSTITUTIONAL FORM AND POLITICAL REALITY*

This paper is narrow in its geographic focus and modest in its scope. And it is concerned more with politics than with law. But the question it addresses is, I believe, significant and of some relevance to other Pacific states facing demands for local autonomy. That question is twofold: what is the substance of 'decentralisation' as embodied in the Papua New Guinea Constitution and Organic Law on Provincial Government; does the political reality of decentralisation correspond to the concept elaborated by the 'founding fathers'?

The concept

In the course of planning the Constitution, the Constitutional Planning Committee (CPC) made an early decision in favour of decentralisation. In its *1st Interim Report* of September 1973 it discerned 'the emergence of some clear majority views', according to which 'a system of district government should be introduced with greater powers for districts than those vested in area authorities' (ibid.).

Two months previously the CPC had been presented with a demand for immediate district government[1] in Bougainville and

* This paper was written for a legal workshop on Pacific constitutions and was first published in Peter Sack (ed.) *Pacific Constitutions* (1982). It makes extensive use of material presented in a consultancy *Report to the Committee to Review the Financial Provisions of the Organic Law on Provincial Government* (May 1981).

[1] 'Districts' were renamed 'provinces' in 1975, though the term 'provincial government' was in widespread use from around 1973.

a detailed draft (prepared by the Bougainville Special Political Committee (BSPC)) of the form which it should take. Referring specifically to the demand from Bougainville the CPC proposed a tripartite meeting between the national government, the CPC and the BSPC 'to find a solution to the immediate Problem of making interim arrangements for district government [in Bougainville], pending the Committee's final recommendations' (CPC 1973a:9-10). In its *2nd Interim Report* of November 1973 the CPC noted that this proposal had been accepted by cabinet 'subject only to the condition that any agreement which might be reached must be within a general legislative framework to be applied to the country as a whole' (1973b:1/7), and on the general question of decentralisation it said:

> We are convinced it is essential that decentralisation of decision-making be political and not merely bureaucratic if the basic objective of involving our people as much as possible in their own development is to be achieved. [ibid.:4/3]

It saw district-level government as:

> an important step towards accommodating strong political pressures for the granting of significant autonomy to particular areas of the country which have been building up over the last five years. [ibid.:4/4]

The *2nd Interim Report* did not resolve the question of what powers should be exercised by provincial governments though it did recommend that there should be a single national public service and that 'certain powers should be vested by law in provincial governments'. The subject was then referred to expert consultants, W. Tordoff and R.L. Watts.

The precise form of provincial government which was finally recommended by the CPC in its *Report* of 1974 drew heavily on the recommendations of the consultants' *Report on Central-Provincial Government Relations* (Tordoff-Watts Report) 1974. Their terms of reference required them to outline options and make recommendations:

> ... bearing in mind the [CPC's] firm commitment to the development of a strong form of provincial government (which is a decentralised form of government within a unitary system, subject to political control at the district [i.e. provincial] level). (1974:i)

And amongst a number of premises which Tordoff and Watts listed before proceeding to the body of their report, the first was that:

> The form of decentralisation advocated by the C.P.C. is a fully decentralised system within a unitary state rather than a federal system. Under the proposed system it is intended ... that provincial governments would enjoy considerable autonomy, but that they would not have coordinate authority with that of the central government (a characteristic of the federal principle). Provincial government would remain subject to final overall policy direction and control from the central government. They would be subordinate governments and the supremacy of the National Parliament would be unimpaired (ibid.:1/3-1/4).

Tordoff and Watts considered three alternative types of decentralised political systems: unitary, federal and confederal. Having dismissed the last two of these ('no-one has advocated a confederal scheme'; 'a federal system would be inappropriate') (ibid.:3/1-3/2) , they distinguished three broad types of unitary system: completely centralised unitary system; unitary systems with administrative devolution and limited political devolution; and unitary systems with moderate or full political devolution. After considering the relative advantages and disadvantages of these alternative types of unitary system the consultants recommended:

> ... that a fully decentralised system of unitary government should

be constitutionally assured as an ultimate goal, but that it evolve by stages, with each province beginning at that stage most consistent with provincial capacity (ibid.:3/9).

The recommendations of the CPC are set out in chapter 10 of its *Final Report* (1974), which also contains a schedule of proposed national, provincial and concurrent powers. It noted:

> Experience in other recently independent states does not incline us towards recommending a federal system for Papua New Guinea. The overwhelming majority of our people favour the maintenance of a unitary state. [1974:10]

The government's 'white paper' *(Proposals on Constitutional Principles and Explanatory Notes* [Papua New Guinea, 1974]) which challenged the CPC recommendations on several points, expressed some reservations about the proposals on provincial government, but 'strongly supported' the principle.

Following the conclusion in March 1975 of the House of Assembly debate on the provincial government proposals, an interparty Follow-up Committee was established to draw up an organic law. The committee was assisted by consultants Watts and W.R. Lederman, who presented a rough draft of the Organic Law in July 1975. The Watts-Lederman draft was intended, in the words of its authors:

> To put the relations of the national government and the provincial governments on a flexible but definite basis that provides a strong central national government along with significantly autonomous provincial governments (ibid.).

The sequence of events concerning provincial government between 1975 and 1977 is well-known and has been documented elsewhere (Conyers 1976; Conyers and Westcott 1979; Standish 1979; General Constitutional Commission 1980; Ballard 1981). There was: the decision of the Constituent Assembly in July 1975 to exclude the provincial government provisions from the Constitution; the preparations, nonetheless, for the introduction of provincial government, including the establishment of the Bougainville Interim Provincial Government in July 1974 and the creation of constituent assemblies in other provinces; the Bougainville negotiations, culminating in the Bougainville Agreement of August 1976; and the eventual decision to reinstate the provincial government provisions through amendment to the Constitution and the passage of the Organic Law.

As I read it, the Organic Law which was passed in 1977 differed from the Tordoff-Watts/CPC recommendations in some significant respects (reflecting some of the differences which emerged between the government and the Nationalist Pressure Group during 1974 to 1975 – already partially taken into account in the draft Organic Law prepared by Watts and Lederman – and some of the particular circumstances of the Bougainville negotiations and agreement); but it retained the broad features of the fully-decentralised-unitary-system model put forward in 1974.

It might be noted, however, that Goldring sees the situation differently:

> The structure of provincial government recommended by the CPC was quite different from that which has emerged in the Constitutional provisions of the Organic Law. [1977:253]

The latter he describes as '*Bulsit bilong mekim bel isi*':

> The machinery established by the Constitutional arrangements is such that if the national government has certain policies which it wants to be carried out by provincial governments, its ability to control provincial administration (by control of manpower) and of provincial finance can ensure that its wishes prevail (ibid.:283).

The political circumstances in which provincial government was proposed, planned, rejected, revived and then haltingly implemented obviously had much to do with people's reasons for rejecting federalism, and opting for what the Tordoff-Watts Report described as 'a fully decentralised system of unitary government', but these circumstances will not concern me here. Nor will I attempt (except by way of an indulgent footnote[2]) the fruitless task of trying to locate Papua New Guinea's Organic Law on Provincial Government on a continuum from confederation to centralised unitary state. The important thing is that the CPC, and subsequently the National Parliament, specifically rejected federalism for a unitary system, and the Organic Law on Provincial Government was intended to give expression to this decision.

What, then, are the essential elements of the relationship between the national government and the Provinces as defined by the Constitution and the Organic Law? The essential elements are to be found in the provisions concerning: the status of the provincial governments; the division of powers between the national and provincial governments; procedures for settling disputes between the two levels of government; intergovernmental financial relations; and administrative relations. The following paragraphs will attempt to sketch briefly what I see as the more important provisions in these five areas. (For a more thorough examination of the constitutional structure of provincial government in Papua New Guinea see Goldring 1977.)

Status of provincial governments

The subordinate status of the provincial governments in Papua New Guinea's constitutional arrangements seems to be clearly reflected in several provisions of the Constitution and Organic Law: e.g., s.187D of the Constitution (inconsistency and justiciability of provincial laws); 55, 28, 29 and 37 of the Organic Law (which respectively secure the power of the National Parliament to make laws for the peace, order and good government of Papua New Guinea; restrict the 'concurrent' legislative powers of provincial governments where there is existing national legislation or in matters of 'national interest', and enable the

[2] For a general critique of attempts to 'define' federalism, see May (1969:10-11). Also see Riker (1969, 1970) on 'the triviality of federalism'.

National Parliament to disallow a provincial law 'if in its opinion the disallowance is in the public interest'); s.187E of the Constitution and ss.86-98 of the Organic Law (suspension of provincial governments), and, as Goldring notes, in relation to the public service and fiscal matters. It is these which identify Papua New Guinea's system of government as unitary.

As against this constitutional statement, however, it might be noted that the Bougainville Charter states that: 'the relationship between Provincial and Central authorities, are [*sic*] founded on principles of complementarity, [and that] one is not inferior in its nature to the other' which, as Goldring comments, 'asserts even more than federalism' (1977:251n) – and that in a submission to the third Premier's Council (PC) conference in 1980 it was stated (by a provincial government – apparently without challenge) that: 'the most important and fundamental principle that both national and provincial governments should bear in mind . . . [is that] both governments are equal partners in the Process of Governing the Country' (PC 3/3/80).

Division of powers

As early as November 1973, when cabinet agreed in principle to interim district government, a Task Force on Interim District government was established to make recommendations on the powers and functions which might be devolved upon or delegated to interim district governments. The Task Force presented, in March 1974, a proposed *Division of Functions Between Central and District governments* which distinguished functions which should remain with the central government (A functions), those which should be concurrent (B functions), and those which could be handed over to the province (C functions). This list was incorporated in the CPC's *Final Report* as the 'Second Schedule'. The philosophy underlying the division is explained in the *Report:*

> The 'A' list provides a minimum framework for development within a unitary state. The 'C' list guarantees a minimal autonomy

> to provincial governments. The 'B' list is as accurate an approximation of the outstanding powers and functions of government in Papua New Guinea as we have been able to secure . . . It is, in intention, a residual list. [1974:10/10]

But while the CPC recommended that final responsibility for all of the powers and functions on the 'B' list be vested in the national government, it expressed the view 'That responsibility should be delegated to, or devolved upon, provincial governments to the maximum practicable extent'.

Commenting on the proposed division Diana Conyers said:

> The list was useful as a preliminary attempt to analyse the present functions of the Central government but as a basis for planning the transfer of functions to provincial governments it had some deficiencies. In particular, it did not consider the implications of transferring these functions, for example, the changes in national laws and departmental procedures which would be necessary, the financial implications and the effects on the relationship between public servants working in the Districts and their headquarters in Port Moresby. Another problem was that it is relatively easy to distinguish between different functions on paper but much more difficult to do so in reality. [1976:44]

Between the proposals of 1974 and the arrangements embodied in Part VI of the Organic Law there is a subtle change of emphasis: Div.3 lists those subjects which are 'primarily "provincial"', within which – subject to s.19 – provincial governments have exclusive legislative power (taxation is covered separately); Div.4 lists 'concurrent' subjects, within which provinces may legislate, provided that such laws are 'not inconsistent with any Act of the [National] Parliament' (s.28) (though s.29 limits the legislative powers of the national government under this division to matters of 'national interest'); Div.5 provides that in '"unoccupied" legislative fields' if the National Parliament has not made exhaustive laws, on any subject, provincial governments may make laws not inconsistent with any national legislation. There is also specific provision for the delegation of powers (Part VIII). However, under s.37: 'The National Parliament may, by a two-thirds absolute majority vote, by resolution disallow any provincial law, if in its opinion the disallowance is in the public interest.'

The Organic Law provisions concerning legislative powers would thus seem to give the provinces potentially wide scope for initiating policy, yet at the same time – subject to the interpretation given to 'national interest' and 'the public interest' – to grant the national government extensive power to overrule provincial legislation. Moreover, although the passage of the Organic Law went some way towards resolving fundamental questions about the division of powers – and a January 1977 decision of the National Executive Council (NEC) which provided a detailed listing of administrative functions divided into national and provincial 'spheres of interest' (NEC 19/77) further clarified the situation – most of the uncertainties listed by Conyers, concerning the question of how to implement provincial government, remained. This, together with a suspicion that some public servants were fighting a rearguard action against decentralisation, resulted in the government's decision to employ the consulting firm of McKinsey and Co. to draw up a programme for the implementation of administrative decentralisation. A programme based on the recommendations of the McKinsey team was accepted by the NEC in September 1977 and an Office of Implementation was created to carry out the programme, which involved a transfer of functions, uniformly for all provinces, in three stages between January 1978 and January 1979. Those functions designated 'provincial' within the Departments of Provincial Affairs, Primary Industry, Education and Commerce were transferred to the provinces in January 1978; those within Health and Information were transferred in July 1978, and in January 1979 the Bureau of Management Services (BMS) was placed under provincial control. (Commencing 1977, all provinces had assumed responsibility for provincial works and maintenance and the Rural Integrated Plan as well as for provincial legislatures and secretariats.) Functions of other departments were expected to be transferred subsequently, but as far as I am aware no coherent programme for further devolution has emerged.

I have argued elsewhere:

> The situation which now exists is ... one in which the real distribution of policy making powers is essentially a political (rather than – as characterises federal systems – a constitutional/judicial) process. Provinces have not legislated in all the areas in which they have authority, but they have used political muscle to achieve policy objectives even in areas in which they do not have a clear competence. [May 1981:18]

The development of an essentially *political* system of decentralised government – in which governments have so far been reluctant to litigate and in which the ability of the national government to discipline the provinces, short of suspension, is in any case limited – is presumably what the former minister for Decentralisation had in mind when in a Ministerial Statement on provincial government, he spoke of 'a concrete implementation of the concept of sharing' (Momis 1979:6). The virtues of such arrangements, in a historical context, have been argued in a *Review of the Constitutional Laws on provincial government* by Yash Ghai and Mani Isana:

> ... it was considered inappropriate, when the Law on provincial government was enacted, to set out much detail, either on the structure of provincial governments, or the relationship between provincial government and the national government. The Organic Law intended to lay down a broad framework for provincial government and the establishment and further evolution of the system was, in large measure, left for consultation between the Provincial and the national governments ... we consider that the Organic Law sets out an essentially flexible system for the de-

> centralisation of political and administrative powers . . . The Organic Law is therefore concerned, in a very large measure, with the relationship of different political authorities and many of the provisions of the Organic Law are concerned, not with narrow legal questions, but with broad fundamental political questions. [1978b:3-4]

Elsewhere, however, Ghal and Isana describe the Organic Law as 'complex, legalistic and difficult to operate' (1978a:l) and comment that:

> The Constitutional amendments to accommodate provincial government, the Organic Law on provincial government and the provincial constitutions, do not add up to a very coherent picture of the status of provincial governments and their place in the overall national system (ibid.:4).

Settlement of disputes

The question of conflict resolution was discussed in a general way in the Tordoff-Watts Report (op. cit.:8/1-8/8). Having observed that, in any system in which there are two or more levels of government, inter-governmental conflicts are bound to arise, the consultants suggested five possible procedures for conflict resolution. These were: an arrangement whereby in any case of conflict the decision of the national government prevails; requirements for consultation between governments; requirements for consent between governments; judicial review; a special commission; a Premiers' Council. The report recommended a combination of the first three and the last procedures and gave qualified support to a special commission. Interestingly, however, it specifically rejected judicial review: 'In our view, the rigidity and legalism involved in such a procedure for settling central-provincial conflicts is for most aspects of a unitary system totally inappropriate' (ibid.:812).

With specific reference to the allocation of grants to provinces,

Tordoff and Watts also recommended the appointment of an advisory expert financial commission *(ibid. 7/33-7/34)*. The CPC *Report* of 1974 broadly followed these recommendations including one for an expert National Fiscal Commission (NFC).

Following these recommendations, the Organic Law on Provincial Government includes four principal provisions for settling disputes: s.30(2) requires the Minister for Decentralisation, if requested, to consult with a provincial executive on proposed legislation in a concurrent field; s.85 requires consultation between the national and provincial governments concerning any major investment; ss.75-78 establish and list the functions of the NFC; and ss.82-84 establish and list the functions of the Premier's Council.

The emphasis which the Organic Law places on 'consultation' reflects the intention of its framers 'that provincial government should embody a spirit of friendly cooperation between the levels of government' (Goldring 1977:256) an intention which is made explicit in s.187D(3) of the Constitution. Goldring expressed the opinion that 'consultation would be regarded as a real consideration by the court', but added: 'Whether or not the consultation must be effective or meaningful is deemed to be a political, rather than a legal question' (ibid.:257).

The body set up under the Organic Law and the *National Fiscal Commission Act* is rather different from that recommended earlier, both in its composition and its functions. Under s.78 it has the functions:

(a) to consider, and to report to the National Parliament and to the provincial assembly concerned on, any alleged discrimination or unreasonableness in provincial taxation and any proposals by the national government to remove or correct it; and
(b) in accordance with Section 79 [principles of allocation of unconditional grants], to consider, and to make recommendations to the National Executive Council on, the allocation of unconditional grants under Section 64

to provincial governments and as between provincial governments; and

(c) to consider, and to make recommendations to the national government and provincial governments on, other fiscal matters relating to provincial government referred to it by the national government or a provincial government.

The NFC has been described as a 'buffer' between the national government and the provincial governments. In introducing the National Fiscal Commission Bill 1977 the minister for Finance said: 'It will mean that a lot of politics is taken out of . . . disputes (between the central government and the provinces) and that solutions will be more readily found'.

Section 187H of the Constitution provides for the establishment of the Premiers' Council (PC) and states that: 'A major function of the Council . . . shall be to avoid legal proceedings between governments by providing a forum for the non-judicial settlements of intergovernmental disputes' (s.187H(S)).

Section 187H(6) provides that an organic law may vest in the PC 'mediatory or arbitral powers or functions in relation to inter-governmental disputes'. Sections 82-84 of the Organic Law provide for the setting up of the PC.

At its first meeting, in Kavieng in 1978, the Council resolved: 'That a Working Committee be established to prepare a report proposing an Organic Law to grant Mediatory or Arbitral Powers to the premiers' Council, and enabling Legislation' (Resolution No.1/78). Draft legislation was submitted to the PC conference in Wewak in 1979 and the subject was raised again in Port Moresby in 1980.

Finally, the *Provincial Governments (Mediation and Arbitration Procedures) Act* was passed early in 1981. It lays down procedures for the non-judicial settlement of disputes, but specifically 'applies to a dispute . . . which is not eligible for reference to the National Fiscal Commission' (s.3(d)).

Intergovernmental financial relations

Notwithstanding the CPC's rejection of federalism, the financial provisions of the Organic Law – which *broadly* follow the recommendations of the Tordoff-Watts Report – are for the most part those of a federal system (indeed the discussion of the principles of fiscal allocation in that Report might have been taken from, say, May 1969). There is provision (rather more generous than that recommended in 1974) for exclusive provincial taxes (ss.56-60); there is provision for conditional and unconditional (including 'derivation') grants, and for the transfer of proceeds of certain national taxation; and provinces are empowered to borrow and to guarantee loans on short-term.

There are, however, at least two significant restrictions on the formal fiscal powers of the provinces. Section 59(4) enables the national finance minister, 'after consultation with the provincial government', to exempt from provincial land taxes, other than taxes on unimproved land value, any mining or industrial activity. Section 61 enables the National Parliament to 'remove or correct' provincial tax laws which it considers to be discriminatory or unreasonable. Before doing so it must refer the matter to the NFC (see above), but its recommendation is not binding and the decision of the National Parliament is non-justiciable.

Also, provinces are required to submit annually to the minister responsible for provincial affairs a full statement of their financial position and of the affairs of the province (s.73), and provinces (but not provincial business enterprises) are subject to inspection and audit by the auditor-general (and incidentally to review by the Joint Committee of Public Accounts of the National Parliament).

Before leaving the subject of financial relations a brief word on the subject of financial autonomy.[3] Between January and July 1978 three provinces – North Solomons, East New Britain and New Ireland – assumed full financial responsibility for the func-

[3] The terms 'financial autonomy', 'full financial autonomy', 'full finan-

tions transferred in 1978-1979. In May 1978 (on the initiative of the Department of Finance) the question of criteria for granting such responsibility was discussed at the PC meeting in Kavieng. The meeting passed a resolution (Resolution No.4/78) which set seven criteria to be met by provinces before full financial responsibility would be devolved (see May 1981:31). It was anticipated that all provincial governments should attain full provincial government status before early 1981. In fact, however, although Eastern Highlands joined the 'club' in July 1979, there was no further grant of full financial autonomy (despite five applications) until 1982 (when it was announced, another four provinces would graduate). Pending the achievement of full financial autonomy, the financial allocation to these provincial functions forms part of the national budget in Div.248. The levels of expenditure are determined after consultation between the provincial and national governments and the former have some authority to reallocate funds between the divisional subheads. However budgetary and financial control over such funds is exercised by the Department of Finance for the minister for Decentralisation. Meanwhile, the present level of Div.248 expenditures relative to the projected level of formula grants has created a situation in which, unless the formula is changed, a number of provinces stand to lose – some substantially – by shifting to fully autonomous status.

---

cial responsibility', 'full financial control' have been used interchangeably. The minister for Decentralisation has given the following definition: 'Full financial control means that the provincial government controls all funds available to the province including public service administrative funds under Division 248, any funds at the end of the financial year which would in the past have returned to Consolidated Revenue would remain with the provincial government. Budgeting would have to come from the provincial government, and the monitoring of expenditure would be done on the financial report under Section 73 of the Organic Law' (Momis, Ministerial Statement on provincial government, 1979:23).

Administrative relations

Section 48 of the Organic Law authorises a province to employ a provincial secretariat of up to six persons, over whom the national government has no power of direction or control. Apart from this secretariat, all provincial administrative staff are members of the national public service; the costs of their employment are borne by the national government, but 'except as provided by any law relating to the National Public Service' (s.47), they are subject to the direction and control of the provincial government.

The picture which emerges from this selective and superficial summary is one of a system which indeed retains many of the essential features of a unitary state but which nevertheless makes substantial provision for devolution of powers to provincial government. Further, the flexibility embodied in the Organic Law, or perhaps its lack of 'coherence' (see Ghai and Isana 1978a, 1978b), and the emphasis placed on consultation rather than litigation as a means of resolving differences between the two levels of government, has produced, as I have already suggested above, a very *political* system of decentralisation.

The reality

Obviously one cannot portray the political reality of provincial government in contemporary Papua New Guinea in the space of a few pages – even assuming that there is a single, objective 'reality' (and that it can be understood by non Melanesians). The intent of this section is simply to offer some comments on the way in which provincial government had developed, and is developing, in a number of areas, particularly those whose constitutional provisions have been discussed above.

Before doing so, however, I would like to suggest that there are several historical reasons why in Papua New Guinea 'politics', as opposed to 'constitutionalism', have been so important in determining the form of provincial government. For one, the whole disjointed and uncertain history of decentralisation from

1973 encouraged provincial governments (at least the more progressive of them, who provided a model for others) to formulate their ideas of what they wanted to do without much regard to the constantly shifting parameters imposed (or not imposed) as the result of successive reports and committee decisions. This was particularly so in those provinces (such as North Solomons, East New Britain, West New Britain, East Sepik, Manus, New Ireland, Simbu and Central) in which experienced public servants or articulate students returned to their provinces to help plan the establishment of provincial government, and in those few (such as Eastern Highlands) where national politicians played a similar role. Second, frustration caused by lack of firm direction on decentralisation before 1977 and frequent lack of cooperation from national departments persuaded some provinces to act unilaterally and negotiate later (e.g. in relation to the provincial secretariat). This tradition has become part of the system; indeed I have the impression that there is a growing antipathy between the provinces and the centre (and particularly between some national politicians and some provincial politicians), which could magnify this tendency. Third, although there appears to be a growing revisionist tendency to play down the role of North Solomons separatism in the process of institutionalising decentralisation, the decision in 1973 that any agreement with Bougainville must be within a legislative framework applicable to the country as a whole ensured that the ultimate form of provincial government reflected strongly the demands of that province which was the most ardent supporter of decentralisation and had the greatest capacity for financial autonomy. Finally (and perhaps most important), with the establishment of provincial assemblies, provinces became politicised, and Papua New Guinea politics became provincialised, to an extent that few people anticipated even as late as 1977, and this appears to have been associated with a similarly unexpected shift of political weight and administrative initiative from the centre to the provinces (May 1981:17).

Status of provincial governments

The first general observation to be made under this heading is that although there has been no formal challenge to the concept of the unitary state, and the implicit dominance of the national government, the rhetoric of provincial politicians and officials seems to reflect a widely accepted view that, as expressed in the submission to the 1980 Premiers' Council (quoted above), the national and provincial governments 'are *equal* partners in process of governing the country', that, in the words of the Bougainville Charter, 'one is not inferior . . . to the other'. This view is put, for example, in arguing for amendment to or ignoring of the Organic Law when it inhibits provincial action (for example, in relation to overseas investment, or taxation) or is simply seen as an affront to provincial autonomy (for example, in relation to measures designed to ensure financial accountability). At a more abstract level I have heard provincial officials argue that the national government has no right to revenue from, for example, coffee, because coffee is grown '*in the provinces*'.

A second general observation is that there have been tendencies to both centralisation and decentralisation in this area. Thus, for example: on the one hand, the declaration of states of emergency in the highlands provinces, the introduction of sectoral programme funding, and pressure on provincial governments (with the implied threat of resort to s.61 of the Organic Law on Provincial Government) to reduce certain provincial tax rates, have all been quoted as evidence of a lack of real provincial autonomy; on the other hand, the realisation that few requirements of provinces (e.g. in relation to financial reporting) carry any effective provisions for enforcement, and the discovery that the original provisions for suspending provincial governments were so complex as to be ineffective, suggest serious weaknesses in the powers of the national government vis-à-vis the provinces. On balance, however, I feel that evolution has favoured the provinces.

Division of powers

The division of legislative powers set out in Part VI of the Organic Law (plus the delegation to provincial governments of executive responsibility in areas in which they do not have legislative power) gives the provinces a potentially wider field of operation than the states or provinces enjoy in most federal systems. At the same time, the fluidity of the provisions by which powers are divided has created uncertainty and confusion over where powers reside in relation to certain administrative decisions taken at the provincial level. To cite two recent examples: in 1978 Simbu provincial government refused to reimburse the national Department of Works and Supply (DWS) in the province for certain works undertaken in Simbu, because, it alleged, DWS had not adequately consulted with the provincial government; in another province the provincial government declined to commit funds to a high school whose construction was said not to reflect provincial priorities.

To date [1982] provinces have not rushed to exercise responsibility in all areas available to them, though most provinces are currently exercising a good deal of autonomy in policy-making and administration. More interesting are the demands expressed by provincial premiers and secretaries at Premiers' Council conferences, in submissions to the General Constitutional Commission, and recently to the committee appointed to review the financial provisions of the Organic Law on Provincial Government. These demands for additional powers to provinces have covered such 'naturally' national responsibilities as foreign investment, overseas borrowing, and aid, not to mention police (in 1979 the East New Britain premier was sentenced to goal for maintaining what was in effect a provincial police force). On the positive side, such demands are, I believe, evidence of a growing shift of policy initiative (and to a certain extent, expertise) from the centre to the provinces; as against this there seems to be an emerging propensity for provincial governments (and their business arms) to act, out of frustration with central government, in areas in which they clearly do not have constitutional or administrative competence.

Settlement of disputes

A distinctive feature of the Papua New Guinea system is the emphasis which is placed, in the Constitution and the Organic Law, on the settlement of disputes through consultation. However, of the three mechanisms provided to this end, none has worked particularly satisfactorily. Of the Constitutional provisions for consultation the General Constitutional Commission has commented:

> Although there has been some consultation between national government and provincial governments the extent to which this has been carried out has been extremely poor. Our experience has shown that there has been no meaningful consultation by national government in a lot of areas in the concurrent field. [1980:31]

And neither the NFC nor the PC has assumed the role apparently intended for it.

In the case of the NFC, to date no question relating to (a) or (c) of its functions (see above) has been referred to it by national or provincial governments, and in allocating the small amount of money made available to it by the national government for unconditional grants it would appear that the NFC has been 'led' by the Department of Finance (which provides its secretariat). This is not necessarily to be condemned. If issues of potential dispute can be negotiated on a government-to-government basis, and if questions of grant allocation can be settled without arousing 'provincial and regional jealousies' (Manning 1979:9) so much the better. However, I see two major problems in the situation which has developed. First, s.79 directs the NFC to base its decision on allocation on equal per capita payments, but allowing also for 'the location and physical nature of a province', 'the lack of development of a province', or 'any other relevant factor'. In practice, the NFC – following submissions from the Department of Finance – has allocated part of the available amount to reducing inequalities between provinces, part to supplement the cost of provincial government (i.e. the 'costs of running the assembly and essential supporting services'), and part to supplement maintenance of capital assets. And funds that might otherwise have been allocated to the NFC have been diverted to the NPEP. This would seem to be in contravention of the spirit, and probably the letter, of the Organic Law. Second, in several instances where provinces might have been expected to refer matters to the NFC (e.g. in cases where the national government has opposed provincial tax increases, and on the question of 're-centralising' sectoral programme funds), they have not done so. In submissions to the Committee to Review the Financial Provisions of the Organic Law on Provincial Government several provinces expressed the view that the NFC is 'in the pocket' of the Department of Finance, and more than one submission called for its abolition.

The PC, on the other hand, has served as a useful forum, and a review of agendas and resolutions of the PC conferences held to date shows that it has dealt with a number of significant issues and has passed important resolutions. There are, however, major questions concerning the extent of follow-up to PC resolutions, and the capacity of the PC secretariat. Few resolutions from the first three conferences have yet been implemented. The minister for Decentralisation has recorded that provinces have:

> . . . expressed disappointment with the attitude of national departments towards these conferences, as reflected in the poor attendance and non-implementation of resolutions passed at these conferences. [Momis 1980:8]

However, provinces also are guilty of non-implementation of resolutions. For example, in an important resolution of the second conference in 1979, the premiers called on the national government to set up a Provincial Finance Inspectorate and undertook to amend provincial finance legislation to give the proposed inspectorate access to all provincial accounts and records: to date, however, only a small number of provinces has made the necessary amendments. The lack of action on resolutions is emerging as a major source of frustration and eventually antagonism in the relations between the national government and the provinces, and, taken with the generally poor service available from the small secretariat, threatens to undermine the effectiveness of the institution. (In this context an interesting recent development is the emergence of four informal regional premiers' conferences.)

Intergovernmental financial relations

The financial arrangements of provincial government are complex, and in 1982 were under review by an interdepartmental/national-provincial committee. (For a more detailed discussion of the subject see the reports of the two consultants to this committee – May (1981) and Chelliah (1981) – and Manning (1979).) I will restrict myself here to three broad comments.

First, provincial governments are, and will continue to be (the recent introduction of provincial retail taxes notwithstanding), heavily dependent for their revenue on grants from the national government. Chelliah (1981:9) calculates provinces' own tax and non-tax revenues in 1980 as constituting one per cent of their total revenues. This situation seems inevitable given the structure of the taxation system (e.g. the critical role of import duties and taxes on a small number of foreign companies, and the fact that the bulk of income taxation is collected in two provinces – National Capital and Morobe) and the very considerable inequalities in taxable capacity between provinces. Nor is it particularly remarkable; it is a situation which, for a number of good reasons, characterises most federal systems. Nevertheless, the heavy dependence on revenue transfers does underline the importance of the methods employed, particularly the distribution as between the richer provinces and the poorer.

Second, in several respects the financial provisions of the

Organic Law either have not worked as intended or have been misinterpreted. The major element of the revenue transfer to provinces comprises a minimum unconditional grant, provided for by s.64 of the Organic Law according to a formula set out in Sch.l. Essentially, the formula gives to each province a base amount equal to the level of expenditure on transferred functions in 1976/77, adjusted annually for variations in the cost of living or in the level of national revenue, whichever yields the smaller amount. An apparently unforeseen aspect of this formula is that it embodies a downward ratchet effect in the payments to provinces. In practice, however, this has not been significant, because the Department of Finance has chosen (consciously or unconsciously) to ignore the 'whichever is less' provision. Another aspect of the grant formula, as we have already noted is that for those non-fully-financially-autonomous provinces funded through Div.248 payments, a number are now receiving larger allocations than would be indicated by application of the formula – such that several provinces stand to lose by achieving autonomy. (I understand that the provinces recently granted autonomy have been guaranteed that they will not lose by doing so; this is a sensible policy decision – which apparently dates back to 1978 (Manning 1979:10) – though the constitutional basis for it is not clear.) We have already commented on the discrepancy between what the Organic Law says about the allocation of grants through the NFC and what actually happens. Referring to the *formal* provisions for NFC grants Manning wrote in 1979:

> This principle [equal per capita grants] will gradually reduce the inequalities between provinces . . . Other government policies, particularly the N.P.E.P. are also working to remove inequalities. [ibid.:10]

In fact, however, there is to date no evidence for such a conclusion. Neither the scale nor the distribution of payments through the NFC has done anything to reduce inequalities, and there has been no significant correlation between per capita

NPEP expenditure by provinces and provincial development indicators. Indeed Berry and Jackson (1981) conclude their survey of inter-provincial inequalities and decentralisation with the comment:

> All in all . . . the financial arrangements for provincial government in Papua New Guinea seem likely to entrench existing inter-provincial inequalities. [ibid.:74; see also Hinchliffe 1980]

A third comment on the subject of financial relations is that financial management and control by some provinces has left a lot to be desired. In several instances where a provincial government has appeared to be in financial difficulties the national government has sought to consult with the province but has been refused access to provincial accounts. In one case national officers were invited in to the province only to have the invitation withdrawn when they arrived. Two provinces have actually run out of money through gross mismanagement and have been rescued by conditional loans from the national government.

Yet although it seems to me that the Organic Law *intended* to provide for national oversight of provincial finances, in fact the national government has been often unable, and sometimes, it would seem, reluctant, to exercise such oversight (see May 1981:33-39). With regard to financial reporting, for example, the Organic Law simply says that provincial governments will submit statements 'as soon as practicable after the end of the fiscal year' (s.73), and carries no penalty for non-compliance. The form in which provinces are required to report has been laid down in provincial government Finance Circulars. However in his 'Statement on the Financial Activities of Provincial Governments', presented to the National Parliament in May 1979, the minister for Decentralisation observed that four provinces had failed to submit their reports for 1978, and in his 1980 report he stated that three provinces had failed to submit their reports 'despite repeated warnings' 15 had submitted their reports after the deadline, and that the remaining province had submitted a report which did not comply with the requirements (Momis 1980:1). He also commented that reports contained a variety of errors and many were simply not put into the correct format (ibid.:10). Problems in this area are likely to be exacerbated as more provinces attain full financial responsibility.

Administrative relations

Administrative relations have been, predictably, another complex issue. However, it would appear that in the effort to reconcile the decision for a single national public service with the demand for provincial autonomy at least three mechanisms have operated in favour of the provinces: an unexpectedly large number of senior public servants have chosen to pursue careers in the provinces rather than in Port Moresby; there has been a strong tendency for provinces (especially the more 'developed' provinces) to recruit public servants from their own province, and several provinces have chosen to ignore the constitutional limitations on the size of the provincial secretariat.

Conclusion

To suggest that constitutional structure does not provide an explanation of the workings of a political system (though it is an element of the system) is not to say anything novel (cf. e.g. May 1966, 1969). Yet in the growing literature about provincial government in Papua New Guinea few writers get far beyond the institutional aspects of the system (the notable exception being Standish 1979). I would argue that in Papua New Guinea more than in most countries it is impossible to understand provincial government without understanding the developing political processes within which it operates. Further I would suggest that recent political developments have tended, on balance, to shift the political weight of the system in favour of the provinces.

Finally, bearing in mind that this paper was written for a legal workshop, I would like to draw attention to the comments above concerning dispute settlement. If in fact the mechanisms provided for consultation cannot be employed effectively to resolve differences between the national and provincial governments as provincial government evolves, there may be an increasing tendency for provincial governments to turn to litigation. In this context, the recent legal challenge over fishing licences in Milne Bay may mark the emergence of a new trend.

8

DECENTRALISATION: TWO STEPS FORWARD, ONE STEP BACK*

Introduction

Local governments were established in Papua New Guinea during the colonial period. By the time of independence in 1975 a new tier of sub-national bodies, area authorities, had been created to provide some coordination of local government activities at the administrative district level.[1] Following independence a system of provincial government was introduced, within a unitary constitution. In each of the former administrative districts, renamed provinces, an elected provincial assembly was established, and substantial powers were transferred to the provincial governments, though the national government maintained overriding authority.

From the outset, however, provincial governments came under attack, both from local government councillors, who attributed an accelerated decline in the local government system to indifference or hostility on the part of provincial politicians, and from national politicians who saw the provincial government system as undermining their local power bases. Many bureau-

* This paper was presented at a workshop at the University of Canberra in 1997. It was subsequently published in Mark Turner (ed.), *Central-Local Relations in Asia-Pacific. Convergence or Divergence* (1999) and is reproduced with the kind permission of Polgrave Publishers.

[1] At the end of the colonial period there were 18 administrative districts, each headed by a district commissioner. In 1975 one of the larger provinces was divided into two. Somewhat confusingly, what were previously sub-districts were renamed districts. A National Capital District was also created for the capital, Port Moresby.

crats also resisted the decentralisation of policy making and implementation. In 1995 new legislation was passed, in the face of some opposition, to substantially 'reform' the provincial and local-level government system. The new arrangements, whose stated objective was to achieve a further decentralisation of the political system, did away with elected provincial governments, replacing them with assemblies comprising the national MPs from each province, representatives of elected local-level governments, and a small number of sectoral and community representatives. It was intended to hold elections for the local-level governments concurrently with national elections in June 1997, but the local elections were postponed. Meanwhile, there is a great deal of discussion about how the new system is intended to work, and suggestions that in many provinces it is not working at all. In the lead-up to the 1997 national elections some candidates promised, if elected, to repeal the 1995 legislation.

This paper examines the rationale, structure and performance of the former provincial government system, which operated for about two decades,[2] and attempts to describe the new scheme of decentralisation, which is still in the process of articulation and whose future is by no means assured.

Early devolution: local government councils

As in most colonial territories, local government councils were introduced into Papua New Guinea by the Australian colonial administration primarily as a tutelary device to give Papua New Guineans experience in the operation of formal democratic-style institutions. The first local councils (initially termed 'village councils'), established under the *Native Local Government Councils Ordinance, 1949*, were given some of the powers previously en-

[2] For a more detailed analysis of the previous provincial government system see Conyers (1976), Ballard (1981), Ghai and Regan (1992) and May and Regan with Ley (1997). May and Regan with Ley (1997) also includes an extensive bibliography.

trusted to village constables (in Papua) and *luluais* (in New Guinea), in relation to local peacekeeping and organising certain community activities, as well as more usual local government functions. They were also given authority to raise taxes (their main source of revenue being a head tax, which varied from council to council and frequently set different rates for men and women, and young and old), and to engage in business, and they instituted 'council work days', which involved all adults contributing unpaid labour for community work (principally road building and maintenance) one day a week. A special section was set up within the (then) Department of Native Affairs to oversee the establishment of councils and at the district level patrol officers were assigned as council advisers (*kaunsil kiap*). Subsequently the office of Commissioner for Local Government was created. Although the role of the council advisers was to advise and educate, it was often claimed that some at least exercised a dominant influence over council affairs, and questions were frequently raised as to the extent to which councils were autonomous bodies or merely extensions of the colonial administration in Port Moresby. From the mid 1960s the position of council adviser was progressively localised.

By 1951 five councils had been established, covering a population of around 18 000; by 1960 the number had increased to 36 (covering 250 000), and by 1965 to 114 (1 250 000). In 1961 councils were used in the indirect election of 'native members' for the newly-created Legislative Council.

The 1949 ordinance was replaced in 1963 by a *Local Government Ordinance*, whose preamble foresaw the progressive acceptance by individual councils of increasing responsibilities and authority. Controversially, the new ordinance changed councils from being 'native' to being multi-racial. The 1963 ordinance extended the powers of local government councils to include: the provision, maintenance and management of roads and bridges, parks and gardens, aid posts, ambulance services and public latrines, housing schemes, markets, water, light and power supplies, land reclamation, agricultural, pastoral, horticultural and forestry industries, airstrips, bus services, and fire prevention; the making of rules regulating public health, building, town planning, the control of livestock, and school attendance; the provision of agency functions for the administration, and engaging in business. Further, to improve their performance councils were provided with 'model rules' in several areas, to guide their activities, and were required to formulate five-year plans setting development priorities.

In the early 1960s the population served by a local government council ranged from around 5000 to over 50 000. To provide better linkage between village people and the councils, particularly in the larger council areas, the 1963 ordinance made provision for the creation of ward committees chaired by the elected councillors. Initially essentially advisory bodies, the powers of the ward committees were subsequently widened to include the promotion of community self-help projects and disbursement of funds allocated by the council.

As well as extending links downwards, from around 1959 there were moves to establish links between councils. In that year the first nationwide local government conference was held. Six years later, with the growth in council numbers making national conferences difficult, regional conferences (based on the territory's four supra-district administrative regions) replaced the national conference, though in 1968 the regional delegates created a Local Government Association to represent council interests nationally. In the early 1960s, also, regular council conferences were being organised at district level.

In recognition of this trend a *Local Government (Authorities) Act, 1970* provided for the creation of area authorities at district level. These authorities, consisting mostly of local government council nominees, served as advisory bodies to the district commissioners (progressively replacing the former district advisory councils) and played a role in the provincial allocation of certain development funds (see Conyers 1976:13-15). However, they also helped promote a sense of provincial identity, and in the early 1970s it was principally the area authorities which voiced the demand for provincial government and later provided the membership for interim provincial governments and constituent assemblies.

The provincial government system, 1976-1995

History

With movement towards independence gaining momentum from around the late 1960s, there was some popular advocacy of political decentralisation, and when in 1972 a Constitutional Planning Commission (CPC) was established to draft a constitution for an independent state, decentralisation was on its agenda.

In its *2nd Interim Report* (1973) the CPC supported the idea of district-level government,

> ... as an important step towards accommodating strong political pressures for the granting of significant autonomy to particular areas of the country which have been building up over the last five years. [CPC 1973:4/4]

It argued that decentralisation of decision making should be 'political and not merely bureaucratic', and recommended that 'certain powers should be vested by law in provincial governments' (ibid.:4/3-4). The subject of central-provincial government relations was referred to consultants William Tordoff and Ronald L. Watts in 1974. Bearing in mind the views of the CPC, the consultants' report recommended

> ... that a fully decentralised system of unitary government should be constitutionally assured as an ultimate goal, but that it evolve by stages, with each province beginning at that stage most consistent with provincial capacity. [Tordoff-Watts Report 1974:3/9]

The CPC's final report was presented in 1974. It included detailed recommendations for the establishment of provincial government, including a schedule of proposed national, provincial and concurrent powers. The report was accompanied by a government 'white paper' (*Proposals on Constitutional Principles and Explanatory Notes*, 1974), which challenged the CPC's recommendations on several points. On the subject of provincial government, the white paper 'strongly supported' the principle of decentralisation, but raised four substantive reservations:

> - 'that the CPC proposals could result in an undue concentration of power at the provincial centre';
> - 'that the law should also safeguard the interests of local government bodies . . .';
> - that 'The type of near-federal system proposed by the CPC would create many legal and administrative problems if introduced suddenly';
> - that 'The schedule . . . dealing with the functions and powers of provincial governments should be used only as a guide' (the government also argued that it was not essential for all provinces to reach the same stage of decentralisation). [ibid.:35, 37]

The subsequent discussion of the provincial government proposals attracted considerable controversy, and by the time the relevant chapter of the CPC's report was under debate a compromise had been arrived at, in which the essential principles of provincial government would be included in the constitution but the detailed arrangements would be set out in a subsidiary organic law. But in July 1975, as the proposed organic law on provincial government was under discussion, Prime Minister Somare successfully moved in the national parliament (which was sitting as a constituent assembly) that the provincial government proposals simply be deleted from the constitution.

The demands of Bougainvilleans, whose province (Bougainville, or North Solomons) was home to a vast gold and copper mine, had been a significant factor in the move towards provincial government. A provincial (then called district) government had been set up on Bougainville in early 1974, and an agreement made to pay the provincial government a grant, in lieu of royalties, from revenue from the mine. A *Provincial Government (Preparatory Arrangements) Act, 1974* had been passed to give formal status to what in July became the Bougainville Interim Provincial Government, but, within a policy context of denying special deals with Bougainville, making similar provision for all other provinces. Growing tensions in relations between the national government and Bougainvillean leaders, who were seeking a larger share of mining revenue and talking separatism, probably influenced the Somare government's move in July 1975. However, the Bougainvillean response, on 1 September 1975 – two weeks before Papua New Guinea's independence – was a unilateral declaration of independence.

Negotiations between the national government and Bougainvillean leaders during 1975-76 culminated in the signing of a Bougainville Agreement in August 1976, the reinstating of the provincial government provisions through amendment to the constitution, and the passage of the Organic Law on Provincial Government (OLPG). The provisions of the OLPG were based on the Bougainville Agreement of 1976, which in turn derived largely from the earlier CPC/Tordoff-Watts proposals.

Meanwhile, in most other provinces by 1976 constituent assemblies (generally based on the area authorities' membership) had been established and progress was being made towards the establishment of provincial governments. By the end of 1978 all 19 provinces had been granted charters under the OLPG, though it was another two years before all had elected provincial assemblies.

Political structures

The OLPG provided that all provinces have legislatures of at least 15 members, and an executive; but it left much of the detail concerning political structures for the provincial constituent assemblies to decide. In practice, all provincial constitutions provided for assemblies popularly elected from single member constituencies every four or five years, though most made provision also for the assembly to appoint up to three members to represent specified special interests (women, churches, and business). A 1981 amendment to the OLPG made national MPs *ex officio* non-voting members of their respective province's assemblies.

By the early 1990s four provinces had opted for a presidential-style direct election of the chief executive (the premier) but all other provinces had broadly Westminster-style systems, with the premier elected by the members of the legislature. The small size of the assemblies and the absence (at least in the early years) of a well developed political party system in the provinces frequently made for a personalistic, patronage-based style of government, especially in provinces where a relatively large cabinet (in several cases more than half of the assembly) was used as a means of buying support and stability. As against this, in the absence of parties, provincial assemblies were often characterised by divisions along personal and regional lines and wracked by factionalism and frequent votes of no confidence.

Although, over the years, much was made of the 'cost' of provincial governments, the amount allocated to salaries and overheads for the provincial legislatures and executives (as opposed to the cost of providing services which otherwise would have had to have been largely met by the national government) was calculated in the 1980s at, on average, around 5 per cent of provincial spending (Axline 1988:table 20).

Powers and functions

In allocating powers and functions between the national and provincial governments, the OLPG 'sought to secure the autonomy of provincial government without undermining the role of the national government as guardian of the overall interest'

(CPC 1974:10/23/198). In practice, this principle was embodied in a complex but flexible set of provisions which allowed for the possibility of extensive provincial powers being negotiated with the national government. The OLPG specified a small number of exclusively national powers (essentially, powers needed to implement the constitution and deal with emergencies) and reserved some taxation fields (principally land and retail sales taxes) to the provinces; but the bulk of legislative responsibilities was listed under one of two categories: 'primarily provincial' subjects and 'concurrent' subjects. The first – which included primary education (excluding curriculum), village courts, local government, liquor licensing, housing, and sporting and cultural activities – was open to both levels of government but in the event of any inconsistency provincial laws took precedence. The second and much longer list was also open to both levels of government, but with the national laws prevailing in the event of a clash. This list included education generally, health, agriculture, forestry, community and rural development, land, labour, and transport and communications. Provinces were further empowered to make laws in areas normally covered by national legislation (including national security and international relations) if those areas were 'unoccupied' by national legislation. Provision was also made for each level to delegate powers to the other. Particularly in view of the fact that national legislation on most subjects existed before the creation of provincial governments, provision was made in the OLPG to limit national law-making in the 'concurrent' field to matters of 'national interest' and give provinces the right to seek repeal of national legislation not covering matters of national interest. Nevertheless, reflecting the essentially unitary nature of the Papua New Guinea state, the National Parliament was given overriding power to disallow a provincial law if it considered such action to be 'in the public interest'. (This power was exercised only once – to prevent a provincial government extending the term of its provincial assembly.)

However, while it was intended that provincial governments develop their own body of legislation, initially a range of functions was transferred to the provincial governments by the national government under the arrangements for delegation. These functions were delegated, uniformly to all provinces, in two stages in 1977. They comprised:

- provincial affairs (what had previously been termed 'district administration');
- health (including aid posts, health centres and provincial hospitals, and malaria eradication programmes);
- primary industry (including agricultural extension and forestry management);
- education (including community schools, provincial high schools, and vocational centres);
- business development extension services;
- government information services;
- public works (construction and maintenance);
- the Rural Improvement Programme (which funded small projects through the local government system); and
- government financial and accounting services (the functions of the Bureau of Management Services).

Commenting on this delegation of functions Anthony Regan has noted:

> . . . functions determined for transfer . . . were not based on any coherent concept of the role and responsibilities of provincial government. Rather, they bore all the marks of the series of *ad hoc* decisions that led to their transfer . . . More importantly, the arrangements tend to tie the provincial staff to operating under national government laws and so answering to national departments in a variety of ways, thereby weakening the capacity of provincial governments to plan and manage their activities and organise their staff. [May and Regan with Ley 1997:34]

In fact, after an initial flurry by provincial governments to pass the basic legislation necessary for them to function (in many instances model legislation drafted by national government officials), most provinces were legislatively inactive. Though some enacted new policies and even challenged existing national policies (for example, East Sepik on customary land registration, and Manus on sustainable forestry management [see, respectively, May in May and Regan with Ley 1997:248-52, and Taylor 1991]), others did no more than pass their annual appropriation acts.

Finance

As in most federal-type situations, the perceived need to control major fiscal resources nationally, and the marked inequality of provincial fiscal capacity, dictated that, while provinces were given exclusive revenue sources, their main source of revenue would be transfers from the national government. And as in most federal-type systems, the distribution of grants amongst provinces acknowledged three basic allocative principles: derivation, equity, and needs.

For all provinces the largest single element of the fiscal transfer was a 'minimum unconditional grant' (MUG).[3] Essentially, the MUG was intended to meet the cost, for each province, of the functions transferred from the national government in 1977, with provision for changes in prices and national government revenue. Inherent problems in the MUG grant formula were addressed in a series of reviews, but proposed amendments introduced into the National Parliament were never passed. The national government also paid an annual (uniform) grant to provinces to meet the salary costs of a six-person provincial secretariat.[4]

---

[3] The complexities surrounding the MUG (including the issue of 'full financial responsibility') are discussed elsewhere – see May (1981); Department of Provincial Affairs (1984); Axline (1986:79-84); Ghai and Regan (1992:238-46); May and Regan (1997:39-40).

[4] Public servants in the provinces were assigned from the national public service, and their salaries covered (in effect) by the MUG arrangements. But in recognition of existing arrangements on Bougainville in 1976, each

A third transfer, designed to placate the wealthier provinces (particularly, in 1976, Bougainville) but also to provide an incentive to provincial economic development, was an annual derivation grant. This was calculated at 1.25 per cent of the export value of produce originating in the province, less any royalties paid to the province. (Problems with the derivation grant formula – particularly concerning disparities between mining and timber royalties – were also addressed in the 1990 proposed amendments to the OLPG).

A fourth transfer, 'additional unconditional grants' (AUG) were intended to achieve some degree of equalisation of development amongst the provinces, with funds allocated on the advice of an independent National Fiscal Commission. The amount paid through AUG, however, was never substantial, and after 1984 AUG were not paid. It was considered, by the national government, that the issue of equity could be better addressed through the government's five-year rolling National Public Expenditure Plan (1985-87) and subsequent Public Investment Program, which allocated capital funds for national and provincial development projects; in fact there is no evidence that the NPEP/PIP mechanism achieved equalisation between provinces.

In addition to these four 'unconditional' transfers, provision was made in the OLPG for conditional grants to provinces. However, apart from allocations (through the NPEP/PIP mechanism) to five provinces for integrated rural development programmes under a Less Developed Areas Programme, the only conditional grant paid to provinces was a small amount for town sanitary services in rural areas.

Another element of the fiscal package involved the payment to provinces of the proceeds from certain national revenue-raising measures. The most important of these were royalties, particularly royalties from mining, forestry, and petroleum. Lesser amounts were paid from motor vehicle registration and drivers'

---

provincial government was allowed to appoint up to six people as a secretariat, solely responsible to the provincial government.

licence fees, bookmakers' tax, and, in some provinces, tobacco excise in lieu of provincial retail sales tax on tobacco products. With respect to the distribution of transfers amongst provinces, royalty payments, along with derivation grants, tended to skew the distribution in favour of the wealthier provinces (or those having a major resource project).

Local government

By the early 1970s local government councils in most parts of the country were in decline. Poor management, inability to collect head taxes, the frequent failure of council-run businesses, the unpopularity of council workdays, a general feeling that councils were alien institutions, and, after 1963, opposition to the shift to multi-racial councils, all contributed to this decline. On Bougainville, by 1974 councils had been replaced by village-level community governments.

The CPC noted this dissatisfaction with councils; it recommended that alternative forms of spontaneous local organisation then emerging across the country (see May 1982) be given formal recognition and that all aspects of local-level government be vested in provincial governments.

In the event, the constitutional amendment of 1976 and the OLPG gave full legislative control over local government to the provinces, with the reservation that existing councils could not be abolished without the consent of both provincial and national governments. In 1977 administrative control of councils was transferred by delegation from the national government. Subsequently all but two provinces passed legislation on local-level government (in the remaining two, councils continued to operate under national legislation). Most provinces simply re-enacted the national law as a provincial act; four replaced local government councils by a system of community governments.

Regan (in May and Regan with Ley 1997:28) has suggested that 'in the . . . struggle for power, resources and prestige, local government has been perhaps the biggest loser under the provincial government system'. In a few provinces, local councils continued to operate fairly effectively and their status was maintained. In a few, a new system of community governments functioned satisfactorily. In some the number of councils increased, through subdivision (generally to accommodate internal breakaway movements or in recognition of regionally-based antipathies), but without evidence of increased effectiveness. But in most provinces, lacking skilled manpower and deprived of revenue by diminished tax collection and parsimonious allocations under provincial budgets, local government councils continued to decline from the 1970s through to the mid 1990s. In urban areas, elected urban councils were frequently replaced by appointed statutory bodies.

A significant factor in the demise of local government councils was the fact that provincial politicians frequently saw councils or councillors as threatening their own political base. (This was sometimes exacerbated when local government councillors aligned themselves with national members of parliament.) In such circumstances councils were sometimes deliberately starved of funds and denied their proper status. Not surprisingly, therefore, local government councils made a conspicuous contribution to the opposition to the provincial government system which developed during the 1980s and early 1990s.

Performance

Balanced assessment of the performance of the provincial government system from 1976 to 1995 is not easy. There was certainly no shortage of critics of the system; even its supporters, like John Momis, the acknowledged 'father' of decentralisation and long-time minister for provincial affairs, were frequently scathing in their comments on provincial governments. When, eventually, the auditor-general produced reports on provincial governments' finances the reports pointed to numerous instances of minor and major irregularities. And there was copious documented and anecdotal evidence of lax and inefficient administration, nepotism and outright corruption, some of it confirmed by my own observations in the field.[5] Several premiers and a large number of provincial ministers were charged with various forms of financial mismanagement. By 1994 all but five of the nineteen provincial governments had been suspended, some more than once; three of those five were in the Islands region.

However, the failings of provincial governments have to be seen in the context of a declining level of government performance and a rising level of mismanagement and corruption nationally. There is little doubt that in some provinces, particularly in the Islands region, the performance of governments was generally sound and the delivery of services was better than would have been the case if provincial governments had not existed. In the only detailed sectoral analysis of provincial government performance, in the health sector, the editors of the study concluded:

> . . . decentralisation has brought both benefits and costs to the provinces. On the positive side provinces have greater autonomy in making decisions about their own services. The implementation of local health projects has shown some improvement, as has the ability of provinces to plan for and coordinate their own human and material resources. On the negative side, the political interference in health programs and in the work of public servants has increased considerably. Limited management skills have, in some provinces, led to poor management of services, while inadequate budgetary control has contributed to the continual shortfalls in the recurrent financial allocations for services in recent years.

---

5 For a number of years I have conducted fieldwork in East Sepik Province. In 1991 the East Sepik provincial government was suspended on grounds of financial mismanagement. Soon after this the provincial headquarters were burned down. The outgoing premier was one of several people arrested over the incident. Several members of the provincial cabinet were subsequently charged over misuse of government funds.

> Perhaps the primary question to ask, however, is whether the decentralisation of administrative and political authority for health services has improved the health of the people. This question is impossible to answer with any degree of certainty. [Thomason, Kolehmainen-Aitken and Newbrander 1991:139]

With the added comment that the record varied from province to province, and, within provinces, between activities and over time, much the same might be said of the provincial government system's performance generally.[6]

'Reform' of the provincial government system, 1995–

History

Following the 1992 national elections, the coalition government of Paias Wingti began a new assault on the provincial government system. Within weeks of taking office, Village Services and Provincial Affairs minister John Nilkare introduced a Village Services Programme (see *Post-Courier* 14 August 1992:24-25). The programme, which according to Nilkare represented 'the most fundamental policy shift in our national history', sought to empower some 240 'community governments' through the provision of information, training and resources. Operating through the Department of Village Services and Provincial Affairs, and largely bypassing provincial governments, the programme was to link the national government with village groups through a structure of district centres and community councils; the latter were to comprise representatives from village groups or settlements, national MPs, provincial MPs, and church, women and youth group representatives. Under the programme allowances would be paid to village services personnel, including 'custom-

[6] In the absence of adequate quantitative data, the contributors to May and Regan with Ley (1997) examine in some detail the performance of 11 of the provincial governments.

ary leaders' and village court officials, working in the areas of education, health, agriculture, land mediation, law and order, and women, youth and sports. Ultimately, it was envisaged that the programme would create up to 40 000 new jobs and have a budget of K140 million. (A later statement is given in *Times of PNG* 12 November 1992:32-33).

Subsequently Prime Minister Wingti announced that he intended to overhaul the provincial government system, reduce the number of provincial politicians, and give greater powers to national MPs; he described the provincial government system as costly and divisive and marred by gross mismanagement and corruption (*Post-Courier* 2 October 1992. Also see *Post-Courier* 8 October 1992). Shortly after this it was announced that the National Executive Council had agreed to the abolition of the provincial government system (*Post-Courier* 12, 16 October 1992), a decision which was endorsed by opposition leader Sir Michael Somare (*Post-Courier* 20 October 1992). Legislation for amendment of the constitution to enable the repeal of the Organic Law on Provincial Government was drafted. Around the same time four provincial governments were suspended; three more were suspended in 1993. Some welcomed the Wingti-Nilkare initiatives, but in all four regions there was strong opposition from within provincial governments and in the New Guinea Islands there were threats of secession. The Islands premiers were said to be preparing their own flag and anthem, and a committee of provincial government representatives was to tour the region seeking peoples' views on secession. Solomon Islands Prime Minister Solomon Mamaloni was invited over for talks (*Post-Courier* 20, 23 October 1992).

The national government responded with threats to suspend the provincial governments in the Islands region and to prosecute their leaders. Nevertheless, in the face of this opposition, Wingti modified his stance and in November announced the creation of a Bi-partisan Parliamentary Select Committee on provincial government, headed by Kavieng MP Ben Micah (Peoples

Progress Party), to again review the future of provincial government.

The Bi-partisan Committee presented an initial report in March 1993. The report confirmed that there was widespread disenchantment with provincial governments. It recommended that they be replaced by a system of decentralisation comprising provincial-level authorities (consisting of national politicians and representatives of local government councils, community governments, or traditional authority structures), with more circumscribed powers than provincial governments, and strengthened local-level structures. The NEC endorsed the committee's report and agreed to widen its terms of reference. Five months later the committee presented a second and final report which contained more specific proposals for a comprehensive restructuring of the provincial government system. It also recommended the establishment of a Constitutional Commission to implement and monitor its recommendations and to review the national constitution.

Legislation establishing the Constitutional Review Commission (CRC) was eventually passed in late 1993. The CRC, which was chaired by Micah, comprised representatives from both sides of the parliament as well as representatives from the National Premiers' Council, trade unions, churches, women, and urban authorities, and three 'prominent citizens'. Early in 1994 the CRC presented draft legislation, including a bill for an Organic Law on Provincial Authorities and Local-level Governments. This was tabled in the National Parliament in March and passed the first reading stage.

The provisions of the bill – the so-called 'Bi-partisan model' – involved a substantial reduction in the role of provincial governments. Not only were elected assemblies to be replaced by authorities comprising national MPs and non-elective members, but the law-making powers of the provincial authorities were confined to: the provincial budget; supervision and control of national and local-level governments' development policies;

alcohol licensing; lower-level education; local health centres; tourism; libraries, museums and cultural centres of provincial interest, and 'any other powers which have been delegated to it by law'. In contrast, some thirty powers were given to local-level governments. 'The general principle which underpins the proposed Organic Law', the CRC explained, 'is a system of a greater decentralisation . . . in that more powers are decentralised further to local-level governments' (quoted from a Constitutional Commission brief published in *Times of PNG* 7 April 1994, pp. 31-42). 'The provincial authority', in the words of Prime Minister Wingti, 'would only become a facilitator with limited powers' (*Media Statement* 9 February 1994). Other significant features included a shift from cabinet government at provincial level to a committee system; proposals for a separate 'Provincial and Local Level Governments Support Service' within the national public service (but under a commissioner); provisions for district administrative structures ('electoral development authorities') within each electoral boundary, and tighter financial control through a provincial and district treasury system.

But with continuing opposition from provincial premiers and from some national MPs, the second reading of the bill was postponed pending further public consultation. Meanwhile two prominent members of the CRC resigned, complaining that decisions were being bulldozed through without consultation.

The continuing concerns of the New Guinea Islands region were addressed in April 1994 by a New Guinea Islands Leaders Summit attended by provincial assembly members, senior regional public servants, national MPs from the New Guinea Islands region, and observers from two mainland provinces. The Islands leaders drew up a constitution for a Federated Melanesian Republic (FMR), comprising East and West New Britain, Manus and New Ireland (with Bougainville having an 'automatic right' to join) and demanded greater autonomy; if greater autonomy were not forthcoming they threatened to pursue 'the FMR option' (*Post-Courier* 6, 7, 8, 11 April 1994).

As a result of further consultation, changes were made to the draft legislation: provincial authorities were granted increased legislative powers and renamed provincial governments; financial arrangements for provincial governments were improved; and provisions were included to guarantee consultation between national, provincial and local-level governments and landowners in respect of projects exploiting natural resources. A redrafted Organic Law on Provincial Government and Local-Level Governments was approved by cabinet and legislation was prepared for gazettal, though some equivocation continued (see, for example, *Post-Courier* 29 July 1994).

In August 1994 a mid-term change of government occurred; in a reshuffle of coalition partners, deputy prime minister Sir Julius Chan (PPP) replaced Wingti, heading a coalition which included Pangu and the Melanesian Alliance. Chan was not long in making clear his intention to support the initiative of his New Ireland and PPP colleague. With a change of membership (but with Micah still chairman), the CRC was reactivated. The commission subsequently reported to the NEC in November and in January 1995 the latter approved drafting instructions. The following month a revised bill for an Organic Law on Provincial Governments and Local-Level Governments was gazetted (*National Gazette* No. G19 27 February 1995). Speaking to provincial premiers at a National Premiers' Council conference at that time Chan said: 'The reforms we are putting forward will help bring to an early close a clumsy chapter in the political history of Papua New Guinea' (quoted by Micah, *Post-Courier* 22 May 1995, p.17).

In fact, however, the 'clumsy chapter' was still unfolding. In September 1994 a further meeting of the New Guinea Islands Leaders Forum, deploring the 'appalling financial mismanagement by the national government', resolved to demand 'absolute autonomy' in major areas of government activity (police, public service, agriculture, fisheries, forestry, mining and petroleum, health, education, lands, transport, commerce and industry, and environment and conservation). If their demands were not met, they threatened, they would, by 6 January 1995, declare their independence (see *Post-Courier* 8, 9, 12 September 1994). The demands of the Islands premiers were somewhat overshadowed at the time by volcanic eruptions in Rabaul. However, in October 1994 the government responded, following a meeting of the National Security Council, by ordering that the four Islands premiers and the forum chairman be charged with treason, that staff of the Islands Regional Secretariat be arrested, that expatriates involved in the move be deported, that the provincial secretaries be suspended and charged, and that grants and loan guarantees to Manus Province be frozen (*Post-Courier* 14, 17, 18 November 1994). Although the Islands leaders were not arrested, legal action against them was still proceeding in mid 1995 – though by November 1994 secession was said to be no longer an issue (*Post-Courier* 21 November 1994). Chan rejected calls for further negotiations and maintained a hard line against the premiers and other opponents of the proposed changes to the system.

In March 1995 the redrafted Organic Law and enabling legislation were tabled in the National Parliament and, with minor amendments, passed through the second reading stage with a substantial majority. 'History was made yesterday', Chan said. Papua New Guinea had been freed from the burden of a provincial government system that had handicapped the country for the best part of 20 years.

As against this, the acknowledged father of provincial government in Papua New Guinea, John Momis, urged members to reject the bill. 'At this time in our history', he said, 'attempts to abolish and replace the provincial government system will be deeply divisive and destructive'; there had been 'grossly inadequate public discussion' and 'meetings were stage-managed'. Momis predicted that the new legislation would create 'an administrative nightmare'. Not only was the local government system 'almost dead in most provinces', but the new arrangements 'will make many provincial governments tools in national level conflict on a level and to a degree of intensity never before imagined' (*Post-Courier* 4 April 1995).

Notwithstanding the clear vote for the draft legislation in March, with the third reading adjourned till June 1995 it appeared that others were coming round, at least partly, to Momis's persuasion. In addition to continuing opposition from provincial premiers – particularly the Islands premiers, who at an Islands Premiers' Council meeting in May announced the formation of a new political party, the Movement for Greater Autonomy, and proposed the formation of an Islands State Government (*Post-Courier* 26 April, 8 May 1995) – several national MPs began talking about opposing the legislation at its third reading, and even calling for the rescinding of the first and second readings (see *Post-Courier* 28 April, 1, 5 May, 16 June 1995). Rescinding of the first two readings was also recommended by the Permanent Parliamentary Referral Committee on Justice, which criticised the government for 'bulldozing' the legislation through the house (*National* 1 May 1995; *Post-Courier* 22 June 1995). With two major parties opposing the bill, in early June it was reported that Pangu would call for amendments to the bill, which Somare described as 'grossly deficient' (*Post-Courier* 19 June 1995; also see *Post-Courier* 7, 8, 9, 13 June 1995). In his determination to ensure the passage of the bill Chan urged members to vote for it and move amendments at a later stage, and he threatened to take action against those who were disloyal to him.

In the event, when the legislation came to a vote on 27 June a majority of Pangu members voted to support the bill, and it was passed by 86 votes to 15. Those who voted against the bill or abstained from voting included five cabinet ministers; the following week all five were sacked from cabinet.

While the redrafted Organic Law was before parliament, progress towards reconciliation of the conflict on Bougainville (and the inadvertent lapsing of the suspension of the North Solomons provincial government) resulted in the establishment of a Bougainville Transitional Government (BTG). In recognition of the special circumstances on Bougainville, the BTG was exempted from the provisions of the Organic Law. Special arrangements were also made for the National Capital District.

Political structures

The Organic Law on Provincial Governments and Local-Level Governments (OLPGLLG) effectively abolishes the provincial government system established in the 1970s.[7] In place of the existing elected provincial assemblies the new legislation establishes bodies (still referred to as provincial assemblies) comprising:

- all members of the National Parliament from the province;
- heads of rural local-level governments;
- one representative of the heads of urban authorities and urban councils;
- up to three 'paramount chiefs or their appointed nominees representing local areas where the chieftaincy system is in existence and is accepted';
- one nominated woman representative;
- up to three other members appointed from time to time by the provincial assembly. [OLPGLLG s.10 (3)]

All members, including nominated members, have voting powers.

---

[7] In a briefing paper prepared by the Constitutional Review Commission, however, the question was asked, 'Will provincial governments be abolished?' and it was answered, 'No' (see *Post-Courier* 31 May 1995, pp.18-19). On the other hand, another paper, apparently authored by Micah (*Post-Courier* 22 May 1995) concluded: 'By finally approving the Bills the National Parliament will be sending a clear message to the Nation that provincial governments are subsequent of [*sic*] and not equal to national interest. They are not a second source of political or governmental power. They are part of the national Government, largely delegated, but subject to supervision and ultimate control of the state'.

The chairman of the provincial assembly and head of the provincial government, to be called 'governor', is normally the member of the National Parliament representing the provincial electorate. The governor may be dismissed, however, by a two-thirds majority of the provincial assembly, in which case another person must be elected from amongst the other national MPs. The governor may not be in an executive position in government, or speaker or deputy speaker of the house, or leader or deputy leader of the opposition (s.19). (If the provincial MP accepts such a position, or is otherwise removed, he is to be replaced by another MP.) The governor is constitutionally responsible to the minister for provincial and local-level governments (s.22). The deputy governor is to be elected from amongst the representatives of the local-level governments (as an interim measure existing premiers served as deputy governors).

The former ministerial system was replaced by a committee system; the provincial executive council comprises the governor and deputy governor, and the chairmen of the permanent committees (not exceeding in total a third of the membership of the assembly). Since the governor appoints the committee chairmen, this provision gives the governor considerable authority.

The idea of a separate provincial and local-level service was dropped from the revised legislation. Administratively, provincial departments have been abolished; their operations now come under the relevant national departments through a provincial administrator. The provincial administrator, who is chief executive officer of the provincial government and 'the administrative head of the staff in the province' (ss. 73-74), is chosen by the National Executive Council from a list of persons nominated by the provincial executive council. Below the provincial administrator is a stratum of divisional administrators. The framers of the Organic Law foresaw a decentralisation of administration from Waigani to the provinces and from provincial capitals to the districts. In fact, however, these provisions have been a source of some confusion: although the provincial administrator 'shall maintain overall supervision and direction' over all public servants in the province (excluding law enforcement agencies), and 'shall coordinate and monitor the roles and functions' of the national departments and agencies (s.74(1)(d), (e)), it is not clear how this authority relates to the chain of command within national departments and agencies, nor is it entirely clear what control the provincial administrator exercises over district administrators.

Local-level governments – which form the cornerstone of the new system – are 'in principle' elective bodies representing local communities. They may comprise commissions, urban authorities or councils, community governments, local government councils, 'traditional form(s) of governmental structure', or some combination of these (s.26). The particular form(s) of local-level government is to be determined by the national government on recommendation from the provincial assembly, with a normal maximum of three rural local-level governments in each open (national) electorate.[8] A significant amendment to the Organic Law (s.33A) provides for the establishment, in each district, of a joint district planning and budget priorities committee. Each committee consists of the MP representing the open electorate (as chair), the provincial MP, the heads of the local-level governments in the district, and up to three other members appointed by the open MP in consultation with heads of the district's local-level governments. The provincial administrator is executive officer to the committee. These committees will oversee and coordinate district planning (including a rolling five year development plan) and budget priorities 'for consideration by' the pro-

---

[8] Because the boundaries of local government councils and community governments did not necessarily coincide with those of open electorates, it has been necessary to carry out an extensive redrawing of local-level government boundaries. A number of provinces with more than three local-level governments in an open electorate have also had to amalgamate former councils or community governments. By June 1997 the NEC had approved 284 reformed local-level governments; this did not include Bougainville.

vincial and national governments, determine and control budget allocation priorities for local-level governments, and approve local-level government budgets. Local-level governments are promised full legal status and 'significant funding and manpower'. The shifting of responsibility for local-level government from the provinces to the national government is an important aspect of the 1995 reforms.

Powers and functions

Provinces retain their present primary powers, including financial powers, but concurrent powers revert to the national government. Local-level governments are also given significant law-making powers, covering such subjects as labour and employment, self-help schools (excluding curriculum), dispute settlement, local environment, and local aid posts. (See ss.42-45.) The incorporation in the Organic Law of a list of local-level law-making powers reflects the increased status the new legislation grants to local-level governments. It is on this basis that the CRC argued (in explanatory notes) that 'the reform is not "centralising" powers as claimed by critics. This reform is in fact decentralising powers further to the Local Level Governments'. The argument is less than convincing, however, since the Organic Law also provides that when there is any inconsistency between provincial and local-level laws and national laws, the latter will prevail (s.41(6)).

In some areas of provincial government jurisdiction it has been possible to re-enact the legislation of the former provincial governments (though there is some doubt as to whether the necessary procedures have been observed in all cases). Given the changes in local-level boundaries this is not a straightforward option at the local level. In any case, a huge legislative programme will be required to formally empower the two levels of government. To facilitate the process at least one national department (Health) has drafted model laws to assist provincial legislatures.

The CRC's explanatory notes state that 'There will be no general suspension of Provincial and Local-level Governments except where there is a war or national emergency or where a Provincial or Local-level Government undermines or tries to undermine the authority of the national government'; however, the national government's powers to suspend or to withdraw functions and finances from provincial and local-level governments, though subject to referral to an independent National Investigation Committee set up under the Organic Law, remain substantial (see ss.51-71).

A Provincial and Local-Level Service Monitoring Authority has been established, comprising representatives of several national departments and agencies chaired by a representative of the Department of Provincial Government and Local-Level Government, whose function is to coordinate national policies at the provincial and local level and monitor various aspects of the system, including assessment of 'the effectiveness and efficiency of the provincial governments and local-level governments' (s.110 (4)(e)).

Disputes between and amongst national, provincial and local-level governments are to be referred to a Mediation and Arbitration Tribunal (of undetermined composition).

Finance

The CRC's explanatory notes claim that, 'Provinces will, under the reform, get a lot more finance from the national government and will have full autonomy within powers and functions in the law to apply its finances'. To supplement existing internal revenue sources provinces will receive grants from the national government of six types (ss.91-97): a provincial and local-level administration grant, a provincial infrastructure development grant, and a local-level government and village services grant (all based variously on population and land and sea area); a town and urban services grant (based on urban population); a provincial and local-level staffing grant (related to provincial administrative and teaching service salaries), and the derivation grant (which will be increased from its previous 1.25 per cent to 5 per cent). Part of the annual allocation (not less than K300 000) will be paid directly to districts to fund a Rural Action Programme[9] and urban rehabilitation (s.95A). Estimated outlays for provincial and local-level governments in the first year of the new system were K490 million, compared to K374 million (including K74 million in village service grants and Electoral Development Fund) in 1994. In 1997 this figure had risen to K568 million.

The new Organic Law also provides for the creation of an independent National Economic and Fiscal Commission with broad fiscal and economic functions, including oversight of provincial finances – a successor to the long moribund National Fiscal Commission.

A set of provisions added to the initial draft of the new Organic Law addresses the question of participation of landowners and local leaders in deliberations relating to the exploitation of natural resources and payments to provincial and local-level governments from resource revenues.

Assessment

In May 1997 Provincial and Local Government Affairs Minister Peter Barter told a seminar in Port Moresby,

> . . . in the 22 months since the reforms commenced, little improvement has been achieved in the operations of provincial administrations and almost nothing in most of their sub-units, the districts. [*The Independent*, 30 May 1997]

Earlier he had told the National Parliament that 'it will defi-

[9] The Rural Action Programme replaces the former, controversial, Electoral Development Fund (commonly known as 'slush fund'), which gave each national MP an amount (in 1995, K0.5 million) to allocate, at his/her discretion, in his/her electorate.

nitely take time, may be five years or more before the results of the system are realised' (*Draft Hansard* 11 February 1997, p. 14). Clearly, assessment of the new system would be premature. Some general observations might, however, be offered.

(i) The Organic Law was pushed through parliament hurriedly, and bears the marks of haste. Four sets of amendments have been passed,[10] to meet promises made to get the legislation through in 1995 and to rectify confusion and omissions. A huge programme of legislative amendment, repeal and enactment remains to be completed before the system can be described as operative. Meanwhile, there is much in the new arrangements to cause uncertainty and confusion, not least in the provisions concerning the respective roles of national line departments, provincial administrators and district administrators.[11]

(ii) The avowed purpose of the 'reform' of decentralisation was to shift power towards local-level government. It must be seriously questioned whether local-level government will have the capacity to carry this load. As argued above, local governments in most of Papua New Guinea were in a state of decline by the 1990s and it is difficult to see how the necessary political and administrative expertise can be mobilised, for some 300 local-level governments, in a relatively short space of time. Initial attempts to decentralise by relocating administrative personnel from provincial headquarters to districts have also been constrained by lack of adequate infrastructure (especially housing and offices).

(iii) In the absence of a strong local-level government structure,

[10] Of 141 sections of the original OLPGLLG, 13 had been repelled or replaced and 38 amended, and six new sections had been added.

[11] A workshop was held in Port Moresby in May 1997 to review the status of the implementation of the reforms. Its report summarises the problems and contains a number of recommendations.

the new system is likely to substantially increase the political role of national MPs. Arguably, this was the real objective of the reforms. One of the arguments levelled against the previous provincial government system was that it created competitive tensions between the different levels of government. In fact, however, as Momis warned in 1995 (see above), the new system seems much more likely to foster political intervention and the use of government resources for political purposes, particularly if local-level governments remain weak.[12]

[12] According to a report in the *National* newspaper (7 August 1997) outgoing provincial and local-level government minister Peter Barter, in a brief to his successor, identified four shortcomings in the reform process: first, 'that dominant MPs were directly involved in making decisions on allocating resources just to meet their own political ends' (MPs and local politicians, he said, 'should not be allowed to dominate the decision-making process'); second, that the national government was withholding funds guaranteed to the provinces; third, that there was no clarification of the allocation of responsibilities between the provincial and local-level governments; and, fourth, that there was 'an urgent need to put infrastructure before services, and ensure adequate staffing at all levels of government'.

9

(RE?)DISCOVERING CHIEFS: TRADITIONAL AUTHORITY AND THE RESTRUCTURING OF LOCAL LEVEL GOVERNMENT IN PAPUA NEW GUINEA*

In the 1960s and 1970s, what most people knew – or at least thought they knew – about Papua New Guinea's 'traditional' societies was that they were essentially egalitarian: excepting a few societies which possessed hereditarial chieftaincies, leadership was typically by 'bigmen', who achieved their status through competition, and community decision making was predominantly consensual. Although challenged by a number of scholars from the mid 1970s, this stereotypical view still has a good deal of currency. In recent years, however, stimulated by a series of reviews of the provincial government system and attempts to nurture new local-level political structures, it has come under increasing challenge within Papua New Guinea. In the mid 1990s people are (re)discovering chiefs on a wide front and are looking to traditional 'chiefly' structures as part of a move towards more extensive political decentralisation. This paper looks briefly at the discussion of traditional authority in the anthropological literature, examines the emerging political discourse on 'chiefs' within Papua New Guinea, and comments on its contemporary political significance.

Bigmen and chiefs in pre-colonial society[1]

In the early postwar decades, the period leading up to independ-

---

* This paper was first published as a discussion paper in the *Regime Change and Regime Maintenance in Asia and the Pacific* series in 1997.

[1] The subject of leadership in Papua New Guinea has generated a sub-

ence, Papua New Guinean societies (and most of Melanesia generally) were characterised as 'acephalous', lacking the formal, hereditary chiefly structures which typified neighbouring Polynesia and other small-scale traditional societies in much of Africa and Asia. Leadership was seen to be localised, and normally determined by competition on the basis of skills in warfare, oratory, accumulating wealth and arranging exchanges, or in the possession of special knowledge or personal qualities. Exceptions were noted, mostly amongst Austronesian-speaking coastal societies[2] but these were regarded as deviations from the norm. Thus, in his influential but ultimately controversial article on political types in Melanesia and Polynesia, Sahlins (1966:162) contrasted what he described as 'the Melanesian scheme of small, separate, and equal blocs' with 'the Polynesian polity [of] an extensive pyramid of groups capped by the family and following of a paramount chief'. These differences, which Sahlins argued, were reflections of 'different varieties and levels of political evolution' (ibid.:163), produced two distinct types of leadership: that of the Melanesian bigman and that of the Polynesian chief. Elaborating on the former, Sahlins said:

---

stantial literature by anthropologists and at least one political scientist. It is not intended here to cover a field already well ploughed, but rather to highlight some of the major features of the debate as a basis for the discussion which follows. For an introduction to the literature on traditional leadership in Papua New Guinea see Standish (1978); Chowning (1979); Douglas (1979); Allen (1984); papers by Morauta and Reay in May (1984), and Godelier (1986:chapter 8). There is also interesting comparative material in Berndt and Lawrence (1971), *Anthropological Quarterly* 51(1) (1978) and Strathern (1982a).

[2] The most commonly cited example was the Trobriand Islands, about which there is a large literature. But Leach (1982) argues that traditional leadership structures in the Trobriands were substantially influenced by the early colonial impact and that the title of 'paramount chiefs', used in colonial reports and perpetuated by Malinowski, was 'applied inappropriately in the Trobriands based on misconceptions of the political system' (ibid.:253). Also see Malinowski (1922:chapter 2, 1935:vol.1 33-40); Powell (1960); Uberoi (1962).

> . . . the indicative quality of big-man authority is everywhere the same: it is personal power. Big-men do not come to office; they do not succeed to, nor are they installed in, existing positions of leadership over political groups. The attainment of big-man status is rather the outcome of a series of acts which elevate a person above the common herd and attract about him a coterie of loyal lesser men. It is not accurate to speak of 'big-man' as a political title, for it is but an acknowledged standing in interpersonal relations . . . In particular Melanesian tribes the phrase might be 'man of importance' or 'man of renown', 'generous rich-man' or 'centre-man', as well as 'big-man'. [ibid.:165][3]

This model of bigman leadership was further elaborated in an entry on 'political organisation' in the *Encyclopedia of Papua and New Guinea* (1972):

> Such authority as does exist is based almost exclusively on personal ability, not on inheritance, descent, or supernatural sanction. Leadership is almost always achieved, almost never ascribed . . . It is achieved through personal charisma, by accumulating wealth in the form of pigs and other material goods that can be used to aid others thus placing them under an obligation, sometimes by the possession of specialised knowledge, or through sheer physical power and the ability to direct warfare . . . This pattern of authority – that of the 'big man' or 'man with a name' – is virtually universal in New Guinea . . . Decisions were reached by consensus, with leaders and elders exerting more influence than others. Power and authority were diffuse and non-centralised . . . They were not elaborated into political offices or other specifically governmental institutions. [Langness 1972:927, 933. Also see de Lepervanche 1972; Lawrence 1971]

As several commentators have observed, the 'bigman model'

---

[3] In a footnote Sahlins (1963/1966:171) notes exceptions of 'proto-chiefdoms' in western Melanesia, listing Buka, Manam, 'perhaps Mafulu', and the Trobriands.

was heavily influenced by African segmentary lineage models prevalent in the anthropological literature of the time (see Barnes 1962/1971; Langness 1972; Strathern 1982b) and by one or two major contemporary studies of Papua New Guinea highlands societies – notably Brown's (1963) study of the Siane, which characterised pre-colonial Chimbu society by 'the absence of any fixed authority ("anarchy")', and went on to say:

> The stratification by rank or authority described in some coastal communities is unknown in the highlands . . . We can recognise qualifications for leadership, but there is almost equal opportunity for every man to attain these qualifications. There are no hereditary positions, and few hereditary advantages. [ibid.:3-5]

In time, critiques of the bigman model came from two main directions. On the one hand, Hau'ofa and others reminded their readers that:

> Although [societies which do not fit the Big-man paradigm] are widely regarded as aberrations from the general Melanesian pattern, along much of seaboard Papua from the Purari Delta in the west to the Trobriand Islands in the east, there are many systems with more or less developed hereditary authority structures[4]

and suggested that:

> It is probable . . . that Melanesian societies with hereditary authority structures are more common than we have realised . . . We could more profitably adopt the view that there is a range of leadership structures in the region manifesting all degrees of relative ascription and relative achievement. [Hau'ofa 1981:291-93][5]

[4] Hau'ofa lists, in addition to the Mekeo, the people of the Purari, the Orokolo, Elema, Roro, Kaopo, Nara or Pokao, Kabadi, Doura, Koita, Motu, Sinaugoro and other coastal groups between the Motu and the eastern boundary of the Central Province, the Trobriand Islanders, Kalauna, Mafulu, Kuni, Goilala, Kuma, Chimbu, Murik, Wogeo, Manam, and Buka. Also see Douglas (1979); Chowning (1979).

[5] Hau'ofa's study of the Mekeo was published in 1981, but the thesis from which it derives was submitted in 1975.

On the other hand, there were suggestions that even in the highlands societies portrayed by Brown and others as conforming to the bigman model, leadership was in fact frequently passed on from father to son, and was often more despotic than communalistic. In a reconsideration of the bigman model, Standish (1978) quoted Chimbu informants' statements that in pre-colonial times leadership was commonly hereditarial, and pointed out that such statements were consistent with early accounts of missionary-anthropologists Bergmann in Kamanegu (Chimbu) and Vicedom in Mount Hagen, and more recent studies by Reay amongst the Kuma and Strathern amongst the Melpa (Vicedom's Mbowamb of Mount Hagen). Having reviewed this evidence Standish concluded:

> The central core of the 'Big-man' theory is the open nature of the competition for leadership which is achieved on merit rather than ascription. In the highlands, manifestations of operative hereditary principles have been identified in several areas, and practical demonstration shown not only of the mechanics of advantage for members of certain lineages, but also several instances of succession. 'Hereditary advantage' is perhaps a better term for the findings presented. [Standish 1978:33; similarly see Douglas 1979:9-10]

Chowning (1977) went further: while acknowledging that bigman status is 'largely achieved', she goes on to say:

> . . . it is not true that everywhere in Melanesia any man had an equal opportunity to achieve high status . . . almost everywhere the heirs of a Big Man, if only by virtue of their special wealth and knowledge, have a much better chance of achieving high position than do others. In some societies . . . anyone who is not closely related to a former Big Man is publicly condemned and shamed by the community for trying to achieve such a position. [ibid.:42, 45]

Standish's reconsideration also addressed the subject of leadership styles. According to both early accounts by outsiders and the recollections of informants, he observed, leadership in Chimbu (as in other parts of the highlands)[6] was frequently despotic. Standish cited Bergmann (1971-72:195):

> I have known chieftains who had killed [or had henchmen kill] more than 100 people . . . Nobody dared to contradict them, because they feared to incur the chieftains' displeasure.

'Such behaviour', Standish comments, 'is very hard to reconcile with a "big-man" courting popularity'. Rather,

> It is clear from the evidence presented that the techniques of leadership within clans and more particularly sub-clans varied from conciliation, compromise, persuasion, inspiration and bargaining, to threats and sheer brute force. [Standish 1978:22-23]

Oliver's (1955) account of leadership amongst the Siuai [Siwai] (which Douglas (1979:9) suggests was 'a basis of Sahlins's Melanesian political type'), and references by Salisbury (1964) to the Tolai and Chowning (1979) to the Lakalai, suggest that despotic behaviour was not restricted to the highlands.

Finally, much has been written about social stratification in 'traditional' Papua New Guinea societies which suggests a common pattern of socially, politically and economically differentiated layers, ranging from the *rabisman* or 'slave' (Vicedom and Tischner 1943-48; Oliver 1955) at the bottom, to the bigman or chief at the top, with a variety of categories of 'ordinary men' and minor or specialist leaders in between, overlaid by systemic status differences based on gender and age.[7]

Simplistic versions of the bigman model thus require substan-

---

[6] See, for example Watson (1971), Strathern (1966).

[7] In a volume on *Social Stratification in Papua New Guinea* (May 1984), chapters by Morauta and Reay review the data on social stratification, respectively, for lowlands and highlands societies. Also see Standish (1978); Strathern (1982a). The issue of gender is specifically addressed in Morauta (1984), Reay (1984) and Godelier (1986).

tial qualification to take account of, first, the effective continuum in (and common mix of) leadership patterns, from hereditarial or ascriptive to competitively achieved; second, the range of leadership styles, from the ruthlessly despotic to the leader-as-steward, and third, the existence of varying degrees of social stratification.

This qualification having been made, however, it is probably still true that, compared to other largely 'tribal' societies, including those of neighbouring Polynesia, traditional leadership in Papua New Guinea can be generally characterised as largely dependent on personal qualities (and as a corollary only partially susceptible to inheritance). It is substantially constrained by competition, by specialisation of leadership roles, by the prevalence of communal modes of decision making, and by communal demands on leaders and resentment of leaders who attempt to raise themselves too far above other members of the society. Thus, for example, after pointing out the necessary qualifications to the bigman model, Chowning (1977:46) nevertheless concludes, 'Sahlins is right to stress the contrast between what a Melanesian leader is likely to accomplish . . . and what some Polynesian chiefs could do' (similarly see Chowning 1979:68; Morauta 1984: 9-10). It is also probable that in the great variety of patterns of social organisation amongst Papua New Guinea's traditional societies, there were systematic differences between highlands societies, where leaders frequently seem to have been individualistic and aggressive, and lowlands societies, where there seems to have been generally greater emphasis on mediation and group decision making.

The general pattern of non-hierarchical (or weakly-hierarchical) leadership and essentially communalistic social organisation was probably reinforced by the colonial experience and the particular form which emerging nationalism assumed in the 1970s. The German and British colonial administrations enlisted, respectively, *luluai* (or *kukurai*) and *tultul* (in New Guinea) and village constables (in Papua) as their agents at (roughly) village level, with some 'paramount *luluai*/chiefs' representing groups of villages. These systems were perpetuated under early Australian colonial rule.[8] But though indigenous local officials were initially selected as people of influence in the society, their basis of appointment seems to have had as much to do with personal relationships between the selected individuals and the colonial administration as it did with traditional leadership structures (hence *luluai* and *tultul*, and village constables seem often to have worked as translators and go-betweens for colonial officials, and, later, as former police and administration officers). Moreover, since the role of village official, as intermediary between villagers and the colonial administration, often attracted resentment or abuse from both sides,[9] it was one which traditional leaders often avoided. Thus after ineffective attempts by the early German administration, the German, British and later Australian regimes did not develop a system of 'indirect rule' in Papua New Guinea, as the British and Germans did in other parts of their colonial empires.[10] And given the extreme political and social fragmentation which characterised Papua New Guinea society, there was certainly little prospect of creating an institution like Fiji's Great Council of Chiefs. Moreover, since the activities of missions (which in Papua New Guinea frequently preceded government) were often subversive of traditional authority structures – much as Chinua Achebe has described for Africa in his

[8] For a detailed account of colonial administration see Reed (1943), Mair (1970), Rowley (1958, 1965) and Downs (1980). Also see Blackwood (1935:47-49).

[9] Until well into the 1980s it was not uncommon for villagers to stage 'pantomimes' on festive occasions, in which villagers enacted a visit from the *kiap*, who ordered the village official to line up the villagers, complained of the state of village tidiness, ordered that latrines be dug, and frequently kicked the village official's backside.

[10] Liz Adams has drawn my attention to a 1938-39 patrol report by Ian Downs, then a patrol officer in Madang District, who informed his superiors that in the area between the Gum and Gogol rivers 'there was no native remotely resembling or even fractionally fit for the position [of *luluai*]'.

novel *Things Fall Apart* – the effect of missionising was often to create competing sources of influence in village leadership.

In the postwar period the establishment of local government councils and cooperatives, and eventually of the national parliament, coupled with the growth of cash cropping and paid employment, and the spread of schools, ensured that leadership in the newly emerging political system was likely to go to a new group of younger, educated people, often experienced in government administration or business, at the expense of traditional leadership (even though a number of traditional leaders remained influential in national politics for some time).

It is notable that in many of the 'second generation' and later studies by anthropologists, reference is made to the decline of traditional leadership. Chowning (1979:66), for example, notes that the chiefs mentioned in W.E. Bromilow's early study of Dobu are not mentioned in Reo Fortune's later study; Blackwood (1935:47-49) comments on the impact of colonial administration on the role of traditional lineage heads, and Hogbin (1978:11) notes that on revisiting Wogeo in 1974-75, 40 years after his initial fieldwork, 'These hereditary headmen were also no more'. (Also see Oliver 1955:423; 1973:196-98; Chowning and Goodenough 1971:162; Sarei 1974:50; Douglas 1979:5, and more recently, Sabin 1988 [quoted below] and Deklin 1992.)

Such tendencies were reinforced by the communalistic national ethos which emerged in the early 1970s. Elaborated in the concept of 'The Melanesian Way', this philosophy emphasised, often in a somewhat romanticised way, the egalitarian, communalistic nature of Papua New Guinea societies and what it saw as the essentially consensual nature of traditional decision making. The principal exponent of the Melanesian Way, lawyer, philosopher and member of parliament Bernard Narokobi, declined to define the concept (though a collection of writings on the subject by Narokobi and his critics, entitled *The Melanesian Way*, was published in 1980 [Narokobi 1980]), but the late Gabriel Gris described the essence of the Melanesian Way: '. . . our peoples are communalistic and communalism is the basis for our traditional way of life' (Gris 1975:137).[11] The philosophy of the Melanesian Way was strongly reflected in the reports of the Constitutional Planning Committee (CPC), which provided the basis for Papua New Guinea's independence constitution. Its *Final Report* (1974) states that 'our people are firmly against "elitism" which is both unjust and undemocratic' (p.2/7), and a section entitled 'Papua New Guinean Ways' endorses 'those practices of participation, of consultation and consensus, and sacrifice for the common good' which it attributes to traditional societies (p.2/14). These principles were subsequently written into the constitution, notably in the preamble, which acknowledges 'the worthy customs and traditional wisdoms of our people', and includes in a statement of 'National Goals and Directive Principles' specific proposals on 'equality and participation' and 'Papua New Guinean ways'. Under the directive principle of equality and participation, the constitution asserts that no citizen should be deprived of the opportunity to exercise his (*sic*) personal creativity and enterprise, consistent with the common good, 'because of the predominant position of another'; under 'Papua New Guinea Ways' the constitution states as one of its goals, 'to achieve development primarily through the use of Papua New Guinean forms of social, political and economic organisation'. In 1975 the Melanesian Way was given royal approval when in a speech on the occasion of Papua New Guin-

[11] A later, but more comprehensive, statement of the concept has been given by Papua New Guinean lawyer Tony Deklin. Deklin (1992) lists amongst the essential features of 'the Papua New Guinean Way': a 'relatively high degree of participation . . . in general communal life'; 'the absence of authoritarian regimes (such as chiefs) in most PNG village communities'; the high values placed on consultation and consensus ('Both consultation and consensus . . . are crucial elements in decision-making processes in Melanesia. Consensus is valued so much that the process of reaching it can sometimes involve days, weeks, even months . . .'); and social equality ('. . . the society is classless. With the disappearance of the traditional Big Man, social equality is complete'). Also see Samana (1988:*passim*); Momis (1973).

ea's independence, Queen Elizabeth II said:

> Great store is rightly placed on the ability of your people to solve problems by consensus and discussion. That is the Melanesian Way. I am sure it will lead to success. [Quoted in Narokobi 1980:184]

In the early post-independence years the egalitarian ethos remained strong, at least in rhetoric. Nine years after independence the then foreign minister and later prime minister, Rabbie Namaliu, in an address at The Australian National University in Canberra, referred to an advertisement in the Australian press the previous year, which depicted a Papua New Guinean dressed in traditional finery, with a caption which referred to 'the big chiefs'; 'The advertisement was misleading', Namaliu said,

> in suggesting that traditional leaders in Papua New Guinea can rightly be called 'Chiefs', when most, in fact, are properly called 'Bigmen', who gain power through personal achievement rather than accession to office.' [Namaliu 1984:1]

Some time during the 1980s, however, the egalitarian ethos of the Melanesian Way seems to have waned,[12] or at least to have undergone some revision. By 1991, in the face of growing problems of law and order, former prime minister Sir Michael Somare told an Australian journalist that what Papua New Guinea needed was a benevolent dictator: 'Dictatorship would go a long way to solving the country's problems', Somare was reported as

---

[12] Standish (personal communication) sees the controversy over amendments to the Leadership Code in 1980 – a controversy which led to a split in the coalition government and the first post-independence change of government in Papua New Guinea – as something of a turning point. But there were earlier symptoms – for example, increasing involvement of national politicians in business, and some evidence of corruption, from the 1970s, and widespread calls for the deployment of the Papua New Guinea Defence Force to assist police in the highlands in the same period. The truth is that the principles of egalitarianism, communalism and consensus probably always coexisted with the common practice of inequality and coercion.

saying. The 'hard line' of Singapore's former prime minister, Lee Kuan Yew, was needed in Papua New Guinea, he said; 'Papua New Guineans need discipline' (*Sunday Herald* [Melbourne] 17 March 1991). Shortly after this Somare presented a paper to the XVIIth Pacific Science Congress in Honolulu, on the subject of 'Melanesian Leadership'. In it Somare argued that

> . . . most of the men who were first called on to lead our Pacific countries were, in fact, traditional leaders in their own right. They were all *big men, taubada,* chiefs of paramount clans, *sanas* [Somare's own title], *ratus, lohia bada* . . . Some of these leaders came from long lines of hereditary chiefs and were recognised aristocrats or members of chiefly families. Others were heads of paramount clans or the founders of clan dynasties. And yet others again, because of outstanding personality, and their ability to articulate the unspoken aspirations of their people, assumed a role they seemed destined to fill. [Somare 1991:105]

(Here he referred specifically to Papua New Guinea's first governor-general, Sir John Guise, who, Somare suggested, '. . . drew his authority, partly from the mantle passed on to him from Reginald Guise, his grandfather, who came from a noble county family in England'.) As against the virtues of traditional Pacific leadership, Somare deplored the 'tyranny of the ballot box'; under the colonially-introduced democratic processes involving one person one vote, Somare said, 'our traditional leaders . . . were virtually pushed to one side. They saw their influence and their authority quietly and slowly eroded by a process that was foreign, arbitrary, and very disruptive', adding: 'Some of us think great danger lies in the blind acceptance of the ballot box and what they ['Westerners'] call "majority rule"' (ibid.:106). Somare praised Fiji's Ratu Mara as 'The man who challenged and has survived the "tyranny of the ballot box"'. At the same time, Somare argued, 'what made our chiefs so effective . . . was what we might call *concern for people* – for *their* people that is' (ibid.:107).

This nostalgic regard for the more authoritarian aspects of

traditional leadership was invoked in frequent demands by national and provincial politicians and others for tighter social control (with Singapore, Malaysia and Indonesia mentioned as models), for more draconian measures to deal with the problems of breakdown in law and order, and for censorship of the media.

By the early 1990s popular references to 'chiefs' had become increasingly commonplace.[13] When I commented on this, first in Port Moresby in 1991 and later at a seminar in Canberra attended by several Papua New Guineans, I was told that Papua New Guinean societies had always had chiefs, though foreign anthropologists had failed to recognise this, and that indeed many of

---

[13] By way of illustration, the following have been randomly selected from recent newspaper reports. (They do, however, exclude Bougainville, from whence references to chiefs are commonplace.)

- 'Revive traditional system of leadership – village chief' (*Post-Courier* 27 April 1993) (reporting the proposal by 'a village chief' from Rigo, Central Province, to establish 'a village body or authority based on traditional village leadership system', to deal with problems of lawlessness and lack of coordination at village level).
- 'Chiefs ban sports since fatal fight in Mumeng' (*Post-Courier* 11 May 1993) (reporting a decision by 'village elders' in Mumeng, Morobe Province, following a 'tribal fight' sparked by a local soccer match).
- 'Sir Charles – chief of two cultures' (*Post-Courier* 17 January 1994) (on the investiture of Sir Charles Maino, former Justice secretary and chief ombudsman, as KBE (Knight of the British Empire) and 'paramount chief of the Inaui [Mekeo] people').
- 'Tapini chief dies in road slip' (*Times of PNG* 3 March 1994) reporting the death, in a road accident, of 'the Paramount Chief of Tapini').
- 'Chiefs set to boycott prince's visit' (*Post-Courier* 8 June 1994) (reporting the threat of 'New Ireland traditional chiefs' [*maimai]* to boycott a visit by Tonga's crown prince unless compensated for 'past performances with similar dignitaries' visits', including, apparently, the initiation of Prime Minister Wingti as a *maimai* in 1986; said the chiefs' spokesman: 'We are an elite group with traditional power. To call us out from our village, you must pay each of us with traditional shell money worth K10').
- 'PM praise for Sepik chiefs' (*Post-Courier* 10 July 1995) (reporting Prime Minister Chan's response to a welcoming ceremony in Wewak attended by national MPs from the Sepik and outgoing provincial assembly members).

the people with whom I spoke – whose origins ranged from Bougainville to Enga – were themselves chiefs or the sons or daughters of chiefs.

In what follows I do not intend to enter into a debate about the 'authenticity' of chiefs, but rather to briefly trace the emerging discussion in three specific instances:

(a) in calls for chiefly institutions in East Sepik (a province with which I have had a long association);

(b) in the emergence of a chiefly political structure in Bougainville; and

(c) in proposals for the incorporation of traditional authority structures in measures (recently legislated) to replace (or reform) the provincial government system.

A concluding section will look at the political implications of these developments.

Chiefs in East Sepik

East Sepik is not an area renowned for chiefly status, though hereditary chiefs appear to have been common along the north coast. Hogbin (1978) describes a system of hereditary headship amongst the Wogeo (an Austronesian group in the Schouten Islands north from Wewak):

> The office of headman is ascribed; that is to say the title [*kokwal*] descends by hereditary right, though not necessarily to the father's firstborn. [ibid.:37]

Having noted that 'birth by itself does not ensure distinction', and having discussed the 'basic qualifications' for leadership, Hogbin concludes:

> In other words, the successful Wogeo leader, apart from his hereditary right, must be the same sort of individual as a big-man in those areas of Papua New Guinea and Melanesia generally, where titles are wholly acquired. [ibid.:42]

However, Hogbin presents a picture of the headman which is very different from that of a stereotypical 'chief' or despotic bigman:

> A traditional saying runs that a stranger can easily discover who is the headman by looking for the person with dirty hands and muddied feet . . . It is said that at a feast he should leave the most succulent taro, the slabs of lean pork, and the strips of white fat and be content with the bones . . . 'The host should see that ordinary folk depart with full bellies; he himself holds back and tightens his belt'. [ibid.:40]

Aufenanger (n.d.:250-51) refers to hereditary leadership, *kokal*, on another Schouten island, Koil, and a similar pattern is described by Wedgwood (1933-34) and Lutkehaus (1990) for the Manam, also in the Schouten group (but administratively part of Madang Province).[14] On the mainland, Aufenanger (n.d.:18) describes a hereditary chieftainship system in the (non-Austronesian-speaking) Wewak-Boikin area:

> One family in the village is the *kinyau* family. It possesses the highest rank in the village. The chieftainship is hereditary . . . The highest *kinyau* has the title of *kokal*.

In his 1975 autobiography former prime minister Sir Michael Somare describes his ascendance to the traditional chiefly title of *sana*, a title held by his father and grandfather before him. Somare is from Karau village in the Murik Lakes at the mouth of the Sepik River, but he records that his people migrated there from the upper Sepik and that his great-grandfather, 'a big fight leader and peacemaker', was the first *sana* (Somare 1975:16).

Elsewhere in the East Sepik Province various forms of 'bigman

---

[14] Recently, Bernard Narokobi, having rejected an Order of the British Empire in the New Year's Honours List, accepted the gift of a necklace, *sawai*, from Sup villagers from Mushu Island. 'One who wears this,' it was reported, 'is recognised as the son of a wealthy chief and can marry a number of women' (*Post-Courier* 6 July 1995).

model' seem to predominate. In a survey of 'social control' for the *Encyclopaedia of Papua and New Guinea* (Ryan 1972) Berndt groups the recorded Sepik cultures together as 'Type IV leadership' – 'illustrating one kind of leadership, focused on the "big man" who gains ascendancy through personal achievement, including, in many cases, aggression' (Berndt 1972:1053). In a later overview of Sepik (East and West) politics, Mitchell (1978:6) distinguishes between the 'eastern section of the Sepik River Basin', in which 'hierarchical political systems predominate' and the western section, in which 'all the societies are egalitarian'. In the same volume Metraux (1978:50) observes: 'The Iatmul [a Middle Sepik River group] do not have chiefs but they do have a kind of incipient aristocracy'. But whatever traditional leadership structures may have existed, by the mid 1970s they appear to have been substantially disrupted by the impact of missions, the colonial administration and the national government, including local government councils, and by the effects of migration, education, and *bisnis* (business). One would expect that the general effect of these developments has been to undermine chiefly authority (as Hogbin suggests has been the case in Wogeo) though more recently Errington and Gewertz (1990) have described the emergence of a 'chief' amongst the previously chiefless Chambri.[15]

In the early 1980s, with the local government council system in East Sepik already in a state of advanced decline, there was some discussion about the possibilities of reviving local-level government through the establishment of community governments (as had been attempted with some success in the North Solomons Province). In the Boiken area, north of the provincial capital Wewak, a proposal had been discussed in some detail and a constitution was being drafted for a movement known as Arapesh Kita Muna by the national parliamentary member for

[15] For a more extensive discussion of leadership patterns in the Sepik see *Anthropological Quarterly* 51(1) 1978, Lutkehaus (1990), and Lutkehaus et al. (1990:*passim*).

Wewak Open and author of *The Melanesian Way*, Bernard Narokobi, and lawyer Peter Donigi. This development, and a move to incorporate a formal chiefly structure in the Trobriand Islands, were referred to in a national review of local-level government chaired by Narokobi in 1981:

> In these two provinces [East Sepik and Milne Bay] there is a move to cater for both the traditional leadership based on heredity, and new leadership based on popular voting. There is emerging an English type bicameral system, with the hereditary chiefs occupying the Upper House and the popularly elected occupying the Lower House. [Department of Decentralisation 1981:11]

The Trobriands initiative was written into the Milne Bay provincial constitution (see Anere and Ley 1997:116) but the Narokobi-Donigi proposals appear to have foundered (though the Arapesh Kita Muna was still in existence in the early 1990s).

Ten years later, following a period of fractiousness within the East Sepik provincial government and increasing antipathy between the provincial government and East Sepik national MPs, the East Sepik provincial government was suspended. Subsequently, part of the provincial headquarters was burned down, the former premier was charged with arson and other offences, and several members of the suspended government were charged with misappropriation (see May 1997a). This series of developments confirmed the generally negative popular view of provincial government in East Sepik[16] and strengthened a growing cynicism towards politicians and political parties.

In Port Moresby, the burning of the provincial headquarters prompted East Sepik students at the University of Papua New Guinea to call a meeting of resident Sepiks to discuss the political situation in the province. The meeting, convened by Narokobi (then attorney-general in the Namaliu government), was held at

[16] See, for example, the progress report of the parliamentary Select Committee on Provincial Government Review on its tour of East Sepik Province (PNG National Parliament 1990:volume 2).

the National Parliament in June 1991; Donigi was chosen to chair the meeting. An interim committee was elected at the meeting and given the task of preparing the terms of reference 'of a permanent committee to look after the affairs of the Province and its people' (letter from Donigi to Somare 17 June 1991). The committee produced a set of recommendations which were amended and approved at a second meeting of Sepiks the following week.

The resolutions of the second meeting called for the establishment of an East Sepik Promotion Commission (ESPROC), whose object was 'to promote social, economic and political welfare of the people who originate from the East Sepik Province of Papua New Guinea'. ESPROC was to have an executive arm, to be known as the Council on Economic, Social and Political Development of East Sepik Province (CESPODES); CESPODES' first objective was listed as

(a) To continually review and recommend ways of improving the social, economic and political structures, norms, practices, policies and their implementation for a better and improved government and development of the East Sepik Province and its people.

Within CESPODES there were to be three permanent committees (political, economic, and social). The terms of reference of the Permanent Political Committee were:

(a) To review and recommend a political structure for East Sepik Province which shall take into account the traditional political structures that existed prior to the advent of europeans and which shall supercede the provincial government system.

(b) To recognise and recommend measures to promote the establishment of the title of *Kokal* (Chief) to precede the names of all clan leaders in the Province.

(c) To recommend measures to promote the establishment of a register of all *Kokals* in the Province which register shall include the names of their clans, clan land, village and language group.

(d) To recognise and recommend measures to promote the legitimisation of the traditional powers of the *Kokals* or Clan Chiefs in matters concerning:
   (i) politics,
   (ii) control and use of land,
   (iii) dispute settlement,
   (iv) law and order issues, and
   (v) environmental protection and management of resources.

(e) To recommend measures to promote the establishment of a Council of *Kokals* or Council of Chiefs in the Province to be composed of four (4) *Kokals* elected to the Council by all *Kokals* in each language group.

(f) To recognise and recommend measures to promote the establishment of the position of 'B. . .' [sic] to be elected by the Council of *Kokals* to hold office for a period of five years and who shall:
   (i) be the esteemed political head of the Province;
   (ii) preside over all meetings of the Council of *Kokals*; and
   (iii) counter-sign all agreements between foreign investors and the clan *Kokal* on behalf of the landowning clan.

There seems to have been general support for the proposal to replace the provincial government by a 'Council of *Kokals*', but not universal support: a distinguished former national and provincial government officer and member of the provincial assembly, Peter Waliawi, objected to the proposed composition of ESPROC as 'creating an elite group', and on the proposed political structure commented:

> I do not think we should confuse the situation to take ourselves back to the Traditional Chieftain System which is clear in some areas while not in others . . . [and] which could lead to revival of unsocial [*sic*] and malpractices of the past as these were the sources

> which kept some of them in the authority . . . [Letter from Waliawi to Donigi 27 June 1991]

Another Sepik colleague observed that, since leadership roles in his (Boiken) village were specialised, with different clans having different traditional roles, it was far from clear which clan leader was the 'chief' (Joe Naguwean, personal communication, April 1993).

In the event Donigi went overseas and though Narokobi told the National Parliament late in 1991 that he believed strongly 'that we should reintroduce the chieftain system' and hoped to introduce legislation to this effect (*Daily Hansard* 5 November 1991), the recommendations endorsed by the meeting of Sepiks in Port Moresby seem to have lapsed. In 1993 a new provincial government was elected according to the provisions of the provincial constitution. The model proposed by the Donigi committee, however, resurfaced in 1992 in the recommendations of the Bipartisan Committee (see above).

Chiefs in the North Solomons (Bougainville)

The North Solomons Province was the first to replace local government councils by a system of community governments. Initially, the process appears to have been spontaneous. Peasah records that,

> Local traditional, political culture had a substantial impact on the composition and operation of the community and village governments, which were spontaneously and unofficially established by the people in the 1970s to replace the unpopular local government councils. [Peasah 1994:184. Also see Connell 1977]

In 1978 this development was formalised with the passage of a provincial *Community Government Act* which sought, *inter alia*, 'to promote and recognise traditional leadership and authority while merging these concepts with those of the modern government ideals and structures' (Togolo 1986).

Members of the community governments were variously elected or appointed by communities. Each had an assembly and executive headed by an elected president or chairman[17] and a full-time community government officer was appointed in each sub-district. The head of the community government was paid a retainer (of around K1000 per annum) and expected to spend two days a week on the job (Griffin and Togolo 1997:366-67).

By the early 1980s the number of community governments had grown to over 70, and they were becoming a source of some disgruntlement, especially in areas where they were seen as challenging traditional authority. The provincial Division of Local Government subsequently initiated steps to reduce the number of community governments through amalgamation. At the time, several communities moved to create 'councils of chiefs'. By the end of 1987 there were councils of chiefs for (at least) Tahetahe, Hanahan and Hakets, Malasang and Hangan, Solos (Gagan) and Buka (see Sabin 1988:2).

In 1987 the North Solomons Provincial Assembly passed a resolution (6/87) calling for an investigation into the establishment of a council of chiefs system in the province and the abolition of village courts. A Bougainvillean then at the University of Papua New Guinea, Ephraim Manhi Sabin, was commissioned to prepare a report for the assembly; this was completed in early 1988 (ibid.).[18]

The proposal to establish a council of chiefs system seems to have been generated specifically in response to dissatisfaction with the way in which the village court system and community

[17] A 1981 Committee of Review into Local Level Government reported that: 'In the North Solomons, a Community Government is a collection of several villages . . . Members of the government are usually hereditary chiefs who amongst themselves, elect a Chairman' (Department of Decentralisation 1981:11).

[18] There appears to have been a subsequent redrafting of this document within the provincial administration; the later draft is referred to by Peasah (1994) as the Tsereha Report.

government system were functioning. As expressed by Sabin (ibid.:28):

> The provincial government has taken this initiative to establish Council of Chiefs primarily because of problems faced with and created by the Village Courts in the province . . . It was originally intended that Village Courts use traditional methods in dealing with cases and settling disputes. However . . . Village Courts avoid traditional punishment in preference [for] the Western standards of punishments . . . They refuse to use our traditional laws . . . [which] govern customary land rights, customary marriages, customary ceremonies, and many other areas of our Bougainvillean or Melanesian society.

Sabin went on to suggest that the village court system had become 'too formal' and that 'The people have lost trust and confidence in the system' (ibid.:28, 29). More specifically, Sabin reported that traditional leaders saw village courts as 'a foreign power which is undermining chieftain authority':

> Village Courts do not allow our chiefs to settle disputes amongst their people – to make decisions on matters that affect them and their people. Village Courts leave 'no room' for our traditional leaders to move. Everytime they want to 'rise', the Village Courts are always [there] to discourage or stop them . . . Our Chiefs see Village Courts as a great threat to their very existence – it could wipe them out. [ibid.:29]

Sabin's view of traditional leadership on Bougainville appears to have been heavily influenced by a reading of Blackwood (1935) and Oliver (1955).[19] But he also undertook an extensive survey of traditional leadership in communities throughout the province. Summarising the results of this survey Sabin concluded:

> The whole position has been fundamentally altered by the new system introduced by the Germans, continued by the Colonial

[19] See especially pp.29-31. Sabin quotes with apparent approval the observation of Blackwood (1935:49): 'It is certain he [the lineage head or *tsunaun*] possessed power of life and death over those under his jurisdiction'.

> government . . . and devastated by the present Village Courts and Community Government system . . . Although there exists a traditional form of leadership, it is quite difficult to ascertain. In some areas of the province, this leadership can be easily identified, whereas in other areas it is very difficult. For instance, a person cannot differentiate between an ordinary person and a chief. In such areas this traditional leadership is virtually 'dead'. [Sabin 1988:30-31]

However, Sabin said, traditional leadership '*can be* revived and practised in the light of today's social, economic, and political development' (ibid.:30-31).

Progress towards the establishment of a council of chiefs system was disrupted by the conflict on Bougainville which erupted in 1988 and by the general breakdown of administration which occurred following the withdrawal of national government personnel and security forces in 1990 (see May and Spriggs 1990; Spriggs and Denoon 1992). The withdrawal of government services and collapse of formal political structures in 1990, however, created a vacuum of authority which was largely filled by clan elders or chiefs. Village councils of elders or 'chiefs' became the effective form of government in many parts of the province and played an increasing role in organising communities and subsequently in responding to initiatives for reconciliation and reconstruction.[20] In 1991, as part of the national government's efforts to reestablish government and restore services on Bougainville, a *Bougainville Interim Authorities Act* was passed, establishing (initially) six interim authorities.[21] Section 4(4) of the act provided that 'the people of the area [of the interim authority] may select

[20] See, for example *Post-Courier* 22 July 1992, 27 April 1993; *Times of PNG* 8 October 1992, 22 April 1993.

[21] These were for Nissan/Atolls, Buka, North-east Bougainville, North-west Bougainville, Central Bougainville and South Bougainville. Subsequently the South Bougainville interim authority split into two – Telei (Buin) and South-west Bougainville – and later still the Banoni and Nagovisi split from the South-west to form a Bana Interim Authority, making a total of eight.

or recommend their representatives to the Minister'. A subsequent report on progress from the South Bougainville Interim Authority presented the following picture for South Bougainville:

> The Council of Chiefs System of Government is now emerging in South Bougainville. The Area Chiefs Council (ACC) and the Clan Chiefs Council (CCC) is now fully participating in the restoration of Peace. As a result of these changes, a division is established to coordinate the activities of the Chiefs.
>
> The Division has now established ACC in areas previously under community governments and CCC in villages. The Chairman of ACC would now form the combine [*sic*] Chiefs Assembly (CCA) and they would report direct to the Interim Authority.
>
> The priorities of the division is to re-establish village courts system and to re-appoint village court magistrates. This would assist in settling disputes and other Social Disturbances in the Community.
>
> The co-ordination of the Chiefs to fully participate in the rehabilitation programme is well underway . . . [South Bougainville Interim Authority 1992:5]

In Central Bougainville, also, informally-constituted CCC emerged as effective units of government, though on major issues affecting the whole village most of the population of the village attended meetings, effectively providing a village assembly (A.J. Regan, personal communication, June 1995). In other areas such as Telei, Siwai and North-west Bougainville similar village-level councils were termed 'Village Councils of Chiefs' (VCC). In most parts of the province groups of CCC/VCC formed a second level of government to deal with issues of a larger scale or on which villages wanted an outside conciliator. These were known variously as village, community or area councils of chiefs. In Telei and Central Bougainville a third tier, called ACC, was created (ibid.).

When in 1995 provincial government was restored on Bougainville, in the form of the Bougainville Transitional Government (BTG), with one representative on the BTG from each of the old provincial government electoral constituencies, the area councils of chiefs acted, in effect, as electoral colleges, selecting from amongst the nominations of village-level councils the BTG representative for the constituency.

The (re-)emergence of chiefly structures in the North Solomons has not been without controversy.[22] There have been disputes both about who the 'chiefs' are and about whether traditional chiefs provide an appropriate form of leadership for the 1990s. Nevertheless, in a relatively short space of time councils of chiefs appear to have become well entrenched on Bougainville, and when this paper was being written [1995] proposals were being drafted for a formal, province-wide, structure of councils of chiefs. Under the proposed arrangements village councils of chiefs, or elders, would be elected (having regard to the existence and form of traditional authority) by village assemblies; above these would be area councils. This would replace the previous structure of community governments and directly-elected provincial assembly.

Chiefs in the political system

From around 1990, considerable stimulus was given to consideration of traditional leadership by renewed debate over the future of provincial government (see May and Regan 1997:chapter 4, Postscript). In July 1990 a parliamentary Select Committee on Provincial Government Review (Hesingut Committee) delivered a progress report,[23] in which it recommended that the Organic Law on Provincial Government be amended to replace existing, elected, provincial governments with bodies compris-

[22] See, for example, *Post-Courier* 13, 18 October 1993; *Times of PNG* 23 February 1995.

[23] Before reporting, the committee canvassed public opinion in four provinces 'which, in the opinion of the Committee, were better managed than the rest'; these included East Sepik and North Solomons.

ing presidents or chairmen of local government councils or community governments (PNG National Parliament 1990:13). The Hesingut Committee's final report was tabled the following year but the recommendations predictably met with strong opposition from provincial government sources and little progress had been made towards implementing them before the term of the parliament expired in 1992.

Soon after the new government came to office it made clear its intention to overhaul the provincial government system. In August 1992 Village Services and Provincial Affairs Minister John Nilkare announced a Village Services Programme designed to 'empower' some 240 community governments and link them to the national government through a structure of district centres and community councils.[24] A specific feature of the programme was its proposal to incorporate in the new system a formal role for 'traditional leaders', who were to receive a monthly allowance of K40 for their contribution to the programme (*Post-Courier* 18 November 1992).

Two months later Prime Minister Wingti announced that the National Executive Council had agreed to the abolition of the provincial government system (*Post-Courier* 12, 16 October 1992) and legislation to enable the repeal of the Organic Law on Provincial Government was drafted. However, continued opposition from the provinces – especially the provinces of the New Guinea Islands Region, which threatened secession if provincial government were abolished – forced the government to modify its position, and in November 1992 a Bipartisan Parliamentary Select Committee on Provincial Government (headed by Kavieng MP Ben Micah) was appointed to carry out a further review of the system.

After touring the country, the Bipartisan Committee submitted a preliminary report early in 1993 and a final report in

[24] The Village Services Programme is described in statements published in *Post-Courier* 14 August 1992:24-25 and *Times of PNG* 12 November 1992:32-33.

August. The general thrust of the Committee's recommendations was to replace the elected provincial governments by authorities comprising national MPs, heads of local-level governments (local government councils, urban authorities and community governments), and a small number of sectoral representatives; to reduce the legislative powers of provincial governments, and to substantially increase the role of local-level governments. In addressing the latter, the committee commented that:

> ... in the decades leading up to independence, the colonial government ... emphasised local autonomy and self-determination. This has resulted in the creation of the system of local-level government councils throughout Papua New Guinea. As a consequence, the indigenous forms of leadership, political structures and decision-making processes have been largely pushed aside.
>
> Because of the strong evidence that indigenous forms of leadership and decision-making processes are inherent to the social fabric of the village communities inhabited by eighty-five percent of Papua New Guineans, we are of the opinion that this traditional leadership system must be encouraged as one of the options of local-level government. [PNG National Parliament 1993:64]

The committee proposed two options for local-level government: elected community governments, and 'non-elected representation – chiefs and traditional bigmen' (ibid.:67-68). Under the second option community governments would comprise 'traditional bigmen or chiefs and women' (thereafter referred to in the report as 'councils of chiefs'), but with provision to include 'limited elected representatives and nominated representatives of churches, youth and women, 'if and only when traditional bigmen and chiefs require them' (ibid.). The report went on to say that 'the council of chiefs/bigmen who comprise the legislature shall be direct representatives of their lineages, clans, communities and tribal groups' (ibid.:68); and on the subject of 'election/selection' stated:

- The position of chief is acquired by birthright, by the customs of the people, and by community recognition.
- The position of chief is held for life and shall be appointed as chief to the community government by the council of chiefs of the area and according to the custom of the area.
- A bigman assures his leadership by achievements through a system of reciprocity. A bigman shall be appointed by a method of selection determined by the custom of the tribal groups.
- A bigman is known as bigman by custom of the tribal groups. [ibid.]

The local-level governments so constituted were to have law-making powers on local matters of concern, 'powers to make the customary laws of the area', and authority for village court functions.

There was considerable opposition to the Bipartisan Committee's proposals from some sources (particularly within the Islands Region)[25] and confusion between Nilkare's Village Services scheme and different initiatives for change in the provincial government system[26] (at one stage there appear to have been three different pieces of draft legislation on the same subject). However in June 1995 an Organic Law on Provincial Governments and Local-Level Governments, based on the recommendations of the Bipartisan Committee, was pushed through the National Parliament. It states that provincial assemblies shall

[25] As against this, a former East New Britain premier, in a joint statement with a provincial MP, welcomed the legislation, commenting that 'their village chiefs and councillors would resume their "rightful roles as traditional leaders" . . . and be given the respect they have been denied for the last 20 years . . . '(reported in *Post-Courier* 7 April 1995).

In the highlands, a meeting of highlands premiers presented a position paper to the prime minister which, in criticising the proposed reforms, called for a major overhaul of the political system, including 'special consideration' of the role 'chiefs' could play in a restructured provincial government system (*National* 3 March 1995).

[26] The details of these developments are recorded in May and Regan with Ley (1997:Postscript).

consist of all national MPs from the province, heads of rural local-level governments and urban councils or authorities, an appointed representative from women, up to three members appointed by the provincial assembly, and:

> where the chieftaincy system is in existence and is accepted in a province, paramount chiefs from the province not exceeding three in number or their duly appointed nominees, who shall be appointed by the Minister responsible for provincial government and local-level government matters on the recommendation of the Provincial Executive Council. [S.10(3)(d)]

The anticipated effects of this will be a shift of political power to the local level and a significant increase in the role of 'chiefs'.

Conclusion

The (re)discovery of chiefs in Papua New Guinea, and attempts to incorporate traditional authority structures into the national political system, raise several questions.

An initial, if perhaps peripheral, question concerns the 'authenticity' of the chiefly status currently being claimed in some communities. As will be clear from the first section of this paper, many pre-colonial societies in Papua New Guinea did have hereditary chieftains, and, even in those which did not, bigman leadership frequently, if not normally, rested on a mixture of ascription and what Standish (1978) has called 'hereditary advantage'. The fact that many early accounts of Papua New Guinea societies, highlands as well as coastal, identified 'chiefs' when later accounts denied their existence perhaps says as much about the administrative and theoretical predispositions of early European contact and ethnographic scholarship as it does about social actualities: those who expected to find 'chiefs' often found them; those who did not expect to find chiefs found 'bigmen'. What is clear – unsurprisingly, when one considers patterns of leadership in other societies – is that heredity normally bestowed an advantage on the children of political leaders in traditional societies, even where leadership was not actually ascriptive, and that even in ascriptive chiefly societies heredity did not ensure security of tenure. Moreover, leadership styles clearly varied considerably from community to community and were susceptible to individual personality and circumstance; they probably also varied significantly over time. In this context discussion of 'authenticity' is particularly problematic. Nevertheless, there is no doubt that some creative rewriting of traditional social structures is currently in progress – Errington and Gewertz's account of the rise of Chief Mathias Yambumbe providing a nice example – and contemporary claims for the previous existence of chiefly structures appear to be only weakly correlated with the recorded occurrence of chiefs in administrative and anthropological sources.

A more interesting question concerns why the dominant rhetoric of egalitarianism and consensus, enshrined in the constitution, is being increasingly outweighed by one which emphasises instead hierarchical structures and social discipline.

In fact, the discourse on chiefs is part of a broader tendency in Papua New Guinea politics towards a more assertive national leadership and an increasing inclination towards authoritarian forms of social control. This is encapsulated in the 1991 speech by Sir Michael Somare, quoted above, but has been manifested also in the demand for more draconian measures to deal with problems of law and order, in attempts to impose media censorship, in more widespread use of the military in internal security operations, in a growing status consciousness amongst many of Papua New Guinea's political leaders, and in frequent calls for tighter social control, with Indonesia, Singapore and Malaysia as models.[27] Such sentiments spring in part from a widespread belief that 'imposed' Western institutions of parliamentary democracy were not well suited to Papua New Guinean society, and

[27] In 1992 a group of NGOs and church organisations placed a full-page advertisement in the *Post-Courier* (7 August 1992) urging Papua New

that problems of breakdown in law and order, specifically, reflect the inappropriateness of Western-style democracy. These arguments run counter to the view, dominant in the 1970s and well expressed by Deklin (1992), that democratic government is consonant (*marit tru*) with traditional politics; they also challenge the general belief of the 1970s and early 1980s, that the Papua New Guinea constitution which in 1975 defined the features of the independent state was 'home-grown'.

The argument that Papua New Guinea's political institutions are 'inappropriate', however, is compatible with the fact that at the time of independence most Papua New Guineans had a very weak sense of identification with 'the state'. In the 1970s, I used the term 'micronationalism' to describe a tendency, in many parts of the country, for organised local or regional groups to 'disengage' or 'withdraw' from the larger, national, community, 'seeking in a sense of common identity and purpose, and through some combination of traditional and modern values and organisational forms, an acceptable formula for their own development' (May 1975, 1982; the quotation is from May 1982:1). Amongst the larger of these groups were the separatist Papua Besena, the Highlands Liberation Front, and the separatist movement on Bougainville. By the 1980s micronationalism and broader separatist tendencies in Papua and the North Solomons appeared to be on the wane and there was some evidence of a greater sense of national identity. But unfulfilled expectations, an increasing incidence of 'tribal fighting' and *raskolism*, declining levels of government provisions in rural areas, tensions created by big resource-exploiting projects (most notably on Bougainville and at Ok Tedi), reports of police brutality, well-publicised evidence of corruption amongst political leaders, and a growing cynicism towards politicians at both national and provincial level, have tended to erode popular perceptions of the legitimacy of the state (cf. Standish, 1992, 1995). Against this background, a return to

Guineans to resist what they described as 'overwhelming evidence [of an] increasing and dangerous trend towards the militarisation of society'.

'traditional' forms of social organisation and control, albeit often romanticised, has an obvious appeal to communities who believe they can deal with their problems more effectively than a distant, and largely 'foreign', state. As Chief Vere Bau of Kwalimurubu village, Rigo said, in proposing 'a "mini" sort of government . . . based on traditional village leadership system':

> Today, the disintegration of traditional village leadership system and non recognition or respect of village customs and culture of village level create confusion and frustration amongst village people. Leadership roles played by some individuals . . . even some elected members of the highest level of government are creating all sorts of confusion amongst the ordinary village people . . . consequently law and order problems become more confounded (*sic*) . . . there has been no sign of development at village level. [Quoted in *Post-Courier* 27 April 1993]

The appeal of 'traditional authority', in other words, has much the same attraction as micronationalist withdrawal had in some parts of the country two decades ago. It is, consequently, no coincidence that calls for councils of chiefs are strongest on conflict-torn Bougainville, were most vociferous in East Sepik following the burning of the provincial headquarters, and have emerged most recently on Lihir as that island's vast gold and copper mine is about to start operations.

This points to a final set of questions: if there is a shift to traditional forms of authority, how is traditional leadership to be defined and how effective is it likely to be in 'people empowerment' and restoring law and order?

The new Organic Law on Provincial Governments and Local-Level Governments implicitly assumes that traditional leaders will emerge (the questions of 'election/selection' of chiefs and bigmen/women was addressed in the Bipartisan Committee's report – see above), and indeed this seems to have happened on Bougainville – though not, as noted above, without some dispute. But it cannot be assumed that Bougainville's example can be easily replicated elsewhere, least of all in those areas, including much of the highlands, where competition for leadership was traditionally intense. Moreover, qualities on which traditional leadership was based, such as prowess in war and ritual knowledge, are not necessarily the qualities needed for leadership in the late twentieth century. What seems likely is that the introduction of 'traditional' leadership into formal political arrangements will provide another arena for political contestation and that this is as likely to weaken local-level government as it is to strengthen it.

As to its likely effectiveness, amongst communities which have become relatively remote from the reach of the state, or have chosen to disengage, there may be virtue in a revival of traditional leadership, just as many villagers gained from the introduction of village courts and community governments. But as Morauta (1984:28) warned over a decade ago: 'Traditional systems may not . . . be the panacea . . . that they are sometimes made out to be'. For one thing, advocates of the chiefly system, in arguing that the colonial administration 'pushed out' traditional leadership, perhaps dismiss too easily the possibility that in shifting from traditional to introduced political systems ordinary village people were expressing a preference for the new forms; such a possibility is suggested by Waliawi's reference (quoted above) to the 'unsocial and malpractices of the past' which kept some leaders in power, and by the recurring references in the ethnographic literature to the despotism of certain chiefs and bigmen. For another, the welfare of village people today depends in part on their ability to capture a share of the goods and services flowing from the state; chiefly or bigman leadership will only be effective to the extent that it ensures access to these benefits, and that implies its articulation with the state.

It remains to be seen whether the shift towards traditional leadership represents a substantial and permanent change in the nature of Papua New Guinea's political system or whether, like the Melanesian Way, it is primarily philosophical and semantic. One should not underestimate the capacity of Papua New

Guinean politics for creative adaptation; however, any attempt at a wholesale (re)introduction of chiefly structures seems fraught with problems, not least that it is unlikely to meet the more optimistic expectations placed upon it.

10

THE PNGDF IN TROUBLED TIMES*

The Papua New Guinea Defence Force (PNGDF) has been through difficult times in recent years. A gradual deterioration in standards of equipment, training and discipline, and its failure to contain the rebellion on Bougainville which began in 1988, have severely lowered morale. The national government's decision in 1996-97 to employ foreign mercenaries in a covert operation against the rebel leadership on Bougainville resulted in a 'quasi-coup', in which the PNGDF commander, Brigadier General Jerry Singirok, intervened to terminate the contract with Sandline International and call for the resignation of the prime minister and two of his colleagues. The 'Sandline Affair' briefly pushed the Defence Force into the centre stage of Papua New Guinea politics, but Singirok was sacked and currently faces a charge of sedition. The affair has left a legacy of division and mistrust within the Force.

The reappointment of General Singirok in late 1998, under a new government, in the context of substantial improvement in the prospects for peace on Bougainville, has raised hopes in some quarters that the PNGDF is about to address the problems of discipline, capability and conditions, and restore its tarnished image as a professional force. But the events of 1997 have left deep scars within the Force and there are concerns that, having been increasingly politicised since the 1980s, the PNGDF may not have completely withdrawn to the barracks.

---

* This paper was initially written for *The Asia-Pacific Magazine* in 1997, shortly before the magazine ceased publication.

The PNGDF – a colonial legacy

On the eve of independence in 1975, there was a serious debate amongst Papua New Guinea's emerging nationalist elite about whether the independent state should have a defence force. Not only was there no obvious external threat, but it was recognised that if there were, a Papua New Guinea Defence Force could do little more than provide token defence until support arrived from Papua New Guinea's allies.

It was acknowledged that a defence force might have a role to play in supporting civilian authorities in the maintenance of internal security, but there was some apprehension that in a divided, fragile new state a disciplined, cohesive armed force might itself pose a threat to a democratic government (as armies had done in much of post-colonial Africa and Asia).

In the event, a Papua New Guinea Defence Force, established and built up during the Australian colonial period, was retained. The Force was substantially localised but received significant support from Australia, which saw a direct self-interest in maintaining Papua New Guinea's defence capability.

External defence and internal security

In terms of its external role, the PNGDF's principal task has been patrolling the country's western border, in association with the Royal Papua New Guinea Constabulary (RPNGC, the police), primarily to prevent infiltration by the separatist *Organisasi Papua Merdeka* (*OPM*, Free Papua Movement) operating in the neighbouring Indonesian province of Irian Jaya, but also to check on cross-border movement more generally. Apart from this, the Force's small maritime element has the ambitious task of policing the country's EEZ (in which illegal fishing has not been uncommon). A brief but much celebrated external venture in 1980 also saw the PNGDF play a decisive role in bringing to an end a separatist uprising on the island of Santo in neighbouring, newly-independent Vanuatu.

From an early stage, however, it has been clear that the PNGDF's major role was in relation to internal security.

As early as 1977 there were calls for the deployment of the PNGDF to assist police in dealing with 'tribal fighting' and criminal activity in the highlands, but there was resistance to this both from within and from outside the PNGDF. There were further demands, from national politicians and others, to use the PNGDF to quell tribal fighting in the highlands in the following years, but it was not until 1984 that the army was called out to assist police. This followed the declaration of a state of emergency, in response to rising urban crime and violence in the national capital, Port Moresby. The operation lasted for about four months, and was generally seen as a success. Two months later the PNGDF was called out again, for an operation in the National Capital District that lasted five months.

Soldiers were involved in several more operations to assist police in law and order operations in various parts of the country in 1987-88 – including a major operation in the highlands and north coast provinces, which attracted a good deal of negative publicity; police and soldiers were accused of using excessive, and sometimes arbitrary, force.

In 1989 the PNGDF was called out to assist the police on Bougainville, where a dispute by local landowners around the province's large gold and copper mine was about to grow into a rebellion.

Notwithstanding the growing role – and apparent acceptance – of the PNGDF's role in internal security operations during the 1980s, there was a reluctance to acknowledge it officially. In 1989 a Defence General Board of Inquiry (appointed to investigate a riot by PNGDF personnel) referred to the deployment of the PNGDF in this capacity as 'premature'; the same year the defence minister stated that internal security was the responsibility of the RPNGC. This changed, however, the following year.

Facing an escalating law and order problem across the country, and with the situation on Bougainville deteriorating, the national government set up a Security Review Task Force and subsequently a National Summit on Crime. Out of these came a report which suggested that 'the most serious, foreseeable threats facing Papua New Guinea are internal' and that the priorities of the PNGDF 'should be reviewed and, as may be appropriate, reordered'. The proposed change of priorities was endorsed by the Defence minister, who in 1991 told a PNGDF passing out parade that 'The real future of our Defence Force is to assist the civil authorities deal effectively with these threats'. Contemporaneously, following a review of the Australian government's security assistance to Papua New Guinea, the two governments announced that Papua New Guinea was to give highest priority to internal security needs, and that Australian assistance would be geared to this.

By this time the PNGDF had become heavily committed to the conflict on Bougainville, where the combined efforts of the PNGDF and RPNGC were proving incapable of containing the activities of the rebel Bougainville Revolutionary Army (BRA). (Indeed, as a result of some undisciplined behaviour, the security forces probably contributed to the spread of the rebellion beyond the vicinity of the mine.)

Military-civil relations

Already before 1988 there had been several isolated instances of indiscipline and defiance of government by PNGDF personnel. Conditions generated by the Bougainville conflict increased tensions between Defence Force personnel and politicians.

For one thing, as successive national governments shifted between negotiated political settlement and military action, PNGDF personnel felt (as soldiers often do in protracted guerilla war situations) that the government lacked commitment to fighting the rebels, and that 'political interference' in the conflict was a betrayal of its soldiers. Moreover, as peace negotiations between the national government and the rebels gained some ground,

PNGDF (and RPNGC) personnel were deeply suspicious of those who came across from the rebel side to help create a Bougainville Transitional Government (BTG). (The first premier of the BTG, lawyer Theodore Miriung, was murdered by a group of assailants who included military personnel.)

Second, there had been a steady deterioration in PNGDF conditions, equipment, training, and discipline for a number of years, and the Bougainville conflict put new pressures on the Force without a corresponding increase in funding. From 1987 Defence spending regularly exceeded its budget allocation (in 1991 by a massive 81 per cent). Despite this, not only were soldiers frequently not paid allowances but troops on the ground were often not adequately provisioned, and aircraft and boats were regularly out of commission because funds were not available for fuel or repairs. A Defence White Paper, finally tabled in 1996, proposed some major restructuring and generated expectations of improvements, at least in equipment and training. [Few of the recommendations of the 1996 White Paper had been implemented by 1997, when events were overtaken by the 'Sandline Affair' and a subsequent change of government. A new White Paper was presented in 1999.] Morale has been understandably low.

The blatant politicisation of the position of the commander, from the early 1980s, and the build-up of a large number of senior colonels has also contributed to growing factionalism and rivalry at the senior officer level.

The Sandline Affair

In mid 1996, frustrated at the lack of progress in negotiations with the Bougainville rebel leadership, Prime Minister Chan authorised an operation ('High Speed II') against the BRA in southern Bougainville. The operation resulted in a defeat for the security forces, and several PNGDF personnel were taken hostage by the BRA. Angered by this (and facing a national election in June

1997), the Chan government became involved in negotiations which culminated in the signing of a contract with 'military consultants' Sandline International for a covert operation against BRA leaders. The contract was subsequently exposed, and widely criticised, both within Papua New Guinea and beyond [the Sandline Affair has been discussed in detail in Dinnen, May and Regan (1997), Dorney (1998) and O'Callaghan (1999).

In March 1997, less than four weeks after the exposure of the Sandline deal, the PNGDF commander, Brigadier General Singirok, delivered an address to the nation, in which he denounced the contract, saying that he had cancelled all further activities involving the PNGDF and Sandline (the Sandline personnel had in fact been detained and were deported soon after), and called on the prime minister, deputy prime minister, and defence minister to resign. There has been some speculation about Singirok's motives in this. The commander had been a party to the negotiations with Sandline International from an early stage, and had apparently initially accepted their proposed action on Bougainville. By mid March he clearly had second thoughts about the impact of such an operation in Bougainville, and its wider political repercussions. Several commentators have suggested, however, that a more significant factor was Singirok's resentment at Sandline's effectively taking charge of the operation.

Prime Minister Chan accused Singirok of 'gross insubordination bordering on treason', and dismissed him. He subsequently appointed as commander a controversial officer, Leo Nuia, who had attracted a degree of notoriety while commander on Bougainville and had been decommissioned by General Singirok.

Singirok's actions, however, won widespread popular approval, and after some initial resistance, and with volatile crowds demonstrating outside the National Parliament, the three ministers agreed to step down pending an enquiry. The enquiry reported in May 1997; Chan declared that it had cleared him of any wrongdoing and resumed office. But in the national elections the following month both Chan and his defence minister lost their seats. This was the first time in Papua New Guinea's political history that an incumbent prime minister had failed to gain re-election.

Another fallout from the election was the arrest of Major Walter Enuma – the officer who had led the operation to oust the Sandline personnel – and thirteen soldiers under his command. Enuma (who earlier had been seconded to the Electoral Commission to help coordinate security during the elections) had been in the highlands, where he and his troops were said to have provided support to particular candidates favoured by Singirok. The soldiers were charged with setting up an unauthorised force. Subsequently armed soldiers forced their way into a police station in Port Moresby where Enuma and others were being held, released them, and then proceeded to PNGDF HQ where they briefly placed General Nuia under 'house arrest'.

By this time, divisions within the PNGDF, partly along regional, 'ethnic' lines, had become a serious threat to the cohesion of the Defence Force. The Special Forces Unit, which had been set up by General Singirok in 1996 following a recommendation of the 1996 Defence White Paper, and had played a prominent role in the operation against Sandline, was effectively disbanded under Nuia, and a Special Operations Group, set up by Nuia, was allegedly used to harass Singirok supporters within and outside the PNGDF.

The aftermath of Sandline – increased politicisation?

The incoming coalition government was headed by former National Capital District governor (and self-confessed former *raskol*[1]) Bill Skate. Skate had been a strong supporter of Singirok in March 1997.

Towards the end of 1998, amid talk of an imminent parliamen-

---

[1] The term *raskol* is used in Papua New Guinea to refer to members of criminal gangs.

tary vote of no confidence against him, Skate announced that he could no longer work with General Nuia, and reappointed Singirok.

Singirok's reappointment brought mixed reactions. Apart from the fact that some elements within the PNGDF, mobilised in the wake of the Sandline Affair, were now opposed to him, Singirok still faced a charge of sedition (a charge which was quickly re-activated by police following his re-appointment). A group of former PNGDF commanders called on him to step down until the sedition charge had been settled. More significantly, the revelation, in July 1997, that prior to the Sandline Affair General Singirok had received payments from a British arms dealer, substantially undermined the moral high ground on which Singirok had stood.

Against this background, there were rumours in Port Moresby in late 1998 that Prime Minister Skate had reappointed Singirok to strengthen his hand in the event the parliamentary vote of no confidence proceeded; there was talk of a possible military coup, and expressions of concerns that the Special Forces Unit had been reconstituted and was in training outside Port Moresby. The threat of a no confidence vote was averted when in December 1998 Skate adjourned the National Parliament for six months.

Rumours of an imminent coup surface from time to time in Papua New Guinea, but in a country which is culturally and geographically fragmented, with no dominant ethnic group, a robust tradition of challenging authority, and relatively low levels of urbanisation, it is difficult to conceive of a military coup being sustained. By early 1999 fears of a coup had subsided.

On reappointment, Singirok promised 'a massive clean-up' to restore standards and improve conditions for personnel, and to refocus on the PNGDF's role in civic action and nation building. With respect to the latter, construction of a long-promised engineers base in the highlands commenced in early 1999. With progress towards peace on Bougainville (a paradoxical by-product of the Sandline Affair), it is anticipated that troops released from there can be used to increase the PNGDF's presence on the border with Indonesia (patrols having effectively lapsed in 1988).

But the commander faces an uphill task. For a start he has to deal with problems of factionalism and rivalry within the Force. In January 1999 six senior colonels (not known for their support of Singirok during the events of 1997) were sacked, and several others promoted, though this has produced some legal challenges. A programme of reconciliation and confidence building within the Force has been initiated. Second, he has to address the task of restructuring and upgrading the Force. Commencing in 1999 some 700 PNGDF personnel (in a force of around 4200) will leave through retirement or redundancy. Without a significant injection of funds any restructuring will be difficult, and in the present budgetary climate, funds are scarce. If these two issues can be addressed, progress may be made in respect of another critical issue – that of reversing the decline in PNGDF morale.

Beyond these issues, however, is a bigger question. The role of the PNGDF in internal security is now well established, though the respective responsibilities of police and army have never been clearly defined, and, even after years of joint operation on Bougainville, antipathy between the two services persists. But in a situation in which the army, and increasingly the police, have been politicised, and in which coalition governments are continually pushing the limits of their constitutional powers to stay in office, it is not entirely clear what subservience to the civilian authorities entails. A full-scale military coup still looks highly improbable, but another 'Sandline Affair' certainly cannot be ruled out.

11

THE MILITARY FACTOR IN THE EVENTS OF MARCH 1997*

In his address to the nation on 17 March, in which he called on the prime minister, deputy prime minister, and defence minister to resign, Brigadier General Singirok claimed to be acting 'as senior citizen and a responsible Departmental Head'. But it is clear from his statement that Singirok's primary concern was, as commander of the PNGDF, with the terms of the contract between the government and Sandline International. 'As a professional military officer', he said:

> I have kept quiet and followed orders from this government as I would for any serving government of the day without questioning their orders and directives. And this included the Sandline International project which has brought into question the issues of sovereignty and the credibility of the PNG Defence Force and our own professionalism which the government has greatly undermined . . .
>
> [But] I have cancelled all further activities involving the PNG Defence Force with the Sandline International . . .
>
> It is my professional and ethical view that it is wrong to hire Sandline International to carry out the operations on Bougainville . . .
>
> The amount of money spent on hiring Sandline should be used to buy much needed logistical support and capability to sustain

---

* This paper was first published in S. Dinnen, R.J. May and A.J. Regan (eds), *Challenging the State: the Sandline Affair in Papua New Guinea* (1997).

current efforts on Bougainville and the other roles of the Defence Force within the country.

These concerns were in part specific to the Sandline contract; but they reflected a much deeper, longstanding, and growing malaise in relations between the government and the armed forces (May 1993).

In the lead-up to independence in 1975 there was a good deal of discussion about whether Papua New Guinea should have an army. At least some people saw a cohesive, well-resourced and disciplined armed force as a potential threat to the government of an independent state. Concerns were also expressed about the prospect of using the military in law and order operations 'in aid to the civil power', and about the relative size and funding of the police and army. Ultimately, however, the decision was taken to have a defence force, and after some resistance to earlier demands, in 1984 the PNGDF was called out to assist police following the declaration of a state of emergency in Port Moresby, in response to rising crime and violence in the capital.

The Defence Force was involved in several more law and order operations before being deployed, in a similar capacity, on Bougainville in 1989. Meanwhile, however, the PNGDF's reputation as a well-resourced and well-disciplined force was coming increasingly into question. Well before the Bougainville campaign it was frequently being observed that the level of training and standards of discipline in the PNGDF were declining, that equipment and accommodation for personnel and their families were deteriorating, and that morale was slipping. As early as 1984-85 a *Defence Report* commented that the standard of discipline in the PNGDF was 'below that required' and some 190 soldiers were discharged. The same year a number of Transport Squadron ground crew staged a strike over pay and conditions. In 1988 the Defence Force defied a government decision to relocate the Air Element from Lae to Nadzab, and the following year between 100 and 200 soldiers marched on the Parliament to voice their disappointment at lower than expected pay increases. The latter incident resulted in a Defence General Board of Inquiry, which reported a serious decline in discipline, some misuse of funds and equipment, and low morale.

By the mid 1980s, too, the position of PNGDF commander had become politicised and there was growing evidence of factionalism at senior officer levels.

The inability of the security forces to contain the conflict on Bougainville provided further evidence of the PNGDF's limited capacity, though it also reflected the inherent difficulties of this sort of guerilla warfare. Analyses of the Bougainville campaign have pointed to inadequate logistic capacity, poor intelligence, questionable strategy, and poor discipline (see, for example, Liria 1993). Although, according to the late Graeme Kemelfield, the PNGDF was initially welcomed by most Bougainvilleans, after the first few PNGDF casualties the soldiers became increasingly alienated from the people and human rights abuses multiplied.[1]

With the Bougainville conflict dragging on, and morale amongst the troops low, members of the security forces, and their families, accused the political leadership of indecision and lack of commitment to a resolution of the conflict, which some in the Defence Force felt could have been achieved, given the necessary resources and political will, by military means. Security forces personnel resentment resulted in several confrontations with government ministers and officials.

In each year from 1988 actual Defence expenditure exceeded the budget allocation by a significant margin; in 1991 expenditure, at K92 million, exceeded the appropriation by a massive K41.2 million. Notwithstanding this, the PNGDF was unable to meet the cost of its operations on Bougainville. The refusal of local suppliers to keep extending credit for such purposes as air charters, fuel, and general supplies, and the inability of the Defence

---

1 Parliament of Australia, Joint Committee on Foreign Affairs, Defence and Trade, Hearing, 22 October 1990, p. 793.

Force to provide adequately for the maintenance of its naval and air craft, meant that its operations on Bougainville were frequently hampered. Shortage of funds also resulted in the non-payment of allowances, and occasionally in delayed salary payments, to soldiers; this became a source of increasing resentment. A *Defence Ten-Year Development Plan* approved by cabinet in 1991 provided for an increase in force size and re-equipment of the Defence Force, but little was done to implement the plan, and in 1993, in presenting a budgetary review of the law and order sector, the Minister for Finance announced that the PNGDF was to be 'scaled down' and directed more towards civic action. A subsequent *Defence White Paper* was tabled in the National Parliament in July 1996; its proposals – more modest than those of the *Ten-Year Development Plan* – remained to be implemented at the time of the 'Sandline affair'. Requests for additional assistance through the Australian Defence Cooperation Program, in particular for upgraded equipment, received little sympathy; this became a point of contention in Australian-Papua New Guinea relations, and added to the growing sense of grievance within the PNGDF.

At the time of the October 1994 Peace Talks in Arawa, hopes for at least substantial progress towards a settlement were high. The failure of the Bougainville Revolutionary Army (BRA) leadership to attend the talks clearly annoyed Prime Minister Chan, and although discussions continued after Arawa, leading to the formation of the Bougainville Transitional Government (BTG), Chan seems never to have been enthusiastic about the BTG, while the military remained at best suspicious of it and at worst openly hostile. Notwithstanding this, progress was being made in talks between the BTG and the rebels until January 1996 when, following a second round of talks in Cairns facilitated by the Australian government, members of the BRA/BIG delegation were fired upon while returning to Bougainville via Honiara. In the aftermath of this incident, Prime Minister Chan said there would be no further discussions outside Papua New Guinea, and the armed conflict resumed. Obviously frustrated, annoyed, and anxious for a 'solution' to the Bougainville problem, Prime Minister Chan ordered *Operation High Speed II* against the rebels in June 1996.

Operation High Speed II ended disastrously for the security forces, further lowering morale and, it seems, straining relations between Chan and Singirok.

Whatever less worthy motives there may have been behind the Sandline contract, the failure of *Operation High Speed II* promoted the attempt to boost central government's military capacity. The then National Capital District governor, Bill Skate, subsequently described the contract as 'a slap in the face for the PNGDF'; without doubt it was concrete evidence of the government's lack of faith in the security forces' ability to deal with the situation on Bougainville.

Singirok's role, as PNGDF commander and a member of the National Security Council, in the negotiations with Sandline International, is not entirely clear. He was involved in the Sandline negotiations from at least April 1996 and apparently went along with the rather draconian military estimate contained in the December 1996 Project Contravene proposal; within the terms of Project Contravene all personnel 'would be tasked under the full command of Commander of PNG Forces'. The prospect of additional funding and equipment for the security forces' operations must have held some attraction to the Defence Force commander, whose troops, in his own words, had been operating on Bougainville for nine years with 'depleted resources . . . and lack of funding for vital allowances and supplies from successive governments'. In his own words, Singirok initially 'followed orders' on the Sandline contract. But at some point in February-March 1997 he decided that the contract undermined the role of the security forces – specifically the PNGDF (and Singirok's personal position as PNGDF commander) – and impinged upon the sovereignty of the Papua New Guinea state. It also cost money which might be better spent on the PNGDF. More significantly, perhaps, Singirok appears to have become concerned at 'the expected backlash as a result of any major military operations on Bougainville which will for ever remain with us' ('Address to the Nation' 17 March 1997).

Another factor in Singirok's change of attitude may have been a letter he received from the acting secretary of the Department of the Prime Minister and National Executive Council dated 20 January 1997, in which he was informed that the prime minister had directed that the 'PNGDF Rapid Reaction Force' (presumably the recently established Special Forces Unit) 'be formalised, strengthened and commanded by Police' and be brought administratively under the Department of the PM and NEC. Singirok objected to the shifting of control over the unit to the prime minister, subsequently telling the Sandline inquiry:

> I believed strongly that if Sandline is engaged and if the Prime Minister has personal interests in the SFU and Sandline, obviously the SFU will be amalgamated with Sandline and we will have a palace guard. We will not have a Defence Force that represents the Constitution. [*Post-Courier* 10 April 1997]

In making a stand against the Sandline contract, and against those most closely responsible for it, Brigadier General Singirok was thus ostensibly motivated by both moral outrage and by the corporate interests of the military.[2] Both of these are factors which feature large in the literature of military coups.

There was substantial popular support for Singirok's action, but there were also many, including some within the PNGDF itself, who condemned the move as setting a dangerous precedent.

Two of the questions most frequently asked by the foreign media at the time were, 'Is this a coup?' and 'Is the military, "having tasted power", likely to seek a continuing role in politics, as

[2] In the light of subsequent revelations, concerning payments received by Singirok from British arms dealers J & S Franklin, there may also have been more personal and perhaps venal motives.

in many African [curiously, few journalists said 'and Asian'] countries?'

The answer to the first question ultimately comes down to defining what constitutes a coup. But it is significant, not only that Singirok himself specifically denied that his actions constituted a coup (a claim, however, that many coup leaders make), but also that *Operation Rausim Kwik* (as the action was called) involved no attempt to detain political leaders[3] or occupy the Parliament, nor any attempt to seize radio or TV stations or influence the press – the initial steps of any normal coup. It is also worth bearing in mind that, with national elections only weeks away, there were means close to hand of resolving the issue, within the classic democratic paradigm, 'through the ballot box', and that, when dismissed, Singirok accepted his dismissal. Thus, without in any way downplaying the seriousness of Singirok's action, to describe it as a 'coup' would be to stretch that term well beyond its normal usage.

In addressing the second question, it is well to remember, first, that, though this may be the most serious, it is not the first (and probably will not be the last) confrontation between the elected government and the security forces in Papua New Guinea, and, second, that successive elected governments have tempted such intervention insofar as they have deliberately politicised the position of Defence Force commander – though it is ironic that Singirok, appointed by Chan in October 1995 over several more senior officers, was seen at the time as 'Chan's man'. For some years, most professional observers have been dismissive of the likelihood of a military coup. This view has been based on consideration of logistic factors and the demonstrated incapacity of the small force, even with government support, to resolve the

[3] Singirok's 17 March statement did contain the statement: 'If the PM and his deputy and Minister for Defence do not step down within 48 hours then I will plea to Papua New Guineans [*sic*] to join hands to force them to resign'; but when the three had not resigned within 48 hours no direct move was made against them.

Bougainville conflict or (with the police) to maintain peace and order in other parts of the country. On the other hand, increasingly we have tended to concede the possibility that the PNGDF (or at least factions of it), perhaps in collaboration with disgruntled or ambitious politicians, might seek to exercise selective influence over government decision making.

In the fallout from the events of March-April 1997 this position remains sustainable. The prime minister, deputy prime minister, and defence minister 'stood aside' pending an enquiry, and two of them subsequently lost their parliamentary seats in the June 1997 election; Singirok was dismissed and in September 1997 was facing charges of sedition. Contrary to the expectations of many people, the PNGDF generally showed remarkable discipline during the popular demonstrations against the Sandline contract, and was largely responsible for defusing a potentially explosive situation outside the National Parliament on 25-26 March (when Prime Minister Chan and his two ministers were persuaded to step aside) after the police had departed the scene, leaving an agitated crowd of demonstrators. A Defence Board of Enquiry has since been set up to review the PNGDF's role in the events of March.

Papua New Guinea's robust democratic system appears to have survived another crisis intact. Nevertheless the March 1997 incident has clearly placed further strains on relations between the government and the military, and has exacerbated divisions within the PNGDF.

12

CHALLENGING THE STATE*

Sharing borders with Indonesia, Australia, the Solomon Islands and Micronesia, Papua New Guinea looks west and north to Asia, south to its former colonial administrator, and east to the island Pacific. Though it has experienced occasional tensions along its land boundary with Indonesia and, recently, in the waters which separate it from the Solomon Islands, Papua New Guinea's geographical location has left it relatively free from external security concerns, able to follow what was initially stated to be a 'universalist' foreign policy and to maintain an open economy while continuing to enjoy a 'special relationship' with Australia.

For some years, however, Papua New Guinea has faced growing problems of internal security and these problems appear to have escalated in the early 1990s. A resurgence of tribal fighting, an increasing incidence of criminal activity, and since 1988 an armed separatist rebellion on the island of Bougainville, have tested the capacity of the Papua New Guinea state, and brought a shift in the priorities of the Papua New Guinea Defence Force (PNGDF) from external defence to internal security.

Consolidating the independent state

Papua New Guinea enjoyed an easy and amicable transition from Australian colonialism to its independence in 1975. However, as

* This paper was written in 1996 for a volume on regional security, published as W.A. Hermann (ed.), *Asia's Security Challenges* (1998).

one of the world's last colonies, and as a small country fragmented by geography and ethnicity, independent Papua New Guinea faced substantial challenges. With a rapidly growing population of almost four million, speaking around 800 separate languages, it lacked a tradition of political organisation beyond the village community and temporary alliance of common language (*wantok*) group, and the essentially Westminster-style institutions created in the latter stages of colonial rule were seen by many as a fragile basis for stable democratic government. Within and outside the country, there were many who forewarned of a military coup or transition to single-party rule.

On the eve of independence, separatist movements in Papua and in the gold-and-copper-rich North Solomons Province, and the emergence of a variety of micronationalist movements in different parts of the country, posed more obvious threats to the nation's viability.

Economically, the emerging state's future seemed more promising; but dependence on volatile returns from export cash crops and, initially, the output of one very big mine, together with low levels of domestic capital and a low-skilled workforce, underscored the need for continuing external assistance and sound fiscal and economic management.

Externally, Papua New Guinea had defined its foreign policy prior to independence in terms of a policy of 'universalism' – friends to all and enemies to none but racist regimes. The existence, however, in the neighbouring Indonesian province of Irian Jaya, of a Melanesian separatist movement, *Organisasi Papua Merdeka* (OPM), whose freedom fighters occasionally sought refuge in the dense jungle on Papua New Guinea's side of the border, created a potential for difficulties in relations with Indonesia, particularly when the Indonesian military pursued OPM sympathisers across Papua New Guinea's border.

Notwithstanding such challenges, and contrary to the expectations of some, Papua New Guinea weathered the early years of independence fairly well, and in some respects it has continued to do so.

In the two decades since independence Papua New Guinea has had six changes of government – two as a result of general elections, three as the result of parliamentary votes of no confidence, and one as the outcome of a judicial ruling; all have taken place smoothly. Moreover, between 1975 and 1996 Papua New Guinea has had only four prime ministers. The country has had regular elections, with a fairly high turnover (on average just over 50 per cent) of members of parliament. There has been no evidence of the tendency towards single-party dominance predicted by some observers in the 1960s on the basis of experience in Africa and Asia; indeed, contrarily, political parties have remained fluid, loosely disciplined, and differentiated more by personal and regional loyalties than by ideology. All governments since 1975 have been coalition governments, with almost every major party having cohabited with every other at some stage and individual 'party hopping' not uncommon. This situation is reflected in the incidence of votes of no confidence, and has contributed to a pork-barrelling style of politics which has made commitment to difficult policy objectives hard to maintain.

The separatist and micronationalist tendencies which came to the fore in the mid 1970s appeared to have been effectively dealt with by the end of the decade. A settlement was reached with separatist leaders in the North Solomons (Bougainville) in 1976, several of whom became members of the national government after the 1977 general elections, and the Bougainville Agreement became the basis for a system of provincial government within the unitary state, along lines which had been recommended by the Constitutional Planning Committee in 1974 but initially rejected. Elected provincial governments were set up on a common basis in all provinces in the late 1970s and a substantial decentralisation of powers was effected.

From the start, however, there was opposition to the provincial government system, both from national bureaucrats who resisted the transfer of decision making to inexperienced provincial politicians, and from national MPs and local government councillors who saw their power bases being eroded by provincial governments. In some provinces, political inexperience, lack of administrative capacity, nepotism, and local rivalries resulted in financial mismanagement and administrative breakdown. By 1995 (following a relaxation of the enabling legislation over a decade earlier) 15 of the country's 19 provinces had been suspended, some of them twice. Continuing demands for the dissolution of provincial governments culminated in new legislation in mid 1995 which substantially alters the system created in 1976-77. Under this legislation elected provincial governments are replaced by assemblies comprising the national MPs from the province (with the members from the provincial electorates designated 'governor'), heads of local-level governments (including, where appropriate, 'customary leaders'), and several sectoral representatives. Though presented as a move towards greater decentralisation, shifting power to the people, most commentators see the move as part of an attempt to strengthen central government control.

More seriously, unsatisfied demands by landowners around the Bougainville gold and copper mine from 1988 revived secessionist sentiments in the North Solomons, which, following often heavy-handed measures by police and the military, escalated into an armed conflict. Apart from forcing the closure of the mine, with major financial implications nationally, the conflict has caused substantial loss of life, dislocation of people, and damage to property and gardens, and has so far defied settlement (see below).

On the economic front, declining export crop prices through most of the late 1970s and early 1980s were largely offset by the commencement of several large mining and petroleum developments and, more recently, the controversial expansion of the logging industry. However, the closure of the Bougainville mine in 1989, and industrial and landowner unrest at other mine sites, have demonstrated the fragility of this form of development, and a high rate of population increase has restricted gains in per capita income. Although around 85 per cent of Papua New Guinea's population is still largely dependent on subsistence agriculture, urban unemployment (estimated at around 35-40 per cent) and disaffected rural youth have contributed to a growing problem of lawlessness in town and countryside (see below).

In 1981 Papua New Guinea changed its foreign policy from one of universalism to one of 'active and selective engagement'. However, there was little change of substance in its external outlook, which remained essentially non-aligned but pro-Western. In 1984 nationalist unrest in Irian Jaya and consequent military action by the Indonesian armed forces resulted in the movement of some 10 000-12 000 Irianese across the border into Papua New Guinea seeking refuge. There were also several incursions by Indonesian military personnel into Papua New Guinea territory during this period. Indonesia's failure to respond satisfactorily to Papua New Guinea's protests at the border incursions and to attempts to repatriate the border crossers, and Papua New Guinea's refusal to engage in joint patrols of the border area, soured relations between the two countries and culminated in Papua New Guinea voicing its concerns before the United Nations General Assembly. Relations gradually recovered, however, and in 1986 the two countries signed a Treaty of Mutual Respect, Friendship and Cooperation, which addressed their common security concerns and endorsed arrangements already in place for border management and liaison. Although the Treaty did little more than confirm existing arrangements and past undertakings, the formalisation of relations was seen by some as a step forward, and in fact relations between Indonesia and Papua New Guinea have improved in recent years, to the point where several recent border incursions by Indonesian troops have gone largely unreported.

Having formalised relations with Indonesia (and following an incident in which, for domestic fiscal reasons, Australia unilaterally reduced its aid to Papua New Guinea shortly after negotiating a new aid programme), Papua New Guinea also moved to formalise its relations with Australia. The outcome of this initiative was the signing in 1987 of a Joint Declaration of Principles Guiding Relations Between Papua New Guinea and Australia. Included in the joint declaration was an undertaking by the two signatories to 'consult about matters affecting their common security in the event of external armed attack threatening the national sovereignty of either country'. This was widely interpreted as a firmer commitment by Australia to safeguarding Papua New Guinea's external security. There is little doubt, however, that over recent years relations between the two countries have not been as close as they used to be. In particular, a shift in Australia's development assistance programme in Papua New Guinea from general budgetary support to programme assistance has drawn repeated adverse comment from Papua New Guinea leaders. A third important development in external relations was the formalisation in 1988 of Papua New Guinea's relationship with its Melanesian neighbours, the Solomon Islands and Vanuatu (together, the Melanesian Spearhead Group) through a set of Agreed Principles of Cooperation. Also in this period Papua New Guinea acceded to the ASEAN Treaty of Amity and Cooperation, and joined the non-aligned group of countries. Under the subsequent Wingti government (1992-94), the announcement of a 'Look North [to Asia] Policy' signalled a further development in Papua New Guinea's external outlook, which recognised the growing significance of its economic links with Asian countries.

Security issues for the 1990s

Papua New Guinea thus survived the early years of independence as a secure, democratic state, but not without increasingly visible problems. These have been primarily in three areas: increasing lawlessness across the country; a deteriorating climate of political decision making and implementation, contributing to economic crisis; and the rebellion on Bougainville. This in turn brought a formal shift in the priorities of the Papua New Guinea Defence Force from external defence to internal security.

Law and order

Warfare was endemic amongst Papua New Guinea's fragmented pre-colonial communities. The Australian colonial regime achieved a remarkable degree of 'pacification', but it now appears that, like the colonial presence in much of the country, the *Pax Australiana* was shortlived. Already by the early 1970s there was concern that 'tribal fighting' was undergoing a resurgence, particularly in the populous highlands provinces, whose contact with the colonial government was comparatively recent. In 1977 an *Inter-Group Fighting Act* was passed in an effort to deal with the situation, but its more radical proposals did not survive legal challenge. (The relevant provisions were revived, however, following a constitutional amendment, in 1991.) The early 1970s also saw the development of what came to be referred to as *raskol* gangs – groups of mostly young men engaged in petty crime. Initially such gangs consisted largely of unemployed youth from ethnically based squatter settlements around the major towns of Port Moresby and Lae. But by the late 1970s *raskolism* was well established in rural areas and well developed *raskol* networks, including former police and PNGDF personnel, were spread across the country, some with links to national and provincial politicians, and the incidence of more serious crimes appeared to be escalating. Police mobile squads were employed to confront the growing problems of tribal fighting and criminal activity, but having acquired a reputation for undisciplined and sometimes partisan behaviour, the police tended to become as much a part of the problem as a solution to it. There were also calls, from around this time, for the deployment of the PNGDF to assist police.

In 1979, with an accelerating deterioration in the law and order situation, a state of emergency was declared in the five highlands provinces. This was the first of a number of such states of emergency. Five years later the government announced a list of measures to deal with law and order problems; these included the use of PNGDF soldiers. Later that year the PNGDF was called out to assist police during a state of emergency, occasioned by rising urban crime and violence in the national capital. This operation, and another shortly after, together lasted for some nine months. A later operation, 'LOMET 88', in which the PNGDF also participated, covered four provinces and lasted for over three months. The following year (1989) the military was committed to the emerging crisis on Bougainville.

In 1990, facing problems of lawlessness across the country and with the Bougainville conflict no closer to resolution the national government set up a Security Review Task Force and, shortly after, convened a National Summit on Crime. A consequent report, entitled *Security for Development* (1991) observed that the disciplined forces had not been able to cope with 'sources of law-breaking and disorder' and suggested that 'the most serious, foreseeable threats facing Papua New Guinea are internal'. Amongst recommendations contained in the report were, that a Joint Services Command Centre be established; that an Office of Security Coordination and Assessment be created within the Prime Minister's Department, and that the police and military be progressively integrated. Amongst other measures introduced around this time were the reimposition of the death penalty for crimes of murder and gang rape, and the institution of community auxiliary policing. Following a change of government in 1992, more draconian measures were proposed. These included the creation of a Police Tactical Force to respond effectively to 'armed criminals, hostage situations, gang activities, tribal fights and civil unrest', and the passage of an Internal Security Act along Malaysian-Singaporean lines. The first of these proposals was explored with British security contractors

Defence Systems Ltd, and there was renewed discussion of a suggestion made two years earlier, that Gurkha troops be recruited; but the idea lapsed, probably through lack of funding. An *Internal Security Act* was passed in 1993, but it was widely criticised and a challenge by the Ombudsman Commission resulted in the Supreme Court declaring parts of the legislation unconstitutional. Also in 1993 a National Law, Order and Justice Council was established and a five-year National Law and Order Programme was announced.

After almost five years, few of the recommendations of the 1991 security report have been implemented, though there has been an increased allocation to the Police Department. Meanwhile both tribal fighting and *raskolism* appear to have grown in scale and intensity. Few parts of the country do not suffer from a breakdown of law and order, and the use of modern weapons (some home-made) is becoming more widespread. Police intelligence reports suggest that the internationalisation of criminal activity (specifically the export of marijuana and stolen vehicle parts, and the import of firearms) is becoming a serious threat. Observers of the last (1992) national election and subsequent provincial elections have reported that, in some parts of the country, physical threats to candidates, voters and officials, and other electoral irregularities, have jeopardised the legitimacy of the results. With over 50 per cent of members elected in 1992 with less than 20 per cent of their constitutency's vote, this becomes a serious issue. Well-publicised instances of corruption and nepotism on the part of national and (until 1995) provincial politicians, combined with such developments, tend to undermine the legitimacy of the state itself.

The year 1996 was declared the 'Year of Law Enforcement', but a series of events which occurred as this chapter was being written (February 1996) illustrates the sorts of problems confronting the government in this area. A bus from the Eastern Highlands, travelling along the highlands highway (the country's main arterial road), was stoned by villagers from the Markham

Valley; as payback some Eastern Highlanders killed a Markham youth; groups of Markhams thereupon blocked the highway demanding compensation of K200 000 (about $US150 000); failing to get this, they blew up a bridge, using explosives from unexploded World War II bombs, and prevented movement between the highlands and the port city of Lae. Police from the Eastern Highlands responded by raiding Markham villages, allegedly burning more than 200 houses and attacking a prominent national member of parliament who was attempting to mediate. The provincial police commander was subsequently removed from his post and PNGDF personnel were brought in. Pending resolution of the dispute, the highway was effectively closed, with potentially serious implications for, amongst others, the Porgera gold and copper mine, the Kutubu oilfields, and the nation's largest coffee producing region.

Administration and the economy

In the early post-independence years Papua New Guinea maintained unspectacular but steady rates of economic growth, with sound economic management and a policy framework which emphasised agricultural development (including the strengthening of subsistence agriculture), self-sufficiency, and an equitable distribution of the benefits from development. Declining commodity prices undermined this trend and between 1980 and 1984 real GDP fell. With population officially estimated to be growing at 2.5 per cent per annum, the impact of the decline in per capita incomes was exacerbated. The rate of economic growth recovered somewhat in the latter part of the 1980s but in 1989 the economy was hit by the closure of the Bougainville mine, which at that stage contributed around 40 per cent of the country's exports and 17 per cent of government revenue. In 1990 the Papua New Guinea government was forced to negotiate an external assistance package and undertook to introduce a number of structural adjustment measures, including a 10 per cent cut in government spending. The commencement of production at other big mining and petroleum ventures at Ok Tedi, Porgera, Misima and Kutubu, helped lift GDP in the early 1990s, and expansion of the forestry industry boosted growth.

Despite the resource-based surge in national income, however, by 1993 the Papua New Guinea economy began to show further signs of emerging fiscal crisis. Although the loss of revenue from the Bougainville mine was offset by the gains from the new mining ventures, these too have been subjected to stoppages due to industrial and landowner disputes, highlighting the vulnerability of an economy dependent on big resource-exploiting projects. At the same time, the expansion of logging, largely by overseas companies and commonly bypassing environmental safeguards, has brought increasing protest from both landowners and conservation groups. Moreover, the revenue generated by these activities has done little to offset inequalities in the distribution of benefits, which most social indicators suggest have widened, and rising levels of government spending and of foreign debt have underlined problems of economic management.

In many parts of the countryside the delivery of government services, in fields such as health, education, and agricultural extension, has declined and physical infrastructure, such as roads and housing for government employees, has deteriorated. Government officers, at national and provincial levels, are frequently unable or unwilling to visit the more remote parts of the countryside. One attempt to address this – the allocation to MPs of money from an Electoral Development Fund for discretionary spending – has been widely criticised and has reinforced a growing cynicism towards politicians. The declining visibility, and, for many, legitimacy, of the state has contributed to the growth of *raskolism*. It also helps explain an upsurge in compensation demands against government, both for land acquired earlier by government (for schools, roads, airstrips, town development, etc.), and, more recently, for losses suffered as a result of police actions (in which the burning of houses, killing of pigs, theft, and physical abuse of women and men have been reported).

In towns and at mine sites there has been a burgeoning recourse to private security firms (which sometimes employ reformed *raskols*); but the general deterioration of law and order has impeded recruitment of outsiders and deterred longer-term foreign investment.

The economic situation reached a crisis point in 1994-1995 with several branches of government unable to meet debts or salary commitments. The government was forced to seek further World Bank assistance and to commit itself to a programme of microeconomic reforms, at least some of which are politically unpopular.

While attempts are now being made to address the country's economic problems, there are many who believe that the decline in standards of economic management since the 1970s is irreversible. The revenue generated by big resource projects has not been used productively, unemployment is high, and while a small number of Papua New Guineans have become very wealthy, the expectations of the vast majority of the population remain unfulfilled. Compared to other Third World countries, literacy and general education rates are low, nutrition levels are poor, infant and maternal mortality rates are high, and life expectancy is low. In some parts of the countryside there is a visible decline in living standards. This has contributed to social unrest and helped undermine the state's capacity to deal with such unrest.

The Bougainville rebellion

In 1975, separatist elements on Bougainville, reluctant to see the bulk of the returns from the Bougainville copper mine flowing out of the province, announced their independence as the Republic of the North Solomons. In doing so they appealed to a longstanding sense of differentiation from the 'redskins' of the mainland and of resentment at perceived neglect by the government in Port Moresby. The negotiation of the Bougainville Agreement and the introduction of provincial government (with financial provisions including a derivation grant to return some of the mining revenue to the province), together with the renegotiation of the agreement with the operating company, Bougainville Copper Ltd (BCL), appeared to have succeeded in reconciling Bougainvilleans to their membership of the Papua New Guinea nation; Bougainvilleans became prominent in national politics and administration, and the North Solomons provincial government became probably the most successful of the country's second-tier governments.

In 1988, however, a split within the Panguna Landowners' Association (PLA) – which represented landowners around the mine site – brought to the fore a group of younger, more militant people, who campaigned against environmental damage from the mine and sought substantially increased compensation from BCL. When their demands were ignored, the new group embarked on a campaign of sabotage against mine installations, and harassment of mine workers and members of the officially recognised faction of the PLA. Ultimately, this led to confrontation, in which the militant landowners, joined by other disgruntled groups in south and central Bougainville and, initially, with support from sympathisers elsewhere in the North Solomons province and beyond, were ranged against the security forces – police and military – of the Papua New Guinea state.

After an early period of failed negotiation with what became the Bougainville Revolutionary Army (BRA), in 1990 the Papua New Guinea government withdrew its personnel and imposed an effective blockade of the province. Its hope appears to have been that an ensuing collapse of administration and disappearance of services would undermine support for the BRA and generate demand for the return of the national government. In fact the situation worsened. The BRA failed to establish any sort of order, there was widespread destruction of property and dislocation of people, and resentment against the government culminated in a declaration of independence. Division between 'hawks' and 'doves' in the national government (the former led by former PNGDF commander Ted Diro), did not help the situation.

Towards the end of 1990 the security forces returned to the north of the province and attempts were made to re-establish government services. In so doing, the national government made use of local 'resistance' forces opposed to the BRA and of an emerging structure of councils of chiefs. But continued opposition from the BRA and its supporters, exacerbated by well-publicised reports of human rights violations by the security forces (involving, in one instance, the use of Australian-supplied helicopters), proved a barrier to resolution of the conflict.

With BRA activists and supporters coming and going between south Bougainville and the nearby Solomon Islands, and PNGDF naval vessels attempting to prevent such movement, it was not long before clashes occurred between members of Papua New Guinea's security forces and the Solomon Islands' Police Field Force. Relations between the two Melanesian states deteriorated in 1992 after Papua New Guinea security forces personnel killed two Solomon islanders during a raid on a Solomon islands village believed to be harbouring BRA rebels, and the Solomon Islands island of Oema was 'annexed' by PNGDF troops. While Papua New Guinea's prime minister apologised to his Solomon Islands counterpart over these incidents, he nevertheless commented that if the Solomon Islands did not cooperate in preventing the use of its territory by the BRA, 'this sort of thing is bound to happen'.

With the national government gradually regaining control in the province, towards the end of 1994 peace talks were arranged on Bougainville in the presence of a multinational South Pacific Peacekeeping Force and a UN observer. The non-attendance of the top leadership of the BRA and its political arm, the secessionist Bougainville Interim Government (who alleged there were plots to assassinate them) meant that no settlement could be reached. However, some prominent members of the BRA did attend and those present – particularly women community leaders – called on both sides to end the conflict. A dialogue has since been established and some progress has been made towards peace and reconstruction. As part of this process a Bougainville Transitional Government has been created, with a former national court judge and BRA supporter as its premier. But even if peace is restored in the near future, there will be lingering bitterness between different factions on Bougainville and a massive problem of restoring health, education and other services in the province, let alone reviving the mine.

The role of the PNGDF

In the years preceding independence there was a good deal of discussion amongst Papua New Guinea's emerging national leaders as to whether the independent state should maintain a defence force; some saw a relatively well-provisioned and cohesive military as a possible future threat to democratic government. In the event, it was decided to maintain a defence force, separate from the police constabulary, and having rejected suggestions that it be given a political role (along the lines of the Indonesian military's *dwifungsi*), the principle of subordination of the military to the civil authority was established in the constitution and emphasised in military training. In effect, the PNGDF was maintained, in the independent state, in essentially the form in which it had been inherited from Australia. It has continued to receive substantial support through the Australian government's Defence Cooperation Program, but has also signed status of forces agreements or memoranda of understanding with New Zealand, the United States, Indonesia and Malaysia. In 1992, the Defence Secretary said, 'We may be able to learn from Malaysia on handling domestic security and from Indonesia on civic action'.

Foremost amongst the functions of the PNGDF listed in the constitution was the defence of Papua New Guinea, though it seems to have been generally accepted that, if attacked, Papua New Guinea could do little more than mount a holding operation awaiting assistance from Australia and other allies. The PNGDF's role also included provision of assistance to the civilian authorities, but only under certain specified, limiting conditions.

In 1980 the PNGDF, with logistic support from Australia, assisted the newly independent Vanuatu government in putting down a local rebellion, but apart from that, patrolling the borders with Indonesia (to deny access to the OPM) and later the Solomon Islands (to prevent the movement of the BRA between Bougainville and Solomon Islands), and policing the waters of its 200-mile economic zone against illegal fishing, the PNGDF has not had an external role to play.

As foreseen by many commentators in the 1960s and 1970s, on the other hand, the PNGDF has been called upon increasingly to assist the civil authorities in maintaining law and order. Since the 1980s, it has been employed regularly to assist civilian authorities, including, in 1992, to help maintain order during the national elections. More substantial involvement in internal security operations came in 1988 with the beginning of the armed rebellion on Bougainville. The subsequent inability of the security forces to resolve the conflict has been seen by many within the military as due to political indecision – or, as some put it, 'political interference' – which has restrained the security forces at key periods. Since 1989 there have been several public altercations between senior military personnel and politicians. A more balanced assessment, however, might point to well-documented instances of inefficiency and lack of discipline, to human rights abuses which alienated large segments of the local community, and to the impossibility, in situations like that on Bougainville, of achieving a military solution without a political settlement.

The 1991 report, *Security for Development*, observed that, 'the most serious, foreseeable threats facing Papua New Guinea are internal' and recommended that the PNGDF's priorities be reordered. This was done the same year; towards the end of 1991 the Papua New Guinea and Australian governments released a joint statement announcing that Papua New Guinea was to give highest priority to internal security needs, and that Australian assistance would be geared to supporting Papua New Guinea's disciplined forces in maintaining internal security.

Persistent over-budget spending by the Defence Department, largely as a result of the Bougainville operation (in 1995 operations came to a virtual standstill because the PNGDF was unable to pay local creditors), and its inability to pay allowances due to servicemen, have strained relations between the PNGDF and the government. A 10-year programme to reorganise force structure, increase force size (from around 4000 to 5200 in 1995), and replace major equipment was drawn up in 1988 but did not receive cabinet approval until 1991 and was never implemented. Meanwhile, a law and order sectoral programme presented with the 1993 budget proposed to cut force size and place primary emphasis on civic action work.

Since the early 1980s, when the force's first Papua New Guinean commander resigned to contest elections, there has been a politicisation of senior ranks of the PNGDF. Several senior officers have left to stand for parliament and there is now a well-established pattern of changing commanders when governments change. Notwithstanding this, relations between senior military officers and the government have gone through some tense periods, with the PNGDF defying the government on at least two significant policy decisions affecting its interests. Discipline within the Force has also been a problem. There have been several incidents in which PNGDF personnel have gone on a rampage against civilians, and one in which soldiers marched on the National Parliament following a pay dispute.

Nevertheless, despite rumours of possible coups in 1977 and 1987, and an incident in 1990 in which the police commissioner, apparently under the influence of alcohol, called for an uprising of police and soldiers, the army has politically remained in the barracks. Considering the small size of the PNGDF and the country's geographical and social fragmentation, early fears of a military coup seem unrealistic.

Overview

Given its geographical location and its historically close ties with Australia, Papua New Guinea has, since independence, enjoyed a fairly stable and benign security environment, enabling it to develop a universalist foreign policy while assuming something of a leadership role amongst the Melanesian states and acting as a 'bridge' between Asia and the island Pacific. Despite occasional tensions in its relations with Indonesia, arising from the activities of the OPM and the Indonesian military in the border area, and recently in its relations with the Solomon Islands, over the activities of the BRA and its supporters (who have maintained an office in the Solomon islands capital Honiara), Papua New Guinea has been free from external threat and has generally enjoyed good relations with its neighbours. Internal problems of social unrest, however, exacerbated by poor economic management and growing popular cynicism towards politicians, have come to pose a serious challenge to the country's social, economic and political development, particularly since the outbreak of rebellion on Bougainville. These developments have been recognised in a formal shift in the priorities of the PNGDF, from external defence to internal security, and have been acknowledged in Australia's development assistance and Defence Cooperation Programs. Although successive Papua New Guinea governments have attempted to address the problems of law and order through a series of measures, sometimes draconian, a poorly developed sense of nationhood and state legitimacy, and limited state capacity, have substantially constrained such efforts. This has created some problems for Australia, as Papua New Guinea's closest neighbour and its major source of development assistance and defence support, and it has clearly troubled some

Indonesian security analysts, who, placing a high premium on political stability, see Papua New Guinea's lack of tight social control as a potential security problem for the region.

By 1996 there had been significant progress towards a resolution of the conflict on Bougainville but little progress towards the solution of broader problems of social order. The picture of a weak state, heavily dependent on the disbursement of favours to remain in office, is by no means unique to Papua New Guinea, however. In Papua New Guinea's case a robust, if poorly coherent, democratic polity seems unlikely to pose any significant security threat to its neighbours.

13

THE BOUGAINVILLE CRISIS*

The Bougainville mine, in Papua New Guinea's North Solomons (formerly Bougainville) Province, is one of the world's largest gold and copper mines. In recent years it has accounted for around 40 per cent of Papua New Guinea's exports and between 17 and 20 per cent of government revenue. Ever since mining exploration began on Bougainville in the 1960s, however, the presence of the mining company has been a source of resentment amongst the local people in the Panguna area, as well as for many Bougainvilleans not directly affected by the mining operations. Opposition to mining development was a major factor in the emergence of a secessionist movement on Bougainville in the late 1960s. Melanesian people have a deep attachment to their land and, notwithstanding a complex structure of compensation payments, many Bougainvilleans feel that the development of the mine has robbed them of their land, irrevocably changed their way of life, and left them with little of the wealth they believed the mine would bring. As a prominent member of the Panguna landowner group said in 1989: 'Land is marriage – land is history – land is everything. If our land is ruined our life is finished' (Perpetua Serero, quoted in *Post-Courier* 1 May 1989).

---

* This paper was written in 1990, in what proved to be an early stage of the Bougainville conflict, and describes the origins of the conflict (it draws on a 1989 consultancy report by the author). It was published in *The Pacific Review* 3(2) 1990:174-77, and is reproduced by kind permission of the publishers, Taylor and Francis. A later account of the Bougainville Crisis was written for the Australian Parliamentary Research Service (May 1996).

Towards the end of 1988 the longstanding antipathy of landowners towards the mining company, Bougainville Copper Limited (BCL), erupted into violence. A group of militant landowners took to the bush and began a campaign of sabotage and harassment of mine employees. In December the mine was forced to close, briefly, and subsequently a curfew was imposed in the main towns and the mine area in an attempt to contain the conflict.

In March 1989 riots broke out in the town of Arawa after a Bougainvillean woman was killed by migrant workers from the Papua New Guinea mainland and two mainlanders were killed in retaliation. Although these incidents were not directly related to the dispute between landowners and BCL they revived separatist sentiments on Bougainville and strengthened popular support for the militant landowners. There was considerable tension on the island following these riots and Papua New Guinea Defence Force (PNGDF) personnel were brought in to support the already augmented police forces in maintaining law and order while representatives of the national and provincial governments attempted to negotiate with the militants. Shortly after, an army patrol which had arrested several dissidents was ambushed and two soldiers and two villagers were killed. It was subsequently reported that security forces had launched a 'full-scale military operation' against the rebels.

On 12 April 1989, *Niugini Nius,* one of Papua New Guinea's two daily newspapers, published an undated letter from the leader of the militant landowner group, former BCL employee Francis Ona. In it he set out the revised demands of the militant group, which included compensation of Kina 10 billion (about $US12 billion) for environmental and other damage caused by BCL's operations (BCL claims that this is more than double the total revenue generated by the company since mining commenced in 1967), 50 per cent of all profits, and the withdrawal of security forces. The letter went on to state: 'We are not part of your country any more . . . We belong to the Republic of

Bougainville and we are defending our island from foreign exploitation.'

Despite a substantial police and military presence, continued guerilla activities against mine installations and employees forced the closure of the mine in May 1989, and it remained closed throughout the year. With the security situation largely unchanged, in January 1990 the mine was placed on a 'care and maintenance' basis and the company began to evacuate its employees from Bougainville. Although the national and provincial governments and representatives of the landowners agreed on a 'peace package', which promised increased compensation and development funds to both landowners and the provincial government, the militant landowner group rejected the terms of the government's offer and maintained an effective guerilla campaign against the mine and in defiance of the government security forces.

In March 1990 a ceasefire was negotiated and the national government began a withdrawal of its security forces. The government also promised a further transfer of powers to the provincial government.

The basis of landowner demands

When, in 1964, Conzinc Riotinto of Australia (CRA) began mineral exploration in the area of the Bougainville mine, it met with resistance from landowners, some of whom were arrested for damaging CRA property. There was also resistance to the forced appropriation of village land for the development of port facilities for the mine. However, with the promise of compensation, assurances that the mine would bring benefits to the people, and threats that the government would act against troublemakers, most of the villagers became, in the words of the CRA consultant anthropologist, Douglas Oliver, 'resigned more or less disconsolately to what they regard as another example of the white man's cupidity, deceit and irresistible power' (Oliver 1973:162).

In the early stages of mining exploration and development, compensation was paid to landowners under a series of ad hoc arrangements and provisions of the amended *Papua New Guinea Mining Ordinance.* Between mid-1966 and the end of 1969 some 350 claims for compensation were heard by mining warden's courts and a schedule of compensation payments was drawn up. Following the company's decision to go ahead with the mine development, separate leases were negotiated to cover access roads, the mine area, and an area for mine waste (tailings) disposal. The leases were granted despite a legal challenge by villages in the mining area which was disallowed in the High Court of Australia. In response to a demand for royalties, the Bougainville Agreement of 1967 between BCL and the Papua New Guinea administration provided for payment of 1.25 per cent of the value of exports, of which 5 per cent was to be distributed amongst landowners and 95 per cent paid to the government (initially the national government but after 1974 the provincial government).

The construction of the mine and the mine access road produced a new spate of claims for compensation. Bedford and Mamak estimated that between 1968 and 1974 some 2654 compensation payments were made to Bougainvilleans, amounting to $A1.6 million (Bedford and Mamak 1977). The system of compensation payments which developed in the years from 1968 was, however, extremely complex and highly contentious. Most of the payments, moreover, were quite small and in many cases were once-off payments. Their distribution amongst communities, and within communities (most payments being made to a head of family) amongst individuals, was very uneven.

In 1979, a Panguna Landowners Association (PLA) was formed amongst customary landowners in the roads, mine and tailings lease areas, primarily to press for a review of the compensation arrangements. Following a confrontation between landowners and BCL, which resulted in a minor riot and the looting of the Panguna supermarket, an agreement was drawn up in 1980 which incorporated all existing compensation payments, introduced some new forms of compensation and a price indexing formula for recurring payments, and established a Road Mine Tailings Lease Trust Fund (RMTLTF) into which portions of certain payments were to be made. The intention of the new agreement was to consolidate the various forms of compensation that had developed, discourage new claims, and achieve a greater degree of equity in the distribution of payments.

The 1980 agreement, however, did not resolve longstanding dissatisfaction with the level and direction of compensation payments. Moreover, it created another problem. The RMTLTF was created as a fund into which certain payments would be directed with a view to establishing capital for income-generating investments and other benefits for landowners in the lease areas. It comprised 75 landowner representatives and was administered by an eight-person executive committee. Initially, with a capital of Kina 1.3 million, the fund appears to have run harmoniously, investing in interest-bearing deposits and making loans to its members. There was, however, a substantial write off of bad debts in these early years and when in 1983 the chairmanship of the RMTLTF changed, a non-Bougainvillean manager was appointed and a stricter financial regime was instituted. Fewer loans were made to members and funds were mainly invested in local businesses, real estate and plantations. But, while the RMTLTF's assets and income increased under this new regime, members themselves received less and soon began to complain that the executive was not using RMTLTF funds for the benefit of the landowners; executive members were accused of mismanaging the fund and taking the money for their own purposes.

This disagreement within the landowner group reflected in part a growing split between an 'old guard' and the younger generation of people who not only resented the presence of BCL but also believed that the older generation had largely acquiesced in BCL's takeover of their land and had diverted what compensation had been received to their own ends. Some, like Francis

Ona, had indeed received little from the compensation payments.

It was in this context that a challenge to the leadership of the PLA took place in 1988 and a new phase of landowner militancy began. But the divisions within the landowner group also help explain the difficulties which the government faced in attempting to negotiate a settlement, and the tensions which became apparent amongst villages in the mine area. (One of the first victims in the armed conflict was a prominent PLA executive member, Mathew Kove, who is believed to have been murdered by his nephew. Other landowners who supported a settlement with the government in 1989 were attacked by the militant landowner group.)

Thus, in a pattern not unfamiliar to students of Melanesian politics, what appears at first to be a straightforward case of a landowner group seeking increased compensation from a mining company turns out to be a multi-layered mass of shifting elements whose motivations range from a broad Bougainville nationalism to internal family fighting.

The move from protest to insurgency

As early as March 1988 a delegation of some 500 landowners, organised by the militant faction of the PLA, marched on BCL with a petition of demands. Not satisfied with the company's response the group organised a number of protests including a sit-in at the mine which caused production to stop for several hours. Explosives were stolen from the BCL magazine in April 1988, and proposed action to shut down the mine was narrowly averted late in 1988 following a visit by the national minerals and energy minister.

But things came to a head in November at a public meeting organised to discuss a consultants' report on alleged pollution from the mine. When the report refuted claims by villagers that mine pollution was responsible for the death of fish and the disappearance of flying foxes (popular as food), Ona and others stormed out. A few days later armed men held up the BCL magazine and took a large quantity of explosives. In the following weeks mine installations were subjected to a series of arson and sabotage attacks: power pylons were blown up, a repeater station was damaged, and there was a fire at one of the company's maintenance depots. Workers repairing lines were threatened by armed men. Early observers expressed some surprise at the professionalism of the saboteurs; it was later revealed that one of Ona's fellow militants was a former PNGDF officer and explosives expert, Sam Kauona (a Bougainvillean, but not from the immediate mine area).

In the early phase of confrontation there appears to have been a good deal of sympathy towards Ona and the militant landowner group. The premier of the North Solomons, Joseph Kabui, himself from the tailings lease area, said in February 1989: 'The people see Ona as some kind of folk hero and champion of the Panguna land rights cause' (*Times of Papua New Guinea* 2-8 February 1989). Kabui later declared: 'I also support what he was fighting for, but not his terrorist methods' (*Post-Courier* 20 February 1989). However, as the conflict escalated, as additional police and later PNGDF reinforcements arrived, and as the inevitable toll in human lives and the destruction of houses and property increased, the extent of support for Ona seems to have become more problematic. Moreover, it became increasingly less clear who 'the militants' were. Reports suggest that by about March 1989 there were at least three elements: the original militant faction of the PLA together with a number of sympathetic (mostly younger) villagers in the mine area; members of the anti-government, cultic movement, the 'Fifty Toea Association', led by Damien Damen, from the Kongara area south of the mine, with whom the militants took refuge; and so-called *raskol* elements, gangs of petty criminals, concentrated in south Bougainville, who were ready to take advantage of the general disruption caused by the conflict. Estimates of the number of people involved have ranged from a 'hardcore' of 75 to around 1000 (effectively, the adult population of villages in the lease area). Early in 1989 the hardcore militants began referring to themselves as the 'Bougainville Revolutionary Army' (BRA). As with many Melanesian organisations, the BRA appears to have no formal structure, but its actions against the security forces and the mine – and specifically its ability to successfully resist the PNGDF for over 12 months – suggest that it has been unusually well organised.

Initially the demands of the militant landowner group had to do with compensation – though, as noted, their figure of K10 billion was unrealistic, and the demand for 50 per cent of profits, retrospectively, scarcely less so. Failing in this, they called for the closure of the mine, and adopted terrorist activities to secure their objective. At least as early as February 1989, Ona was calling for secession and in April he claimed to speak for an independent Bougainville Republic and demanded the withdrawal of troops from 'our country'. Although the Papua New Guinea government persisted in attempts to negotiate a settlement with the landowners, as the military confrontation escalated Ona must have realised that he was on a one-way track; in response to calls to surrender he replied that he would only surrender 'in a coffin'. In June, the national government declared a state of emergency in the North Solomons, and in September a leaked cabinet document was published, which said: 'Cabinet is now firmly of the view that a state of insurgency exists' (*Niugini Nius* 22 September 1989).

Moreover, as so frequently happens in such situations, the security forces, brought in to restore law and order, soon became a major part of the problem. As early as April 1989 some 50 police had been sent from Bougainville for various breaches of discipline. There were reports of villages being burned and innocent villagers being harassed. The provincial premier, who had already been assaulted by militants, was beaten up by security force personnel, and the deputy premier was partially blinded after being poked in the eye with a rifle barrel. A subsequent Amnesty International report confirmed claims of human rights violations and police and army brutality. More recently it has been alleged that in February 1990 several suspected militants, including a Uniting Church pastor, were murdered by security forces and their bodies dropped into the sea from a helicopter (*Sydney Morning Herald* 8 March 1990). Such reports have shocked Papua New Guineans and longtime observers of Papua New Guinea, and have undoubtedly damaged the reputation of the police and the PNGDF. They also raise questions about the extent of government control over the security forces. More specifically, the actions of the security forces served to strengthen secessionist sentiments on Bougainville and reinforce demands for the removal of the security forces from the island.

The issue of secession

The development of the Bougainville mine coincided with the emergence in Papua New Guinea both of a pro-independence nationalism and of a number of regionally based 'micro-nationalist' movements. On Bougainville, a broad sense of ethnic separateness, which drew on a clear difference in physical appearance between Bougainvilleans and mainlander 'red skins' and a feeling that Bougainville had been neglected by the administration, encouraged the growth of such movements from as early as the 1950s. During the late 1960s and early 1970s, subnationalist sentiments became more widely and more firmly established in Bougainville and there were frequent calls, if not for secession and independence, at least for autonomy. The development of the Bougainville mine was not the sole cause of this subnationalist movement but the activities of the mining company and the administration, particularly in relation to land acquisition, and the broader social impact of the mine development, most obviously the huge influx of non-Bougainvillean people, were inextricably tied up with it.

In 1972, a Bougainville Special Political Committee (BSPC) was created, representative of local government councils, subnationalist movements and others in the (then) Bougainville District, to consider Bougainville's future political status. The BSPC subsequently made a submission to the Constitutional Planning Committee, calling for the establishment of a Bougainville District Government. When the national government rejected these demands there was talk of secession and thinly veiled threats were made about closure of the mine (Mamak and Bedford 1974). The Constitutional Planning Committee subsequently recommended the establishment of an interim district government on Bougainville and in 1974 this was done. When, the following year, the national parliament acting as a constituent assembly resolved to omit the provincial government provisions from the constitution, Bougainville's political leaders unilaterally declared the independence of the Republic of the North Solomons. Bougainville member of the House of Assembly, John Momis (currently national minister for provincial affairs), travelled to New York to press Bougainville's claim to independence before the United Nations Trusteeship Council. Under pressure, the national government resumed negotiations, the interim provincial government was reinstated, and an agreement was signed with Bougainville's leaders in 1976 which provided the basis for an Organic Law on Provincial Government under which a nationwide system of provincial government was established.

With the introduction of provincial government, and following the renegotiation of the Bougainville Copper Agreement in 1974, Bougainville subnationalism appeared to have declined, though a widespread feeling of separateness remained, along with general antipathy towards BCL, and pockets of active secessionist sentiment.

Thus, in early 1989 when Francis Ona challenged the authority of the national government and spoke out for Bougainville independence, he struck a sympathetic chord amongst many Bougainvilleans. In April, a meeting of provincial assembly members and community leaders discussed the situation in the province and reports suggested that the mood of the meeting was in favour of secession. Subsequently a committee of the provincial assembly, headed by John Bika, prepared a report on the Bougainville situation. It did not support secession but called for full provincial autonomy in all areas except defence, currency and foreign affairs. (Six weeks later, on the eve of the signing of an agreement between the national and provincial governments and landowner representatives, Bika was murdered by militant landowners.)

The significance of recent developments on Bougainville

Until 1988 the North Solomons Province was, as well as the richest, one of the more orderly and peaceful provinces in a country beset by problems of law and order. Its slide into militant advocacy, insurgency, and now a virtual abdication of governmental authority, raises serious questions about the capacity of the national government, and specifically about its control over the country's security forces.

One of the effects of the unrest which developed in 1988-89 was a massive migration of non-Bougainvilleans from the mine area and from plantations and towns across the province. With this, and especially following the deaths of police and army personnel in encounters with the BRA, has come a good deal of antipathy towards Bougainvilleans in other parts of the country. Many Bougainvilleans, fearing retribution, have left jobs on the mainland, and even in places such as the two university campuses in Port Moresby and Lae, Bougainvilleans have been subjected to abuse, notwithstanding a good deal of early sympathy for the landowners' demands against BCL. Within the North Solomons, too, tensions have arisen amongst Bougainvilleans which will not quickly disappear. Families have been divided over the issue of compensation and the tactics of the BRA, provincial leaders have been killed and beaten, and some Bougainvilleans who have lost homes and property blame the militants for resorting to violence.

More particularly, the behaviour of the security forces has not only tarnished the (already questionable) reputation of police and the military but has seriously damaged relations between the national government and the people of the province. The withdrawal of the security forces and the granting of increased autonomy to the provincial government may have done something to prevent a further deterioration in national-provincial relations, but it has done little if anything for the general law and order situation on the island and appears to leave the provincial government a hostage to the BRA (or perhaps a faction of the BRA, since Kauona seems to have replaced Ona as spokesman for the militants).

Economically, the closure of the mine and the exodus of non-Bougainvilleans has had a devastating effect on business and the plantation economy within the province. Nationally, the impact of the mine's closure was cushioned by the existence of gold and copper reserves and of a Mineral Resources Stabilisation Fund. But, by late 1989, the economic effects of the conflict had become apparent, in part through an across-the-board cut of 25 per cent in national government expenditures. Optimists point to other major resource projects about to come on-stream in Papua New Guinea, but the effects of the militant landowners' campaign have not been lost in other parts of the country. Already there have been renewed demands by landowners in the area of the Ok Tedi mine, and forewarnings from the premier of Enga, where a major gold and copper prospect at Porgera is currently under development, that if Engans do not receive a satisfactory settlement they too can bring a prospective mine to a standstill. This in turn must have negative effects on potential foreign investors.

Politically, the Namaliu government wisely persisted with a strategy of negotiation with landowners and the provincial government, while attempting – with little success, it seems – to keep the military on a tight rein. But others around the prime minister have been inclined to show less patience, and the failure of the government quickly to resolve the issue has done little to build confidence in a coalition government which already looked shaky.

In 1990 there was some optimism about the prospects for maintaining the ceasefire and reopening the mine. But even if this were achieved, there will be scars from the conflict, nationally and provincially. In retrospect the events of 1988-90 may well appear as something of a watershed in Papua New Guinea's political history.

14
'MUTUAL RESPECT, FRIENDSHIP AND COOPERATION'? THE PAPUA NEW GUINEA-INDONESIA BORDER AND ITS EFFECT ON RELATIONS BETWEEN PAPUA NEW GUINEA AND INDONESIA*

In October 1986 the foreign ministers of Indonesia and Papua New Guinea signed a *Treaty of Mutual Respect, Friendship and Cooperation*. Under the terms of this treaty the two countries agreed not to threaten or use force against one another and not to cooperate with others in hostile or unlawful acts against each other or allow their territory to be used by others for such purposes. Provision was made also for consultation and negotiation in the event of any dispute. The treaty was hailed by President Suharto as 'another milestone in the history of both countries,' while Papua New Guinea's prime minister and foreign affairs secretary said it would give direction for the future and inspire confidence in Papua New Guinea and its regional neighbours (*Niugini Nius* 28 October 1986).

More sceptical opinion, however, observed that that there was nothing in the new treaty which either had not been the subject of earlier and repeated verbal assurances, or was not already adequately provided for in the existing agreement on border administration. Some opposition politicians in Papua New Guinea went further, describing the treaty as 'naive and misconstrued,' 'sinister,' and 'an exercise in hypocrisy' (*Post-Courier* 29 October 1986; *Times of Papua New Guinea* 31 October–6 November 1986).

In an attempt to throw some light on these conflicting viewpoints, and to promote a better understanding of the nature of

* This paper was first published in the *Bulletin of Concerned Asian Scholars* 19(4) 1987, and is reproduced by kind permission of the *Bulletin*.

relations between Papua New Guinea and Indonesia, this paper looks at the problems that have arisen over the common border between Indonesia and Papua New Guinea and at the effects of these problems on relations between them.

The border

The land boundary between Indonesia and Papua New Guinea stretches for some 750 kilometres. In the south it passes through dry savannah and swampy rain forest before ascending into the precipitous limestone ridges of the rain-soaked Star Mountains. North of the Star Mountains it traverses the Sepik floodplain, another series of formidable limestone ridges and raging mountain streams, and a thickly forested swampy plain before rising again into the Bougainville Mountains, which ultimately fall, in a succession of limestone cliffs, into the sea at Wutung. The border itself is poorly defined. Until the 1980s there were only fourteen markers along the entire length of the border.

Except for parts of the border area roughly from the Fly River bulge to 100 kilometres north of it, the region is sparsely populated by people who are shifting cultivators with small groups of predominantly hunter-gatherers. In the north and south respectively taro and yam provide the main staples, and in the higher altitudes some depend on sweet potato; for the rest sago is the main staple, supplemented by hunting. As in other countries whose borders are the product of arbitrary decisions by past colonial regimes, language groups and traditional rights to land as well as relations of kin and of trade extend across the border. Indeed, border surveys during the 1960s established that the border ran right through the middle of at least one village and that several villages which had been administered by the Dutch were in fact in the Australian territory. As recently as 1980 a village included in Papua New Guinea's National Census was found to be inside the Indonesian province of Irian Jaya [which in 2000 President Wahid renamed Papua]. The situation is made more complex for administering authorities by the tendency, amongst these shifting cultivators, for whole villages to shift, re-form and disappear over time.[1]

The land border is defined by an Australian-Indonesian border agreement of 1973, and is the subject of an agreement between Indonesia and Papua New Guinea concerning administrative border arrangements. The latter was originally drawn up in 1973 (when Australia was the administering authority in Papua New Guinea, though the agreement was signed by Michael Somare as chief minister), and was renegotiated, with minor but significant amendments, in 1979 and 1984. The agreement contains provisions relating to definition of the border area, the establishment of a joint border committee and consultation and liaison arrangements, border crossings for traditional and customary purposes and by non-traditional inhabitants, customary border trade and the exercise of traditional rights to land and waters in the border area, border security, quarantine, navigation, exchange of information on major construction, major development of natural resources, environmental protection, and compensation for damages. There is, however, no provision for hot pursuit across the border, and Papua New Guinea has repeatedly resisted proposals for joint military patrolling of the border.[2]

Border problems

Since earliest colonial times New Guinea's borders have been an occasional source of friction between the neighbouring administrations. In recent years problems between Papua New Guinea and Indonesia over the border area have arisen from four sources.

---

[1] A population survey of the border census divisions of Papua New Guinea's Western Province by the Papua New Guinea Institute of Applied Social and Economic Research (IASER), provides some documentation of this fluidity (see Pula and Jackson 1984).

[2] The agreement is reproduced in May (1979).

Border crossers

In principle, one can distinguish four broad classes of border crossers. First, there are villagers from the border area who cross from time to time, as they have always crossed, to make sago, to hunt, or to visit kin. As mentioned above, provisions are specifically made for such traditional movement in the border agreement. Traditionally, such movement was two-way and sometimes, in response to drought or disputes, for example, was more or less permanent. Within comparatively recent times there has been continuous substantial movement across the border. During the Dutch period many Papua New Guinean villagers from the border area travelled across into what was then Dutch New Guinea, attracted by the superior facilities available, especially at centres such as Hollandia (now Jayapura), Mindiptanah, and Merauke. Lately, it seems, movement has tended to be in the opposite direction, though greater formality of border administration and the existence of different *lingua franca* has inhibited such movement. The IASER survey referred to above (footnote 1) has documented extensive cross-border ties for the people of Western Province: in the North Ok Tedi and Moian census divisions, for example, 47.8 and 30.3 per cent respectively of adults surveyed were born in Irian Jaya (Pula and Jackson 1984:35). In view of the frequency of movement in the past, the IASER report ventured the opinion that 'a good proportion of these border crossers [i.e. those who crossed in Papua New Guinea in 1984] could have good claim to Papua New Guinea citizenship' (ibid.:33). Much the same situation exists in Papua New Guinea's northern Sandaun Province. In 1984 the Sandaun premier, Andrew Komboni, accused the Australian, Indonesian, and Papua New Guinean governments of ignoring the 'family aspects' of the situation created by border crossing: 'The traditional ties amongst the border villages in the northern sector have not changed since the white man declared an invisible border line', he said: 'A good number of the current refugees . . . have run this way with the natural inclination to seek family refuge. It must be shocking . . . to see blood relatives being jailed or being held at camps' (*Post-Courier* 12 April 1984). As the IASER report observed: 'As time has passed and as the rule of national laws has reluctantly spread to the border area so people going about their business as they have done for centuries are slowly being made into law-breakers at worst or "problems" at best' (ibid.:32).

Second, there has been a comparatively small number of Irianese nationalists seeking political asylum in Papua New Guinea. Some of them have been allowed to resettle in Papua New Guinea but increasingly in the 1980s those granted refugee status were passed on, with the assistance of the United Nations High Commission on Refugees (UNHCR), mostly with considerable difficulty, to third countries such as Sweden and Greece.

Third, from time to time, as a result of military activity in Irian Jaya, groups of Irianese villagers have crossed over into Papua New Guinea seeking temporary refuge often with kin or *wantoks*.[3]

Fourth, the OPM [*Organisasi Papua Merdeka*, or Free Papua Movement] guerrillas operating in the border area have on occasion crossed over into Papua New Guinea seeking refuge from Indonesian military patrols; this, however, is a special class of border crosser and will be considered in more detail below.

Papua New Guinea policy on border crossers was established during the colonial period. As I described it some years ago:

> People crossing the border are required to report to one of the several patrol posts along the border and state their reason for crossing. If their purpose is 'traditional' (the most common is sago making) they are normally allowed to stay until they have finished what they came to do and are then expected to return across the border. If they apply for political asylum they are held

[3] *Wantoks* are literally members of the same language group, but in more general usage, friends.

> until a decision is taken and then either granted permissive residence or told to return. In all other cases they are told to return. If they refuse, they are arrested and charged as illegal immigrants, after which they may be deported. [May 1979:98-9]

The essential features of this policy have not changed since the 1960s, though in early 1984, in an apparent effort to discourage movement across the border, the Papua New Guinean government charged all adult male border crossers as illegal immigrants. In practice, as I noted in 1979, the stringency with which this policy has been applied has varied since 1962. However there is nothing to support the claim that while Papua New Guinea was a colony Australia kept the border pretty well sealed but that since 1975 administration of the border has been relatively lax. In fact a close look at the available evidence suggests that from about 1972, when the first Somare government came to office, Papua New Guinea has taken an increasingly hard line against border crossers in all of the above categories (ibid., also see May 1986).

With regard to numbers: before 1984 the best estimate of Irian-born residents in Papua New Guinea was around 2000 to 3000; many of these must have slipped across the border prior to 1962, and taken up residence in villages or towns, without acquiring formal residential status. Of this number, by 1986 217 had been granted citizenship in Papua New Guinea – 157 in 1976 and another 60 in 1977. No Irian-born person had been granted citizenship after 1977.

But while, 'in principle', border crossers may be classified in four categories, in practice, of course, border crossers are not always so easily distinguishable. Until 1984 the number of border crossers was sufficiently small that this was not a major problem. In 1984 this changed. Following an abortive local uprising by Irianese nationalists in Jayapura in February, and a subsequent military crackdown, hundreds and eventually thousands of Irianese began to pour across the border into Papua New Guinea.

By 1986 there were between 10 000 and 12 000[4] border crossers in camps along the border, few of whom showed any inclination to return in the foreseeable future, and many of whom claimed traditional land rights. Most of these people were 'refugees' in the broad sense that they crossed the border to take refuge from conditions they found threatening. The Papua New Guinea government was reluctant to refer to them as refugees, however, because of what this implied with regard to the UN 1951 Convention and 1967 Protocol Relating to the Status of Refugees, and preferred to see them as Indonesian citizens who would soon return to their own side of the border. In fact, the Papua New Guinea government has tried to persuade groups to return, and even forcibly repatriated some, in the face of ongoing domestic reaction. Border crossers themselves, especially those from the border area, were also reluctant to have themselves classified as refugees, for fear that they too might be sentenced to resettlement in Sweden.

The handling of the refugee problem during 1984-85 has been documented elsewhere.[5] It is a story that does not reflect well on either Indonesia or Papua New Guinea, nor on regional neighbours who have shown no willingness to help resettle those who are eventually granted refugee status. Indonesia, having initially refused to acknowledge that an influx of border crossers had occurred, hampered efforts at repatriation by its reluctance to formally guarantee the safety of returnees, its refusal for some time to agree to UNHCR involvement in repatriation, and its insistence that Papua New Guinea provide a list of names of the border crossers. Indonesia's foreign minister Mochtar subsequently made

[4] The exact number was difficult to measure, since quite large groups of people appear to have moved back and forth across the border. Towards the end of 1984, however, the official estimate was about 12 000. Following a change of government in Papua New Guinea in late 1985 the figure generally quoted officially was 10 000 (though there was no apparent reason for the reduction, except perhaps an earlier Indonesian claim, never verified, that 2000 border crossers had returned to Irian Jaya).

[5] See chapters by May and by Smith and Hewison in May (1986).

it quite clear that he had little interest in the return of the border crossers. In an interview with Peter Hastings (*Sydney Morning Herald* 16 August 1986) Mochtar is reported to have said: 'The biggest problem of these Irianese . . . is . . . they want to go through life doing nothing at all. We don't need people like that'. On the other hand it is clear that, having failed to force a large number of border crossers to return by withholding assistance, during 1984-85 the Papua New Guinea government made little effort to screen the refugee camp inmates with a view to sorting out 'genuine refugees' from potential returnees. The government of Paias Wingti, which came to office in Papua New Guinea in late 1985, elaborated a new policy on border crossers, which included greater UNHCR involvement, greater commitment to the screening of border crossers, and the possibility of some resettle-ment of refugees within Papua New Guinea.[6]

The OPM

Since the early 1960s groups of Irianese nationalist rebels have operated in the border area of Irian Jaya, in the name of the *Organisasi Papua Merdeka*, and have occasionally crossed over into Papua New Guinea for 'R & R' (rest and recreation) or to escape Indonesian military patrols. There have also been isolated instances of OPM sympathisers within Papua New Guinea seeking to materially assist the OPM, but usually without effect. Two notable cases were a rather naive letter of 1981 seeking arms from the USSR, which was returned – and intercepted – because the address ('Mr George, c/o Poste Restante, Turkey') was

[6] The financial cost of maintaining the border camps was met in part by the UNHCR, to which Australia contributed $2.9 million, and in part by church organisations. The Indonesian government contributed only about $50000 for the support of its citizens; according to a former Papua New Guinea foreign minister, 'most of our requests have gone unanswered.' (*Post-Courier* 20 August 1984). [Subsequently many of the border crossers were resettled at East Awin, in Papua New Guinea's Western Province.]

insufficient, and an unsuccessful attempt in 1984 to obtain weapons through an Australian mercenary soldier.

Successive Papua New Guinea governments, however, have consistently reiterated their denial of Papua New Guinea soil to OPM rebels, and Papua New Guinean police and military and administrative personnel patrol the border area in an effort to discourage movement across the border in general and to deny the use of the border area to OPM guerrillas in particular. In 1983 and again in 1984 budgetary allocations for police and military border patrols were increased, and it was announced that an infantry company would be stationed at Kiunga. In addition several Irianese granted permissive residence in Papua New Guinea were deported for violating their promise, as a condition of their residence in Papua New Guinea, not to engage in political activity relative to their nationalist sentiments. Indeed since the late 1970s the Papua New Guinea government's actions against OPM supporters have brought retaliatory threats from the OPM. For example, in 1984, in protest against planned repatriation of border crossers, specific threats were made against the Ok Tedi mining project and against individual Papua New Guinean politicians and bureaucrats, and in 1985 government officers were pulled out of refugee camps in the Western Province following threats from the OPM's regional commander, Gerardus Thomy.

Notwithstanding this, Papua New Guinea has been accused of not devoting adequate resources to the task of 'sanitising' the border. Whether or not Papua New Guinea should spend more on border patrolling depends on judgements about priorities. Personally, given the nature of the terrain and the small number of OPM guerrillas involved, I see little reason why a country whose main concerns are with the economic and social development of its people should divert scarce resources away from development in an attempt to deal with a problem of internal security that a large, militaristic neighbour has been unable to resolve – especially when that neighbour has in turn denied that there is conflict in Irian Jaya, told Papua New Guinea that affairs in Irian Jaya are none of its business, and denied the existence of the OPM itself. But whatever one feels on this issue, it is simply not accurate to accuse Papua New Guinea, as some have, of not taking firm action against the OPM.

Border violations

Although it has occasionally been proposed by Indonesia, Papua New Guinea has stopped short of the sort of border agreement that Indonesia has with Malaysia, which allows 'hot pursuit' across the border, and on a number of occasions Papua New Guinea has indicated its unwillingness to enter into joint military patrols along the border. On several occasions since the late 1960s, however, Indonesian troops or aircraft have crossed the border, intentionally or unintentionally. In mid 1982, for example, Indonesian military patrols crossed into Papua New Guinea on seven occasions, despite Papua New Guinea protests, and a helicopter flying the regional military commander to Wamena, 240 kilometres southwest of Jayapura, landed 'off course' at a mission station 10 kilometres southeast. In March 1984, two Indonesian aircraft appear to have violated Papua New Guinea's air space over the Green River station, and the following month there were three border violations, during one of which Indonesian troops destroyed houses and gardens in a hamlet on the Papua New Guinea side of the border.

Such incursions are perhaps inevitable given the nature of the terrain, the poor demarcation of the border, and the circumstances of a guerilla campaign. But such 'incidents' have been magnified rather than minimised by the refusal of the Indonesian government, or the inability of its civil and military elements, to deal credibly with Papua New Guinea's diplomatic protests or requests for explanation. In the instance of the 1982 border violations, for example, the Indonesian government denied that the incursion had occurred, saying that some

Indonesian hostages taken in an OPM raid had been recovered from the Papua New Guinea side of the border by Irianese villagers, and accusing Papua New Guinea of not honouring its obligations under the border agreement; in fact, the hostages – who had been held on the Indonesian side of the border – were subsequently released to Irianese villagers, who escorted them across to Papua New Guinea for repatriation. In the case of the 1984 air violations the Indonesian ambassador in Papua New Guinea initially denied that the planes were Indonesian (despite the fact that the Antara News Agency had already reported an exercise by the Indonesian air force in the vicinity of Jayapura); and though the possibility of an unintentional incursion appears to have been admitted privately in Jakarta (*Far Eastern Economic Review* 12 August 1984; *Niugini Nius* 30 March 1984) a belated official response to Papua New Guinea's diplomatic protests again denied that an incursion had taken place. And with respect to the military incursions of mid-1984 (which occurred during military exercises in the border area, of which – despite earlier Indonesian assurances – Papua New Guinea had not been informed), in the face of all evidence Armed Forces Commander Benny Murdani denied the violation, suggesting that perhaps the offenders were OPM guerillas in Indonesian army uniforms. About the same time the governor of Irian Jaya was reported as saying, 'There have never been any clashes between the Indonesian defence forces and the OPM rebels. There have been no clashes, never' (*Times of Papua New Guinea* 31 May 1984).

Such response to legitimate concerns of the Papua New Guinea government have created tensions in the relations between the two countries which might easily have been avoided by a more honest response. In mid-1984, Papua New Guinea's foreign minister stated that while Papua New Guinea did not want to interfere in Indonesia's internal affairs the border crossers were not simply an internal affair. Since they had a direct effect on Papua New Guinea, the means by which Irian Jaya was governed and developed was of immediate interest to Papua

New Guinea (*Times of Papua New Guinea* 24 May 1984; *Post-Courier* 24 July 1984). In late 1984, frustrated and 'bloody angry', the Papua New Guinea foreign minister expressed his dissatisfaction with the border situation in a speech to the UN General Assembly. The Indonesian ambassador in Washington, it was reported, was 'painfully surprised'.

Border development

Except perhaps at its northern extremity, the border area is poorly endowed and poorly developed. On the Papua New Guinea side, apart from the fortuitously placed Ok Tedi mine, what development there has been – a little basic infrastructure (schools, aid posts, minor roads) – is largely the result of the attention the border area has received during periods of OPM-Indonesian military confrontation. Agricultural development has been inhibited by the government's policy on quarantine. A modest border programme was included in Papua New Guinea's 1980-83 National Public Expenditure Plan, but the allocation for border development was cut in 1983 as a consequence of declining revenue from domestic sources and Australian aid.

On the Irian Jaya side, the construction of the trans-Irian Jaya highway and the transmigration programme are seen as major contributions to development, and there have been announcements of plans to improve communications in the border area (including, according to one report, colour TV sets) in the hopes of persuading Irianese border dwellers to stay on their side of the border. More recently it has been reported that under a three-year plan for development in the border area, commencing in 1986, Indonesia will spend about $US66 million on highway construction, airstrips, health and education services, industrial and agricultural developments, and the establishment of trading centres to improve living conditions in the border area. A further $US2 million is to be spent on border security, including an army base.

From time to time joint border development has been proposed as the solution to problems of Irianese separatism and of border crossers. Indeed in 1983, before thousands of Irianese began flooding over the border into Papua New Guinea, Peter Hastings observed that Papua New Guineans from the Vanimo area were visiting Jayapura and suggested that greater development efforts on the Irian Jaya side could soon produce a situation where the predominant flow of border crossers was from Papua New Guinea to Irian Jaya (*Sydney Morning Herald* 2 May 1983). In fact, however, border development programmes on the Papua New Guinea side, and it seems on the Irian Jaya side, have not made much progress, and since 1984 the Papua New Guinea government has been more concerned with sustaining (and eventually getting rid of) border crossers than with providing the improved conditions along the border that might attract more crossers. In the longer term there is some concern in Papua New Guinea that if large-scale transmigration to Irian Jaya takes place, and unless it proves more successful than it has to date in Irian Jaya, the resultant tensions could aggravate the problems of border crossing.

Relations between Indonesia and Papua New Guinea

In the 1980s there was some discussion of the broad defence and security aspects of Indonesia-Papua New Guinea relations.[7] The informed consensus seemed to be that Indonesia does not have expansionist ambitions towards Papua New Guinea (past expansionist ventures being the product of particular historical circumstances that cannot be projected onto the Papua New Guinea case), but that there might be other imaginable circumstances that would worry Indonesia and perhaps lead to intervention in one form or another, specifically the emergence of a

[7] See, for example, the chapter by J.A.C.M. Mackie in May (1986) and Crouch (1986).

hostile (communist-sympathetic) regime in Papua New Guinea or some kind of breakdown in Papua New Guinea's political system, perhaps caused by regional dissidence.

I have no fundamental quarrel with this analysis, except perhaps a logical quibble about the 'particular-historical-circumstances' argument: granted that the particular historical circumstances of Indonesia's original claim to West Papua, of *konfrontasi* over Malaysia, and of East Timor do not apply to independent Papua New Guinea, can Papua New Guineans be blamed for sometimes wondering whether *another* set of particular circumstances, domestic and/or external, might be seen by Indonesia as justifying another expansionist venture? It is in this context (and perhaps also in view of recurring Indonesian claims that it has acted with 'restraint') that some of us find the discussion of possible Indonesian 'intervention' in the event of a 'hostile' or 'unstable' regime in Papua New Guinea disquieting. I hope we may assume that those who present such scenarios agree that the emergence of an 'unstable' regime (whatever that means) in Papua New Guinea, or even one hostile to Indonesia, would provide no justification for Indonesian intervention. Having said that, I suggest that the more immediate concerns in Indonesia-Papua New Guinea relations have to do not with possible invasion or intervention but with the problems arising over administration of the common border. Administration of the border takes place within the framework of the border agreement and in the context of a mutual commitment to good relations. Since 1981 there have been annual Joint Border Committee meetings, irregular meetings of a Border Liaison Committee, and a number of meetings of technical subcommittees.

In fact, however, relations between the two governments over the border have been marked by short cycles of tension followed by self-conscious cordiality. When 'incidents' have occurred, the machinery of border liaison has generally proved ineffective. For example, when in 1983 it was discovered that Indonesia's trans-

Irian Jaya highway crossed into Papua New Guinea at three points, it took more than three months to secure an acknowledgement that the incursion had taken place and 16 months before the offending sections of road were closed off. (Incidentally, the incursion might have been established several months earlier had Indonesia not withdrawn from a joint survey exercise, because of inadequate funds.) Again, in February 1984, with refugees flooding across the border, Indonesian officials told the Papua New Guinea foreign minister that they knew nothing of reported events and assured him that things in Jayapura were 'normal', even though residents on the Papua New Guinea side of the border confirmed that Jayapura was in darkness and its government radio station silent. At this time there had not been a border liaison meeting for over a year – allegedly because of lack of funds – and the Vanimo-Jayapura 'hot-line' had been out of service for several months. And when in April 1984 Papua New Guinea sought a meeting of the Joint Border Committee to attempt to achieve some resolution of the situation, its foreign secretary found himself sitting down with a local *bupati* who was apparently uninformed on the subject of the border crossings and had no authority to make decisions. A scheduled meeting the following month was cancelled at short notice when the Irian Jaya governor withdrew from the Indonesian delegation due to 'over commitment'. This sort of situation, combined with evasive responses to Papua New Guinea's protests over border violations as described above, did much to generate the strains that characterised Indonesia-Papua New Guinea relations throughout most of 1984-85.

There has been a tendency amongst distant commentators on Indonesia-Papua New Guinea relations to refer to the problems, and to urge greater 'understanding', as though the Indonesia-Papua New Guinea relationship is symmetrical. Obviously it is not: border crossing has been essentially one way; border violations have been entirely at Papua New Guinea's expense; Papua New Guinea does not have a domestic insurgency problem overflowing its border; it has been Papua New Guinea rather than Indonesia that has had to seek explanations for external disturbances, and responsibility for the frequent ineffectiveness of liaison machinery has been largely on the Indonesian side. Moreover, the huge disparities in size and military capacity between the two countries create an obvious imbalance in the relations between them. One might be excused for wondering too, when Indonesia's foreign minister defends *transmigrasi* on the grounds that Indonesia does not intend to preserve Irian Jaya as 'a human zoo', if there are not also imbalances in cultural attitudes. Any sensible discussion of possible improvements in Indonesia-Papua New Guinean relations must begin by recognising this imbalance.

Conclusion

In view of this analysis, it is difficult to see what the *Treaty of Mutual Respect, Friendship and Cooperation* can hope to achieve that could not be achieved just as easily without it. It is, as one Papua New Guinean described it, '*bilas tasol*' ('just ornament'). At the most, it might give an assurance of goodwill on both sides that will help ease the tensions that emerged during 1984-85. Ultimately, however, relations between the two countries are likely to be determined less by the rhetoric of diplomats than by the day-to-day problems of administering a border that divides an independent Melanesian nation from an Indonesian province in which a Melanesian liberation movement remains active after some two decades of Indonesian rule. In this context it is perhaps worth noting that in the same week as the much-heralded *Treaty of Mutual Respect, Friendship and Cooperation* was signed, a Joint Border Committee meeting in Bandung broke up after four days, having failed to reach agreement on proposals for joint search-and-rescue operation in the border area.

15

FROM PROMISE TO CRISIS: A POLITICAL ECONOMY OF PAPUA NEW GUINEA*

The island of New Guinea was one of the last parts of the globe to be subjected to European colonisation,[1] and when the eastern half of the island became independent as Papua New Guinea, in 1975, the extent of colonial penetration remained limited.

In the latter part of the nineteenth century there was some land alienation and development of European plantations in the territories that were to become Papua New Guinea, principally in the New Guinea islands (New Britain, New Ireland and Bougainville) and along parts of the north and south coast. Much of the commercial interaction between Europeans and the Melanesian population, however, involved trade: principally the exchange of copra, pearl and trochus shell, and bird of paradise skins for European goods.

Following World War I there was further plantation development, primarily by big companies, and a system of head taxes on Papua New Guineans encouraged them to produce copra and

---

* This paper was first published (in French) in *Revue Tiers-Monde* XXXVIII (149), 1997.

[1] The northeastern part of New Guinea was annexed by Germany in 1884. The same year Britain annexed the southeastern portion. The western half of the island (now the Indonesian province of Irian Jaya) had earlier become part of the Dutch East Indies. British New Guinea (renamed Papua) was transferred to Australian protectorate status in 1906, and German New Guinea was occupied by Australia in 1914 and subsequently became a UN Trusteeship under Australian administration. The two were administered jointly during World War II and continued to be governed as a single entity after the war.

to engage in wage labour. In the 1920s, discoveries of major gold deposits brought a new influx of prospectors and by the early 1930s gold had surpassed copra and coconut products as the territories' major export. At the outbreak of World War II, however, the European presence in Papua and New Guinea was still largely confined to the New Guinea islands and a thin coastal fringe; the populous hinterland of the New Guinea highlands, which in the postwar years became the main focus of the colonial administration's development efforts and a reservoir of labour for coastal plantations, had only recently been contacted by miners, missionaries and government officers, and was still largely unknown territory to Europeans.

After World War II the pace of development accelerated. The colonial administration was gradually re-established and extended into more remote areas.[2] Pre-war copra, cocoa and rubber plantations were at least partly rehabilitated and new plantations, largely in the hands of individual Australian settlers, were established. Much of the new development took place in the highlands, where coffee ('brown gold') was the main crop.

In the new, postwar, political climate, however, government policy was directed more specifically to ensuring that economic development benefitted the Papua New Guinean population. In presenting the *Papua New Guinea Provisional Administration Bill 1945*, Australia's Minister for External Territories told the Australian parliament:

> This Government is not satisfied that sufficient interest had been taken in the Territories prior to the Japanese invasion . . . the Government regards it as its bounden duty to further to the utmost the advancement of the natives . . . In future, the basis for the economy of the territory will be native and European industry with the limit of non-native expansion determined by the welfare of the natives generally. [*Commonwealth Parliamentary Debates*

[2] Much of the interior was declared 'restricted' until well into the 1950s, however, and some areas were still restricted in 1970.

(House of Representatives) vol.183:4052-54, 4 July 1945]

Settler plantations, on leased land, were seen in part as a means of stimulating Papua New Guinean smallholder cashcropping, and by the mid 1960s smallholder production of coffee exceeded plantation output. Government expenditures on education, health and physical infrastructure expanded markedly; cooperatives and local government councils were established, and early steps were taken to identify and assist entrepreneurs.

In 1950 the first of a series of UN visiting missions came to Papua New Guinea to review Australia's performance of its mandate in New Guinea. It called for increasing participation of Papua New Guineans in the economy and in politics. A Legislative Council was established the following year. Shortly after this the Australian government commissioned a team from The Australian National University to review the development needs of Papua and New Guinea; their report recommended that priority be given to the development of smallholder agriculture, the establishment of a road system, and fiscal reforms; they also endorsed the administration's policy of limiting land alienation (Spate, Belshaw and Swan 1953).

Development proceeded on a broad front during the 1950s and 1960s, though there was considerable ambiguity about the objectives of Australian policy, with many in Australia and Papua New Guinea believing until well into the 1960s that incorporation of Papua New Guinea as a seventh state of Australia was a serious option, and that economic self-sufficiency must precede political independence (see, for example, Parker 1970). In 1962 another visiting UN mission criticised Australia for its lack of clear forward planning (an initial five-year plan had been drawn up the previous year). Partly in response to this criticism the Australian government invited the IBRD to carry out an economic survey of the territory, and this was done in 1964.

The so-called World Bank report of 1964 (IBRD 1965) became a major focus for debate about Papua New Guinea's economic future.[3] In essence, it supported a development strategy based on maximising the growth of areas of greatest export agricultural potential, through the provision of infrastructure, credit and extension, and the encouragement of foreign private capital. It also urged investment in human capital, and advised that the level of government services (which largely reflected Australian standards) be geared to local conditions. Little was said about either mining or the possibility of industrialisation.

Although the World Bank report provided a more comprehensive review than had been previously attempted, its recommendations suggested no real substantive change of direction in existing policy. Following the appointment of an Economic Adviser (Bill McCasker) to the administration in Port Moresby, in 1967-1968 two major economic policy papers were produced[4] which, in effect, sought to provide a basis for implementing the administration's economic development strategy in broad conformity with the World Bank report. These documents provoked a lively debate, particularly amongst academics in Port Moresby and Canberra, progressives within the Reserve Bank of Australia's Papua New Guinea Department, and Papua New Guinea's emerging nationalist elite.[5]

---

[3] See reviews of the report by P.W.E. Curtin, in *New Guinea* 1(1) March/April 1965:52-58, and by H.C. Coombs and B. Schaffer, in *New Guinea* 1(2) June/July 1965:62-69, 72-79.

[4] *Territory of Papua and New Guinea, Economic Development of Papua and New Guinea, prepared by direction of the Administrator* (Port Moresby, 1967); *Programmes and Policies for the Economic Development of Papua New Guinea,* prepared by direction of His Honour the Administrator (Port Moresby, 1968). Also see *Papua New Guinea, The Development Programme Reviewed. Prepared in the Office of Programming and Co-ordination by Authority of the Administrator's Executive Council* (Port Moresby, 1971).

[5] R. Kent Wilson, 'Priorities in development', *New Guinea* 2(4) January 1968:40-46; P.W.E. Curtin, 'How to be inconsistent', *New Guinea* 3(1) March/April 1968:19-24; R. Crocombe, 'That five year plan', *New Guinea* 3(3) December 1968/January 1969:57-70; J. Kaputin, 'Australia's carpetbaggers', *New Guinea* 4(1) March/April 1969:35-42; H. Arndt, R. Shand and E.K. Fisk, 'An answer to Crocombe – I, II, III', *New Guinea* 4(2) June/

The existence, in the late 1960s of an articulate nationalist group was itself a reflection of the increasing pace of political development. From the largely administration-dominated Legislative Council, Papua New Guinea had progressed to its first national elections in 1964 and its second in 1968. Although the first two parliaments continued to be heavily influenced, if not actually dominated, by appointed and elected expatriates, and although a sense of national purpose was still embryonic, the lead-up to the 1968 election saw the emergence of Papua New Guinea's first major political party, the Papua and New Guinea Union (PANGU Pati), and growing demands for increased Papua New Guinean participation in politics and the economy and for early independence. Expectations of political change were further stimulated by the 1969 visit of Australian parliamentary opposition leader Gough Whitlam, who promised that if elected he would grant Papua New Guinea independence. By the late 1960s, also, construction had commenced on what was to be one of the world's largest gold and copper mines, at Panguna on Bougainville. Though there was early opposition from local landowners, the Bougainville mine promised to give the young nation a degree of economic security substantially greater than was implicit in dependence on export agriculture.

In 1972 Whitlam became prime minister in Australia. The same year Papua New Guinea's third national elections brought to office the territory's first truly Papua New Guinean government, a coalition headed by Pangu Pati's Michael Somare. The following year Papua New Guinea became self-governing and in September 1975, in the face of some opposition from leaders in the more recently-contacted highlands (who feared economic and political domination by the better educated coastals), it achieved independence.

July 1969:54-71; R. Crocombe, 'Crocombe to his critics', S. Epstein, 'The plan's assumptions', M. Reay, 'But whose estates?', *New Guinea* 4(3) September/October 1969:49-68.

Within Papua New Guinea the period of transition to independence, from around 1969 to 1975, was one of intense debate and, relative to the preceding decades, very rapid change. Increasing political awareness, and rising levels of education (the University of Papua New Guinea produced its first graduates in 1970) was reflected in widespread public discussion of Papua New Guinea's development options, including alternative models of economic development from Tanzania and China.[6] Following Somare's election in 1972 as chief minister (a position which in 1975 translated into prime minister) the office of the economic adviser was closed and a new Central Planning Office was established. The same year a team led by Michael Faber from the Overseas Development Group, University of East Anglia, was contracted by the IBRD to prepare a report on development strategies for Papua New Guinea over the next five years.

The Faber Report, as the team's report became known, marked a departure from the comparative orthodoxy of previous reports. In its opening paragraphs, its authors stated:

> The model of development proposed, and the balance of development strategies recommended will be seen to be different from those incorporated in the last programme of the Papua New Guinea administration. This should not be regarded as a criticism of the last programme so much as a recognition that the situation has changed profoundly, both economically and politically . . . whatever the merits of the past programme, the consultants . . . found that the need for a marked change in emphasis was now widely recognised by those in public life and in the public service both within the Papua New Guinea administration and within the Commonwealth government. [Overseas Development Group 1973:2]

As reflected in its recommendations, the main elements of this change in emphasis were: (i) increased indigenous control of the economy and indigenisation of many forms of economic activ-

[6] See, for example, Clunies Ross and Langmore (1973); May (1973).

ity (including the public service); (ii) increases in opportunities for employment, especially income-generating self-employment; (iii) emphasis on 'projects and policies that will directly increase the incomes of PNG nationals, and of the poorest sections amongst PNG nationals'; (iv) greater emphasis on rural development, including food production and the development of urban-centres in the countryside; and (v) a progressive reduction in dependence on aid and, ultimately, foreign capital. Underscoring the change in emphasis, the authors said: 'Maximisation of the growth of Papua New Guinea's domestic product has not, of itself, been set as a long term objective . . . we believe that the emphasis of the next plan should be on localisation/indigenisation, rather than growth' (ibid.:4, 13).[7] Other recommendations included: procedures to release land for development; removal of a wide range of regulations 'imposing western-style standards of design, safety, etc.' on small scale operators; broadening of the tax base; a 'regional development package' (which included strengthening local government and cooperatives, decentralisation of service centres and development of growth points in less developed areas, and the promotion of self-help at village level); and a review of the Bougainville mining agreement.

The Faber Report resonated the predominant nationalist economic discourse of Papua New Guinea in the early 1970s. The approach was further endorsed in late 1972 by the announcement of the Somare government's eight-point 'Improvement Program'. The government's eight aims were listed:

(1) a rapid increase in the proportion of the economy under the control of Papua New Guinean individuals and groups and in the proportion of personal and property income that goes to Papua New Guineans;

(2) more equal distribution of economic benefits, includ-

[7] In support of this priority the Faber Report quoted estimates which showed the indigenous share of domestic product declining from 32 to 28 per cent (or 68 to 56 per cent including subsistence production) between 1965/66 and 1969/70 (ibid.:13).

ing movement toward equalisation of incomes amongst people and toward equalisation of services amongst different areas of the country;

(3) decentralisation of economic activity, planning and government spending, with emphasis on agricultural development, village industry, better internal trade, and more spending channelled to local and area bodies;

(4) an emphasis on small scale artisan, service and business activity, relying where possible on typical Papua New Guinean forms of business activity;

(5) a more self-reliant economy, less dependent for its needs on imported goods and services and better able to meet the needs of its people through local production;

(6) an increasing capacity for meeting government spending needs from locally raised revenue;

(7) a rapid increase in the equal and active participation of women in all forms of economic and social activity;

(8) government control and involvement in those sectors of the economy where control is necessary to achieve the desired kind of development.

The eight aims were subsequently incorporated in the five 'National Goals and Directive Principles' included in the preamble to the constitution of the independent state in 1975. These were listed as:

1. Integral Human Development;
2. Equality and Participation ('. . . all citizens to have an equal opportunity to participate in, and benefit from the development of our country');
3. National Sovereignty and Self-reliance ('. . . Papua New Guinea to be politically and economically independent, and our economy basically self-reliant');
4. National Resources and Environment ('. . . national resources and environment to be conserved and used for the collective benefit of us all . . .');

5. Papua New Guinean Ways ('... to achieve development primarily through the use of Papua New Guinean forms of social, political and economic organisation').

They also provided the basis for a new economic plan, *Strategies for Nationhood* published by the Central Planning Office in 1974.

While the emphasis on localisation, equitable distribution, and decentralisation addressed issues of real and practical importance in the early 1970s, it also served broader political ends. As one who was closely involved in policy development in the early 1970s later commented: the statement of the eight aims 'was probably the closest the ministry came to expressing a general ideological stance... [though] like the Bible, the Eight Aims could be quoted in support of almost any proposal' (Lynch 1981:13).[8] There was, clearly, an element of romanticism in elaboration of the new development strategy, as there was in the broader contemporary philosophy of 'the Melanesian Way' (Narokobi 1980), and it was frequently observed that the eight aims did not provide a specific guide for policy formulation, and even implied conflicting directions. Moreover, McCasker and others could rightly point out that the *extent* of change in policy objectives was often overstated, since issues such as localisation, equitable and regionally balanced development, and priority to rural development had long been recognised in policy documents.

Nevertheless the strong endorsement of these values in the lead-up to independence was important, and the rhetoric was given concrete form in a number of new institutional arrangements in the 1970s.[9] These included the publication of 'Investment Guidelines' in 1973 and the creation of a National Investment Development Authority (NIDA) to regulate the direction

[8] Lynch was secretary to the cabinet from 1972 to 1979.

[9] The development of the institutional framework for economic policy-making between 1972 and 1977 is described by R. Garnaut in Ballard (1981:157-211). A more comprehensive account of policy development during the colonial period is contained in Downs (1980).

and level of foreign equity investment; the establishment of a Village Development Task Force and an Office of Village Development; the funding of a Rural Improvement Programme to support development initiatives by local government councils; the preparation of a feasibility study of regional growth centres; the creation of a National Cultural Council and provision of funding for regional cultural activities; and the promulgation of a Leadership Code and creation of the office of Ombudsman.

Responding to demands by Bougainvillean politicians and the advice of the Faber Report, in 1974 the government renegotiated the Bougainville mining agreement, securing what was generally accepted as a better formula for the government. At the same time a Mineral Resources Stabilisation Fund was created, to even out the impact on the budget of fluctuations in the flow of revenue from the mine.

On independence, then, Papua New Guinea could count, on the positive side: a reasonably diversified, and generally healthy, export-based agricultural industry; one of the world's largest copper and gold mines already in operation, and other mining and petroleum projects in prospect; a framework of soundly based policy-making and financial institutions; a healthy subsistence economy; and an ideological commitment to an open economy – though with some provisions aimed at achieving increased local participation in business – and to policies of interpersonal and inter-regional equity in the distribution of benefits from development. The negotiation of a five-year development assistance agreement with Australia also gave the independent government the initial security of fairly generous budgetary support.

As against this, amongst a number of negative factors, Papua New Guinea inherited: a workforce which was, relative to other countries in the region, low-skilled and highly paid (making industrialisation a difficult development option);[10] a large and

[10] For a critical discussion of wages, productivity, non-wage costs, and the possibilities for industrial manufacturing see Mannur and Gumoi (1994).

mostly inexperienced public sector workforce and a level of government service provision which could not be sustained without external assistance (in 1975/76 28 per cent of government income came from the Australian aid grant, and in 1976/77 39 per cent); an economy heavily dependent on commodity prices over which Papua New Guinea had no control; a high population growth rate (around 2.4 per annum between 1970 and 1975); and an emerging problem of maintaining law and order.

During the first decade or so of independence, economic performance was generally satisfactory: although increases in real GDP were small (averaging 1.4 per cent over the period 1976-1985) they were, except for one year, positive; there was a gradual diminishing of dependence on aid; and, under the government's 'hard kina' strategy,[11] economic management was sound. In 1982 a second large gold and copper mine had come into production at Ok Tedi, and further mining and petroleum prospects were being developed or investigated at Porgera, Mt Kare, Misima, Lihir, Kutubu and Hides. Notwithstanding this, the rate of growth in real GDP declined each year from 1987, with negative growth rates in 1989 and 1990 after a rebellion led by disgruntled landowners in the Panguna area forced the closure of the Bougainville mine. GDP then increased strongly in the early 1990s before slumping again in 1994.

In the period of accelerated development between 1945 and 1975, the government sector was a major contributor to growth, particularly in promoting agricultural development and small business. In 1974/75 government spending represented 36 per cent of market GDP and public sector employment accounted for 28 per cent of the formal workforce. Following independence, government spending was sustained at what were, by regional standards, fairly high levels by development assistance from Australia, mostly in the form of general ('untied') budgetary assistance. In the early post-independence years, consistent both

[11] For an early discussion of the hard kina strategy see Dahanayake (1982 Part V), and Garnaut and Baxter in consultation with Krueger (1983).

with the Papua New Guinea government's stated aim of self-sufficiency and with the policy of the Australian government, the level of development assistance was progressively reduced, falling from around 40 per cent of government revenue at independence to 25 per cent in 1985 and 17 per cent in 1988. This was substantially offset by increases in taxation revenues, principally from the Bougainville copper mine, which in 1988, before its forced closure, contributed around 17 per cent of government revenue.

The closure of the Bougainville mine deprived Papua New Guinea of a major source of government revenue and export earnings. Nevertheless, government spending continued to rise. Already in 1986 there were warnings about excessive government spending and of a bias to recurrent spending at the expense of maintenance and new capital expenditure. Nevertheless, in many rural areas, from at least the mid 1980s there was a visible deterioration of roads, schools, aid posts, and other capital. The effects of this were often exacerbated by destruction of assets as a result of tribal fighting, 'payback' for non-payment of demanded compensation, or vandalism. Problems of maintaining law and order had emerged in the 1970s, but reached new levels in the 1980s; the first of several states of emergency was declared in the national capital, Port Moresby in 1984 and the Papua New Guinea Defence Force (PNGDF) was called in to provide assistance to civilian authorities.[12]

Following a change of government in 1985, which brought highlander Paias Wingti to the prime ministership, there was also an increasing politicisation of the public service. This was underlined in 1986 by the introduction of a *Public Services (Management) Act*, which effectively emasculated the quasi-independent Public Services Commission and greatly facilitated the government's control over public service matters (see Turner 1991).

As well as cutting off revenue from the mine, the Bougainville

[12] This was authorised by Section 202 of the constitution. For a discussion of the PNGDF's role in assisting the civilian authorities, see May (1993).

crisis made additional demands on expenditure: defence spending rose from K40 million in 1988 to K92 million in 1991, and from 4.3 to 7.7 per cent of total government expenditure; moreover the Defence budget was repeatedly overspent (by a massive 81 per cent in 1991). Notwithstanding this, in 1993-94 PNGDF aircraft and boats could not be used because the PNGDF could not pay for fuel and maintenance.

With expenditure growing in excess of revenue, government borrowing expanded to cover the resulting deficits. By 1994 debt repayment and servicing represented about one third of government spending and the government was facing a fiscal crisis.[13] In March 1994 the government introduced a 'mini budget' and three months later negotiated a loan of $US102 million from a group of overseas private lenders based in the Cayman Islands on the condition that interest on and repayment of the loan have first call on mining and petroleum revenues which would otherwise be directed to the Mineral Resources Stabilisation Fund. By this time the government owed substantial amounts to local creditors (including members of the Papua New Guinea Defence Force) and its international credit rating was being downgraded.

In August 1994 there was a further change of government which brought in a new coalition headed by former finance minister and prime minister Sir Julius Chan. Within weeks of taking office the Chan government first devalued and then floated the kina, but persistent fiscal and foreign exchange difficulties forced the government in 1995 to negotiate an emergency loan brokered by the World Bank. Popular protest at some elements of a structural adjustment package attached to the loan was expressed in public demonstrations. The following year a World Bank-led

---

[13] For a more detailed commentary on developments in the early 1990s see *Pacific Economic Bulletin* 10(1) 1995, Special Issue on Papua New Guinea; AIDAB, *The Papua New Guinea Economy. Prospects for Sectoral and Broad Based Growth*. International Development Issues No. 30 (Canberra, 1993), and AusAID, *The Economy of Papua New Guinea. 1996 Report*. International Development Issues No. 46 (Canberra, 1996).

mission visited Papua New Guinea but after an acrimonious exchange with Papua New Guinea officials left without completing consultations, and payment of the second tranche of the loan was postponed.

In 1994 Papua New Guinea's per capita GNP was $US1474, about three times the level at independence, placing it amongst the middle range of developing countries (above Indonesia and the Philippines). However, on a range of social indicators Papua New Guinea was ranked amongst the lower-income developing countries, and in most areas covered by these indicators improvements from 1975 were more modest.

Given its fortunate resource endowment, its early aspirations, and its generally sound beginnings, why has Papua New Guinea's economic performance been so disappointing, and what are its future prospects?

Before addressing these questions at a broader level it is necessary to make an initial point about the principal economic aggregates. Although commodity prices generally improved in the early 1980s, low levels of growth in GDP, a steady decline in the real value of Australian development assistance, a high population growth rate, and high expectations on the part of Papua New Guinea's citizens, placed severe strains on government financing. Papua New Guinea's second large gold and copper mine, at Ok Tedi, came into production in 1982, but because of tax concessions written into the Ok Tedi agreement the mine did not make a direct contribution to public revenue until 1987. Soon after this the Bougainville crisis took away the revenue from the Bougainville mine and imposed new costs of maintaining internal security and providing for restoration and rehabilitation. As a result, the additional revenue from Ok Tedi and other minerals projects coming on stream in the early 1990s did little more than fill the gap created by the loss of revenue from Bougainville and the continuing decline, in real terms, of Australian aid. In other words, the so-called 'mining boom' was largely illusory; the real effect of the boost from new mining and petroleum projects was not so much to finance new levels of expenditure as (at least initially) to prevent a fiscal collapse.

However, the failure of successive governments to deal effectively with an emerging fiscal crisis reflects more systemic factors in Papua New Guinea's political economy.

As noted above, during the colonial period, and especially in the period of accelerated development from 1945 to 1975, government played a major role in development. It promoted agricultural development (especially smallholder development) and marketing; it encouraged small-scale indigenous business; it financed the provision of education and health services (with continued assistance from the churches); and it provided basic infrastructure.

In the post-independence period smallholder agriculture continued to expand, though certainly not evenly across the country. But plantation agriculture had mixed fortunes: while plantation-based oil palm production flourished, the traditionally dominant plantation crops – copra, cocoa and rubber – languished. In the pre-independence period many foreign-owned plantations were run down in anticipation of expropriation or sale to Papua New Guineans; many were sold, often subdivided, and with agricultural commodity prices generally down in the latter part of the 1970s, and frequently inexperienced management, many plantations performed poorly.[14] Apart from agriculture: for a number of reasons, largely cultural, small business ventures, including cooperatives, had very limited success,[15] and manufacturing growth was predictably modest. Consequently, while some Papua New Guineans prospered as a result of salaried employment, income from small business or self employment, rent from urban land, or smallholder agriculture (especially coffee, but increasingly also betel nut and food crops),

---

14 Plantation agriculture was the subject of a conference in Port Moresby in 1980; see Walter (1982).

15 Indigenous business ventures were the subject of extensive studies in the late 1960s and early 1970s. See, for example, Wilson (1972) and Andrews (1975), and references cited therein.

most found themselves with small cash incomes, increasing demands for cash (e.g. for education and transportation), and, in many rural areas, deteriorating infrastructure and diminishing access to government services. Often these problems were compounded by increasing pressure on land and growing rural and urban lawlessness.

In this context, the prospect of substantial revenue and infrastructural development from large-scale mining and petroleum prospects, and subsequently from logging, had an obvious appeal to a national government facing heavy demands for public expenditures, a weak tax base, and declining real levels of development assistance. For some communities, also, the immediate prospect of payments from minerals and forestry projects outweighed considerations of longer-term costs. But for those communities which did not have the prospect of large-scale resource exploitation, development options were fewer; and when government failed to meet their developmental demands, they often turned away from, or against, government.

In the lead-up to independence there was a general assumption that political parties would develop in Papua New Guinea to match the country's essentially Westminster-style parliamentary system, and that the emerging nationalism of the early 1970s would provide the basis for a developing sense of national identity. In fact, neither expectation was fulfilled. While three parties – Pangu (notwithstanding two major splits), the Peoples Progress Party and the Melanesian Alliance – have been a significant force now for more than two decades, other parties have proved transient; the major parties have never been sharply differentiated ideologically, nor have they developed a substantive mass base; mostly they have revolved around a few key individuals and have displayed strong regional biases; party discipline has been weak and membership fluid. Since the first Papua New Guinean government emerged from the elections in 1972, every government has been a coalition government and both 'party hopping' and changes within coalitions have been fairly common. Of the six changes of government which have occurred since 1972, three have been the result of votes of no confidence precipitated by coalition shifts. Moreover, each successive election has seen a larger number of candidates contesting. Along with this there seems to have been an increasing tendency for candidates *not* to align themselves with parties (or to loosely align themselves with more than one), in order to maximise the bargaining power of successful candidates in the post-election horse-trading that accompanies attempts to put together a winning coalition. Taken in conjunction with the high turnover of MPs at election time (in all but one election since 1972, 50-55 per cent of members have failed to gain re-election), this has produced a system strongly inimical to rational long-term policy making and particularly prone to politicians seeking short-term advantage. Political candidates outlay relative large sums to get elected and incur debts to their supporters; if elected they naturally seek to recoup these outlays, with interest, and to reward their supporters. In implicit recognition of this in early 1996 each MP was receiving K0.5 million from an Electoral Development Fund for discretionary allocation within his electorate.

Popular realisation that most politicians seek election for personal and parochial gain, and that those who have 'their' MP in parliament stand to do better than those who do not, has encouraged the view that politics is a form of *bisnis*. While this has brought about increased (and increasingly confrontational) competition for parliamentary office, it has also produced considerable popular cynicism about politics and politicians. Such cynicism has tended to undermine the perceived legitimacy of the state – a legitimacy already challenged by Papua New Guinea's poorly developed sense of nationhood and the continuing political salience of parochialism, regionalism – Papuan, Highlands and Islands – and (in the case of Bougainville) separatism.

In 1975 Nigerian scholar Peter Ekeh suggested that the colonial experience in Africa had produced 'a unique historical configuration'. Ekeh distinguished two public realms in post-colonial Africa: a 'primordial' public realm, governed by 'primordial groupings, ties, and sentiments', and a colonially derived 'civic' public realm. Most educated Africans, Ekeh argued, are members of both these public realms:

> On the one hand, they belong to a civic public from which they gain materially but to which they give only grudgingly. On the other hand they belong to a primordial public from which they derive little or no material benefits but to which they are expected to give generously and do give materially ... their relationship to the primordial public is moral, while that to the civic public is amoral. The dialectical tensions and confrontations between these two publics constitute the uniqueness of modern African politics ... The unwritten law of the dialectics is that it is legitimate to rob the civic public in order to strengthen the primordial public. [Ekeh 1975:108]

The effects of this confrontation, according to Ekeh, included 'tribalism' and corruption.

The recent political economy of Papua New Guinea suggests that the African situation is less unique than Ekeh suggested. In a 1996 speech to a conference in Port Moresby, former finance secretary and central bank governor, Mekere Morauta said: '... the most corrosive and intractable problem we face now is corruption'. Morauta went on to talk about 'the institutionalisation of short-term ad hoc decision-making and the catastrophic decline in the power, status, morale and productivity of the bureaucracy', a development which he dated to the mid 1980s (Morauta 1996). [In July 1999 Morauta became prime minister.]

In the past decade or so corruption has become entrenched in Papua New Guinea, notwithstanding the restraining influences of the Leadership Code and the Ombudsman Commission. Such corruption takes two forms: that in which individuals use their position within the state for personal gain, and that in which individuals use their position to transfer resources, in Ekeh's terms, from the civic public to the primordial public. The first of these, as Ekeh suggests also for Africa, is unlikely to be sustainable in the longer term unless individuals can isolate themselves from the demands of their primordial publics. The second form, on the other hand – the transfer of resources from the civic to the primordial public realm – is, with some exceptions, regarded as corruption only by those who are not beneficiaries. It is expected of politicians that they will reward those who voted for them, and where a sense of nationhood and of loyalty to the state is poorly developed, and expectations of political longevity are low, it is accepted that politicians will squeeze as much as possible out of the state, and will do so within a short time frame. Moreover, once this pattern of behaviour becomes established amongst politicians, it is likely to spread within the public service: bureaucrats will tend to favour their *wantoks* in the provision of services or to seek special favours from those to whom services are provided. Such factors largely explain the increasing competition for political office, noted above, and the increasing politicisation of decision-making.

Such behaviour is not restricted to those with direct access to the resources of the civic public realm. Across the country, in rural and urban areas, citizens demand additional compensation for land purchased earlier by government for schools, airstrips, roads, towns, and other public facilities, and often threaten violent action if their demands are not met. (In one case which I have observed at close quarters over a number of years, villagers have claimed large amounts of additional compensation for land on which a provincial high school was built some years ago. They have pressed their claims by attacks on the school and its students and teachers, at one stage burning down a building. Unable to meet the villagers' demands, the provincial government eventually proposed to close the school and relocate it elsewhere. At this stage the villagers – many of whose children attend the school – dropped their claims; but following the election of a new provincial government the demands were revived.) In recent years, also, the judicial system has upheld the demands of villagers for compensation from government for damages inflicted by police in raids on villages.

In a more extreme form, the breakdown of law and order is itself a form of challenge to the state. *Raskols* frequently justify their actions by reference to corruption amongst those in power and the failure of government to meet the needs of its citizens. The inability of the police and defence force to deal with the incidence of crime, 'tribal fighting', and the rebellion on Bougainville underlines the weakness of the state, and the scale of raskolism (and the occasional murder, by his kin group, of a *raskol* who oversteps communal propriety attests to the symbiosis between *raskols* and their primordial public).

Beyond the public sector, similar processes operate. In areas of large-scale resource development, communities have often, initially, welcomed the presence of big companies; particularly in remote areas, they tend to see them as a source of not only income but also infrastructure and development more generally. But they are quick to demand renegotiation of agreements if they think they can get a larger share of the profits, and have used or threatened force to back their demands; the Bougainville mine was the first to be forced to close, but others have been forced to close temporarily and all are vulnerable to local protest action (and local politics is often complex).

In recent years there has been a growing literature on 'weak states', 'collapsed states', 'predatory states', and so on, and attempts, by the World Bank and others, to address the problems of such states in terms of creating 'good governance'. Papua New Guinea displays the typical characteristics of a weak state. What this paper suggests is that unless Papua New Guineans acknowledge and respect the legitimacy of the state – in Ekeh's terms acknowledge moral obligations to the civic public realm which outweigh primordial obligations – the state will remain weak and policy-making will be characterised, to use the words of Oil Search Ltd chairman Trevor Kennedy in May 1995, by 'inconsistency and lack of discipline'.[16] Ultimately the unpredictability of policy-making and its subservience to primordial interests, and the inability of government to maintain a secure economic environment, will not only discourage foreign investment but will inhibit indigenous enterprise as well. (Already, in some parts of the country coffee and cocoa buyers do not go out on buying trips because they fear attacks by *raskols*.)

Judged against the eight aims elaborated in 1975, Papua New Guinea's economic achievements have been modest. Though less dependent on overseas development assistance, the economy remains heavily dependent on imports of goods and services and its major industries remain substantially foreign-owned. Inequality in incomes and access to government services, both personally and regionally, has probably increased. Outside the subsistence sector, women play a minor role in economic and political affairs [at the time of writing, in late 1996, there was not a single woman in the 109-seat National Parliament; two women were elected in 1997]. And changes to the provincial government system in 1995 appear to be designed to centralise rather than decentralise decision making. The situation in 1996, 21 years after independence, was described by Morauta in the following terms:

> Despite the five-fold growth in government expenditure and revenue, the country's infrastructure is breaking down. Government services have declined to the point of being non-existent in many areas. Public assets, whether they be schools, hospitals, offices, roads or bridges, are all in a state of disrepair. Our exports earn more than three billion kina each year, yet we have an underlying shortage of foreign currencies. GDP has grown five times but the distribution of income is more skewed and less equitable than in 1975. Nominal per capita income has more than doubled, but 80 per cent of the population actually earn less than the 1975 average. Corruption, both petty and profound, permeates society today. Society is ravaged by crime. There is a general inability to

[16] 'Chairman Trevor Kennedy's Address. Oil Search Ltd. Annual General Meeting, Port Moresby – Tuesday 9 May, 1995'.

> enforce or maintain law and order. Social inequity and poverty are rampant. [Morauta 1996]

In this paper I have argued that Papua New Guinea's failure to capitalise on its fortunate resource endowment and its early promise of sound and equitable policies is not just a question of 'bad management', but reflects the non-emergence in the post-independence years of a sense of national identity and purpose. The persistence of predominant loyalties to locality and kin, and the historical image of the state in Papua New Guinea as a provider of free goods and services, has promoted a political culture in which, as Ekeh has argued for Africa, those with direct access to the state tend to use their positions to benefit themselves and their 'primordial publics', and those who receive rents from large-scale resource projects continuously seek to renegotiate more favourable agreements. Such a situation has all the hallmarks of a weak state: policy making tends to be short-term and often capricious; governments have difficulty implementing decisions, and corruption and lawlessness are becoming endemic.

There are, nevertheless, positive elements in the Papua New Guinea case: the country has maintained a robust democracy, there are strong redistributive elements in local cultures, and although population growth rates threaten the long-term well-being of some agrarian communities, the country is resource rich. If the present perception of economic crisis can precipitate a commitment to rational long-term policy making perhaps the present worrying trends can be reversed. But before that can happen there needs to be a major change in political perceptions.

16

STATE, SOCIETY AND GOVERNANCE: A PHILIPPINES–PAPUA NEW GUINEA COMPARISON*

For some time students of comparative politics, as well as aid donors and international agencies such as the World Bank, have been concerned with the poor performance of many states in Africa, Asia, the Pacific, Latin America, and more recently Eastern Europe and Central Asia. This has been reflected in the proliferation of such terms as 'weak states', 'collapsed states', and (going back some years) 'broken-backed states'. Since the appearance of Joel Migdal's *Strong Societies and Weak States* (1988) the ideas of weak states and strong (and weak) societies have been employed frequently in analyses of Southeast Asian and island Pacific polities, where state–society relations have long been a focus of scholarly and policy-oriented attention.

This chapter attempts to relate the concepts of weak state, strong–weak society, and state capability (which might be roughly equated with 'governance') in two countries of the region, both democratic, one with a weak state and strong society (the Philippines) and one with a weak state and weak society (Papua New Guinea). Essentially, it asks how far similarities and differences in the configuration of states and societies can explain similarities and differences in state capabilities. It finds – employing Migdal's (1988:32–3) indicators of social control – that in both countries *compliance* is weak and *participation* is in some sense strong, but, paradoxically, that *legitimation* appears to be higher

* This paper was presented at a workshop at The Australian National University in 1977 and was published in P. Dauvergne (ed.), *Weak and Strong States in Asia Pacific Societies* (1998).

in Papua New Guinea than in the Philippines. This finding is related to questions of who occupies the institutions of the state and how representative the interests of those occupants are; it is suggested that the apparently higher level of legitimation in Papua New Guinea might be explained in terms of its greater 'representativeness', given the absence of major class or ethnic cleavages and the frequent turnover of state office holders. While at any point in time a substantial section of the population may be indifferent to the state, seeing it as largely irrelevant to their lives, over time virtually all of the population feel they have a stake in the state, as an institution which delivers public goods and services. This appears to be consistent with the trend of recent constitutional reforms and proposals in the two countries, which have tended to be state-limiting in the Philippines and state-strengthening in Papua New Guinea.

Comparing the Philippines and Papua New Guinea

At first glance, the Philippines and Papua New Guinea are not obviously comparable. The Philippines, with a well-educated and internationally mobile population of around 70 million, has experienced over four centuries of colonial rule, a relatively long period of integration into the world economy, and half a century of independence, and now sees itself as an 'Asian Tiger' cub. Papua New Guinea, on the other hand, once referred to as 'the last unknown' (and more recently described somewhat cryptically by its national airline as 'like no place you've never been') had a comparatively brief contact with the outside world before achieving independence in 1975, and its roughly four million people, who speak some 800 different languages, are still predominantly subsistence farmers, with comparatively low levels of formal education and technical skills.

Notwithstanding these differences, in political terms the two countries share a number of more or less common features.

- Both enjoyed a relatively smooth and amicable transition to independence, without, therefore, creating the sorts of 'heroic' leaders, parties or armed forces that have emerged in countries which had to fight for their independence.[1]

- Although the Philippines inherited, from the US colonial regime, a presidential-style system while Papua New Guinea chose (largely from a reading of Westminster-style African models) a parliamentary system, unusually for the Asia–Pacific area both countries – with the comparatively brief exception of the Philippines under President Marcos (from martial law in 1972 till his downfall in 1986) – have maintained robustly democratic systems.[2]

With the same (but qualified) exception for the Philippines under Marcos, both countries:

- have competitive political party systems, though parties have tended to be fluid, for the most part not sharply ideologically differentiated, and often rooted in the politics of personality or region (Wurfel 1988:93–106; Landé 1965, 1996; Villanueva 1996; May 1984 [see chapter 5 above]),
- have held regular and (albeit with some manipulation)[3] genuinely contested elections,
- have experienced regular and constitutionally mandated changes of leadership,
- have maintained quite strong traditions of judicial inde-

[1] The Philippines fought its revolution, and produced its heroes, in the nineteenth century struggle for independence from Spain, but with no great practical relevance for politics in the second half of the twentieth century (which is not to say that the country's revolutionary heroes are not still revered).

[2] The latest available Freedom House index rates Papua New Guinea (on a scale of 1 [most free] to 7 [least free]) 2 for Political Rights and 4 for Civil Liberties, and the Philippines 2, 3.

[3] On the Philippines see Carbonell-Catilo, de Leon and Nicolas (1985) and Santiago (1991).

pendence and – at least in rhetoric – popular support for the rule of law, and

- have enjoyed a free and active press.
- While both countries – particularly the Philippines, but to a minor extent also Papua New Guinea – have seen the military exercise political influence, both have substantially upheld a tradition of Huntingtonian military professionalism (Huntingdon 1957) and neither has succumbed to a military coup[4] (though some people interpreted the 1986 'People Power Revolution' in the Philippines as a military coup to restore democracy – incorrectly in my view).
- Both have embraced political decentralisation, with limited success (though Papua New Guinea is currently in the process of reversing this – ostensibly in the name of further decentralisation) (Tapales 1993; May and Regan with Ley 1997).
- Both countries have maintained relatively open, capitalist economies, in which government has played an important developmental role (Golay 1961; Doronila 1992; de Dios and Fabella 1996; Connell 1997; May 1997b).
- Both countries have experienced armed regional separatist rebellions (the Philippines in the Muslim south and to a lesser extent in the northern Cordilleras; Papua New Guinea on Bougainville), which they have attempted to deal with by a mixture of military and political means (Che Man 1990; May 1990; Wesley-Smith 1992; May 1996).

If this list of similarities does not impress, then one might consider the comparison of the Philippines and Papua New Guinea against, say, that of the Philippines with any of its Association of Southeast Asian Nations neighbours and that of Papua New Guinea with such other South Pacific Forum member states as Fiji, Samoa or Tonga.

[4] See, for example, chapters by Selochan and May in May and Selochan (1998).

With so many apparent similarities in what might be termed 'political performance indicators', it would seem reasonable to expect to find some parallels in political institutions and/or 'political culture'. To the extent that these can be measured, to what extent is this so?

The state[5]

The state in the Philippines

There seems to be general consensus that the Philippines state, in terms of its capacity 'to *penetrate* society, *regulate* social relationships, *extract* resources, and *appropriate* or use resources in determined ways' (Migdal 1988:4), is relatively weak.[6] Its weakness may be traced to the country's colonial history. 'The state' in the Spanish colonial period was a loose structure, essentially Manila-centred and substantially reliant on the clergy and private enterprise to sustain the colonial enterprise beyond Manila. Apart from the Muslim sultanates in Mindanao and Sulu, and the few bastions of Muslim influence in the Visayas and Luzon which were quickly overthrown, pre-colonial society was politically fragmented into largely autonomous *barangays* (hamlets). Spanish colonialism effectively created a sense of

[5] 'The state' is used here – as in Migdal (1988:xiii fn. 2, 19–20) and in other contributions to this volume – in an essentially institutional, Weberian sense. This broadly corresponds with the usage employed by Stepan (1978:xii), where the state is seen as 'the continuous administrative, legal, bureaucratic and coercive systems that attempt not only to structure relations *between* civil society and public authority in a polity but also to structure many crucial relationships *within* civil society as well'. For further discussion see Migdal (1994:11–18, 1988, 1997); Stepan (1978:chapter 1); Goulbourne, ed. (1979); Evans, Rueschemeyer and Skocpol, eds (1985); Hall (1986); Mann (1986); Bratton (1989); Navari (1991); and Evans (1995).

[6] See, for example, Villacorta (1994), Rivera (1996) and Kerkvliet (1998). For a more detailed discussion of state and society in the Philippines see Wurfel (1988:chapter 3); Hutchcroft (1991); Timberman (1991); Hawes (1992); Gutierrez, Torrente and Garcia (1992); McCoy (1994); Rivera (1994). Also see Machado (1972) and Carroll (1994).

Filipino identity, promoting the growth of prominent local families, in part through intermarriage and the integration of immigrant Chinese. By the end of the Spanish period there was a well-developed, locally based, *ilustrado* (élite) class. During the American colonial period this class consolidated its position through political leadership in the democratic system promoted by the Americans (the Philippine literature commonly uses the term 'élite democracy') and economic dominance based on land ownership and the translation of this into equity in a burgeoning industrial sector.

In the post-independence period, social tensions, particularly between import-substitution manufacturing interests and those supporting an export-oriented development strategy, not only hampered coherent policy making but created the political instability which facilitated the election of Ferdinand Marcos in 1965. However, the increasingly authoritarian regime of President Marcos did little to improve the capability of the state to achieve its leader's objectives (except perhaps the objective of enriching the Marcos family); indeed, it might be argued that Marcos became entrapped in a kleptocracy of cronies in much the same way as previous governments had been constrained by self-seeking élite competition. The People Power Revolution of 1986 only partly changed this, the Aquino regime being heavily dependent on winning the support of local élites just as Marcos had been (indeed in some places the local élite simply switched allegiance from Marcos to Aquino). Only under President Ramos (1992–98) does there appear to have been some strengthening of the state (see Miranda 1993).

What is interesting about the Philippines, however, is that even under Marcos, the *institutions* of the state remained largely intact: apart from the early years of martial law, elections were held (albeit being heavily manipulated), parliament met (though it was dominated by Marcos loyalists and much policy making was done by presidential decree), and the judiciary maintained a measure of independence. Moreover, political parties operated (albeit under various constraints), and an active press and radio were tolerated. Thus, when the challenge to Marcos came in 1986 (significantly, as the result of an election), the opposition had leadership, organisation, and the means of mobilising popular support; in the event, it was also able to call on a degree of Huntingtonian military professionalism.[7] (The contrast with what happened in Burma two years later is striking.)

The state in Papua New Guinea[8]

Pre-colonial Papua New Guinea was also intensely fragmented into small-scale political entities, with little overarching organisation or hierarchical leadership. (Traditional society in Papua New Guinea has commonly been referred to as 'stateless' and 'acephalous'.) The state was very much a colonial creation and for much of Papua New Guinea's population the experience of colonial administration was brief (in some parts, less than two decades). Although the colonial administration has been described as highly centralised,[9] district officers frequently exercised considerable autonomy. After independence in 1975, separatist movements on Bougainville and elsewhere resulted in the establishment of a system of provincial government, decentralising political power and in the process inevitably creating tensions between provincial politicians and national Members of Parliament (MPs).

A legacy of the latter years of the colonial experience has been the widespread view of 'the state' as a provider of goods and services. With limited mobilisation of resources outside the government sector, access to those goods and services is best achieved by occupying the institutions of the state. Politics is thus

---

[7] See, for example, Mackenzie (1987), May (1989).

[8] For a more detailed discussion of state–society relations in Papua New Guinea see Dinnen (1998) and Standish (1994).

[9] See, for example, the report to the Constitutional Planning Committee, on central–provincial government relations, by William Tordoff and Ronald Watts (Tordoff and Watts 1974:2/2).

seen as a major form of *bisnis*, with elections eagerly contested (despite a high cost of contesting, frequently upwards of forty candidates compete, in a first-past-the-post poll, in 89 single-member open constituencies of around 25 000 to 50 000 voters),[10] and around 50 to 55 per cent of members losing their seats at each election. Since 1972, all governments have been coalitions, and in every parliament since 1977 government has changed in mid term as a result of shifts within coalitions. The consequent concentration on factional dealing and pork barrelling has contributed significantly to the inability of the Papua New Guinea state to commit itself to policies with a longer-term perspective, and to the growth of corruption and nepotism. The state's ability to deliver services and to maintain its presence, especially in more remote rural areas, is limited by the capacity of its bureaucracy, availability of resources, and difficulties of terrain. The outbreak of armed rebellion, beginning in 1988, in Papua New Guinea's relatively prosperous North Solomons (Bougainville) Province, primarily over unsatisfied demands by landowners for a larger share of revenue from the huge gold and copper mine at Panguna, tested the coercive powers of the state; after almost a decade, the conflict has not been fully resolved.

Society in the Philippines and Papua New Guinea

If the 'state' is sometimes an ambiguous and contested concept, 'society' is analytically even more difficult. 'Society' is used here, loosely, to refer to what Woods (1992:77) has described as 'patterns of political participation outside of formal state structures and one-party systems'.[11] In this sense, there is an overlap between 'society' and what below I refer to as 'regime'.

The 'strength' of society in the Philippines lies in two, largely

[10] In a parliament of 109 seats there are also twenty provincial seats, of around 25 000 to 400 000 voters.

[11] For a more detailed discussion, see, for example, Bratton (1989), White (1994), Diamond (1994), Hutchful (1995-96).

opposing, directions: the existence of essentially locally based patrons, *caciques*, dynasties or warlords (all four terms, and others, recur in the Philippines literature) on the one hand, and on the other, the existence of a vibrant 'civil society' which includes a mind-boggling array of non-governmental organisations (NGOs), a strong labour movement, a powerful church (especially the Roman Catholic Church) network, a highly politicised academic community, and a strong Left incorporating worker, peasant, church and other sectoral groups and a Communist Party. The former, with some rotation of players, have over time substantially penetrated and appropriated the resources of the state; the latter ('civil society') has been less successful in capturing government, but has asserted itself in other ways, including 'everyday politics' (Kerkvliet 1990) and armed insurgency, and in these ways exercised a restraining influence on an élite-dominated state (most dramatically in the overthrow of Marcos in 1986).

In Papua New Guinea, on the other hand, 'society' is arguably weak: traditional social groups are small and often in conflict; the labour movement (in a country where formal sector employment is relatively small and dominated by government) is at a low level of development. NGOs are embryonic (and having been partly co-opted by government following the June 1997 elections seem less likely to act as a restraint on the state). Christian churches play an important role socially but are not particularly active politically and are divided by denomination. And political parties lack a mass base. Yet the high rate of turnover of members of parliament, and the necessity for national MPs to deliver to their local constituencies, suggest that civil society exercises some influence over the state.

In terms of Migdal's matrix (1988:35, Table 1.1), Papua New Guinea would seem to be a clear case of weak state, weak society; but it is doubtful whether it can be described, as Migdal labels this cell, as 'anarchical'. Indeed, in terms of the classic criteria – regularity of elections, number of changes of government, and the constitutionality of those changes – it has been a remarkably stable polity.

State, society and governance

Having provided these thumbnail sketches of one country with a weak state and strong society and one with a weak state and weak society, where do we go from here? Can we explain similarities and differences in state capabilities in terms of these characteristics?

An obvious approach would be to examine government performance in several comparable policy areas as a measure of state capability. This might reveal, for example, that both states, for more or less similar reasons (to do with the difficulties of placing long-term development strategies above short-term gains) have been poor managers of their economies; that both, for more or less similar reasons (to do with the limited reach of the state) have had difficulties maintaining law and order, and so on. I would expect, however, that on any measure the Philippines would have a better record on policy formulation and a somewhat better record on policy compliance. But I suspect that the more detailed the examination, the more difficult it would become to measure capability, to reconcile the indicators of compliance, participation and legitimation, and to disentangle state from society.

This suspicion appears to have been borne out in several chapters in Dauvergne (1998), which have concluded from studies of particular countries that the 'strength' or 'weakness' of the state can vary both from one policy area to another and one region to another, and, within a single policy area or region, over time (see, for example, Kerkvliet 1998). If this is the case (and there is little doubt that it is), do the concepts of state and societal strength or weakness retain any analytical usefulness?

Some of us, at least, would feel that, despite the inherent problems of definition, the ideas elaborated by Migdal in 1988 have provided sufficient analytical insights that we should be wary of throwing out the conceptual baby with the proverbial bath water. But some development of the initial analytical framework is clearly needed. Two conservationist strategies might be considered.

One would involve the compilation of an index of overall 'state strength' (and perhaps an index of 'societal strength'), along the lines of the Freedom House Index of democracy or the Wall Street Journal/Heritage Foundation Index of Economic Freedom, which would make it possible to locate states (and societies) along a scale of strength–weakness according to the characteristics identified by Migdal (1988) or some other basket of indicators.[12] While such an index might find a ready market, my impression is that, like the Freedom House Index and the Index of Economic Freedom, in the process of aggregation it would conceal as much as it revealed.

A second strategy would be to pursue the difficult task of clarifying the relationship between state and society (a task which Migdal and others have already addressed in Migdal, Kohli and Shue 1994, and Migdal 1997).

Thus, to return to the Philippines–Papua New Guinea comparison: it has been argued that the Philippine state has been dominated by a landed capitalist élite (Villacorta 1994) which has largely (though not exclusively) used the state to promote its own social and economic interests; as against this, the contrasting societal forces of a strong democratic ethos, arguably grounded in the Philippines pre-hispanic culture but certainly nurtured under American colonial rule, and locally based power structures which penetrate but do not coincide with the Philippine state, have for the most part exercised fairly effective restraint over autocratic tendencies in the Philippine state. In consequence, with reference to Migdal's indicators of state strength, policy making

[12] Migdal (1988:279-86) seems to have had this possibility in mind in including an appendix on (quantitatively) 'Assessing Social Control'.

is vigorously debated and legislative programmes (somewhat less vigorously)[13] enacted but implementation and *compliance* is frequently weak – especially (in areas such as land reform, forestry, and environmental management) when the interests of local power brokers do not coincide with nationally legislated policies. The inability of successive Philippine governments, notwithstanding pressures from the International Monetary Fund, to enact much needed tax reforms is a striking case in point.

On the other hand – and apparently contrary to Migdal's (1988:32) notion of '[i]ncreasing levels of social control' – *participation*, on almost any measure, is quite high, with a wide range of civil society organisations active in formal and informal politics, and public demonstrations and strikes (*welga*) over policy issues reasonably frequent and largely tolerated by government. Nevertheless, although elections are well contested and voter turnout is comparatively high, political patronage remains important in the continuing dominance of prominent families – for example, see Soriano (1987) on the first post-Marcos election – and there is widespread popular cynicism about politics, especially as directed towards 'traditional politicians' (*trapos*). Correspondingly, popular perceptions of the state's legitimacy (*legitimation*) in the Philippines appear to be mixed. The common claim that 'Filipinos respect a strong leader' suggests a high degree of state legitimation, but evidence for this is weak. President Marcos held on to power, from 1972 to 1986, only through the declaration of martial law and systematic state repression in the face of growing opposition. Successive governments have faced armed insurgencies from the Communist New Peoples Army and the Muslim Moro National Liberation Front and Moro Islamic Liberation Front (and for a while also the Cordillera Peoples Liberation Army); and after the 1986 change of government President Aquino faced a series of attempted coups by rebel fac-

13 Dickson-Waiko (1994:134) records that during 1987–91 just over five per cent of 104 bills and resolutions introduced into Congress (some, admittedly, addressing the same subject) were enacted into laws.

tions of the armed forces. Moreover, strong public reaction to moves to amend the constitution to enable President Ramos to seek a second presidential term (see below) suggests that even a successful and generally popular president, who appears to have significantly raised perceptions of state legitimacy in the Philippines, exercises a limited mandate.[14]

In Papua New Guinea, the state has been more broadly representative, and in the absence of the sort of major class or ethnic cleavages which have characterised many other societies, and with a relatively high turnover of members of parliament, it is arguable that no substantial social group (except women as a gender group) feels itself to be systematically excluded from the possibility of sharing in state power. State and society are thus more broadly integrated. *Participation* is, in this sense, comparatively high, and is reflected in the large number of candidates contesting elections, the high voter turnout, the demands made on members of parliament by their constituents, and ultimately, the relatively high turnover of members.

A notable feature of state–society relations in Papua New Guinea, on the other hand, is the very low level of development of formal civil–society organisations (apart from churches) between the local community and the state.[15] The integration of state and society and the high rate of participation in politics, however, makes for the 'pork-barrelling' style of politics noted above. With all national governments in Papua New Guinea's political

[14] A more systematic analysis of legitimacy would need to distinguish, at least, between performance-based and moral or 'democratic' concepts of legitimacy.

[15] This observation was made during the Workshop on Weak and Strong States in Melanesia and Southeast Asia (12–14 August 1997), by Michael Ong of the Australian Parliamentary Research Service. It is not obvious whether the low level of civil society development reflects a low level of ('modern') political development generally, the satisfactory working of electoral representation, or simply a high level of political indifference at the national level.

history being coalitions – with generally weak, poorly disciplined, and not ideologically sharply differentiated parties – candidates have increasingly stood as independents (in order to maximise their bargaining position, should they be elected, in the process of government formation) and elected MPs engage in an ongoing process of bargaining to maximise the benefits from office to themselves and their line (as noted above, every Papua New Guinea parliament since independence has changed government in mid term as a result of shifts within coalitions).

As I have argued elsewhere (May 1997b) [see chapter 14 above], employing Ekeh's (1975) notion of 'primordial' and 'civic' realms, this is not an environment favourable to sound policy making and *compliance*. Problems of compliance are further exacerbated by the limited capabilities of many administrators, which inhibits government service delivery,[16] and the frequency of political interference in administration at the local level. In such a context there is a good deal of cynicism about politics and politicians, and perceptions of state *legitimacy* tend to be low amongst those who are not currently recipients of state benefits. But while, at any time, most people have little regard for the state, there has not been (apart from Bougainville) the sort of direct opposition posed to the state that the Philippines has faced with the Moro National Liberation Front and the New People's Army, since those who at present have poor access to the state and its benefits might, at the next election, be the winners. Thus, paradoxically, with a weak state and a weak society Papua New Guinea has enjoyed a generally higher level of state legitimation and political stability than the Philippines.

This Philippines–Papua New Guinea comparison suggests two propositions of more general application. First, consistent with the approach of defining the state in institutional terms and

[16] Compare the comments of Kabutaulaka and Dauvergne (1997) concerning the administrative incapacity of the state in the Solomon Islands.

seeing it, in neo-Weberian terms, as mediating conflicting claims and establishing social values, it is necessary to distinguish the state from those who, at any time, occupy or control the institutions of 'the state'. In a research project on Regime Change and Regime Maintenance in Asia and the Pacific, we have attempted to accommodate this by distinguishing between *the state* (defined in institutional terms), *government* (those who occupy the legislative and executive offices of the state at any time), and *regime* (as in popular usage – for example, 'the Marcos regime' – those who at any time occupy the institutions of the state or exercise significant continuous political influence over it).[17] In practice, governments may change relatively frequently (in democratic systems principally as the result of regular elections) without any change in the state; regime change, on the other hand, occurs less readily and usually involves a dramatic event, such as a military coup, revolution, or foreign invasion. Changes of regime, unlike changes of government, generally imply changes in state structures. In the Philippines, the declaration of martial law marked a regime change (the ascendance of President Marcos, backed by the military, a political machine – the *Kilusang Bagong Lipunan* (KBL), New Society Movement – and a 'crony' business élite) and a change in the state (the suspension of the constitution). The 'People Power Revolution' of 1986, and subsequent passage of a new constitution, brought another change of regime (and state). The Philippine state under the authoritarian rule of Marcos was very different, in its relations with society, from the essentially democratic Philippine state under Aquino or Ramos. In contrast, there have been several changes of *government* in Papua New Guinea, but without a fundamental change of regime the role of the state in society has been essentially unchanged (though there have undoubtedly been differences in governing style).

---

[17] See also Calvert, ed. (1987:248), Fishman (1990:428) and Lawson (1991).

Second, having established who occupies the institutions of the state, it is necessary to ask how representative that group is. There is little doubt, for example, that the Philippine state under Marcos placed considerable weight on the interests of the Marcos family and its supporters ('the Marcos regime'). While many would argue that the Philippine state under Aquino and Ramos was still dominated by the interests of a landed capitalist oligarchy, few would dispute that under Aquino and Ramos the Philippine state was representative of a much broader range of interests (though many Muslims would argue that no Philippine state has really represented their interests).

In much of the writing about the state – even when the diversity of society is recognised – there is a tendency to assume that 'nation building', the creation of a sense of *national* identity (and thus identification with the nation-state) amongst socially diverse populations, can be achieved as a by-product of 'modernisation' or through specific policies of national ideology.[18] The evidence to support such a view, particularly in the Asia–Pacific region, however, is weak. Most states are systemically biased in their representativeness, whether in privileging the interests of dominant ethnic, religious, class or cultural majorities (as in Fiji's 'paramountcy of Fijian interests', or Malaysia's 'New Economic Policy') or in making concessions to minority groups (as in the creation of an Autonomous Region of Muslim Mindanao and the recognition of indigenous 'ancestral domain' in the Philippines). In many states, moreover, there are significant groups who regard themselves as permanently denied the possibility of exercising political power at the national level (the Muslims in

[18] Migdal (1998), for example, speaks of the 'naturalisation' of the state, as a 'shared sense that the state is as natural as the rivers and the mountains'. Similarly see Migdal (1988:16). It is not clear, however, how much 'coherence' states must have in order to survive; sometimes, indeed, they survive through the political disinterest of their citizens, or through the superior coercive force of the national government. Like families, states may be dysfunctional, yet survive.

the Philippines, and perhaps workers, peasants and indigenous cultural communities provide examples). Sometimes such groups simply disengage from the state (compare May 1982); where they are sufficiently large and can be organised politically there is always the possibility of insurrection against the state.

This has implications for the assessment of state strength or weakness: different elements of society may judge indicators of state strength differently. The mining industry in the Philippines, for example, may see delays in the passage of mining regulations as evidence of state weakness where an indigenous minority may see the state's concern over ancestral domain (a major cause of this delay) as evidence of state strength. Similarly, a government's performance on decentralisation may be judged to be strong or weak depending on whether one takes the perspective of a national planner or a provincial governor. Performance on land reform may be judged differently by a land owner and a peasant. Performance on export-oriented industrialisation may be judged differently by workers and the owners of capital. And, ultimately, a state may be judged 'strong' if it successfully counters an insurgency, regardless of the moral justification for such action.[19] It is for this reason that democratic theory emphasises such factors as turnover and tolerance of minorities.[20]

---

[19] Kerkvliet (1998) recognises this in proposing that 'perspective' be added to Migdal's (1988) indicators of state strength. But while compliance, participation and legitimation are, at least in principle, quantifiable, perspective is inevitably subjective. Kerkvliet (fn.22), moreover, sets aside consideration of Muslim separatism in the Philippines on the grounds that it 'challenged the legitimacy of the very idea of the Philippine nation', unlike the two political legitimacy crises he considers, 'which accepted the nation but challenged the legitimacy of those governing it'.

[20] It is notable that the Philippines, which is generally regarded as a weak state, felt able to make constitutional provision in 1987 for autonomous regions in Muslim Mindanao and the Cordilleras, while Indonesia, generally regarded as a strong state, has refused to consider substantive autonomy to East Timor, Irian Jaya or Aceh, on the grounds that such action could precipitate a fragmentation of the Republic.

Reforming the state

In this context (perceptions of whose interests the state represents), it might be instructive to briefly consider and compare recent debates in the Philippines and Papua New Guinea concerning constitutional reforms.

Following the fall of President Marcos in 1986, a Constitutional Commission was created to draft a new constitution. The new constitution was ratified in 1987. One outcome of the Marcos experience was a new provision to limit terms of public office. Under the 1935 constitution presidential office was limited to two terms. It is generally believed that it was the ineligibility of Marcos to stand for a third term in 1974 that precipitated his declaration of martial law and suspension of the constitution in 1972. A new constitution, pushed through in 1973, removed this constraint. Under the 1987 constitution a president was granted only one term (of six years). Senators are allowed two consecutive terms of six years and members of the House of Representatives three terms of three years. In 1997, with President Ramos's term of office due to end in 1998, Ramos supporters campaigned to 'change the charter' to allow the president to recontest in 1998 (and to extend the allowable term of other offices). Despite Ramos's considerable popularity, the move provoked heated opposition from across a broad political spectrum, with accusations that Ramos intended to reimpose martial law. The president's popularity plummeted, and the move was defeated. (Earlier proposals during the Ramos presidency for a shift from a bicameral, presidential system to a unicameral, parliamentary system, ostensibly in the interests of greater efficiency and democracidity, were similarly opposed as covert moves to prolong Ramos's term in office.)[21] A second aspect of the 1987 constitution concerned the role of political parties. Prior to martial law the Philippines had had a broadly two-party system, though

[21] For a summary of, and commentary upon, this debate see Bolongaita (1995).

the two major parties were not sharply differentiated ideologically, were élite-dominated, and membership was fluid. (Marcos himself had stood in the presidential election of 1965 as a Nacionalista Party candidate after being denied nomination by his chosen Liberal Party.) Under martial law, parties were initially banned and then allowed to re-establish under restrictive conditions; Marcos's KBL dominated politics from its establishment in 1978 till 1986, when it virtually collapsed. In the wake of 1986, some commentators confidently predicted the re-emergence of a competitive two-party system (see, for example, Landé 1987:31–2). Amongst Filipinos, however, there was a good deal of hostility towards 'traditional politics' and the party system. This was reflected in the 1987 constitution (Art. VI S.5(1), (2)) which provided that a fifth of the membership of the House of Representatives should be elected through a party-list system of registered national, regional and sectoral parties or organisations. As a transitional measure (for three consecutive terms after ratification of the constitution), however, half of the seats allocated to party-list representatives were to be filled 'by selection or election from the labour, peasant, urban poor, indigenous cultural communities, women, youth, and such other sectors as may be provided by law, except the religious sector'. In a detailed study of the party-list system as it operated during the eighth congress (1987–92), Violeta Corral described the objectives of the party-list system in the following terms:

> The party-list provision was proposed to open up the political system to a pluralistic society through a multiparty system . . . The party-list system . . . in effect, equalises political power such that the traditional two-party system in Philippine politics is dismantled . . . The party-list system, with its transitory provision of sectoral representation, institutionalises people power and broadens participatory democracy. [Corral 1993:6–7]

Corral's study suggests that the provisions may not have yielded the results hoped for by their proponents – even apart from the fact that during the first two post-1987 congresses all seats were allocated to sectoral representatives, with some members representing more than one sector – but the system has been retained and the first election under the full party-list system is planned to take place in 1998. (Further evidence of hostility towards 'traditional politics' was the inclusion in the 1987 constitution's 'Declaration of Principles and State Policies' of a statement (S.26): 'The state shall guarantee equal access to opportunities for public service, and prohibit political dynasties as may be defined by law'; to date no such legislation has been enacted.) A third element of the post-1986 reform in the Philippines was a major effort at political decentralisation through a new Local Government Code (1991). Although progress in some areas has been slow (and notwithstanding a belated concern that decentralisation might deliver political power into the hands of local warlords and political oligarchs), decentralisation has gathered pace over recent years. A significant aspect of this decentralisation has been the formal involvement of NGOs.

In all three areas the predominant rationale for reform has been to prevent the re-emergence of a dominating central state. When in 1992 Singapore's President Lee Kuan Yew advised Filipinos that what they needed was discipline rather than democracy, he was quickly reminded, by President Ramos, of the Philippine's 'ill-fated flirtation with authoritarianism' (see *Far Eastern Economic Review* 10 December 1992:29).

In contrast, much recent debate in Papua New Guinea has been concerned with ways of strengthening the state. At independence Papua New Guinea adopted an essentially Westminster constitution, which included provision for removing the prime minister or other ministers by a parliamentary vote of no confidence. In 1991, following repeated votes of no confidence in successive prime ministers, the constitution was amended to give an incoming government a grace period of 18 months (previously only six months) before facing a vote of no confidence, in the interests of political stability. In contrast to the opposition to charter change in the Philippines in 1997, there was no significant opposition to this amendment. In a second significant initiative, prior to the 1987 national elections in Papua New Guinea, concern over the growing number of candidates contesting elections (and the consequent decline in the percentage of the vote gained by winning candidates) prompted a move to raise the candidate deposit from K100 (then roughly $US90) to K1000. Although this proposal (which would have given Papua New Guinea, with average per capita GNP of $US1130 in 1993, one of the highest candidate deposits in the world) was dropped, on legal advice, it was successfully revived in 1992 and retained in 1997, when there were suggestions that it be increased to K2000. (Despite this, the number of candidates has continued to rise.) A third topic of discussion has been possible ways to strengthen the party system, with the aim of promoting accountability, discipline and stability; favoured measures have been legislation to discourage 'party hopping'[22] and public funding for political parties. There have also been proposals (which were to have been put into effect in 1997) to shift from a first-past-the-post electoral system to a preferential voting system. In 1997, leading opposition figure, Sir Rabbie Namaliu, left the opposition to join the government in order, he said, 'to strengthen the government and provide good governance to the people' (*National* 16 December 1997). With respect to political decentralisation, the pre-independence Constitutional Planning Committee in Papua New

[22] In June 1997, as votes were being counted in the national election, Papua New Guinea's Electoral Commissioner Reuben Kaiulo announced that he would prepare and publish a list of all newly elected members showing their political party affiliation according to their nomination form, so that any member changing party allegiance could be identified. Kaiulo proposed to distribute this list to the chief ombudsman, the police commissioner, churches, and the press (*Independent* 27 June 1997). Legislation to prevent 'political turncoatism' has also been introduced into the Philippine Congress, but to date has not been enacted.

Guinea recommended a system of decentralisation to provincial governments. Although initially dropped from the independence constitution, provincial governments were put into place in 1976–77 following separatist demands from Bougainville. Early opposition from members of the National Parliament and local government councillors, both of whom saw the new political tier as a threat to their local power bases, resulted in several attempts to shift power back to the centre. In 1995, the Organic Law on Provincial Government was replaced by a new Organic Law on Provincial Governments and Local-Level Governments, which abolished the elected provincial assemblies. Although the rationale for the provincial government reforms was stated in terms of greater decentralisation (increasing the powers of local-level governments) the general consensus has been that the new legislation represents a recentralisation of authority to the national government. Other evidence of centralist tendencies might include the increasing use of the army in law and order operations and the frequent expression, in political circles, of admiration for models of 'social control' drawn from Singapore, Indonesia and Malaysia. While such centralist tendencies might be partly explained as attempts by sitting politicians to consolidate their authority and perpetuate their terms in office, the fact is that there has been little public opposition to them and, indeed, a good deal of popular support.

The general hostility towards state-strengthening reforms in the Philippines and apparent widespread acceptance of the need for state-strengthening measures in Papua New Guinea is consistent with the suggestion above that, notwithstanding a relatively low level of *compliance*, the state in Papua New Guinea enjoys greater *legitimation* than that in the Philippines, and that this may be explained by the closer integration of state and society, or greater representativeness of the state, in Papua New Guinea.

Afterword

Migdal (1994:14–15) has argued for a 'new "anthropology of the state"'. In his earlier study, Migdal (1988:xvi) characterised the literature on the Third World, critically, as generally falling into two categories: one which 'often remain[ed] enmeshed in the intricacies of social life at the local level', with scant attention to the state; the other which focused 'on life amongst the most influential elements', which by implication tended to produce overly state-centred accounts. It is doubtful whether this criticism can be sustained for either Papua New Guinea or the Philippines. Studies of politics in Papua New Guinea – where state and local politics are deeply interpenetrated – have often been criticised for being too 'anthropological' and insufficiently engaged with grand theory. To a lesser extent the same 'criticism' might be levelled at those who write about Philippine politics, in which the state and local oligarchies are often difficult to disentangle. Insofar as they have focused on the complex interaction of state and society, however, the literatures on Philippine and Papua New Guinea politics provide a fertile ground for comparative studies of 'the state'.

17

NUGGET, PIKE, ET AL.: THE ROLE OF THE RESERVE BANK OF AUSTRALIA IN PAPUA NEW GUINEA'S DECOLONISATION*

Much of the literature on decolonisation suffers from a tendency to overgeneralise, in particular to portray the colonial power as monolithic and its motives as simple. This propensity tends to vary directly with commentators' distance in time and space from the decolonisation process. Increasingly, I read references to decolonisation in Papua New Guinea which describe events that, as someone involved on the margins of the decolonisation process, I have difficulty recognising. In fact, in virtually all decolonisation processes different actors, both colonisers and colonised, occupy a range of positions, from opposing independence to being in its vanguard. This was true of Papua New Guinea. In the movement towards independence there were Papua New Guineans who resisted the transition, as well as those who promoted it, and colonial officials who sought to hasten it, as well as those who sought to delay it; and amongst both these were people whose position changed over time.

This paper recalls one aspect of Papua New Guinea's decolonisation: the transfer of control over the banking and monetary system. Specifically, it focuses on the role played by the Reserve Bank of Australia. The Bank's interest in the future of Papua New Guinea began early, on the initiative of its governor from 1949 to 1968, Dr H.C. ('Nugget') Coombs – a man who has been in the vanguard of much of what has been good in Australian life in the

* The paper was presented at a conference on Decolonisation in the Pacific at The Australian National University in 1996. It was published in 1998 as a North Australia Research Unit Discussion Paper.

twentieth century. Coombs recruited Dr P.W.E. Curtin to carry forward the Bank's work in Papua New Guinea, and in subsequent years the Bank's Papua New Guinea Department, under Curtin and M.J. Phillips, became closely involved with Papua New Guinea, pursuing a strategy of development which sometimes met resistance from the Australian government, the Papua New Guinea Administration and even within the Bank itself.

In the beginning

In his autobiography, *Trial Balance,* Coombs records that during the latter years of World War II the Department of Post-War Reconstruction (of which Coombs became director-general in 1943) gave thought to a number of issues of postwar regional planning, including plans for the development of Papua New Guinea. Coombs notes:

> As Director-General of Post-War Reconstruction I had been involved in the planning of the transition in Papua-New Guinea from military Government to civil administration, and in the measures to rehabilitate those residents of the Territories adversely affected by the war and to promote the economic and social reconstruction generally.
>
> By 1946 these gave primary emphasis to the development and welfare of the indigenous inhabitants. [Coombs 1981:172]

This 'primary emphasis' was expressed in the Commonwealth Parliament in 1945 by External Territories Minister Eddie Ward:

> This government is not satisfied that sufficient interest had been taken in the Territories prior to the Japanese invasion, or that adequate funds had been provided for their development and the advancement of the native inhabitants . . . In future the basis for the economy of the territory will be native and European industry with the limit of non-native expansion determined by the welfare of the natives generally. [*Commonwealth Parliamentary Debates (House of Representatives),* vol.183:4052, 4054, 4 July 1945]

I do not know what influence Coombs may have had in the formulation of this policy statement, but there is certainly some coincidence in the views recorded by Coombs and those expressed by Ward.[1]

In 1949 Coombs became governor of the Commonwealth Bank of Australia[2] and, as he puts it, 'brought to the banking problems of the Territories some familiarity with their economic and social contexts' (ibid.). At that time, Papua New Guinea was an extension of the Australian banking system; initially two commercial banks operated there: the Commonwealth Banking Corporation and the Bank of New South Wales (now Westpac); in the 1950s they were joined by the Australian and New Zealand Bank and the National Bank of Australasia. The business of all four banks was overwhelmingly directed towards the 'expatriate' sector and the administration, although the Commonwealth Savings Bank made early efforts to mobilise Papua New Guinean savings.[3] Any attempt to extend banking to Papua New Guineans would in any case have been hampered by the *Transactions With Natives Ordinance*, which (until 1963) rendered transactions in excess of $100 'unlawful and void as against a native'. Monetary policy also applied uniformly across Papua New Guinea and Australia.

In 1953 a New Guinea Committee was set up within the Commonwealth Bank. Its responsibilities were: to ensure that funds deposited in 'New Guinea' were 'reasonably employed' in the

---

[1] Geoff Gray discounts the link, pointing to the role of Alf Conlon and the Australian Army's wartime Directorate of Research and Civil Affairs (personal communication and see Gray 1996). Also see MacWilliam (1996). Coombs seems to have had a fairly close personal association with Conlon.

[2] In 1949 the Commonwealth Bank included the Commonwealth Savings Bank, the Commonwealth Trading Bank and the central bank. In January 1960 the central banking functions were separated and transferred to the Reserve Bank of Australia which was created by legislation in 1959. Coombs became governor of the Reserve Bank.

[3] For an account of banking in Papua New Guinea to 1969, see Phillips (1972:54-59).

interests of 'New Guinea itself'; to consider what action the Bank could take to promote the development of village cooperatives; and to oversee long-term educational and training measures to enable the 'natives' to participate in the administration of the Bank.

The same year a working committee of The Australian National University (comprising Oskar Spate, Cyril Belshaw and Trevor Swan) was commissioned by the Australian government, 'to investigate the economic structure of the Territory with a view to suggesting gaps in knowledge which it is most essential to fill and lines of advance which hold most prospect of producing positive results' (Spate, Belshaw and Swan 1953:Foreword). Again, I do not know whether Coombs played a part in initiating this study (his relations with ANU were, of course, close), but an economist from the Bank (Don McKenna) was attached to the working committee in Canberra for several months, acting as general liaison officer between the committee and the Department of Territories (which had been established eight years earlier) and undertaking a major part of the committee's statistical work – and [presumably] keeping Coombs in touch with the committee's work. Although the working committee acknowledged the work of 'numerous committees in the past', and suggested that it had 'found little to say which has not been said before' (ibid.), its report in fact provided an important critique of past policies and its discussion of future prospects and proposals for a 'native-oriented polity' and 'native-based production' anticipated much of developments to come.[4] Coombs recalls that the Spate, Belshaw and Swan report 'criticised all the banks for the failure to support New Guinea development, particularly the native agriculture upon which they believed the development should be based'[5] and says that following the report:

---

[4] The working committee identified three major developmental needs: roads; the strengthening of agricultural work; and fiscal reform and the fostering of financial responsibilities.

> . . . the Commonwealth Bank carried out studies of the native economy to test how far the existing state of knowledge and experience of the money economy provided scope for lending

and that a 'modest beginning' was made to the employment and training of indigenous staff (Coombs 1981:172).

In 1959 the Bank commissioned a study of 'the use of money and the need for credit by the indigenous people of TPNG', to inform its efforts at developing a financial system appropriate to the changing economic and social conditions. The study, carried out by J.R. Thomas, an economist with the Bank, and Sydney University anthropologist Dawn Ryan (Thomas and Ryan 1959), made a number of recommendations for financial education and development, including the recommendation that the Bank consider the establishment of credit unions (see below).

In the same year, the central banking functions of the Commonwealth Bank were transferred to the newly created Reserve Bank, which commenced operations in January 1960. In August the Bank opened a branch in Port Moresby. In its first report (*Reserve Bank of Australia, Report and Financial Statements* [hereafter *RBA Report*] 1960:28) it was noted that the central bank 'has for some years taken a special interest in Papua New Guinea' and that the opening of a Port Moresby branch 'will enable it to carry out its central banking functions in the Territory and to keep informed of problems that face banks in this changing environment'.

---

[5] I can find no discussion of banking in the report apart from the brief observation that 'net finance from the banking system is negative' (that is, the banks in effect used funds deposited by customers in Papua New Guinea to lend to customers, including the government, in Australia) and comments that 'The importance of agrarian credit [for "native production"] . . . cannot be overstressed' and that 'some suitable form of credit will have to be devised' (Spate, Belshaw and Swan 1953:paras 37.4, 14.3, 28.2).

The Reserve Bank in Papua New Guinea

The Bank's role in financial and economic policy making

Initially, the Bank's central banking functions were largely confined to acting as banker to the Commonwealth government and the administration of Papua New Guinea, distributing notes and coins, assisting the Department of Territories and the administration with loan raising, and maintaining a stock registry; but as political and economic development accelerated, the Bank's role increased. The Bank's 1964 report stated:

> In addition [to providing 'the normal range of central banking services'], research activities in relation to the economic and financial development of the Territory have been expanded and, in association with the Administration and the trading banks, the Bank has been actively engaged in encouraging the development of a financial and banking structure suited to the particular needs of the Territory. [*RBA Report* 1964:25]

In November 1958 Coombs appointed, as senior research economist (international affairs) in the Bank's Research Department, Dr P.W.E. ('Pike') Curtin. Curtin, a fellow West Australian, had worked with Coombs in Post-War Reconstruction and had subsequently been director of the Colombo Plan Bureau in Sri Lanka, and chairman of the Commonwealth Public Service Board. He was an unorthodox economist of Fabian persuasion. Curtin provided the nucleus of what in 1965 became the Bank's Papua New Guinea Division.

Towards the end of 1960 a meeting of the Bank's internal Central Banking Advisory Committee (CBAC) considered a paper on the Bank's activities in relation to Papua New Guinea, drafted by Curtin. On the basis of this, CBAC concluded that the Bank should explore the scope for possible action through: education and training of natives in finance and commerce; employment and training of native staff; financing of promising developmental projects; and collection and publication of basic statistical and economic data. It was also resolved to liaise with CSIRO and other relevant research teams and to continue financing research projects through the Bank's Rural Credits Development Fund.[6] Responsibility for planning of studies and courses of action was given to a CBAC subcommittee, the TPNG Committee, headed by one of the Bank's advisers, A.W. Elvery; the work was to be done primarily within the Bank's Research Department, including that Department's Rural Liaison Service, under Curtin.

Shortly after this Curtin, accompanied by John Phillips[7] from the Bank's Rural Liaison Service and Eric Fleming from the Bank's Bonds and Stock Administration, visited Papua New Guinea. On their return, a further paper was presented to CBAC, which recommended: that credit unions be established; that a meeting of banks and the Department of Territories be organised to plan joint advertising and promotion of savings ('thrift'); that a liaison officer be appointed for Papua New Guinea; and that the Bank make clear its feeling 'that there should be a forward move in lending to indigenes.' On the last point, CBAC was of the opinion:

> . . . that it is likely to be some time before the volume of native borrowing would warrant consideration of a separate advance or credit policy for the Territory . . . However, as we are asking the banks to make special efforts in the Territory, the Committee feels that it should consider what would be involved in having policies differing from those required in Australia.

It proposed a meeting with banks, at which

> . . . we should tactfully suggest means of adapting the structure, staffing and policies . . . to meet the growing requirements of the

---

[6] One of the major beneficiaries under this scheme was a study of cocoa dieback.

[7] Phillips, an agricultural economist, later succeeded Curtin as manager of the Papua New Guinea Department and subsequently became deputy governor of the Bank.

> indigenous people . . . It is important that the banks be persuaded that T.P.N.G. should be regarded as a separate entity rather than merely as an extension of Australia.

A meeting was held with the banks early in 1961, but achieved little.

Subsequently, the Bank announced a programme of education in money, savings, banking and credit for Papua New Guineans, to be carried out in collaboration with the Department of Territories, the Territory administration and the banks in Papua New Guinea, and Phillips was posted to Port Moresby, with the designation 'special duties, monetary development'. In 1962 Phillips's staff was increased and he was joined by a Papua New Guinean, Robin Kumaina, who was seconded from the administration.[8] By then a booklet entitled *Your Money*, in English, Tokpisin and 'Police Motu', had been distributed and other publications were in preparation. (By 1966, 100 000 copies of the English version of *Your Money* were in circulation.) The Bank's Port Moresby staff numbers steadily increased in the early 1960s, with an increasing proportion of Papua New Guinean staff (see below), and in 1964 work commenced on a new building (in the early 1970s the Reserve Bank building dominated the downtown Port Moresby landscape).

By the early 1960s the Reserve Bank had thus established a significant presence in Papua New Guinea and initiated a process of localisation, had embarked on a programme of financial education, and was becoming increasingly involved in research into and monitoring of the Papua New Guinea economy.

In 1963 the Australian government requested the International Bank for Reconstruction and Development (IBRD) to undertake a survey of the Papua New Guinea economy. The controversial 'World Bank Report' (IBRD 1965) was presented the following year. Apart from observing that bank lending to indigenous bor-

---

8 Kumaina later became registrar of savings and loan societies, but eventually left the Bank to return to East New Britain as a businessman.

rowers was small and that 'Indigenous employment in banking, apart from the lowest levels is virtually non-existent' (ibid.:374), and advising that a separate monetary system would not be advantageous (ibid.:368), the Mission had little to say on the subject of money and banking. Its main recommendation was that, to mobilise credit to finance the economic development proposals it recommended, a Territory Development Finance Company should be established (ibid.:381-85). (This was later done, in the form of the Papua New Guinea Development Bank, and a Reserve Bank officer, John Beach, was seconded as deputy managing director.)

Curtin provided one of the first public commentaries on the World Bank Report – concluding, somewhat cryptically, that 'No one with a sense of colonial realities can do other than agree, in the main, with the commendations of this World Bank Mission' (Curtin 1965:58) – and the Council on New Guinea Affairs, of which Curtin was a board member and sometime secretary, and to which the Reserve Bank provided funding, organised two seminars (one in Melbourne, one in Goroka) to discuss it. At the high-profile seminar in Goroka, which was attended by Australian opposition leader Gough Whitlam, Coombs presented a paper. In it, he endorsed the assumption 'that it is the Australian Government's intention . . . to try to keep ahead of the demands of the local people' in the transfer of political power, and expressed dissatisfaction with the World Bank Report's 'lack of precision in dealing with the task of stimulating indigenous enterprise', before going on to outline the work the Reserve Bank was undertaking in creating, developing and guiding an emerging financial system (Coombs 1965:62, 63, 64).

In 1965, in accordance with a recommendation of the World Bank Report, the Australian government created the position of Economic Advisor to the Papua New Guinea Administration,[9]

[9] From 1961 there had been a Central Planning and Policy Committee, but it had no full-time staff. Following the World Bank mission's visit a Projects and Planning Team was created; prior to the appointment of

and an Australian economist then with the Prime Minister's Department in Canberra, Bill McCasker, was posted to Port Moresby. In 1967 and 1968 McCasker's office produced two important policy documents, *Economic Development of Papua and New Guinea* and *Programmes and Policies for the Economic Development of Papua New Guinea*, as a basis for future economic policy direction. They broadly followed the strategy proposed in the 1964 World Bank report, concentrating on areas of high economic potential and assuming a continuing major role for expatriate enterprise. The documents provoked a lively debate, notably in successive issues of the Council on New Guinea Affairs journal, *New Guinea*. One of the first critiques came from Curtin. Curtin argued that by adopting general economic development – as opposed to the development of the indigenous people and their economy – as the overriding policy objective:

> We are in danger of building an economy to which New Guinea society will be unable to adapt itself, and which the New Guinea statesmen of the future will be unable to control. [1968:20]

In early 1964, at Coombs's request, a 'Plan of Work for TPNG' (10 April 1964) was prepared, considering the activities the Bank was likely to become involved with 'over the next few years' (the assumption was that the Territory would move towards self-government in this period), and appropriate administrative structures within the Bank. Amongst subjects addressed in this work-plan and a series a subsequent CBAC memoranda were: separate currency (see below); possible expansion of the Bank's role as adviser to the Administration (which was seen as likely to 'necessitate a major expansion in our research activities' in Port Moresby and Sydney); and a separate monetary policy for Papua New Guinea. Consideration of the last of these culminated

---

McCasker, two Reserve Bank officers – A. MacIntyre and M.J. Phillips – acted as team leaders and a young graduate was seconded to the team. Another Bank officer, Ron White, assisted ANU economists in the preparation of national income accounts.

in a policy decision in 1966 that banks' lending in Papua New Guinea should no longer be subject to the Bank's general lending policies, but should take account of needs and conditions within the Territory (*RBA Report* 1966:25), but without amendment to the *Australian Banking Act*.

Administratively, the position of 'manager' for Papua and New Guinea had been created in 1963 (i.e. Curtin's title had changed) and the following year responsibility for the TPNG Committee shifted from an adviser to the manager of Research Department; in 1965 the Papua New Guinea Division came into being, and the Bank's operations in Papua New Guinea became the responsibility of the Division. Also in 1963 a graduate research officer was appointed to the Port Moresby office.[10]

More importantly, as a result of a proposal first made within the Bank in 1964, in 1966 an Advisory Committee on Central Banking (ACCENT) was established for Papua New Guinea. The advisory committee, which met two or three times a year to confer and advise on local banking and finance matters, comprised a senior Bank official from Sydney (the governor or his delegate), a representative of the Territory Treasury and nine permanent residents of Papua New Guinea (initially five of whom were Papua New Guineans); it was serviced by the Bank's research staff in Sydney and Port Moresby.

The separation of lending policy and the creation of the ACCENT represented substantial moves towards the creation of a separate central bank for Papua New Guinea.

With a view to furthering its central banking role as banker to the Administration, in 1965 the Bank also considered acquiring a small portfolio of Administration securities (it was proposed to subscribe $250 000 to the Territory's loan programme in 1966/67). A proposal went to the Bank's board for approval, but was opposed by Treasury in view of existing 'Commonwealth

---

10 Peter Ferguson joined Phillips in 1964. Ferguson had been working with the savings and loan movement in Rabaul. Later he returned as deputy governor of the Bank of Papua New Guinea.

Government/Papua and New Guinea Administration financial arrangements'; the board decided against the move. Five years later External Territories suggested to Treasury that the Bank give 'more positive' support to the Papua New Guinea loan programme, following undersubscription of a loan raising to finance the first instalment of Papua New Guinea's equity in the Bougainville mine. (The Bank had provided short-term funding of the required $12.5 million.) Treasury remained reluctant but the Bank provided capital funding to the Papua New Guinea Development Bank and later acquired a small Papua New Guinea security portfolio.

From the mid 1960s the Bank's work on and in Papua New Guinea intensified. The Port Moresby office was given greater responsibility, and for the most part operated through the Papua New Guinea Division rather than dealing with individual departments in the Bank. The Division reported half-yearly to the CBAC and annually to the Bank's board. From 1966-67 separate shadow accounts were kept for the Bank's Papua New Guinea operations (this had been proposed as early as 1963) and a TPNG Service staff classification system was introduced. From 1969 the Savings and Loan Registry operations were separated from those of the Bank. Research activities were coordinated between Sydney and Port Moresby. In 1970 the Papua New Guinea Division was upgraded to a full department.

Late in 1968 a memorandum from Curtin argued that the time had come to look at a Papua New Guinea banking ordinance, divorced from Australian legislation.[11] Others argued, however, that separate legislation was not needed to give effect to the development of policies specifically geared to Papua New Guinea's needs, and Curtin's initiative temporarily lapsed (though his call for national financial legislation was repeated in a paper to a Council on New Guinea Affairs seminar in Sydney in 1969 –

[11] A similar proposal had come from Curtin five years earlier, but CBAC had doubted whether the government would accept such a proposal, and did not pursue it.

see Curtin 1969-70:45). A later memorandum from Curtin argued for exemption of trading banks' business in Papua New Guinea from the central bank's statutory reserve deposit requirements and liquidity conventions, again without effect.

Early in 1970 a major research project was initiated within the Papua New Guinea Division to guide the Bank's policy making in the final run-up to self-government and independence.[12] The project envisaged a study in four parts, covering (1) a review of past developments; (2) an assessment of the present situation (including the relevance of Australian legislation and policy, and the adequacy of the financial system); (3) an examination of prospective issues in future development, and (4) an analysis of the implications for the Reserve Bank. Prospective issues were identified as:

- (a) Separate currency.
- (b) The role of a central bank.
- (c) The pattern of institutional development:
    - (1) Foreign entry.
    - (2) Multi-purpose banks.
    - (3) An indigenous bank.
    - (4) The Development Bank.
    - (5) Other specialist banks.
    - (6) The future of the Savings and Loan movement.
- (d) The development of a market in financial assets.

It was intended that Bank staff in both Sydney and Port Moresby be involved in the study.

The study was substantially completed when in July 1971 the Minister for External Territories proposed the establishment of a Committee on Banking in Papua New Guinea, comprising representatives from External Territories, Treasury, the Reserve Bank and the Papua New Guinea Administration.

Shortly before this, the Australian government had accepted the recommendation of the Select Committee [of the Papua New

---

12 'Research Project – Financial System for Papua New Guinea' (Papua and New Guinea Division, 29 July 1970).

Guinea House of Assembly] on Constitutional Development, that Papua New Guinea should be prepared for internal self-government in the period 1972-76. Banking was identified as one of the areas in which 'suitable arrangements would need to be developed' prior to self-government. The Committee's terms of reference directed it to make recommendations on: the major elements of a framework appropriate to banking in Papua New Guinea at self-government and at independence; the lines along which the Papua New Guinea banking system should be developed over the next few years; and the nature and timing of the various steps for setting up an appropriate banking system in Papua New Guinea. Prospective currency arrangements were specifically excluded from the terms of reference (see below).

The committee, which was chaired by Gerry Gutman of External Territories, held its inaugural meeting in Canberra in September 1971. The Bank's representatives at this meeting were J.B. Wright (a former secretary of the Reserve Bank, then holding the title of adviser), J.A. Kirkwood (of the Bank's Banking Department), D.G. McKenna (who had recently joined the Papua New Guinea Department, having previously been on secondment as deputy governor of the Bank Negara Malaysia), and the Bank's then deputy manager, Henry ToRobert; with the exception of ToRobert, these were men of essentially conservative disposition with little direct experience of Papua New Guinea.[13] The senior Treasury representative was Harold Heinrich, a person with no evident empathy for developments in Papua New Guinea.[14] The proceedings of the first meeting were largely devoted to discussing possible extension of the terms of refer-

[13] Wright did not attend later meetings and Kirkwood was replaced by D. Parr, without changing the tenor of the Bank's representation.

[14] The full list of those attending the inaugural meeting was Wright, Kirkwood, McKenna, ToRobert (Reserve Bank); Heinrich, T.W.J. Vear, R. Beetham (Treasury – though both Vear and Beetham were former Reserve Bank officers); H.P. Ritchie, V. Navuru (PNG Administration); G.O. Gutman, P. Kellaway, E. Ingevics and M.J. Hilyard (External Territories).

ence to include currency arrangements (the committee decided not to), and discussing publicity (it was agreed that low key publicity of the Committee's existence was desirable and that banks operating in Papua New Guinea should be approached for their views, but that 'no specific invitation would be extended to academics to express their views').

Three more meetings were held in Australia and Papua New Guinea during 1971, which considered a series of papers, mostly derived from the Reserve Bank's research project and including (for the third meeting) a pro forma banking ordinance.

By this time the desirability of localising banking legislation had been underlined by an 'in principle' proposal from the Bank of New South Wales to register a subsidiary, to be called the First Papua and New Guinea Bank Ltd, which would provide integrated trading and savings bank services in Papua New Guinea. As early as 1963 the TPNG committee had suggested that banks operating in Papua New Guinea be encouraged to transform their Territory branches into local subsidiary companies. In 1971 the Papua New Guinea Department supported the idea of using the Bank of NSW's application as leverage to introduce a separate banking ordinance in Papua New Guinea; but in the event the Bank of NSW was persuaded to hold off on its application pending the report of the Banking Committee. Also, an informal application from the First National City Bank to open a branch in Papua New Guinea – challenging the Australian policy of exclusion of 'foreign' banks – was 'discouraged' following discussion with Treasury, though the Papua New Guinea Department expressed support for the FNCB's entry.

The Banking Committee's progress was, however, slow. A note on the minutes of the fourth meeting of the Committee (written shortly before I left the Bank in January 1972) made the comment:

> It is disappointing, to say the least, to see that by December 1971 – the date initially set for completion of the draft preliminary report – the Committee has made so little progress towards a

> definition of issues, let alone a series of policy recommendations. The account of the fourth meeting reveals a lack of direction on major policy issues and the draft summary of recommendations is so trite as to be virtually useless, its only substantive content being a negative one – that there is no necessity to do anything before self-government.

Such disappointment was heightened by the fact most of the substantive issues canvassed by the Banking Committee had been comprehensively addressed within the Reserve Bank before the Committee had even met.

An interim report was eventually presented in January 1972.[15] It recommended: that control of banking be transferred to local authorities 'as soon as practicable'; that Papua New Guinea should have its own central bank; and that the business of the Commonwealth Banking Corporation in Papua New Guinea should be transformed into a Papua New Guinea institution. However, the Committee did not expect 'any immediate demand for self-government' from the new House of Assembly to be elected in 1972, and proposed a timetable which extended into 1974. Moreover, the Committee commented that 'the full implications of the legislative changes required to implement the transfer of banking powers . . . have yet to be considered' – notwithstanding the fact that extensive documentation had been prepared in the Bank in 1970 – and there were unresolved differences between External Territories, Treasury and the Bank as to the sequencing of transferring general banking powers, establishing a central bank, and granting full central banking powers. Indeed, in its response to the interim report External Territories argued that in recommending a central bank the report went further than the committee envisaged (suggesting that the term 'central monetary authority' be used rather than 'central bank', and that decisions about its nature and powers await dis-

15 'Committee on Banking in Papua New Guinea. Interim Report'. 26 January 1972. Mimeo.

cussion with the IMF). External Territories also stepped back from the committee's recommendation on the Commonwealth Banking Corporation, suggesting that its continued operation in Papua New Guinea was still an option.

On the question of a central bank, the committee presented a number of arguments in favour of a separate central bank, but its recommendation was clearly influenced by consideration that 'an embryo central bank already exists' and that training of Papua New Guinean staff and operation of a local Advisory Committee on Central Banking had been initiated some time ago.

Throughout this period (from the early 1960s to the early 1970s) relations between those responsible for the Bank's Papua New Guinea operations and the personnel of External Territories had been cordial, though not especially close. Curtin, Phillips and later myself had good relations with Gutman – who shared the Bank's generally progressive attitude to the pace of development in Papua New Guinea; on the other hand, Curtin especially had little time, intellectually, for External Territories secretaries Warwick Smith (1960-1970) or Hay (1970-1973), both of whom he saw as essentially conservative. Relations with Treasury, on the other hand, were never close and were sometimes antipathetic, reflecting in part a general ambivalence in relations between the Reserve Bank and Treasury during this period, and in part the Treasury's apparent reluctance to embrace change in Papua New Guinea. In contrast, by virtue of its longstanding presence in Port Moresby, the Bank probably had closer working relations with the Papua New Guinea Administration, and later with Papua New Guineans, then either External Territories or Treasury.

With the change of government which brought Whitlam to office in Australia, and the emergence of the Somare government in Papua New Guinea, from 1972 the pace of change quickened and increasingly the initiative for policy change came not from Canberra or Sydney but from Port Moresby.

In early 1972 a confidential 'Gearing-Up Plan' was prepared

by officials in Port Moresby, listing activities to be carried out before self-government (then anticipated as December 1975); the list included a separate central bank and banking system. The establishment of a central bank and separate currency were identified as areas of potential conflict between Australia and Papua New Guinea (Barnett 1981:49, 53).

The Committee on Banking submitted its final report in December 1972, and four months later the two governments announced their agreement on future banking arrangements. This included transfer of control of banks and financial institutions operating in Papua New Guinea to local authorities; the establishment of a central bank based on the Port Moresby office of the Reserve Bank; the creation of a Papua New Guinea Banking Corporation to take over the bulk of the business of the Commonwealth Banking Corporation; and the merging of trading and savings banking operations. A *Central Banking Ordinance* and a *Banks and Financial Institutions Ordinance* were passed by the House of Assembly in September 1972 and the Bank of Papua New Guinea was launched the following month, with ToRobert as its first governor. At a launching ceremony Prime Minister Somare paid tribute to the Reserve Bank's 'foresight and planning'.

The savings and loan movement

In 1959 the Thomas-Ryan report had recommended the creation of credit unions as an appropriate means of drawing Papua New Guineans into the financial system. A follow-up survey by officers of the Bank in 1960 'found considerable interest and enthusiasm for the idea of credit unions, both in government circles and amongst such indigenous organisations as were contacted on the matter' (Lanes 1969:118), and in early 1961 Curtin and Phillips, accompanied by Elliott Elijah of the Administration's Cooperatives Registry, visited Fiji to examine the experience with credit unions there before making a final commitment. A memorandum, written on their return, 'confirmed the view, already widely held, that the credit union type of activity had distinct possibilities as a primary training ground for the money economy',[16] and recommended that the Bank assist in their establishment. There was support for the idea within the administration, specifically from the Co-operatives Division; but since the latter lacked the resources to set up credit unions the task was left to the Reserve Bank, with the expectation that the commercial banks would provide some support.

Following a change in terminology from 'credit union' to 'savings and loan society', a *Savings and Loan Societies Ordinance* was passed in September 1961. In his second-reading speech on the bill the Territory treasurer, H.H. Reeve, described the savings and loan societies as a 'type of "pre-banking" system', intended to 'supplement' the banking system.[17] It was intended that the societies should:

1. help to foster the habit of thrift amongst the people;
2. provide education for their members in the fields of finance generally and financial responsibility in particular;
3. enable the making of small loans for wise purposes which it would not be practicable for existing financial intermediaries to undertake;
4. play some part in fostering capital formation in the Territory; and,
5. place in the hands of members a valuable means of furthering their own development. [Elvery 1962:30-31]

In its 1964 report (p.25) the Bank described savings and loan societies as:

> . . . in effect, small scale co-operative banks. Their main functions are to mobilise small savings and to provide credit in small amounts. At the same time, they enable the indigenous people to

---

[16] (P.W.E. Curtin and M.J. Phillips) 'Credit Societies for Papua-New Guinea' (internal memorandum, Reserve Bank of Australia, March 1961).

[17] T.P.N.G., *Legislative Council Debates September 1961.*

gain valuable training and practical experience in the running of financial enterprises. [*RBA Report* 1964:25]

The following year, it referred to the savings and loan movement as 'a sub-banking system designed to provide a stepping stone to the use of the established banking system and to an extent to supplement it' (*RBA Report* 1965:28).

The first savings and loan society was formed in 1962 and Papua New Guineans were recruited for training in savings and loan operations. An officer of the Bank was appointed registrar of savings and loan societies and expatriate and indigenous staff were posted to Rabaul and Lae to encourage and assist in the development of savings and loan societies and savings clubs. The commercial banks in Papua New Guinea subsequently seconded several officers to the movement and offices were established in Goroka, Mount Hagen and Kavieng. In June 1963 there were four savings and loan societies, with membership of 209 and funds of $6256; by June 1967 the number had grown to 189, with membership of over 10000 and balances of $0.6 million. In 1966 a national Federation of Savings and Loan Societies was established, with funds from a levy on all society members, to provide some common services, including insurance of members' funds and the channelling of funds between societies to enable a more efficient use of the members' money. Also in 1966 a Gazelle League of Savings and Loan Societies was formed amongst societies in East New Britain, to provide advice, training, and audit facilities to members, and organise a discount purchasing service. In 1969 the Gazelle League employed six staff – all indigenous (one of them being John Kaputin) – and owned a building and vehicles. Another League was formed in the Eastern Highlands in 1967, on a more modest scale. (Amongst its directors were Hari Gotoha and Soso Subi, two of the Gorokans referred to in Finney's *Big-Men and Business* [1973].)

The history of the savings and loan movement has been recounted, at least in part, elsewhere.[18] The movement enjoyed a rapid growth during the 1960s. Although the more successful societies were concentrated in Port Moresby and Rabaul – where better educated Papua New Guineans provided both a pool of relatively skilled manpower and source of income and demand for loans – adventurous young field officers enthusiastically set up savings clubs and societies throughout Morobe and the highlands (some of which could not be relocated years later). By the late 1960s, the movement was represented in fifteen of the country's eighteen districts. However, poor understanding of the functioning of societies and a chronic problem of non-repayment of loans had, in Lanes's words (1969:(iii)), 'tended to undermine the societies' reputation and image amongst members', and with only 41 per cent of members' funds invested in loans to members at June 1969, much of the effect of savings and loan activities was to transfer indigenous savings to the banks for on-lending to non-indigenes. These problems were only partially addressed in the early 1970s.

The development of the savings and loan movement represented an early and innovative initiative in attempting to develop financial institutional arrangements appropriate to the needs of Papua New Guineans, at a time when the commercial banks (with the minor exception of the Commonwealth Savings Bank) showed almost no interest in the development of a Papua New Guinean clientele.[19] In developing this cooperative credit system the Bank created a structure that was based fundamentally on the notion of self-help and was, at all levels of its administration, localised to quite a high degree.[20]

---

[18] One of the Bank's savings and loan officers, Ross Lanes, wrote a MEc thesis on the subject in 1969 (Lanes 1969) and other accounts are given in Elvery (1962), Coombs (1965), Andrews (1969) and Kumaina (1970).

[19] A survey of trading bank lending to indigenous borrowers undertaken in 1972 revealed that the banks' interest was still minimal (see May 1974).

[20] At June 1969, of the 38 staff of the Savings and Loan Societies Registry 29 (including the deputy registrar) were Papua New Guinean.

Staff development

In its second annual report, in 1961, the Reserve Bank noted that two Papua New Guineans had been sent by the Bank to Brisbane, to upgrade their secondary school qualifications. The following year another two were sent to Brisbane and one (Henry ToRobert) was enrolled in the Economics Faculty at Sydney University. In 1963 the Bank's report specifically observed that indigenous officers were being trained to 'assume duties currently undertaken by Australians', and noted that six officers were undergoing further secondary training in Australia, including the first woman. Attempts to allocate further bursaries for study at Sydney University in 1963 were unsuccessful, but a second Papua New Guinean (Nick Bokas) was enrolled in Economics the following year. ToRobert graduated from Sydney University in 1967 (becoming Papua New Guinea's second university graduate) and after attending central banking courses in Sri Lanka and Washington (at the IMF) returned as economic research officer in the Bank's Port Moresby branch, which was already being developed as an embryo central bank. With the establishment of the University of Papua New Guinea in 1965, the Bank's 1967 report recorded that seven officers were undergoing further secondary training in Australia, five were attending tertiary institutions in Papua New Guinea on Bank scholarships, and 18 were taking correspondence courses. The same year the Bank announced the formation, in Port Moresby, of a Territory of Papua and New Guinea Bankers' College, a residential college which provided training courses for officers in the five banking institutions then operating in Papua New Guinea.

In addition to its own trainees, the Reserve Bank's Papua New Guinea Division provided a point of contact for other Papua New Guineans studying in Australia: both Bernard Narokobi (studying law at Sydney University) and Charles Lepani (studying Commerce at the University of New South Wales) spent vacation periods working in the Division, where they gained experience of central banking and economic analysis – and were able to discuss their university assignments with the Bank's research staff. John Kaputin (who, as noted, was briefly employed with the Gazelle League of Savings and Loan Societies) was another occasional visitor to the Bank's headquarters in Sydney.

In 1964 the Reserve Bank had 20 officers in Papua New Guinea, of whom eight were Papua New Guinean; the following year, of a staff of 31, 13 were Papua New Guinean; by 1967 the respective figures were 58 and 44. At a time when serious localisation had barely begun in the administration, let alone in the private sector, and was virtually non-existent in the commercial banking sector,[21] the Reserve Bank had thus achieved a 76 per cent localisation of its staff and had put in place a substantial training programme for its own staff and for the banking system generally.

Moreover, in its Sydney head office, the Bank's Papua New Guinea operations attracted the interest of some of the Bank's brighter young and middle-range staff, thus ensuring a lively intellectual environment for the expanding Port Moresby office and, especially, for its emerging young graduate staff, who were encouraged to take part in public seminars and to publish.[22]

This trend continued in the late 1960s and early 1970s, providing the nucleus for a well trained independent central bank. The first UPNG scholars graduated in 1970. By the early 1970s,

---

[21] As late as 1970, indigenous employment in the banks in Papua New Guinea was as follows:

	male	female	total
Reserve Bank	59	26	85
PNG Development Bank	63	-	63
Commonwealth Banking Corp.	28	2	30
Bank of NSW	30	12	42
ANZ	10	-	10
National	4	-	4

(Figures of total employment are not available, but it should be remembered that the four commercial banks all had several branches.)

[22] An interesting early example of this is ToRobert's paper on 'New Guinea's leadership', published in *New Guinea* 1(3), 1965.

however, it was clear that not all of the Bank's graduates could become governor, and with the administration and private sector making a belated effort to localise, many left the Bank to take positions elsewhere. ToRobert remained, becoming manager in 1972 and the Bank of Papua New Guinea's first governor the following year. Bokas also stayed, later becoming deputy governor. An incomplete list of those who left reveals just how much the Bank's far-sighted staff development initiatives contributed to Papua New Guinea's post-independence leadership: it includes Paul Pora (who later returned to the Western Highlands as a council clerk, subsequently becoming a prosperous businessman and prominent member of parliament), Sinai Brown (later secretary and then premier of East New Britain), Tom Fox (sometime chairman of the Papua New Guinea Investment Corporation), Paliau Lucas (subsequently with the Central Planning Office and then Housing Commissioner, before returning to local politics in his home province of Manus), Elison Kaivovo (who became finance officer in the East New Britain provincial government), Eliakim To Bolton (subsequently a senior officer in the Department of Finance), Longas Solomon (who was seconded as finance officer in the East Sepik provincial government and later served as Papua New Guinea's consul-general in Sydney) and Epel Tito (a savings and loan officer who was later Minister for Defence in the national government).

When the Reserve Bank's Port Moresby office was transformed into the Bank of Papua New Guinea in 1973, 85 per cent of its staff had been localised including the entire female staff.

The issue of separate currency

The question of whether Papua New Guinea should have its own currency was raised within the Department of Territories as early as 1953. At that time the Reserve Bank opposed the idea of a separate currency, on the grounds that it was hard to imagine a Papua New Guinea currency not fixed to the Australian dollar or supported by Australia, that it would be unlikely to yield worthwhile benefits to Papua New Guinea, and that it would introduce confusion in trade, inconvenience to visitors, and additional work for banks and traders.[23] Territories concurred. The issue was raised again nearly a decade later, first in the context of a forthcoming visit by an IBRD mission, and second in relation to the commencement of planning for the introduction of decimal currency in Australia in 1966. On the latter occasion – notwithstanding the opinion of the Reserve Bank's manager in Port Moresby (Phillips), that if separate currency were likely to come within, say, ten years of 1966, its introduction with decimalisation would seem sensible[24] – the prevailing view within the Bank, and the view passed on to the acting treasurer in Port Moresby, was that, 'we consider it better that the Territory should continue to use Australian currency'.[25] The IBRD subsequently coalesced in this opinion, saying, 'at this time a separate monetary system would not be to the economic advantage of the Territory' (IBRD 1964:368).

In introducing legislation to implement decimal currency in 1964, the Papua New Guinea Treasurer told the House of Assembly that, although 'serious consideration' had been given to the introduction of a Territory currency, and although 'It is elementary that working as we are towards the independence of the Territory . . . a local currency will be introduced at some time or another', the Administration believed that the interests of the Territory would be best served at that stage by the adoption of the new Australian decimal currency.[26] (Eight months previously

[23] Letter from Coombs to Territories, 6 October 1953.

[24] Memorandum from manager, Port Moresby 24 June 1963.

[25] Letter from deputy governor to manager, Port Moresby, July 1963. The Bank's analysis was set out in two internal memoranda: 'Establishment of Separate Currency' (Research Department, 19 December 1962) and 'Memorandum for Central Banking Advisory Committee. Action in T.P.N.G. in View of Australian Change to Decimal Currency' (Investment Department, 3 July 1963, with comments by Curtin and Elvery).

the Australian Minister for Territories had denied an ABC report that the Administration was considering a separate currency for Papua New Guinea.)

Over the next few years there was little reference to separate currency. Somare later said that in 1968 he had suggested that Papua New Guinea should have its own currency, and 'hardly anyone took me seriously',[27] and in 1969 Curtin had supported separate currency at a Council on New Guinea Affairs Seminar (Curtin 1969-70). However, when in 1970 the Reserve Bank embarked upon a major study of the future of Papua New Guinea's monetary and banking system (see above), possible future currency arrangements were on the research agenda. In October 1970 a paper entitled 'Separate Currency – What is it All About?' was presented to the Advisory Committee on Central Banking (ACCENT) in Port Moresby. Amongst other things it spelt out some of the advantages and disadvantages of Papua New Guinea's integration into the Australian monetary system. Another ACCENT paper in June 1971 discussed 'The Question of Currency Reserves in a Developing Country'. In May 1971 a paper on 'Separate Currency. A First Look at Questions of Implementation' was discussed at a Reserve Bank staff seminar; it looked at alternative possible currency arrangements and what was needed to implement them. A copy of the paper was sent to External Territories. The same month a visiting UN mission recommended that:

> at a later stage the creation of a territorial currency, fully backed by the Australian dollar and freely convertible into Australian currency, might be considered in order to facilitate the observation of monetary transactions relating to the Territory.

By this time, however, the issue of separate currency had become a point of some contention.

In April 1970, ANU Professor Heinz Arndt had addressed the

---

[26] *House of Assembly Debates* Vol. I No. 1, 11 June 1964, p 51.

[27] *Bank of PNG Quarterly Economic Bulletin* March Quarter 1975:2.

Nuigini Economic Society in Port Moresby on the subject of separate currency. Arndt argued, along the same lines as the Reserve Bank's Port Moresby manager in 1963, that nationalist sentiment would demand a separate currency for an independent Papua New Guinea and saw a strong case for its introduction well before independence, so that the step could be taken in conditions of relative calm.[28] Arndt's view caused concern within the administration, where it was believed that merely talking about the possibility of a separate currency could lead to an outflow of capital. The following month the administration issued a press release (No. 661, 25 May 1970) which denied that any consideration was being given to a separate currency. (Similar denials were repeated in January 1971 and October 1971.) The subject was raised again by academic economists at an ANZAAS conference in Port Moresby in August. About this time, also, the Reserve Bank's Papua New Guinea Department proposed to discuss the subject of separate currency with Treasury and Territories but was informed that senior officials thought this inappropriate; instead, the department arranged with Professor Arndt a seminar at ANU, at which papers were presented by Arndt, Phillips, and Don Stammer. In August 1971 I presented a further seminar on separate currency to the Nuigini Economic Society in Port Moresby, incurring the displeasure of the deputy administrator (Newman) and McCasker. What Newman and others failed to appreciate was that, apart from Newman's own statement in 1964, that 'it is elementary that . . . a local currency will be introduced at some time', the subject had been raised on several occasions, and discussed within the Bank's Advisory Committee, and business people in Papua New Guinea *expected* that such discussion should be taking place; when they denied

[28] Arndt's paper (published as Arndt 1971) was passed on to D.W.C. Allen in the Bank of England, who commented, '. . . we thought that Arndt's paper takes a very practical line and we broadly agree with his analysis and conclusions'.

that any consideration was being given to a separate currency, administration officials simply confirmed business people's fears that a separate currency was to be introduced and that its effects must be bad (why else would the administration deny that consideration was being given to the subject when it was so obviously under discussion?).

For reasons that are not clear to me (but presumably had to do with the general paranoia about the subject), in July 1970 Prime Minister Gorton had issued an edict that no study of currency should be undertaken without reference to him. When in 1971 the interdepartmental Committee on Banking in Papua New Guinea was convened, the subject of currency arrangements was specifically omitted from its terms of reference. At its inaugural meeting, however, External Territories Secretary David Hay suggested 'that the situation had changed considerably since then' [July 1970] and that his minister would be prepared to seek the government's approval for a study of future currency arrangements if the committee thought that this was desirable or necessary. In fact, the administrator of Papua New Guinea had requested that the Committee's work be extended to embrace an examination of future currency arrangements, suggesting that the Administrator's Executive Council would expect to be advised on the currency question.[29] Under pressure from the senior Treasury representative (Heinrich), and with the concurrence of the Reserve Bank representatives, the Committee resolved not to widen its terms of reference; instead, it agreed that the Reserve Bank would prepare a paper setting out the policy options available, to be considered by a working group comprising Treasury, Reserve Bank and External Territories officers.[30] In a handwritten note

[29] Draft letter from External Affairs Minister Barnes to Acting Treasurer (McMahon) (September 1971).

[30] The officers 'tentatively suggested' were myself, Mr Hogget (Treasury) and Mr Ingevics (External Territories).

of 30 September, following a phone conversation with Heinrich about how the issue was to be addressed, Curtin wrote:

> Mr Heinrich seems to be pernickety and ostrich-like about Currency. This question will not go away as a result of verbal quibblings. It's a question which, if ignored creates more troubles (and magnifies itself) than if faced up to and at least ventilated.

Correspondence between Curtin and Papua New Guinea's treasurer, H.P. Ritchie, also reveal that by October 1971 Papua New Guinea's treasurer, at least, had come to the view that 'the sooner Papua New Guinea has its own currency . . . the better'.[31]

In a subsequent letter from Barnes to the acting treasurer (McMahon) (7 October 1971), the External Territories Minister accepted the Committee's decision, but expressed 'full agreement' with the administrator's view and urged that the study be commenced at an early date. Two contemporary developments may have sharpened the minister's focus on the subject. First, Gough Whitlam had asked, in the Australian parliament, whether the Committee on Banking was authorised to inquire into and report upon a separate currency for Papua New Guinea. Second, in the context of rumours of an imminent Australian devaluation, primary producing interests in Papua New Guinea had made representations to the minister pointing out that they would lose from such a realignment and would seek compensation.[32] In a letter worthy of *Yes, Minister's* Sir Humphrey Appleby, the Treasurer (Snedden) responded: 'The question of currency is, as I feel sure you would agree, a delicate one with important political and psychological ramifications . . . For these reasons, I believe that we should be careful not to seek to influence the wishes of the local people . . .'

Shortly after this the Papua New Guinea House of Assembly passed a resolution urging the Australian government to restore

---

[31] Ritchie to Curtin, 11 October 1971.

[32] A paper on 'Effects of Currency Re-Alignments on Papua New Guinea' had been prepared in the Bank in October 1971.

the Australian dollar to its former parity with the United States dollar, and the chairman of W.R. Carpenter Holdings Ltd., at a company annual meeting in Port Moresby, observed that Papua New Guinea was unable to counter international currency manipulation because it did not have its own currency. Barnes again wrote to the Treasurer in early December observing that the government's capacity to respond to questions about separate currency was limited, 'because we have deliberately refrained from studying the subject until recently'; 'I now regard the matter as urgent', the minister wrote, and urged the Treasurer to extend the Committee's terms of reference. But the Treasury maintained its opposition, and was supported by the Bank's senior representative, Wright.

Having finally had its role determined (it was to consider a paper, prepared by the Reserve Bank, to be cleared by Treasury, External Territories and the Bank, shown to the Administration, and then formally submitted to External Territories for submission to the administrator), the currency working group met in Canberra in December 1971. A substantial paper ('Currency Arrangements for Papua New Guinea'), based on the paper discussed at a seminar within the Reserve Bank in May 1971, was considered. A diary note from the meeting records that there was broad agreement on the contents of the paper, though Treasury wanted a comment on prospective profits from currency issue to be qualified 'to take account of the possibility that any profits from a note issue would be taken into account in the determination of the Commonwealth grant to Papua New Guinea' (an improbable possibility which in fact was never contemplated), and considered that comments on timing[33] were 'not appropriate'. It was agreed that a simplified version of the paper should be prepared for forwarding to the administrator, subject to the

[33] 'If Papua New Guinea is ever to have its own currency there is a sound case for introducing it sooner rather than later . . . Deferment of separate currency (and, *a fortiori*, embargo of discussion of the subject) will not prevent speculation and may aggravate the effects of it'.

necessary departmental clearance, and another meeting was set for January 1972. In January, however, the Treasury representative failed to appear; on enquiry Ingevics and I were told that his supervisor (Heinrich) considered him 'too busy' to attend the meeting.

I left the Bank soon after this. In March I was told by former Bank colleagues that Treasury was attempting to either pidgeonhole or substantially dilute the currency working group's paper, and was encountering little resistance from the Bank's representatives on the Banking Committee.

But as 1972 progressed, the action in respect of policy development for Papua New Guinea shifted increasingly from Canberra and Sydney to Port Moresby. In February national Pangu Pati president, Gavera Rea, was reported as saying that an independent Papua New Guinea should have its own currency (*Post-Courier* 3 February 1972). In July ToRobert (who became manager of the Bank's Port Moresby branch in that month) complained that Papua New Guinea was impotent to protect its interests against world currency movements while tied to the Australian dollar (*Post-Courier* 11 July 1972). The same month, encouraged by Curtin, I submitted a paper examining alternative currency arrangements to *New Guinea* (May 1972), and at the request of Paul Ryan (secretary of the Chief Minister's Department), prepared a simplified version of the paper for the Administrator's Executive Council (cabinet).

In July 1973 Finance Minister Julius Chan announced that cabinet had decided that Papua New Guinea should have its own currency as soon as practicable (but not before December 1974, and initially with Australian and Papua New Guinean currencies in joint circulation). A Currency Working Group, chaired initially by Chan and later by ToRobert, was established to coordinate planning for the currency. The new currency was introduced in April 1975. In launching the kina and toea Prime Minister Somare said,' to have our own national money has long been one of my dreams . . . It makes me very proud to see and receive this beautiful money.[34]

The Reserve Bank and decolonisation

Due largely to the foresight of Coombs and the dedication of Curtin, the Reserve Bank became involved in Papua New Guinea early and closely. It sought to assist in the development of a financial and banking system appropriate to Papua New Guinea's needs, particularly through the savings and loan movement; it established the foundations for an independent central bank; it was a pioneer in the training of young Papua New Guineans for senior positions, and, for a while at least, it helped keep alive the discussion of a separate currency. Coombs, Curtin, Phillips and others also promoted intellectual debate, in Australia and Papua New Guinea, through their involvement in and the Bank's support of such institutions as the Council on New Guinea Affairs and the Waigani Seminar.

Frequently the Bank found itself pushing against an essential conservatism in Canberra (and sometimes in Port Moresby). Ironically, as self-government drew near and the future of banking came under inter-departmental review, representation of the Bank's views shifted largely from its Papua New Guinea Department to other parts of the Bank, where attitudes were less progressive. But by 1972 the real action was not in Canberra or Sydney but in Port Moresby, where ToRobert and a staff of Papua New Guineans and committed expatriates carried forward the momentum of Coombs, Curtin and Phillips. ToRobert became probably the longest-serving senior appointment in post-independence Papua New Guinea and the Bank of Papua New Guinea a bastion of financial responsibility in an increasingly challenged financial system. That, perhaps, is the ultimate measure of the Reserve Bank's role in decolonisation.

---

[34] Speeches by Somare, Chan and ToRobert are reproduced in *Bank of PNG Quarterly Economic Bulletin* March Quarter 1975.

18

NATIONALISM AND PAPUA NEW GUINEA WRITING*

Slowly, often reluctantly, Australians are coming to realise that Papua New Guinea is an emerging nation with its own cultures, its own history, and its own ability to express its views on its own future. The development of independent expression in the political sphere (though not at first encouraged by the Australian government) has already made itself felt in the formulation of administration policies and, gradually but inevitably, in Australia's official attitudes to the development of Papua New Guinea towards independence. There is little awareness outside Papua New Guinea, however, (and not all that much inside) of the groundswell of national consciousness reflected in the growth of a specifically Papua New Guinean literature. This review takes the release of several important publications by Papua New Guineans, or with a Papua New Guinea theme, to survey some of the developments in this field.

Albert Maori Kiki's autobiography, *Kiki*, published by Cheshire in 1968 (paperback edition, 1970), was the pathbreaker. In a simple direct manner it revealed something of the thinking and feeling of an intelligent and sensitive Papuan born into traditional society in the early 1930s, dragged into the whiteman's world via a mission school, and after a varied career, mostly with the administration, achieving national prominence in the 1960s as a trade union leader and one of the founders of the Pangu Pati, Papua New Guinea's first important political party. Maori Kiki's

* This review was first published in *Australian Quarterly* 43(2), 1971, and is reprinted by kind permission of the Australian Institute of Political Science.

book was at the same time an entertaining personal history, a valuable record of a disappearing traditional culture, and an often damning commentary on a colonial regime.

In bringing his biography to publication, Albert Maori Kiki was encouraged and assisted by Ulli Beier, then recently appointed to a lectureship in English Literature at the University of Papua New Guinea. Beier, already a catalyst in the development of contemporary indigenous literature and art in Nigeria, arrived in Papua New Guinea in 1967 and played a major role in encouraging young Papua New Guinean writers and helping to make their work available to the public. In 1969, *Kovave, a journal of New Guinea literature*, first appeared under his editorship (published by Jacaranda Press in conjunction with The New Guinea Cultural Centre of the University of Papua New Guinea). The journal presents creative writing in English and Pidgin, translations of traditional poetry and folk tales, some literary criticism, and notes on traditional art (and in two issues, advertisements which bring to the attention of Papua New Guineans a fragment of the rich recent writing of Africa). The first four issues of *Kovave* have included stories by Vincent Eri, John Kadiba, Kumalau Tawali, Peter Lus, Wairu Degoba, John Waiko, the Cook Islander Marjorie Crocombe, Maurice Thompson (New Hebrides) and Lazarus Lami Lami (Australia); poems by Pokwari Kale, Tawali, Allan Natachee and the Indian Chakravarthi; plays by Leo Hannett, Waiko, Rabbie Namaliu and Arthur Jawodimbari; translations of traditional poems and folklore by Maori Kiki, Don Laycock and others; an extract from a forthcoming autobiography by Hannett, and a critique of the poetry of Natachee – the first Papuan poet ever to get into print – by Beier. [*Kovave* ceased publication in 1974.]

Beier also edited two new series of slim paperbacks – *Papua Pocket Poets*, which published Indian, Indonesian, African and Australian poetry as well as that of Papua New Guinea, including poems by Tawali (*Signs in the Sky*), Natachee (*Aia*) and collections by Hannett, Tawali and Murray Russell, and *Pidgin Pocket Plays*. In addition Heinemann have published *Two Plays from New*

Guinea (John W. Kaniku and Turuk Wabei) and Jacaranda a volume of *Five New Guinea Plays* (Hannett, Waiko, Jawodimbari, Tawali and M. Lovori), two of which were produced in Canberra in 1969 and reviewed by Laycock in *Kovave* I(2). Laycock alleges a deliberate lack of media coverage of the performances. In 1971 Thomas Nelson (Australia) released a book, *Home of Man: The People of New Guinea,* by Paul Cox and the ubiquitous Ulli Beier, in which Papua New Guinea poems are used as vignettes for Cox's black and white photographic essay.

In Madang, the Kristen Press has been active in publishing writing ('inspirational, educational and entertaining') by Papua New Guineans and conducts a Creative Writing Centre with courses and workshops for writers, translators and editors.

Subsequently the administration itself entered the field, through the Bureau of Literature, Department of Information and Extension Services, with the publication of a low-cost quarterly, *New Guinea Writing* (No. 1, August 1970). Editor is Donald Maynard, whose *Fragment of the God* (1971) is one of the *Papua Pocket Poets,* and Tawali is assistant editor. Poetry and prose, in English, Pidgin and Motu, have been contributed by a number of writers including Eri, Natachee, Tawali, Waiko, Kadiba, Paulius Matane, Bob Giegao, Jacob Simet, Jack Lahui, Clemens Runawery, Peter Wia Paiya, John Kasaipwalova, Renagi Lohia, Joseph Saruva and Ikini Yaboyang. So far the bulk of the work in *New Guinea Writing* has been confined to stories of village life or retelling of folktales, though a 1971 issue contained a statement on 'cultural reconstruction' by Black Power leader Kasaipwalova. It is a less impressive publication than *Kovave,* but has the advantages of a larger market and lower price.

The Bureau also participated in organising residential creative writing courses and has sponsored literary competitions.

The above survey, brief as it is, gives an indication of the extent of the burgeoning of Papua New Guinea writing in the last couple of years [to 1971]. The pace at which this has taken place is in part traceable to the setting-up of the University (first graduates, 1970), which has provided a training ground and an environment conducive to the development of an indigenous literature; more generally, however, it reflects a growing national consciousness and body of articulate expression. Most of the contributions have come from students at the University of Papua New Guinea, though a number have come from other students, public servants and others. As is to be expected, many of these are political activists who felt strongly about the development of nationalism in Papua New Guinea, though (as with Hannett, for example) this may not be a unified Papua New Guinea nationalism. Sometimes nationalism is expressed through a reassertion of the values of the indigenous cultures or voicing of nostalgia for the traditional life, as is implicit in the translation and retelling of traditional poems, songs and folk tales, and explicit in such writing as Tawali's *The Bush Kanaka Speaks* and the poem of Herman Talingapua:

> Leleki baskets
> hang from the roof of the men's house
> pregnant with secrets
> and power.
> But I,
> the 'modern man',
> complete with suit,
> despatch case and transistor set,
> shall never know
> what hidden happiness or strength
> is tied up in these baskets.
> My age and 'learning' notwithstanding,
> I am excluded.
> Uninitiated,
> condemned to sleep with women,
> unfit to carry shield and spear.

In much of the writing, however, the nationalist sentiment is overtly anti-white. Amongst some of the more powerful of these, the anti-colonialist message lies in the situation created or reported by the writer; for example, in Waiko's play, *The Unexpected Hawk,* after the *kiap* (patrol officer) has burnt down a village whose people had refused to comply with a government order to move to become part of a single large village:

> Son: Why do they treat us like this?
> Mother: No one knows why. We do not understand them, and they do not try to understand us. But every tree has its roots deep down in the ground. Even their actions must have roots. I want you to go to school, so that you can dig out the roots. Do not hesitate to uproot their tree and drink their wisdom.

or from amongst the many enlightening and frequently amusing incidents ('When I was five years old, I thought priests were wonderful, because they wore trousers') in Hannett's autobiographical 'Disillusionment with the Priesthood' (*Kovave* II(1)):

> . . . we also had two different masses: one for Europeans and one for natives. I remember that once a Papuan came into the European mass, and he was literally chased out of the church by the Australian priest, who, incidentally, was a member of the Legislative Council!

Only occasionally is there anything approaching a violence of expression, as in *The Bush Kanaka Speaks,* by the usually restrained Tawali:

> Every white man the gorment sends to us
> forces his veins out shouting
> nearly forces the excreta out of his bottom
> shouting: you bush kanaka.
>
> He says: you ol les man!
> Yet he sits on a soft chair and does nothing
> just shouts, eats, drinks, eats, drinks,
> like a woman with a child in her belly.
> These white men have no bones.
> If they tried to fight us without their musiket
> they'd surely cover their faces like women.

My favourite of the overtly anti-colonialist writings is the delightful Pidgin poem by Leo Saulep, *'Wait Dok na Blak Dok' (New Guinea Writing,* No. 3), with its light but telling thrust at Australian colonialism:

Blak dok i tok: 'Nau brata givim mi
Tumora, wenem tumora mi no laik tumora,
Yu givim me bek nau yu go!'
Tasol wait dok i tok: 'Wet liklik bai mi go.'

At a more populist level, the growth of Papua New Guinea literature has had some counterpart in the presentation of three notable Pidgin/English national newspapers: *Pangu Pati Nius* (first issue, April 1970), *Bougainville Nius* (sponsored by the secessionist Napidakoe Navitu; first issue, July 1970 – '*Dispela niuspepa em i no bilong smok na tu em i no bilong rabim as. Taim yu pinis long ritim you putim gut na bihain bai yu inap long ritim gen*'), and *Wantok* (published by the Wirui Press [Catholic Mission], Wewak, first issue, August 1970). These are geared to a local audience, are a little bit educative and the latter two encourage people to express opinions through letters to the editor. *Bougainville Nius* is also publishing traditional stories.

Late 1970 saw another important development in Papua New Guinea literature, the publication of its first novel, *Crocodile,* by Vincent Eri (Jacaranda Press). Eri, born in the Gulf District of Papua in 1936, a former teacher and one of the first graduates of the University of Papua New Guinea, was in 1971 Acting Superintendent of Primary Education in Papua New Guinea [Eri later became governor-general of Papua New Guinea.]

Crocodile is a well-written and enjoyable novel. It is, however, more than this. It is impossible to review the book without being conscious of two things: first, that it is the first novel by a Papuan writer and, second, that whether intentionally or not it is to a certain extent a political document, as it is a major contribution to the growing body of writing which expresses a specifically Papua New Guinean identity. The central character in the novel, Hoiri Sevese, is born in the Gulf District of Papua between the world wars. After the death of his mother (attributed to sorcery) he is transferred from the Protestant to the Catholic mission school, where he begins his partial induction to the white man's world. As a boy he travels with his father on one of the *Hiri* trading voyages across the Gulf to Port Moresby, where his people trade sago and betel nut for the Motu pottery and where Hoiri experiences the wonder, confusion and humiliation of a Papuan in this European-ruled community. After his return to the village Hoiri gets married and becomes a father. The day after his son is born a patrol officer comes to the village and Hoiri is amongst those chosen to go as carriers and paddlers on a patrol inland.

> No one was more troubled than Sevese [Hoiri's father]. He wished Hoiri had never come into this world. He cursed the government and blamed Tamate [Rev. James Chalmers] for carrying the Word of God to the village, opening up the way for the patrol officers to be ordering his people around. If only the Government officers were like Tamate and other missionaries, who understood people and cared for their feelings, it would not be so bad. Maybe when people die and change their skins, their feelings and ideas also change.

While he is on patrol Hoiri receives the news that his wife has been taken by a crocodile. Refused permission to go back to the village, Hoiri deserts and returns to kill the crocodile and embed his axe in an invisible rider of the crocodile (a sorcerer). Subsequently he is told that his wife was claimed in retribution for two sorcerers killed by his uncle and that in Kerema people saw a man with a big wound on his shoulder. But before this episode is closed the war intervenes ('It seemed a silly idea that the white men and the yellow men should come to Papua to fight one another. Still, there was no clear story about the reasons why they were fighting one another') and Hoiri, and his father, are enlisted by ANGAU to support Australia's war effort. As a carrier on the Bulldog-Wau trail (Eri's own father worked on this trail and died after being returned to his village on a stretcher) and in Lae, Hoiri is exposed to more of European civilisation as well as coming closer to a wider group of his fellow Papuans before being thrown back to his village – the war over, his father dead and the presumed agent of his wife's death killed, with 11 pounds, five sticks of tobacco and the hope that his son might grow up to understand the things that baffle him.

Hoiri is essentially a tragic figure. Already partially alienated from the traditional society by his schooling and the church association of his father, he does not fully comprehend the balance between the material and supernatural worlds of a culture which has no real concept of natural death; still less is he able to come to terms with the reality of a dominant European culture which seems to be reaching out to him yet offers him neither respect nor the gift of understanding. Eri portrays this confusion with sympathy, elegance and power. The hope of resolving the confusion lies with Hoiri's son, yet something recalls a wistful comment in Kiki:

> Of course no custom continues for ever . . . And yet I feel cheated somehow, when I remember that I never underwent the *miro ava akore* festival, that I never sat in the *che eravo*, and that no Orokolo girl ever marked me 'as her tree'.

The 'political' content of *Crocodile* is both in the situation it portrays – the clash of cultures in which an uncomprehending traditional society is manipulated by a technologically superior and culturally arrogant white man's world – and in the characterisation of the people in those worlds. The characterisation of the whites is severe, but not vindictive; this is a novel to probe sensitivities, not to club them down.

The main weakness of the novel is that in both situations and characters Eri has tended to draw stereotypes; they are all there – the exploitative missionary, the indiscreet white mistress, the stupid inexperienced patrol officer, the wise, faithful native sergeant, the hard brusque ADO, the simple good-bloke Australian soldier, the revelatory American negro soldier, the cruel ANGAU officer. Perhaps it is appropriate, however, that a country's first novel should record these types. If *Crocodile* does not have the polish of some African writing with a similar theme (Achebe's *Things Fall Apart* comes to mind) it is nonetheless an admirable beginning.

Shortly after the publication of *Crocodile,* Jacaranda Press released another important novel with a Papua New Guinea setting, *The Stolen Land,* by Ian Downs. Though not an indigenous product, Downs's book is included in the context of this review because it is concerned with New Guinea nationalism, and because Downs's writing carries the authority of his intimate association with the country, as district commissioner, planter, and member of parliament and of the Administrator's Council. It can be read, we are told, as a serious attempt to explain and excuse the development and destruction of the hero, a Melanesian torn by the counter-pressures of the modern world and his own pre-literate society:

> in the hope that some notice can be taken of its warning of future violence so that some of the lessons of our time can be used in an endeavour to ensure that home rule and independence in Papua New Guinea can be orderly and peaceful.

The Stolen Land traces the development of Joseph Makati from his departure to school in Australia ('Joseph had been chosen by his village as an expendable orphan to be given to the Church'), through his return to the New Guinea highlands and entry to politics under the guidance of a king-making European planter:

> 'The first thing', Hardie told Joseph, 'is to remember you are black and then be thankful. You are born in an age when the twilight of the white man in this country is clear and the day of the coloured man very close . . . The honourable and sensible thing for you to do is to lead your people before you are caught up in the middle of the mob, with no choice of direction'.

to the achievement of national prominence and representation of his country at the United Nations and on, eventually, to the end of the story. In this reviewer's opinion *The Stolen Land* is a failure as a novel, unsatisfying as a story and yet well worth reading.

The first half of the book is perceptive, informative and well written, building up tension while offering a good measure of sensitive descriptive writing, sharp commentary on Papua New Guinea society – black and white – and often vitriolic humour:

> No one will ever know what Sir James and Lady Craig privately thought about the social occasions which passed for hospitality at Government House and which it was their duty to provide . . . There were drinks at a table presided over by a bar steward and a tray of anaemic dry sandwiches contrived from some sort of fish-paste on another table further away. There were not many of these and guests were reluctant to seem greedy by rushing them. Those who did investigate them seldom returned and it is possible that some sandwiches survived to be used again.

Always a formidable critic of much of what goes on in administration, in white society generally, and amongst the local people, and with a close knowledge of the landscape and the people, Downs is at his best in building up to the election of Makati.

From this point on, however, the novel deteriorates. It is as though Downs believes that to maintain the pace of the story he must keep increasing the 'bigness' of his setting. In quick succession Makati is selected to visit the UN, scores a gleefully acknowledged verbal coup over a Russian delegate, is kidnapped at gunpoint by a black power leader, is seduced by 'a big ripe [Russian] woman' who restores his manhood and pride in the name of international brotherhood (Makati reciprocates by hopping into bed with another young woman so that she can prove she is not a colonialist), and returns to plot something like a bloody, messianic Unilateral Declaration of Independence. The plausible Hardie turns into some sort of super CIA agent, a believable liberal academic type becomes a stooge of a vast international conspiracy, as does a recognisable administration type (in the hopes of acquiring a rich wife), and Makati himself inexplicably comes to assume a national status which apparently places him next to the administrator.

The result, unfortunately, is like something of a poor man's James Bond. And amidst all this there is a constant allusion to 'alien [especially communist?] intrigue' which at first looks like a satire of the Kingsford Smiths [Kingsford Smith was a prominent member of the planter community in Papua New Guinea in the early 1970s.] et al. of the unworldly conservative clique, but subsequently appears to express Downs's own forebodings. If this is what is meant by 'the lessons of our time' which the dustjacket points us to, it is not clear, at least to this reviewer, precisely what Downs is warning us all against, still less what should be done to ensure that nirvana of orderly and peaceful transition to independence.

The other major Papua New Guinea book to appear within the last few months also has something to do with the clash of cultures, though that is not its main subject. *Hohao* (Nelson, 1971) represents a joint effort by Ulli Beier and Albert Maori Kiki to record something of a declining culture while it is still more or less possible to do so. It is a study of the carved and painted ancestral spirit boards, *hohao,* of the Elema people from the villages of Orokolo in the Papuan Gulf. The pictures and description of the important *hohaos* known to have survived are accompanied by the myths of the various clan heroes portrayed, as retold by Maori Kiki.

The culture of Orokolo survived the onslaught of European civilisation somewhat longer than the cultures of other parts of the Papuan Gulf, but shortly before the Second World War the men's cult houses were burnt down (probably by Christian converts) and they were never rebuilt. 'The traditional Orokolo culture was overcome by a spirit of complete malaise and depression'; the men's cults, initiation ceremonies and mask festivals died out and the distinctive art form almost disappeared. Of the few *hohaos* which survived this assault some were later cast aside by their owners who feared their power now that they were no longer subject to the restraints of traditional ritual. One *hohao* representing a powerful ancestor was, at the request of the ancestral spirit, dressed up in European clothes and buried in the Christian cemetery. Although there has been a recent revival of the art form as a commercial enterprise, the traditional *hohao* and much of the associated mythology is virtually lost.

It is perhaps a little disappointing that the authors have covered only a small segment of the rich culture of this region and that, apparently, they have not gone beyond Papua for examples of this art form. But their approach serves to press home the realisation that we have been left with only the scraps of a culture. *Hohao* is a nicely produced volume and a welcome addition to the sparse literature on the traditional art of Papua New Guinea.

And there are more books by Papuan and New Guinean writers in the pipeline: Albert Maori Kiki has received a Commonwealth Literary Fund award to work full-time on another book and autobiographical works are promised from Paulias Matane, head of the newly created Department of Business Development, and from Leo Hannett. [Michael Somare's *Sana* also appeared in 1975.]

The rapid expansion in Papua New Guinea's indigenous literary output in recent years is important. Apart from providing entertaining reading with a local flavour, it rests with Papua New Guinea writers to record something of their traditional cultures before they disintegrate, and to help to formulate a sense of national identity and to get the country's nationalist demands across to Australia and the world generally. There is no doubt that Papua New Guineans will benefit from this; hopefully it will also contribute to a more sensitive appreciation by Australians of the difficulties and responsibilities of being a retiring colonial power.

REFERENCES

Aberle, D.F., 1962. 'A note on relative deprivation theory as applied to millenarian and other cult movements', in S. Thrupp (ed.), *Millennial Dreams in Action. Comparative Studies in Society and History*, Supp. II. The Hague: Mouton, pp. 209-14.

Adams, R., 1982. 'The Pitenamu Society', in R.J. May (ed.), *Micronationalist Movements in Papua New Guinea*. Political and Social Change Monograph 1. Canberra: Department Of Political and Social Change, Research School of Pacific Studies, Australian National University, pp. 207-45.

Adas, M., 1979. *Prophets of Rebellion. Millenarian Protest Movements Against the European Colonial Order.* Chapel Hill: University of North Carolina Press.

Ake, C., 1967. *A Theory of Political Integration*. Homewood: Dorsey Press.

Allen, M., 1984. 'Elders, chiefs and big men: authority legitimisation and political evolution in Melanesia', *American Anthropologist* 11(1):20-41.

Almond, G.A. and Powell, G.B., 1966. *Comparative Politics: A Developmental Approach.* Boston: Little, Brown.

Almond, G.A. and Verba, S., 1963. *The Civic Culture.* Princeton: Princeton University Press.

Andrews, C. Lesley, 1969. 'Responses to the operation of savings and loan societies in two areas of Papua'. Paper presented to the Third Waigani Seminar. Port Moresby. Mimeograph.

____, 1975. Business and Bureaucracy: a study of Papua New Guinean businessmen and the policies of business development in Port Moresby. *New Guinea Research Bulletin* No.59. Port Moresby: New Guinea Research Unit, Australian National University.

Anere, R. and Ley, A., 1997. 'Milne Bay Province, 1978-1991', in R.J. May and A.J. Regan with A. Ley (eds), *Political Decentralisation in a New State: The Experience of Provincial Government in Papua New Guinea*. Bathurst: Crawford House Publishing, pp. 108-29.

Anggo, D., 1975. 'Kafaina: group action by women in Chuave', *Yagl-Ambu* 2(3):207-23.

Anis, T., 1976. 'The system of village government in Bougainville'. Paper presented to Young Nations Conference. Sydney. Mimeograph.

Arndt, H.W., 1971. 'The future of New Guinea's monetary system', *The Economic Record* 47(117):38-46.

Anthropology Quarterly 51(1), 1978. Special Issue, 'Sepik politics: traditional authority and initiative'.

Aufenanger, H., n.d. *The Passing Scene in North-east New-Guinea.* Collectanea Instituti Anthropos Vol. 2 St. Augustin: Anthropos Institute.

Axline, W. A., 1986. *Decentralisation and Development Policy. Provincial Government and the Planning Process in Papua New Guinea.* IASER Monograph 26. Port Moresby: Institute of Applied Social and Economic Research.

_____, 1988. 'Reform of Intergovernmental Fiscal Relations in Papua New Guinea: Trends in Provincial Government Finance, 1978-1988'. Port Moresby: Institute of Applied Social and Economic Research. Mimeograph.

Bailey, F.G., 1969. *Stratagems and Spoils: A Social Anthropology of Politics*. Oxford: Basil Blackwell.

Baker, J.C., 1970. 'The political education programme of the Papua New Guinea Administration', in M.W. Ward (ed.), *The Politics of Melanesia.* Canberra: University of Papua and New

Guinea and Research School of Pacific Studies, Australian National University.

Ballard, J.A., 1976.'Students and politics in Papua New Guinea'. University of London Institute of Commonwealth Studies Discussion Paper SPNS/76/2. Reprinted in *Journal of Commonwealth and Comparative Politics* 15(2), 1977:112-26.

____, 1981. 'Policy-making as trauma: the provincial government issue', in Ballard (ed.), *Policy-Making in a New State. Papua New Guinea 1972-77.* St. Lucia: University of Queensland Press, pp. 95-132.

Barnes, J.A., 1962/1971. 'African models in the New Guinea highlands', in L.L. Langness and J.C. Weschler (eds), *Melanesia: Readings on a Culture Area,* Scranton: Chandler Publishing Company, pp. 97-107 (reprinted from *Man* 62:59 [1962]).

Barnett, T.E., 1981. 'Policy-making in the transfer of powers from Australia', in J.A. Ballard (ed.), *Policy-Making in a New State: Papua New Guinea 1972-77.* St. Lucia: University of Queensland Press, pp. 48-74.

Bedford, R. and Mamak, A., 1977. *Compensation for Development: The Bougainville Case.* Christchurch: Bougainville Special Publication No.2.

Belshaw, C.S., 1950. 'The significance of modern cults in Melanesian development', *Australian Outlook* 4(2):116-25.

Benedict, B. (ed.), 1967. *Problems of Small Territories.* London: Athlone Press.

Bermann, W., 1971-72. *The Kamanuku: The Culture of the Chimbu Tribes.* Mutdapilly: H.F.W. Bermann.

Berndt, R.M., 1972. 'Social control', in P. Ryan (ed.), *Encyclopaedia of Papua and New Guinea,* Melbourne: Melbourne University Press in association with the University of Papua New Guinea, pp. 1050-65.

Berndt, R.M., and Lawrence, P. (eds), 1971. *Politics in New Guinea: Traditional and in the Context of Change. Some Anthropological Perspectives.* Nedlands: University of Western Australia Press.

Berry, R. and Jackson, R.T., 1981. 'Inter-provincial inequalities and decentralisation in Papua New Guinea', *Third World Planning Review* 3(1):57-76.

Bettison, D.G., 1965. 'The electoral education programme', in D.G. Bettison, C.A. Hughes and P.W. van der Veur (eds), *The Papua-New Guinea Elections 1964*. Canberra: Australian National University Press.

Billings, D.K., 1969. 'The Johnson Cult of New Hanover', *Oceania* 40(1):13-19.

Birch, A.H., 1978. 'Minority nationalist movements and theories of political integration', *World Politics* 30(3):325-44.

Blackwood, B., 1935. *Both Sides of Buka Passage.* Oxford: Clarendon Press.

Bodrogi, T., 1951. 'Colonisation and religious movements in Melanesia', *Acta Ethnographia* 2(1-4):259-92.

Bolongaita, Emil R., 1995. 'Presidential versus parliamentary democracy: rethinking Philippine plans for parliamentary reforms', *Philippine Studies* 43(1):105-23.

Bratton, Michael, 1989. 'Beyond the state: civil society and associational life in Africa', *World Politics* 41(3):407-30.

Brookfield, H., 1972. *Colonialism, Development and Independence. The Case of the Melanesian Islands of the South Pacific.* Cambridge: Cambridge University Press.

Brown, P., 1963. 'From anarchy to satraphy', *American Anthropologist* 65(1):1-15.

_____, 1966. 'Social change and social movements', in E.K. Fisk (ed.), *New Guinea on the Threshold.* Canberra: Australian National University Press, pp. 149-65.

Calvert, Peter (ed.), 1987. *The Process of Political Succession.* London: Macmillan.

Carbonell-Catilo, M.A., de Leon, J.H. and Nicolas, E.E., 1985. *Manipulated Elections.* Manila: n.p.

Carroll, J.J., 1994. 'Glimpses into Philippine political culture: gleanings from the Ateneo Public Opinion Survey data', *Pilipinas* 22:47-61.

Chelliah, R.J., 1981. *Provincial Revenue and Mechanism for Fiscal Adjustments in Papua New Guinea*. New Delhi: National Institute of Public Finance and Policy.

Che Man, Wan Kadir, 1990. *Muslim Separatism: The Moros of Southern Philippines and the Malays of Southern Thailand*. Singapore: Oxford University Press.

Chowning, A., 1977. *An Introduction to the Peoples and Cultures of Melanesia*. Second edition. Menlo Park: Cummings Publishing Company.

_____, 1979. 'Leadership in Melanesia', *The Journal of Pacific History* XIV (part 2):66-84.

Chowning, A. and Goodenough, W.H., 1971. 'Lakalai political organisation', in R.M. Berndt and P. Lawrence (eds), *Politics in New Guinea: Traditional and in the Context of Change. Some Anthropological Perspectives*. Nedlands: University of Western Australia Press, pp. 113-74.

Clunies Ross, A. and Langmore, J. (eds), 1973. *Alternative Strategies for Papua New Guinea*. Melbourne: Oxford University Press.

Cochrane, G., 1970. *Big Men and Cargo Cults*. Oxford: Clarendon Press.

Cohen, R., 1978. 'Ethnicity: problem and focus in anthropology', *Annual Review of Anthropology* 7:379-403.

Colebatch, H., 1979. *Policy, Process and Outcome In Government: A Study of the Rural Improvement Programme*. IASER Monograph 10. Port Moresby: Institute of Applied Social and Economic Research.

Connell, J., 1977. 'The decline of local government councils and the rise of village government', in J. Connell (ed.), *Local Government Councils in Bougainville*. Christchurch: Bougainville Special Publication No. 3, pp. 132-71.

_____, 1997. *Papua New Guinea. The Struggle for Development*. London: Routledge.

Connor, W., 1967-1968. 'Self-determination. The new phase', *World Politics* 20(1):319-55.

_____, 1971-1972. 'Nation-building or nation-destroying?',

World Politics 24(3):319-55.

____, 1973. 'The politics of ethnonationalism', *Journal of International Affairs* 27(l):1-21.

Constitutional Planning Committee (CPC), Territory of Papua and New Guinea, 1973a. *First Interim Report*, September. Port Moresby.

Constitutional Planning Committee (CPC), Territory of Papua and New Guinea, 1973b. *Second Interim Report*, November. Port Moresby.

Constitutional Planning Committee (CPC), Territory of Papua and New Guinea, 1974. *Final Report*. Port Moresby.

Conyers, D., 1976. *The Provincial Government Debate: Central Control Versus Local Participation in Papua New Guinea*. IASER Monograph 2. Port Moresby: Institute of Applied Social and Economic Research.

Conyers, D. and Westcott, R., 1979. 'Regionalism in Papua New Guinea', *Administration for Development* 13:1-28.

Coombs, H.C., 1965. 'Pennies and politics', *New Guinea* 1(2):62-9.

____, 1981. *Trial Balance. Issues of My Working Life*. Melbourne: Sun Books.

Corral, V.P., 1993. 'Sectoral representatives in the Eighth Congress: a documentation', *Congressional Studies Journal* 1(1):6-102.

Crouch, H., 1986. 'Indonesia and the security of Australia and Papua New Guinea', *Australian Outlook* 40(3):167-74.

Curtin, P.W.E., 1965. 'The World Bank Report. A review', *New Guinea* 1(1):52-8.

____, 1966. 'The independence issue. Australian obligation', *New Guinea* 1(6):32-6.

____, 1968. 'How to be inconsistent', *New Guinea* 3(1):19-24.

____, 1969-70. 'Money and self-government. Localising the finance structure', *New Guinea* 4(4):41-56.

Dahanayake, P.A.S. (ed.), 1982. *Post-Independence Economic Development of Papua New Guinea*. IASER Monograph 19. Port Moresby: Institute of Applied Social and Economic Research.

Dahl, R.A. and Tufte, E.R., 1974. *Size and Democracy*. London: Oxford University Press.

Daro, B.B., 1976. 'The Papua Besena movement: *Papua dainai, tano dainai, mauri dainai*', IASER Discussion Paper No. 7. Port Moresby: Institute of Applied Social and Economic Research.

Dauvergne, P., 1998. 'Weak states and the environment in Indonesia and the Solomon Islands', in P. Dauvergne (ed.), *Weak and Strong States in Asia-Pacific Societies*. Sydney: Allen & Unwin.

Davis, M.M., 1970. 'Student hang-ups and student action: student political activity at the University of Papua and New Guinea', in M.W. Ward (ed.), *The Politics of Melanesia*. Canberra: University of Papua and New Guinea and Research School of Pacific Studies, Australian National University, pp. 285-302.

de Dios, E.S. and Fabella, R.V., 1996. *Choice, Growth and Economic Development: Emerging and Enduring*. Manila: University of the Philippines Press.

de Lepervanche, M., 1967-68. 'Descent, residence and leadership in the New Guinea highlands', *Oceania* 38(2,3):134-58, 163-89.

de Lepervanche, M., 1972. 'Social structure', in P. Ryan (ed.), *Encyclopaedia of Papua and New Guinea*, Melbourne: Melbourne University Press in Association with the University of Papua New Guinea, pp. 1065-79.

Deklin, T., 1992. 'Culture and democracy in Papua New Guinea: *marit tru or giaman marit?*', in R. Crocombe et al. (eds), *Culture and Democracy in the South Pacific*. Suva: Institute of Pacific Studies, University of the South Pacific, pp. 35-48.

Department of Decentralisation, Papua New Guinea, 1981. *Committee of Review Into Local Level Government Interim Report*. Port Moresby.

Department of Provincial Affairs, Papua New Guinea, 1984. *Review of Intergovernmental Fiscal Relations in Papua New Guinea. Report of a Committee Established by the National*

Executive Council on the Recommendation of the Premiers Council on 1 December 1983. Two volumes: Port Moresby.

Diamond, L., 1994. 'Rethinking civil society. Toward democratic consolidation', *Journal of Democracy* 5(3):4-17.

Dickson-Waiko, A.N., 1994. 'A Woman's Place is in the Struggle: Feminism and Nationalism in the Philippines', unpublished PhD dissertation, Australian National University.

Dinnen, S., 1995. 'Papua New Guinea in 1994 – the most turbulent year?' *Current Issues in Criminal Justice* 6(3):395-407.

____, 1998. 'In weakness and strength – state, societies and order in Papua New Guinea', in P. Dauvergne (ed.), *Weak and Strong States in Asia-Pacific Societies*. Sydney: Allen & Unwin.

Dinnen, S., May, R.J. and Regan, A.J., 1997. *Challenging the State: The Sandline Affair in Papua New Guinea*. Canberra: Research School of Pacific and Asian Studies, Australian National University.

Douglas, B., 1979. 'Rank, power, authority: a reassessment of traditional leadership in South Pacific societies', *The Journal of Pacific History* XIV(part 1):2-27.

Dorney, S., 1990. *Papua New Guinea. People, Politics and History Since 1975*. Sydney: Random House Australia.

_____, 1998. *The Sandline Affair: Politics and Mercenaries and the Bougainville Crisis*. Sydney: ABC Books.

Doronila, Amando, 1992. *The State, Economic Transformation, and Political Change in the Philippines, 1946-1972*. Singapore: Oxford University Press.

Downs, I., 1980. *The Australian Trusteeship in Papua New Guinea 1945-75*. Canberra: Australian Government Publishing Service.

Druckman, D., 1977. 'The person, role and situation in international negotiations', in M.G. Herman (ed.), *A Psychological Examination of Political Leaders*. New York: The Free Press, pp. 406-56.

Duverger, M., 1954. *Political Parties. Their Organisation and Activity in the Modern State*. London: Methuen.

Ekeh, P.P. 1975. 'Colonialism and the two publics in Africa: a theoretical statement', *Comparative Studies in Society and History* 17:91-112.

Elvery, A.W., 1962. 'Savings and loan societies in the Territory of Papua and New Guinea', *Australian Territories* 2(2):25-31.

Enloe, C.H., 1973. *Ethnic Conflict and Political Development*. Boston: Little, Brown and Co.

Epstein, A.L., Parker, R.S. and Reay, M. (eds), 1971. *The Politics of Dependence. Papua New Guinea 1968*. Canberra: Australian National University Press.

Errington, F. and Gewertz, D., 1990. 'The chief of the Chambri: social change and cultural permeability among a New Guinea people', in N. Lutkehaus et al., *Sepik Heritage. Tradition and Change in Papua New Guinea.* Durham: Carolina Academic Press, pp. 309-19.

Evans, P.B., 1995. *Embedded Autonomy: States and Industrial Transformation*. Princeton: Princeton University Press.

Evans, P.B., Rueschemeyer D. and Skocpol, T. (eds), 1985. *Bringing the State Back In.* Cambridge/New York: Cambridge University Press.

Finney, B.R., 1973. *Big-Men and Business: Entrepreneurship and Economic Growth in the New Guinea Highlands.* Canberra: Australian National University Press.

Fishman, Robert M., 1990. 'Rethinking state and regime: southern Europe's transition to democracy', *World Politics* 42(3):422-40.

Garnaut, R. and Baxter, P. with A.O. Krueger, 1983. *Exchange Rate and Macro-Economic Policy in Independent Papua New Guinea.* Port Moresby.

Geertz, C., 1963. 'The integrative revolution: primordial loyalties and civil politics in the new states', in C. Geertz (ed.), *Old Societies and New States: the Quest for Modernity in Asia and Africa*. New York: Free Press of Glencoe, pp. 105-57.

Gerritsen, R., 1975. 'Aspects of the political evolution of rural Papua New Guinea: towards a political economy of the terminal peasantry'. Canberra Marxist Discussion Group.

Mimeographed. Reprinted in R. Gerritsen, R.J. May, and M.A.H.B. Walter, *Road Belong Development. Cargo cults, community groups and self-help movements in Papua New Guinea.* Working Paper No. 3, Department of Political and Social Change, Research School of Pacific Studies, Australian National University, pp. 1-60.

_____, 1982. 'The politics of ambition: Damuni, from micronationalism to a pressure group', in R.J. May (ed.), *Micronationalist Movements in Papua New Guinea*. Political and Social Change Monograph 1. Canberra: Department of Political and Social Change, Research School of Pacific Studies, Australian National University.

Gesch, Patrick F., 1985. *Initiative and Initiation: a Cargo Cult-type Movement in the Sepik Against its Background in Traditional Village Religion.* St Augustin: Anthropos-Institut.

Ghai, Y.P. and Isana, M., 1978a. Report on Provincial Government, March. Unpublished.

1978b. 'Review of the Constitutional Laws on Provincial Government'. Paper presented to a workshop on Constitutional and Legal Issues in Provincial Government, September. Port Moresby: Administrative College.

Ghai, Y.P. and Regan, A.J., 1992. *The Law, Politics and Administration of Decentralisation in Papua New Guinea.* Monograph 30. Port Moresby: The National Research Institute.

Godelier, M., 1986. *The Making of Great Men. Male Domination and Power Among the New Guinea Baruya.* Cambridge: Cambridge University Press.

Golay, Frank H., 1961. *The Philippines: Public Policy and National Economic Development.* Ithaca: Cornell University Press.

Goldring, J., 1977. '"*Bulsit bilong mekim bel isi*" – the constitutional structure of provincial government', *Melanesian Law Journal* 5(2):250-84.

Goulbourne, Harry (ed.), 1979. *Politics and State in the Third World.* London: Macmillan.

Gourevitch, P.A., 1979. 'The reemergence of "peripheral nationalisms": some comparative speculations on the spatial distribution of political leadership and economic growth', *Comparative Studies in Society and History* 21(3):303-22.

Gray, G.G., 1996. '"The next focus of power to fall under the spell of this little gang"'. Anthropology and Australia's post-war policy in Papua New Guinea', *War and Society* 14(2): 101-17.

Greenstein, F.I., 1969. *Personality and Politics. Problems of Evidence, Inference and Conceptualisation.* Chicago: Markham Publishing Co.

Greenstein, F.I., 1975. 'Personality and Politics', in Greenstein and N.W. Polsby (eds), *Micropolitical Theory, Handbook of Political Science.* Vol.2. Reading: Addison-Wesley Publishing Co.

Griffin, J., 1970. 'Bougainville', *Australia's Neighbours* Fourth Series, 68:7-12.

_____, 1973. 'Movements for separation and secession', in A. Clunies Ross and J. Langmore (eds), *Alternative Strategies for Papua New Guinea.* Melbourne: Oxford University Press, pp. 99-130.

_____, 1974. 'Introduction', in J. Griffin (ed.), *A Foreign Policy for an Independent Papua New Guinea.* Sydney: Angus and Robertson, pp. 3-64.

_____, 1975. 'Ethnonationalism and integration: an optimistic view', *Meanjin Quarterly* 34(3):240-49.

_____, 1976. 'Secessionist movements and their future in Papua New Guinea', *World Review* 15(l):23-36.

Griffin, J. and Togolo, M., 1997. 'North Solomons Province 1974-1990', in R.J. May and A.J. Regan with A. Ley (eds), *Political Decentralisation in a New State: The Experience of Provincial Government in Papua New Guinea.* Bathurst: Crawford House Publishing, pp. 354-85.

Gris, G., 1975. 'Opening speech to the Ninth Waigani Seminar', *Yagl-Ambu* 2(2):133-38 (reprinted in J.H. Winslow (ed.), *The Melanesian Environment.* Canberra: Australian National

University press (1977), pp. 241-43.

Groennings, S., Kelley, E.W. and Leiserson, M. (eds), 1970. *The Study of Coalition Behaviour.* New York: Holt, Rinehart and Winston.

Grosart, I, 1982. 'Nationalism and micronationalism: the Tolai case' in R.J. May (ed.), *Micronationalist Movements in Papua New Guinea.* Political and Social Change Monograph 1. Canberra: Department Of Political and Social Change, Research School of Pacific Studies, Australian National University, pp. 139-75.

Guiart, J., 1951a. 'En marge du "cargo cult" aux Nouvelles-Hébrides: le mouvement coopératif dit "Malekula Native Company"', *Journal de la Société des Océanistes* 7:242-7.

_____, 1951b. 'Forerunners of Melanesian nationalism', *Oceania,* 22(2):81-90.

Gutierrez, E., Torrente, I. and Garcia, N., 1992. *All in the Family: A Study of Elites and Power Relations in the Philippines.* Quezon City: Ateneo Centre for Social Policy and Public Affairs.

Hagai, F., 1966. 'Explaining Hahalis', *New Guinea* 7(l):12-14.

Hall, John A., 1986. 'Introduction' in (ed.), *States in History.* Oxford: Basil Blackwell.

Hannett, L.J., 1975. 'The case for Bougainville secession', *Meanjin Quarterly* 34(3):286-93.

Hastings, P., 1971. 'Thoughts on Taurama: the myth of a "non-political" army', *New Guinea* 6(1):28-32.

Hau'ofa, E., 1981. *Mekeo. Inequality and Ambivalence in a Village Society.* Canberra: Australian National University Press.

Hawes, G, 1992. 'Marcos, his cronies and the Philippines' failure to develop', in R. McVey (ed.), *Southeast Asian Capitalists, Studies on Southeast Asia.* Ithaca: Southeast Asia Program, Cornell University.

Heeger, G.A., 1974. *The Politics of Underdevelopment.* New York: St Martins Press.

Hegarty, D., 1973. 'Australian political chronicle, Papua New

Guinea', *Australian Journal of Politics and History* 19(3): 438-46.

_____, 1975. 'Political Chronicle. Papua New Guinea', *Australian Journal of Politics and History* 21(l):91-4.

_____, 1977. 'Political Chronicle. Papua New Guinea', *Australian Journal of Politics and History* 23(3):453-61.

_____, 1979a. 'The political parties', in A. Amarshi, K. Good and R. Mortimer, *Development and Dependency. The Political Economy of Papua New Guinea*. Melbourne: Oxford University Press, pp. 187-204.

_____, 1979b. 'Parties and political change in Papua New Guinea'. Paper presented to 49th ANZAAS Congress, Auckland. Mimeographed.

_____, 1979c. 'Political chronicle: Papua New Guinea', *The Australian Journal of Politics and History* 25(1):106-11.

_____, 1982. 'Changing the guard at Port Moresby', *New Zealand International Review* VII(6):8-10.

_____, (ed.), 1983. *Electoral Politics in Papua New Guinea. Studies on the 1977 National Elections*. Port Moresby: University of Papua New Guinea Press.

Hegarty, D.W. and King, P., 1982. 'Political Chronicle. Papua New Guinea: January-June 1982', *Australian Journal of Politics and History* 28(3):470-74.

Herlihy, J.M., 1982. 'Decolonisation politics in Solomon Islands: the model that never was', in R.J. May and Hank Nelson (eds), *Melanesia Beyond Diversity*. Canberra: Research School of Pacific Studies, Australian National University, pp. 571-99.

Hermann, M.G., (ed.), 1977. A *Psychological Examination of Political Leaders*. New York: The Free Press.

Hinchliffe, K., 1980. 'Conflicts between national aims in Papua New Guinea: the case of decentralisation and equality', *Economic Development and Cultural Change* 28(4):819-38.

Hobsbawm, E.J., 1959. *Primitive Rebels*. Manchester: Manchester University Press.

Hogbin, H.I., 1958. *Social Change*. London: Watts.

_____, 1978. *The Leaders and the Led. Social Control in Wogeo, New Guinea.* Melbourne: Melbourne University Press.

Hueter, D., 1974. 'The battle for the abundant life: the problems of cults and the church', *Point* 1:123-40.

Huntington, S.P., 1968. *Political Order in Changing Societies*. New Haven: Yale University Press.

_____, 1957. *The Soldier and the State*. The Theory and Politics of Civil-Military Relations. Cambridge, Mass.: The Belknap Press.

Hutchcroft, Paul D., 1991. 'Oligarchs and cronies in the Philippine state: the politics of patrimonial plunder', *World Politics* 43(3):410-50.

Hutchful, Eboe, 1995-96. 'The civil Society debate in Africa', *International Journal* 51(1):54-77.

Hyden, G., 1980. *Beyond Ujamaa in Tanzania. Underdevelopment and an Uncaptured Peasantry.* London: Heinemann.

Inglis, I., 1957. 'Cargo cults. The problem of explanation', *Oceania*, 27(4):249-63.

Inkeles, A. and Levinson, D.J., 1969. 'National character: the study of modal personality and sociocultural systems', in G. Lidzey and E. Aronson (eds), *Handbook of Social Psychology*. Second edition, Vol.4. Reading: Addison-Wesley Publishing Co., pp. 418-506.

International Bank for Reconstruction and Development (IBRD), 1965. *The Economic Development of the Territory of Papua and New Guinea.* Report of a Mission Organised by the IBRD. Baltimore: The Johns Hopkins Press.

Jackman, H., 1977. 'Some thoughts on entrepreneurship in Papua New Guinea', *Australian Outlook* 31(l):24-37.

Jackson, R.T. and Hegarty, D.W., 1983. 'From geography to ideology? The 1982 elections in Papua New Guinea', *Australian Geographer* 15(5):334-36.

Jarvie, I.C., 1963. 'Theories of cargo cults: a critical analysis', *Oceania* 34(1):1-31; 34(2):108-36.

_____, 1964. *The Revolution in Anthropology*. London: Routledge and Kegan Paul.

Kabutaulaka, T. and Dauvergne, P., 1997. 'The Weak State in the Solomon Islands'. Paper presented to a workshop on Weak and Strong States in Melanesia and Southeast Asia, 13 August. Canberra: n.p.

Kaidadaya, K.J., 1974. 'The Island Development Association: a case study', *Administration for Development* 1:35-40.

Kairi, J., 1977. 'The Purari Scheme: some comments', in J.H. Winslow (ed.), *The Melanesian Environment*. Canberra: Australian National University Press, pp. 341-43.

Kaiulo, R.T., 1997. *Report to the Sixth Parliament on the 1997 National Election by the Electoral Commissioner Reuben T. Kaiulo*. Port Moresby: n.p.

Kaman, 1975. 'The community self-help project at Olu-Bus, Minj', *Yagl-Ambu* 2(1):28-50.

Kavanagh, D., 1972. *Political Culture*. London: Macmillan.

Keesing, R.M., 1978. 'Politico-religious movements and anti-colonialism on Malaita: Maasina Rule in historical perspective', *Oceania* 48(4):241-261; 49(1):46-73.

Kerkvliet, Benedict J. Tria, 1998. 'Land regimes and state strengths and weaknesses in the Philippines and Vietnam', in P. Dauvergne (ed.), *Weak and Strong States in Asia-Pacific Societies*. Sydney: Allen & Unwin, pp. 158-74.

Kiki, A.M., 1968. *Kiki: Ten Thousand Years in a Lifetime*. Melbourne: F.W. Cheshire.

Kumaina, R.V., 1970. 'Savings and loan societies in Papua New Guinea', *Journal of the Papua and New Guinea Society* 4(1):81-8.

Landé, C.H., 1965. *Leaders, Factions and Parties: The Structure of Philippine Politics*, Monograph Series No. 6. New Haven: Yale University Southeast Asian Studies.

_____, 1987. 'Introduction: retrospect and prospect' in C.H. Landé (ed.), *Rebuilding a Nation: Philippine Challenges and American Policy*. Washington DC: Washington Institute Press.

_____, 1996. *Post-Marcos Politics: A Geographical and Statistical Analysis of the 1992 Presidential Election*. New York/Singapore: St Martins Press/Institute of Southeast Asian Studies.

Lanes, A.R., 1969. 'Financial Institutions in a Developing Economy. A Study of the Role of Savings and Loan Societies in Papua and New Guinea'. Unpublished MEc thesis, University of Sydney.

Langness, L.L., 1972. 'Political organisation', in P. Ryan (ed.), *Encyclopaedia of Papua and New Guinea*, Melbourne: Melbourne University Press in association with the University of Papua New Guinea, pp. 922-35.

Lanternari, V., 1974. 'Nativistic and socio-religious movements: a reconsideration', *Comparative Studies in Society and History* 16(4):483-503.

Lawrence, P., 1955. 'Cargo cult and religious beliefs among the Garia', *International Archives of Ethnography* 47(l):1-20.

_____, 1964. *Road Belong Cargo*. Manchester: Manchester University Press.

_____, 1971. 'Introduction', in R.M. Berndt and P. Lawrence (eds), *Politics in New Guinea: Traditional and in the Context of Change. Some Anthropological Perspectives*. Nedlands: University of Western Australia Press, pp. 1-34.

____, 1975. 'The Melanesian Way', *Quadrant* 19(6):89-92.

____, 1982. 'Madang and beyond', in R.J. May and Hank Nelson (eds), *Melanesia Beyond Diversity*. Canberra: Research School of Pacific Studies, Australian National University 1:57-72.

Lawson, Stephanie, 1991. 'Some Conceptual and Empirical Issues in the Study of Regime Change', *Regime Change and Regime Maintenance in Asia and the Pacific*, Discussion Paper No. 3. Canberra: Department of Political and Social Change, Research School of Pacific Studies, Australian National University.

Laycock, D.C., 1982. 'Melanesian linguistic diversity: a Melanesian choice?', in R.J. May and Hank Nelson (eds), *Mela-*

nesia Beyond Diversity. Canberra: Research School of Pacific Studies, Australian National University, pp. 33-8.

Leach, J.W., 1973. 'Making the best of tourism: the Trobriand situation', in R.J. May (ed.), *Priorities in Melanesian Development*. Canberra: University of Papua and New Guinea and Research School of Pacific Studies, Australian National University, pp. 357-61.

_____, 1982. 'Socio-historical conflict and the Kabisawali Movement in the Trobriand Islands', in R.J. May (ed.), *Micronationalist Movements in Papua New Guinea,* Canberra: Political and Social Change Monograph 1, Research School of Pacific Studies, The Australian National University, pp. 249-89.

Legge, J.D., convenor, 1973. *Traditional Attitudes and Modern Styles in Political Leadership*. Sydney: Angus and Robertson.

Lini, W., 1980. *Beyond Pandemonium: From the New Hebrides to Vanuatu*. Wellington: Asia Pacific Books.

Liria, Y.A., 1993. *Bougainville Campaign Diary*. Melbourne: Indra Publishing.

Loveday, P. and Wolfers, E.P. 1976. *Parties and Parliament in Papua New Guinea 1964-1975*. IASER Monograph 4. Port Moresby: Institute of Applied Social and Economic Research.

Lutkehaus, N., 1990. 'Hierarchy and "heroic society": Manam variations in Sepik social structure', *Oceania* 60:179-97.

Lutkehaus, N., et.al., 1990. *Sepik Heritage: Tradition and Change in Papua New Guinea*. Durham: Carolina Academic Press.

Lynch, M., 1981. 'Ropes, rules and ring-keepers: the cabinet system as policy maker', in J.A. Ballard (ed.), *Policy-making in a New State: Papua New Guinea 1972-77*. St Lucia: University of Queensland Press, pp. 19-32.

McCoy, A.W., 1994. '"An Anarchy of Families": the historiography of state and family in the Philippines', in A.W. McCoy (ed.), *An Anarchy of Families: State and Family in the Philippines*. Quezon City: Ateneo de Manila University Press.

Mackenzie, A., 1987. 'People Power or palace coup: the fall of

Marcos', in Mark Turner (ed.), *Regime Change in the Philippines. The Legitimation of the Aquino Government*. Political and Social Change Monograph 7. Canberra: Department of Political and Social Change, Research School of Pacific Studies, Australian National University.

McKillop, R.F., 1982. 'Papua Besena and Papuan separatism', in R.J. May (ed.), *Micronationalist Movements in Papua New Guinea*. Political and Social Change Monograph 1. Canberra: Department of Political and Social Change, Research School of Pacific Studies, Australian National University, pp. 329-58.

McSwain, R., 1977. *The Past and Future People*. Melbourne: Oxford University Press.

MacWilliam, S., 1996. 'Papua New Guinea in the 1940s: empire and legend', in D. Lowe (ed.), *Australia and the End of Empires. The Impact of Decolonisation in Australia's Near North, 1945-65*. Geelong: Deakin University Press, pp. 25-42.

Machado, K.D., 1972. 'Changing patterns of leadership recruitment and the emergence of the professional politician in Philippine local politics', *Philippine Journal of Public Administration* 16(2):147-69.

Maher, R.F., 1958. 'Tommy Kabu movement of the Purari Delta', *Oceania* 29(2):75-90.

_____, 1961. *New Men of Papua: A Study in Culture Change*. Madison: University of Wisconsin Press.

Mair, L.P., 1970. *Australia in New Guinea*. Second edition. Melbourne: Melbourne University Press.

Malinowski, B., 1922. *Argonauts of the Western Pacific*. London: Routledge & Kegan Paul.

_____, 1935. *Coral Gardens and Their Magic*. London: Allen and Unwin.

Mamak, A. and Bedford, R. with L. Hannett and M. Havini, 1974. *Bougainvillean Nationalism. Aspects of Unity and Discord*. Bougainville Special Publication No. 1. Christchurch: Department of Geography, University of Canterbury.

Mann, M., 1986. 'The autonomous power of the state: its origins, mechanisms and results', in John A. Hall (ed.), *States in History*. Oxford: Basil Blackwell.

Manning, M., 1979. 'Finance and the Provinces', Institute of National Affairs, *Speech Series*, No. 6. Port Moresby.

Mannur, H.G. and Gumoi, M.T., 1994. *Wages Policy Issues in Papua New Guinea*. Port Moresby: NRI Special Publication Number 20.

Mark, T., 1975. 'Acquisition and redistribution of alienated land: a study in access', *Yagl-Ambu* 2(1):65-70.

May, R.J., 1966. 'Politics and gamesmanship in Australian federal finance', in H. Mayer (ed.), *Australian Politics: A Reader*. Melbourne: F.W. Cheshire, pp. 117-29.

____, 1969. *Federalism and Fiscal Adjustment*. Oxford: Clarendon Press.

____, 1972. 'A New Guinea currency', *New Guinea* 7(3):43-51.

____, (ed.), 1973. *Priorities in Melanesian Development*. Canberra: The University of Papua and New Guinea and the Research School of Pacific Studies, Australian National University.

____, 1974. 'Trading bank lending to indigenous borrowers – summary of a 1972 survey', *Bank of Papua New Guinea Quarterly Economic Bulletin*, June Quarter:1-5.

____, 1975. 'The micronationalists', *New Guinea* 10(1):38-53.

____, 1976. 'The political education programme', in D. Stone (ed.), *Prelude to Self-Government. Electoral Politics in Papua New Guinea 1972*. Canberra: Research School of Pacific Studies, Australian National University and the University of Papua New Guinea.

____, 1979. 'Living with a lion. Public attitudes and private feelings', in R.J. May (ed.), *The Indonesia-Papua New Guinea Border: Irianese Nationalism and Small State Diplomacy*. Working Paper No. 2. Canberra: Department of Political and Social Change, Research School of Pacific Studies, Australian National University, pp. 80-107.

____, 1981. *National-Provincial Government Relations in Papua New Guinea: Consultant's Report to the Committee to Review the*

Financial Provisions of the Organic Law on Provincial Government. Working Paper No. 4. Canberra: Department of Political and Social Change, Research School of Pacific Studies, Australian National University.

____, (ed.), 1982. *Micronationalist Movements in Papua New Guinea*. Political and Social Change Monograph 1. Canberra: Department of Political and Social Change, Research School of Pacific Studies, Australian National University.

_____, 1984. *Social Stratification in Papua New Guinea.* Working Paper No. 5. Canberra: Department of Political and Social Change, Research School of Pacific Studies, Australian National University.

____, (ed.), 1986. *Between Two Nations: The Indonesian-Papua New Guinea Border and West Papua Nationalism*. Bathurst: Robert Brown & Associates.

____, 1989. 'People power and powerful people: regime change and regime maintenance in the Asia-Pacific Region', in R.J. May and William J. O'Malley (eds), *Observing Change in Asia. Essays in Honour of J.A.C. Mackie*. Bathurst: Crawford House Publishing, pp. 194-200.

____, 1990. 'The Moro Movement in Southern Philippines', in K.M. de Silva, S. Kiribamune and C.R. de Silva (eds), *Asian Panorama:Essays in Asian History, Past and Present*. New Delhi: Vikas Publishing House.

____, 1993. *The Changing Role of the Military in Papua New Guinea.* Canberra Papers on Strategy and Defence No. 101. Canberra: Strategic and Defence Studies Centre, Research School of Pacific Studies, Australian National University.

____, 1996. *The Situation in Bougainville: Implications for Papua New Guinea, Australia and the Region.* Current Issues Brief No.9. Canberra: Parliamentary Research Service.

_____, 1997a. 'East Sepik Province, 1976-1992', in R.J. May and A.J. Regan with A. Ley (eds), *Political Decentralisation in a New State: The Experience of Provincial Government in Papua New Guinea*. Bathurst: Crawford House Publishing, pp. 228-61.

_____, 1997b. 'Des promesses à la crise: économie politique de la Papouasie-Nouvelle Guinee', *Revue Tiers Monde* 38(149): 139-56.

May, R.J. and Hank Nelson (eds), 1982. *Melanesia Beyond Diversity*. Canberra: Research School of Pacific Studies, The Australian National University.

May, R. J. and Regan, A.J. with A. Ley (eds), 1997. *Political Decentralisation in a New State: The Experience of Provincial Government in Papua New Guinea*. Bathurst: Crawford House Publishing.

May, R.J. and V. Selochan, 1998. *The Military and Democracy in Asia and the Pacific*. Bathurst: Crawford House Publishing.

May, R.J. and Spriggs, M. (eds), 1990. *The Bougainville Crisis*. Bathurst: Crawford House Publishing.

May, R.J. and Tupouniua, S., 1980. 'The politics of small island states', in R.T. Shand (ed.), *The Island States of the Pacific and Indian Oceans: Anatomy of Development*. Canberra: Australian National University, Development Studies Centre, Monograph No.23, pp. 419-37.

Mazrui, A.A., 1970. 'An African's New Guinea', *New Guinea* 5(3):45-56.

Mead, M., 1956. *New Lives for Old: Cultural Transformation – Manus, 1928-1953*. New York: Morrow.

_____, 1964. *Continuities in Cultural Evolution*. New Haven: Yale University Press.

Melson, R. and Wolpe, H., 1970. 'Modernisation and the politics of communalism: a theoretical perspective', *American Political Science Review* 64(4):1112-30.

Metraux, R., 1978. 'Aristocrary and meritocracy: leadership among the eastern Iatmul', *Anthropological Quarterly* 51(1):47-58.

Middlemiss, B.J.A., 1970. 'Napidakoe Navitu', in M.W. Ward (ed.), *The Politics of Melanesia*. Canberra: University of Papua and New Guinea and Research School of Pacific Studies, Australian National University, pp. 100-4.

Migdal, Joel S., 1988. *Strong States and Weak States: State-Society Relations and State Capabilities in the Third World.* Princeton: Princeton University Press.

____, 1994. 'The state in society: an approach to struggles for domination', in J.S. Migdal, A. Kohli and V. Shue (eds), *State Power and Social Forces: Domination and Transformation in the Third World.* Cambridge/New York: Cambridge University Press, pp. 7-34.

____, 1997. 'Studying the state', in M.I. Lichbach and A.S. Zuckerman (eds), *Comparative Politics. Rationality, Culture and Structure.* Cambridge/New York: Cambridge University Press.

Migdal, J.S., A. Kohli and V. Shue (eds), 1994. *State Power and Social Forces: Domination and Transformation in the Third World.* Cambridge/New York: Cambridge University Press.

Miranda, F.B., 1993. 'Democratisation in the Philippines: recent developments, trends and prospects', *Asian Journal of Political Science* 1(1):85-112.

Mitchell, W.E., 1978. 'On keeping equal: polity and reciprocity among the New Guinea Wape', *Anthropological Quarterly* 51(1):5-15.

Mogu, B. and Bwaleto, K., 1978. 'A study of area communities and village courts in the Kainantu District', *Administration for Development* 10:61-80.

Moi, O., 1979. 'Boera Association: a case study of the impact of the association on the social, economic and political activities and conditions of the village people', *Yagl-Ambu* 6(1):19-30.

Momis, J., 1973. 'The challenge of modernisation in Melanesian society', in R.J. May (ed.), *Priorities in Melanesian Development.* Canberra: The University of Papua and New Guinea and the Research School of Pacific Studies, Australian National University, pp. 447-50.

Morauta, L., 1974. *Beyond the Village. Local Politics in Madang, Papua New Guinea.* Canberra: Australian National University Press.

_____, 1984. 'Social stratification in lowland Papua New Guinea: issues and questions', in R.J. May (ed.), *Social Stratification in Papua New Guinea.* Working Paper No. 5. Canberra: Department of Political and Social Change, Research School of Pacific Studies, Australian National University, pp. 3-28.

Morauta, M., 1996. 'The Papua New Guinea economy: the past record, the current dilemma, the future challenge', dinner speech, NCDS/NRI Conference, Port Moresby, 5 August.

Moulik, T.K., 1973. *Money, Motivation and Cash Cropping.* New Guinea Research Bulletin No.53. Port Moresby: New Guinea Research Unit, Australian National University.

Munster, J., 1975. 'A band of hope', *Point* 2:132-46.

Mwayubu, B., 1973. 'The Kabisawali Association', Newsletter of the Economics Students Association of the University of Papua New Guinea, July.

Nadkarni, M.S., 1970. *Indigenous Entrepreneurs for Papua and New Guinea.* Port Moresby: United Nations Industrial Development Organisation.

Namaliu, R., 1984. 'The content and context of the special relationship between Papua New Guinea and Australia', Keynote address to the conference on 'Papua New Guinea and Australia: the Papua New Guinea Perspective', Australian National University, September. Mimeograph.

Narokobi, B., 1980. *The Melanesian Way.* Port Moresby: Institute of Melanesian Studies.

Nation, J., 1978. *Customs of Respect: The Traditional Basis of Fijian Communal Politics.* Canberra: Australian National University, Development Studies Centre, Monograph No.14.

Navari, Cornelia, 1991. 'Introduction: the state as a contested concept in international relations', in Cornelia Navari (ed.), *The Condition of States.* Milton Keynes: Open University Press.

Nayacakalou, R.R., 1975. *Leadership in Fiji.* Melbourne: Oxford University Press.

Nelson, H., 1972. *Papua New Guinea. Black Unity or Black Chaos?* Harmondsworth: Penguin Books.

O'Callaghan, M-L., 1999. *Enemies Within: Papua New Guinea, Australia, and the Sandline Crisis: The Inside Story*. Sydney: Doubleday.

Oliver, D.L., 1955. *A Solomon Island Society. Kinship and Leadership Among the Siuai of Bougainville*. Boston: Beacon Press.

_____, 1973. *Bougainville. A Personal History*. Melbourne: Melbourne University Press.

Oram, N.D., 1967. 'Rabia Camp and the Tommy Kabu Movement', in N.E. Hitchcock and N.D. Oram, *Rabia Camp: a Port Moresby Migrant Settlement*. New Guinea Research Bulletin No. 14, Port Moresby: New Guinea Research Unit, Australian National University, pp. 3-14.

Overseas Development Group, University of East Anglia, 1973. *A Report on Development Strategies for Papua New Guinea*. Port Moresby: Office of Planning and Co-ordination.

Papua New Guinea, General Constitutional Commission, 1980. *Interim Report*. Port Moresby.

Papua New Guinea National Parliament, 1990. Progress Report of the Select Committee on Provincial Government Review.

_____, 1993. Bi-partisan Select Committee on Provincial Government. Report, 3rd March, 1993.

Papua New Guinea, Office of Information, 1976. *Hood Lagoon Sibona durua gaukara/Helpim ol yet long Hood Lagoon*. Port Moresby.

Papua New Guinea, 1974. Proposals on Constitutional Principles and Explanatory Notes, Government Paper. Port Moresby.

Papua New Guinea, Select Committee on Constitutional Development, 1971. *Final Report*. Port Moresby.

Pardy, R., Parsons, M., Siemon D. and Wigglesworth, A., 1978. *Purari. Overpowering PNG?* Melbourne: International Development Action.

Parker, R.S., 1966-67. 'Political parties in developing countries', *Journal of the Papua and New Guinea Society* 1(1):40-7.

____, 1967a. 'Shaping parties in New Guinea', *Dissent* 21:3-8.

____, 1967b. 'Interest articulation and political parties in Papua and New Guinea'. Paper presented to Department of Political Science, IAS seminar, Canberra. Mimeograph.

____, 1971. 'Economics before politics – a colonial phantasy', *Australian Journal of Politics and History* 17(2):202-14.

Parker, R.S. and Wolfers, E.P., 1971. 'The context of political change', in A.L. Epstein, R.S. Parker and M. Reay (eds), *The Politics of Dependence: Papua New Guinea 1968*. Canberra: Australian National University Press.

Parliament of the Commonwealth of Australia, Joint Committee on Foreign Affairs, Defence and Trade, 1991. *Australia's Relations with Papua New Guinea*. Canberra: Senate Publishing and Printing Unit.

Peasah, J.A., 1994. *Local-Level Government in Papua New Guinea. A Study in Change and Continuity in the Development of Liberal-Democratic Self-Determination at the Local Level*. Monograph 31. Port Moresby: The National Research Institute.

Phillips, M.J., 1969. 'Institutional aspects of monetary transition in Papua New Guinea'. Paper delivered to PNG Society of Victoria, June.

____, 1972. 'Banking', in P. Ryan (ed.), *Encyclopaedia of Papua and New Guinea*. Melbourne: Melbourne University Press, pp. 54-9.

Pokawin, S.P., 1976. 'Politics of village level development organisations in Manus'. Department of Political and Administrative Studies, University of Papua New Guinea. Mimeograph.

Powell, H.A., 1960. 'Competitive leadership in Trobriand political organisation', *Journal of the Royal Anthropological Institute* 90(1):118-45.

Premdas, R.R., 1974. 'The case against the no-party state in Papua New Guinea', *Yagl-Ambu* 1(2):117-34.

_____, 1975. 'Towards a one-party system in Papua New Guinea: some problems and prospects', *Australian Outlook* 29(2): 161-79.

_____, 1977. 'Secession and political change: the case of Papua Besena', *Oceania* 47(4):265-83.

Premdas, R.R. and J.S. Steeves, nd. 'Political parties and electoral politics in Papua New Guinea. The case of the Moresby North-East Electorate'. Port Moresby: University of Papua New Guinea.

Pula, A. and Jackson, R., 1984. 'Population Survey of the Border Census Divisions of Western Province'. Port Moresby: Papua New Guinea IASER.

Pye, L.W., 1962. *Politics, Personality, and Nation Building: Burma's Search for Identity.* New Haven: Yale University Press.

Pye, L.W. and Verba, S.(eds), 1965. *Political Culture and Political Development.* Princeton: Princeton University Press.

Quiros, L., 1979. 'Decentralisation in Chimbu – conflicts, costs and changes' (review of Standish 1978b), *Post-Courier* 1 October.

Reay, M., 1974. 'Generating political conflict: some consequences of economic exploitation of the New Guinea highlands', *Anthropological Forum* 3(3-4):295-305.

_____, 1979. 'Social transformation and inequality: the Olu Bus experiment', in R.R. Premdas and S. Pokawin (eds), *Decentralisation: the Papua New Guinea Experiment.* Port Moresby: University of Papua New Guinea Printery, pp. 217-23.

_____, 1984. 'Pre-colonial status and prestige in the Papua New Guinea highlands', in R.J. May (ed.), *Social Stratification in Papua New Guinea.* Working Paper No. 5. Canberra: Department of Political and Social Change, Research School of Pacific Studies, Australian National University, pp. 29-52.

Reed, S.W., 1943. *The Making of Modern New Guinea.* Philadelphia: The American Philosophical Society.

Regan, A.J., 1997. 'East New Britain Province, 1976-1992', in R.J. May and A.J. Regan, with A. Ley (eds), *Political Decentralisation in a New State: The Experience of Provincial Government in Papua New Guinea.* Bathurst: Crawford House Publishing, pp. 304-53.

Riker, W.H., 1962. *The Theory of Political Coalitions*. New Haven:Yale University Press.

_____, 1969. 'Six books in search of a subject or does federalism exist and does it matter?', *Comparative Politics* 2:135-46.

_____, 1970. 'The triviality of federalism', *Politics* 5(2):239-41.

Rimoldi, M., 1971. 'The Hahalis Welfare Society of Buka', unpublished PhD dissertation, Australian National University.

_____, 1976. 'Concepts of development in the Hahalis Welfare Society of Bougainville'. Paper presented to Young Nations Conference. Sydney. Mimeograph.

Rimoldi, M. and Rimoldi, E., 1992. *Hahalis and the Labour of Love: a Social Movement on Buka Island*. Oxford/Providence: Berg.

Rivera, T.C., 1994. *Landlords and Capitalists: Class, Family and State in Philippine Manufacturing*. Quezon City: UP Centre for Integrative and Development Studies and University of the Philippines Press.

_____, 1996. *State of the Nation. Philippines*. Singapore: Institute of Southeast Asian Studies.

Roth, G., 1968. 'Personal rulership, patrimonialism, and empire-building in the new states', *World Politics* 20(2):194-206.

Rowley, C.D., 1958. *The Australians in German New Guinea 1914-1921*. Melbourne: Melbourne University Press.

_____, 1965. *The New Guinea Villager. A Retrospect from 1964*. Melbourne: F.W. Cheshire.

_____, 1969. *Australian Bureaucracy and Niuginian Politics*. Inaugural lecture. Port Moresby: University of Papua New Guinea.

Ryan, P. (ed.), *Encyclopaedia of Papua and New Guinea*. Melbourne: Melbourne University Press in association with the University of Papua and New Guinea.

Sabin, E.M., 1988. 'Traditions and customary law and council of chief system – North Solomons Province. Research into the establishment of council of chiefs and the traditions and customary law'. Mimeograph.

Saffu, Y., 1995. 'Papua New Guinea in 1994. Reaping the Whirlwind', *Asian Survey* 35(2):221-25.

_____, (ed.), 1996. *The 1992 PNG Election*. Political and Social Change Monograph 23, Department of Political and Social Change, Research School of Pacific Studies, Australian National University.

Sahlins, M.G., 1966. 'Poor man, rich man, big man, chief: political types', in I. Hogbin and L.R. Hiatt (eds), *Readings in Australian and Pacific Anthropology*, Melbourne: Melbourne University Press, pp. 159-79 (reprinted from *Comparative Studies in Society and History* 5(3)([1963]:285-303).

Salisbury, R., 1964. 'Despotism and Australian administration in the New Guinean highlands', *American Anthropologist* Special Publication: 'New Guinea, the Central Highlands' 66(4, part 2):225-39.

Samana, U., 1988. *Papua New Guinea: Which Way?* Melbourne: Arena Publications.

Santiago, M. Defensor, 1991. *How to Fight Election Fraud*. Makati: Movement for Responsible Public Service.

Sarei, A.H., 1974. *Traditional Marriage and the Impact of Christianity on the Solos of Buka Island*. New Guinea Research Bulletin No. 57. Port Moresby: New Guinea Research Unit, Australian National University.

Schwartz, T., 1962. 'The Paliau Movement in the Admiralty Islands, 1946-1954', *Anthropological Papers of the American Museum of Natural History* 49, part 2.

Sexton, L.D., 1980. 'From pigs and pearlshells to coffee and cash: socioeconomic change and sex roles in the Daulo Region, Papua New Guinea', unpublished PhD dissertation, Temple University.

Shils, E., 1957. 'Primordial, personal, sacred and civil ties', *British Journal of Sociology* 8(2):130-45.

_____, 1963. 'On the comparative study of the new states' in C. Geertz (ed.), *Old Societies and New States. The Quest for Modernity in Asia and Africa*. New York: The Free Press, pp. 1-26.

Skeldon, R., 1977. 'Regional Associations in Papua New Guinea', IASER Discussion Paper No. 9. Port Moresby: In-

stitute of Applied Social and Economic Research.
Smith, A.D.S., 1979. *Nationalism in the Twentieth Century*. Canberra: Australian National University Press.
Somare, M., 1970. 'Problems of political organisation in diversified tribes in Papua-New Guinea', in M.W. Ward, (ed.), *The Politics of Melanesia.* Canberra: The University of Papua New Guinea and the Research School of Pacific Studies, Australian National University, pp. 489-93.
_____, 1975. *Sana. An Autobiography of Michael Somare.* Port Moresby: Niugini Press.
_____, 1977. 'The role of political parties in Papua New Guinea', *Administration for Development* 9:3-8.
_____, 1991. 'Melanesian leadership', in *Proceedings of the XVII Pacific Science Congress,* May 27-June 2. Honolulu.
Soriano, J.C., 1987. 'The Return of the Oligarchs', *Conjuncture* 1(1):6.
South Bougainville Interim Authority, 1992. *South Bougainville Administration Progress Report – May, June, July.* Konga Head Office, Siwai, South Bougainville. Mimeograph.
Spanier, J., 1978. *Games Nations Play.* New York: Rinehart and Winston/Praeger.
Spate, O.H.K., Belshaw, C.S. and Swan, T.W., 1953. 'Some Problems of Development in New Guinea. Report of a Working Committee of the Australian National University'. Canberra. Mimeograph.
Spriggs M., and Denoon, D. (eds), 1992. *The Bougainville Crisis. 1991 Update.* Political and Social Change Monograph 16, Department of Political and Social Change, Research School of Pacific Studies, Australian National University. Bathurst: Crawford House Publishing.
Standish, W., 1977. 'Independent Papua New Guinea's first national elections: an interim report', *Dyason House Papers* 4(1):1-6.
_____, 1978. 'The "Big-man" model reconsidered: power and stratification in Chimbu', IASER Discussion Paper 22. Port

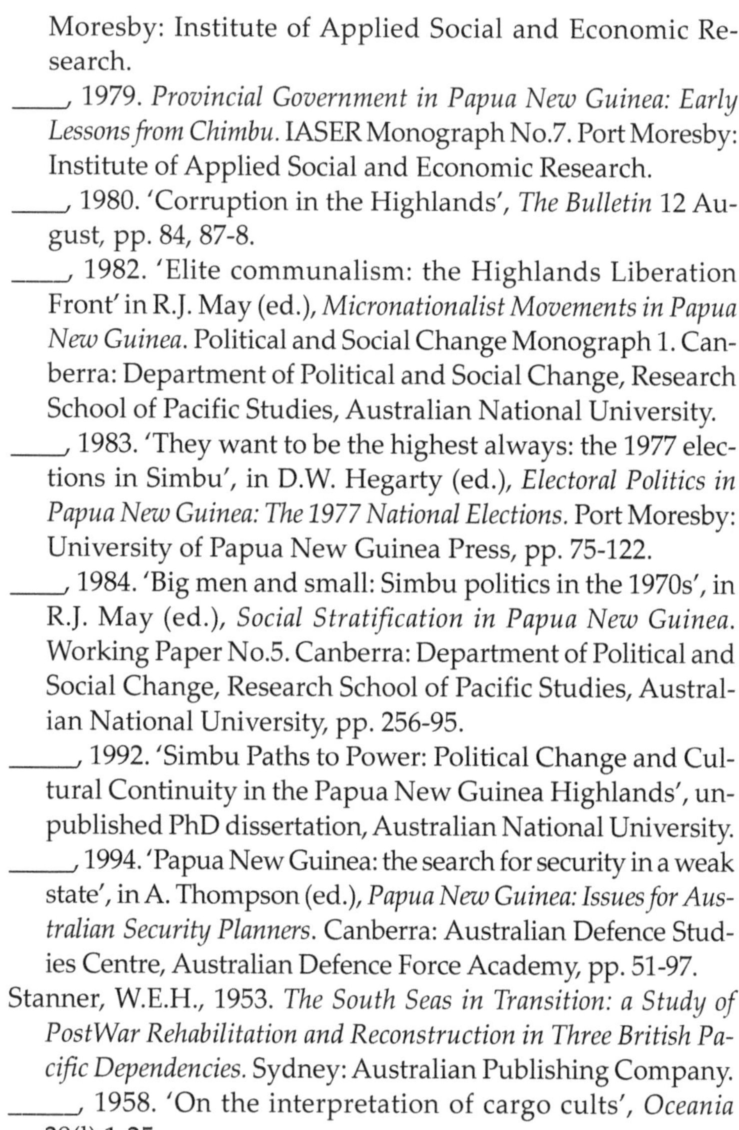

Moresby: Institute of Applied Social and Economic Research.

____, 1979. *Provincial Government in Papua New Guinea: Early Lessons from Chimbu.* IASER Monograph No.7. Port Moresby: Institute of Applied Social and Economic Research.

____, 1980. 'Corruption in the Highlands', *The Bulletin* 12 August, pp. 84, 87-8.

____, 1982. 'Elite communalism: the Highlands Liberation Front' in R.J. May (ed.), *Micronationalist Movements in Papua New Guinea.* Political and Social Change Monograph 1. Canberra: Department of Political and Social Change, Research School of Pacific Studies, Australian National University.

____, 1983. 'They want to be the highest always: the 1977 elections in Simbu', in D.W. Hegarty (ed.), *Electoral Politics in Papua New Guinea: The 1977 National Elections.* Port Moresby: University of Papua New Guinea Press, pp. 75-122.

____, 1984. 'Big men and small: Simbu politics in the 1970s', in R.J. May (ed.), *Social Stratification in Papua New Guinea.* Working Paper No.5. Canberra: Department of Political and Social Change, Research School of Pacific Studies, Australian National University, pp. 256-95.

_____, 1992. 'Simbu Paths to Power: Political Change and Cultural Continuity in the Papua New Guinea Highlands', unpublished PhD dissertation, Australian National University.

_____, 1994. 'Papua New Guinea: the search for security in a weak state', in A. Thompson (ed.), *Papua New Guinea: Issues for Australian Security Planners.* Canberra: Australian Defence Studies Centre, Australian Defence Force Academy, pp. 51-97.

Stanner, W.E.H., 1953. *The South Seas in Transition: a Study of PostWar Rehabilitation and Reconstruction in Three British Pacific Dependencies.* Sydney: Australian Publishing Company.

_____, 1958. 'On the interpretation of cargo cults', *Oceania* 29(1):1-25.

Stent, W.R., 1973. 'The Peli Cargo Cult – an interpretation', Economics Discussion Paper No. 17/73. Economics Department, La Trobe University. Mimeograph.

Stepan, Alfred, 1978. *The State and Society: Peru in Comparative Perspective*. Princeton: Princeton University Press.

Stephen, D., 1972. *A History of Political Parties in Papua New Guinea*. Melbourne: Lansdowne Press.

Stephen, M., 1977. 'Cargo cult hysteria: symptom of despair or technique of ecstasy'. Occasional Paper No. 1, Research Centre for Southwest Pacific Studies, La Trobe University.

Stone, D. (ed.), 1976. *Prelude to Self-Government. Electoral Politics in Papua New Guinea 1972*. Canberra: Research School of Pacific Studies, Australian National University and the University of Papua New Guinea.

Strathern, A.J., 1966. 'Despots and directors in the New Guinea highlands', *Man* 1(1):356-57.

_____, (ed.), 1982a. *Inequality in New Guinea Highlands Societies*. Cambridge: Cambridge University Press.

_____, 1982b. 'Two waves of African models in the New Guinea highlands', in A. Strathern (ed.), *Inequality in New Guinea Highlands Societies*, Cambridge: Cambridge University Press, pp. 35-49.

Strelan, J.G., 1977. *Search for Salvation. Studies in the History and Theology of Cargo Cults*. Adelaide: Lutheran Publishing House.

Talmon, Y., 1966. 'Millenarian movements', *European Journal of Sociology* 7(2):159-200.

Tapales, Proserpina D., 1993. *Devolution and Empowerment: The Local Government Code of 1991 and Local autonomy in the Philippines*. Quezon City: UP Centre for Integrative and Development Studies in cooperation with the University of the Philippines Press.

Taylor, R., 1991. 'Intergovernmental disputes and the concurrent legislative subjects: lessons from the Manus forestry dispute', *Melanesian Law Journal*, Special issue 199:57-70.

Thomas, J.R. and Ryan, D., 1959. 'Report of a Survey on the Use of Money and the Need for Credit by the Indigenous People of the Territory of Papua and New Guinea.' Sydney:

Commonwealth Bank of Australia. Mimeograph.
Thomason, J.A., Newbrander, W.C. and Kolehmainen-Aitken, R-L. (eds), 1991. *Decentralisation in a Developing Country: The Experience of Papua New Guinea and Its Health Service.* Pacific Research Monograph No. 25. Canberra: National Centre for Development Studies, Australian National University.
Thompson, A. (ed.), 1994. *Papua New Guinea. Issues for Australian Security Planners.* Canberra: Australian Defence Studies Centre, Australian Defence Force Academy.
Thrupp, S.L. (ed.), 1962. *Millennial Dreams in Action. Comparative Studies in Society and History. Supp. II.* The Hague: Mouton.
Timberman, D.G., 1991. *A Changeless Land: Continuity and Change in Philippine Politics*. Singapore/New York: Institute of Southeast Asian Studies/ME Sharpe.
Timbi, B., n.d. [c.1977]. 'Pipilka Development Corporation'. Port Moresby. Typescript.
Togolo, M., 1986. 'Provincial government in Papua New Guinea: The North Solomons Experience'. Typescript.
Tonkinson, R., 1980. 'National identity and the problem of *kastom* in Vanuatu'. Paper presented to Development Studies Centre seminar, Australian National University, Canberra. Mimeograph.
Tordoff, W., and Watts, R.L., 1974. Report on Central-Provincial Government Relations. Port Moresby.
ToRobert, H. ('Henry Roberts'), 1965. 'New Guinea's leadership: problems of the prestige period', *New Guinea* 1(3):12-16.
Townsend, D., 1975. 'Distance and participation in the cash economy in a small area of PNG'. Paper presented to Institute of Australian Geographers, Wollongong Conference. Mimeograph.
_____, 1980. 'Disengagement and incorporation – the post-colonial reaction in the rural villages of Papua New Guinea', *Pacific Viewpoint* 21(1):1-25.

Tupouniua, S., Crocombe, R. and Slatter, C., 1975. *The Pacific Way*. Suva: South Pacific Social Sciences Association.

Turner, M., 1990. *Papua New Guinea: the Challenge of Independence*. Melbourne: Penguin Books Australia.

____, 1991. 'Issues and reforms in the Papua New Guinea public service since independence', *Journal de la Société des Oceanistes* 92-93 (1 and 2):101-3.

Uberoi, J.P.S., 1962. *Politics of the Kula Ring*. Manchester: Manchester University Press.

United Nations, 1968. *Report of the United Nations Visiting Mission to the Trust Territory of New Guinea*, document T/1678. Also published in Canberra by the Government Printer.

____, 1971. *Report of the United Nations Visiting Mission to the Trust Territory of New Guinea*, document T/1717. Also published in Canberra by the Government Printer.

Uyassi, M., 1975. 'Improving access: the Komuniti Kaunsils', *Yagl-Ambu* 2(l):51-64.

Van den Berghe, P.L. (ed.), 1965. *Africa: Social Problems of Change and Control*. San Francisco: Chandler Publishing Co.

Vicedom, G.F. and Tischner, H., 1943-48. *Die Mbowamb: die kultur der Hagenberg – Stämme im ötlichen Zentral-Neuguinea*. Hamburg: Museum für Volkerkunde und Vorgeschichte, Monographien zur Volkerkunde.

Villacorta, W.V., 1994. 'The curse of the weak state: leadership imperatives for the Ramos government', *Contemporary Southeast Asia* 16(1):67-92.

Villanueva, A.B., 1996. 'Parties and elections in Philippine politics', *Contemporary Southeast Asia* 18(2):175-92.

Voutas, A.C., 1970. 'Elections and communications', in M.W. Ward (ed.), *Politics of Melanesia*. Canberra: University of Papua and New Guinea and the Research School of Pacific Studies, Australian National University, pp. 494-508.

Waddell, J.R.E., 1973a. 'Constitutions and the political culture', in A. Clunies Ross and J. Langmore (eds), *Alternative Strategies for Papua New Guinea*. Melbourne: Oxford University

Press, pp. 86-98.

____, 1973b. 'Political development: a plea for lateral thought', in R.J. May (ed.), *Priorities in Melanesian Development*. Canberra: The University of Papua and New Guinea and the Research School of Pacific Studies, Australian National University, pp. 27-31.

Waiko, J., 1976. 'Komge Oro: land and freedom or nothing', *Gigibori* 3(1):16-19.

_____, 1977. 'The people of Papua New Guinea, their forests and their aspirations', in J.H. Winslow (ed.), *The Melanesian Environment*. Canberra: Australian National University Press, pp. 407-27.

Wallace, A.F.C., 1956. 'Revitalisation movements', *American Anthropologist* 58(2):264-81.

Wallerstein, I., 1960. 'Ethnicity and national integration in West Africa', *Cahiers d'Etudes Africaines* 3(1):129-39. Reprinted in P.L. van den Berghe (ed.), *Africa: Social Problems of Change and Control*. San Francisco: Chandler Publishing Co., 1965, pp. 472-82.

Walter, M.A.H.B., 1981. 'Cult movements and community development associations: revolution and evolution in the Papua New Guinea countryside', IASER Discussion Paper No. 36. Reprinted in R. Gerritsen, R.J. May and M.A.H.B. Walter, *Road Belong Development. Cargo cults, community groups and self-help movements in Papua New Guinea*. Working Paper No. 3. Canberra: Department of Political & Social Change, Research School of Pacific Studies, Australian National University, pp. 81-105.

_____, (ed.), 1982. *What Do We Do About Plantations?* IASER Monograph 15. Port Moresby: Institute of Applied Social and Economic Research.

Ward, M.W. (ed.), 1970. *The Politics of Melanesia*. Canberra: University of Papua and New Guinea and Research School of Pacific Studies, Australian National University.

_____, (ed.), 1972. *Change and Development in Rural Melanesia*.

Canberra: University of Papua and New Guinea and Research School of Pacific Studies, Australian National University.

Ward, R.G., 1982. 'The effects of scale on social and economic organisation', in R.J. May and Hank Nelson (eds), *Melanesia Beyond Diversity*. Canberra: Research School of Pacific Studies, The Australian National University, pp. 181-92.

Ward, R.G. and Ballard, J.A., 1976. 'In their own image: Australia's impact on Papua New Guinea', *Australian Outlook* 30(3):439-58.

Warren, N., 1976. 'The introduction of a village court', IASER Discussion Paper No. 2.

Warry, W., 1987. *Chuave Politics. Changing Patterns of Leadership in the Papua New Guinea Highlands*. Political and Social Change Monograph No. 4. Canberra: Department of Political and Social Change, Research School of Pacific Studies, Australian National University.

Watson, J.B., 1971. 'Tairora: the politics of despotism in a small society', in R.M. Berndt and P. Lawrence (eds), *Politics in New Guinea: Traditional and in the Context of Change. Some Anthropological Perspectives*. Nedlands: University of Western Australia Press, pp. 224-25.

Watts, R.L. and Lederman, W.R., 1975. 'A Proposal for the Provisions of the Organic Laws Necessary to Define the Authority and Relations of the National Government and Respective Provincial Governments of Papua New Guinea after Independence'. Port Moresby.

Wedgwood, C.H., 1933-34. 'Report on research work on Manam Island', *Oceania* 4(4):373-403.

Weiner, M., 1971. 'Political integration and political development', in J. Finkle and R.W. Gable (eds), *Political Development and Social Change*. New York: Wiley, pp. 551-62.

_____, 1973. 'National integration vs. nationalism' (review article), *Comparative Studies in Society and History* 15(2): 248-54.

Wesley-Smith, Terence (ed.), 1992. 'A Legacy of Development: Three Years of Crisis in Bougainville', Special Issue, *Contemporary Pacific* 4(2).

White, G., 1994. 'Civil society, democratisation and development (I): clearing the analytical ground', *Democratisation* 1(3):375-90.

Wilson, B.R., 1973. *Magic and the Millenium*. London: Heinemann.

_____, (ed.), 1970. *Rationality*. Oxford: Basil Blackwell.

Wilson, R.K., 1972. 'A review of village industries: the urban--rural choice in entrepreneurial development', in M.W. Ward (ed.), *Change and Development in Rural Melanesia*. Canberra: The University of Papua and New Guinea and the Research School of Pacific Studies, Australian National University, pp. 520-29.

Wilson, R.K. and Garnaut, R., 1968. *A Survey of Village Industries in Papua New Guinea*. New Guinea Research Bulletin No.25. Port Moresby: New Guinea Research Unit, Australian National University.

Wolfers, E.P., 1968. 'Social and political assumptions', in J. Wilkes (ed.), *New Guinea . . . Future Indefinite?* Sydney: Angus and Robertson for Australian Institute of Political Science, pp. 33-64.

_____, 1970. 'A short history of political party activity in Papua New Guinea', in M.W. Ward (ed.), *The Politics of Melanesia*. Canberra: University of Papua and New Guinea and Research School of Pacific Studies, Australian National University, pp. 439-88.

Woods, D., 1992. 'Civil society in Europe and Africa: limiting state power through a public sphere', *African Studies Review* 35(2):77-100.

Woolford, D., 1976. *Papua New Guinea. Initiation and Independence*. St. Lucia: University of Queensland Press.

Worsley, P., 1957. *The Trumpet Shall Sound. A Study of 'Cargo' Cults in Melanesia*. London: McGibbon and Kee.

Wurfel, D., 1988. *Filipino Politics: Development and Decay*. Ithaca: Cornell University Press.

Yaman, C., 1975. 'Case study of the Kumusi and Ioma Timber development proposals in the Northern District', *Administration for Development* 4:36-46.

INDEX

www.ingramcontent.com/pod-product-compliance
Lightning Source LLC
Chambersburg PA
CBHW041129280326
41928CB00059B/3288

* 9 7 8 1 9 2 0 9 4 2 0 6 9 *